Philosophy of Language

This unique textbook introduces linguists to key issues in the philosophy of language. Accessible to students who have taken only a single course in linguistics, yet sophisticated enough to be used at the graduate level, the book provides an overview of the central issues in philosophy of language, a key topic in educating the next generation of researchers in semantics and pragmatics. Thoroughly grounded in contemporary linguistic theory, the book focuses on the core foundational and philosophical issues in semantics and pragmatics, richly illustrated with historical case studies to show how linguistic questions are related to philosophical problems in areas such as metaphysics, epistemology, and ethics. Students are introduced in Part I to the issues at the core of semantics, including compositionality, reference and intentionality. Part II looks at pragmatics: context, conversational update, implicature and speech acts, whilst Part III discusses foundational questions about meaning. The book will encourage future collaboration and development between philosophy of language and linguistics.

ZOLTÁN GENDLER SZABÓ is Professor of Philosophy and Linguistics at Yale University. His research focuses on philosophy of language. He is an editor of the *Studies in Linguistics and Philosophy* series and associate editor of the *Journal of Semantics*.

RICHMOND H. THOMASON is Professor of Philosophy, Linguistics, and Computer Science at the University of Michigan. He has written two logic textbooks and edited several books in areas related to logic and linguistics. He is a fellow of the Association for the Advancement of Artificial Intelligence and a managing editor of *Studia Logica*.

CAMBRIDGE TEXTBOOKS IN LINGUISTICS

Philosophy of Language

In this series:

R. CANN *Formal Semantics*
J. LAVER *Principles of Phonetics*
F. R. PALMER *Grammatical Roles and Relations*
M. A. JONES *Foundations of French Syntax*
A. RADFORD *Syntactic Theory and the Structure of English: A Minimalist Approach*
R. D. VAN VALIN, JR, and R. J. LAPOLLA *Syntax: Structure, Meaning and Function*
A. DURANTI *Linguistic Anthropology*
A. CRUTTENDEN *Intonation* Second edition
J. K. CHAMBERS and P. TRUDGILL *Dialectology* Second edition
C. LYONS *Definiteness*
R. KAGER *Optimality Theory*
J. A. HOLM *An Introduction to Pidgins and Creoles*
G. G. CORBETT *Number*
C. J. EWEN and H. VAN DER HULST *The Phonological Structure of Words*
F. R. PALMER *Mood and Modality* Second edition
B. J. BLAKE *Case* Second edition
E. GUSSMAN *Phonology: Analysis and Theory*
M. YIP *Tone*
W. CROFT *Typology and Universals* Second edition
F. COULMAS *Writing Systems: An Introduction to their Linguistic Analysis*
P. J. HOPPER and E. C. TRAUGOTT *Grammaticalization* Second edition
L. WHITE *Second Language Acquisition and Universal Grammar*
I. PLAG *Word-Formation in English*
W. CROFT and A. CRUSE *Cognitive Linguistics*
A. SIEWIERSKA *Person*
A. RADFORD *Minimalist Syntax: Exploring the Structure of English*
D. BÜRING *Binding Theory*
M. BUTT *Theories of Case*
N. HORNSTEIN, J. NUÑES and K. GROHMANN *Understanding Minimalism*
B. C. LUST *Child Language: Acquisition and Growth*
G. G. CORBETT *Agreement*
J. C. L. INGRAM *Neurolinguistics: An Introduction to Spoken Language Processing and its Disorders*
J. CLACKSON *Indo-European Linguistics: An Introduction*
M. ARIEL *Pragmatics and Grammar*
R. CANN, R. KEMPSON and E. GREGOROMICHELAKI *Semantics: An Introduction to Meaning in Language*
Y. MATRAS *Language Contact*
D. BIBER and S. CONRAD *Register, Genre and Style*
L. JEFFRIES and D. MCINTYRE *Stylistics*
R. HUDSON *An Introduction to Word Grammar*
M. L. MURPHY *Lexical Meaning*
J. M. MEISEL *First and Second Language Acquisition*
T. MCENERY and A. HARDIE *Corpus Linguistics: Method, Language and Practice*
J. SAKEL and D. L. EVERETT *Linguistic Fieldwork: A Student Guide*
A. SPENCER and A. LUÍS *Clitics: An Introduction*
G. CORBETT: *Features*
A. MCMAHON and R. MCMAHON: *Evolutionary Linguistics*
B. CLARK: *Relevance Theory*
B. LONG PENG *Analyzing Sound Patterns*
B. DANCYGIER and E. SWEETSER *Figurative Language*
J. BYBEE *Language Change*
S. G. THOMASON *Endangered Languages: An Introduction*
A. RADFORD *Analysing English Sentences* Second edition
R. CLIFT *Conversation Analysis*
R. LEVINE *Syntactic Analysis*
I. PLAG *Word-Formation in English* Second edition
Z. G. SZABÓ and R. H. THOMASON *Philosophy of Language*

Earlier issues not listed are also available

Philosophy of Language

ZOLTÁN GENDLER SZABÓ

Yale University, Connecticut

RICHMOND H. THOMASON

University of Michigan

CAMBRIDGE
UNIVERSITY PRESS

CAMBRIDGE
UNIVERSITY PRESS

University Printing House, Cambridge CB2 8BS, United Kingdom

One Liberty Plaza, 20th Floor, New York, NY 10006, USA

477 Williamstown Road, Port Melbourne, VIC 3207, Australia

314–321, 3rd Floor, Plot 3, Splendor Forum, Jasola District Centre, New Delhi – 110025, India

79 Anson Road, #06-04/06, Singapore 079906

Cambridge University Press is part of the University of Cambridge.

It furthers the University's mission by disseminating knowledge in the pursuit of education, learning, and research at the highest international levels of excellence.

www.cambridge.org
Information on this title: www.cambridge.org/9781107096646
DOI: 10.1017/9781316156353

First published 2019

Printed in the United Kingdom by TJ International Ltd. Padstow Cornwall

A catalogue record for this publication is available from the British Library.

ISBN 978-1-107-09664-6 Hardback
ISBN 978-1-107-48062-9 Paperback

Web pages for this textbook containing supplementary material that instructors and students may find useful can be found at www.cambridge.org/PhilLang

Contents

Preface

This is a book on philosophy written for linguists and for philosophers who have some familiarity with linguistics. Our primary aim is to offer a text that can be used in graduate-level or advanced-undergraduate courses educating the next generation of researchers in semantics and pragmatics. The ideal audience for such a course would consist of students who have already taken their first class in semantics and/or pragmatics, and are seeking a better grasp of the foundational issues in these fields. It can also be used for undergraduates who have had a course in linguistics or several courses in philosophy. We have used the draft of this book successfully in classes attended by both graduates and undergraduates.

Over the last forty years, linguistic research in semantics has become increasingly technical, and this has changed how philosophers must think about meanings and theories of meaning. Although formal semantics, as practiced by linguists, began in the crucible of philosophy, many philosophers are not acquainted with the technical details. And some linguists who may be interested in this book may not have been exposed to the topic. For readers who want to learn more about formal semantics, the most commonly used textbook is Heim and Kratzer (1997). We also recommend Gamut (1991a,b), as a reliable and readable source of information about the relevant logical and linguistic theories.

Having said this, we very much hope that the book will be read by philosophers as well. From their perspective, the distinctive feature of this book is that, unlike previous introductions to philosophy of language, it is thoroughly grounded in contemporary linguistic theory. Philosophers will be aware that many of the issues we discuss are controversial. We both have opinions (which occasionally diverge) on these, and they no doubt show. Still, it was our aim to present the live options in these debates fairly and charitably.

Philosophy gave birth to modern semantics and pragmatics. This is not surprising – the same can be said for physics, economics, and psychology. Like those older siblings, semantics and pragmatics have become independent disciplines, pursued by researchers with well-accepted theoretical tools and with aims that are now detached from the philosophical interests that initially gave rise to their development. Most physicists, economists, and psychologists flourish in their work while (and perhaps even because) they manage to keep philosophy at arm's length. So, if you are a linguist why bother with the philosophy of language? There are three main reasons.

First, the boundaries between philosophy and science are much more fluid in semantics and pragmatics than, say, in biology. Linguists working in these fields will bump up against philosophical problems quite often. Do semantic theories tell us what sorts of things there are in the world? Does communication require knowing other people's minds? Is vagueness a semantic phenomenon or a feature of reality? When this happens, it is good to be clear about the status of the relevant philosophical debates.

Second, the philosophical literature of the last hundred years is filled with valuable but largely unsystematized insights about natural language. This literature may still serve to inspire novel linguistic theories. But this is only possible if the texts can be properly understood, which in turn requires an appreciation of the distinctively philosophical concerns.

Finally, thinking philosophically about the subject matter of a scientific inquiry is useful because it can free the mind from the tyranny of custom. If you study the semantics of cleft-constructions or the pragmatics of scalar implicatures, you won't spend a lot of time thinking about why you seek a compositional semantics or what exactly it means for speaker and hearer to coordinate their behavior in conversation. You have a working knowledge of these things and they serve you well – most of the time. But every now and then, an unexamined assumption or an insufficiently clear concept will lead you to a theoretical dead-end. And when you are stuck, you need to take a step back. Philosophy will help.

The first two parts of the book deal with core foundational and philosophical issues in semantics and pragmatics. These are illustrated with historical case studies showing how linguistic questions are related to philosophical problems in areas such as metaphysics, epistemology, and ethics. Part I introduces students to core issues in semantics such as compositionality, reference, intensionality, and intentionality. Part II deals with pragmatics: context, conversational update, implicature, and speech acts. And Part III discusses foundational questions about meaning.

We recommend reading the four case studies and Chapter 1 on Frege and Tarski in any course that uses this book. Other than this, the book can be used flexibly. A course concentrating on semantics could read Chapters 2, 3, 4, 5, and perhaps 7, perhaps supplementing this with source readings from the literature as well. A course concentrating on pragmatics could read Chapters 6, 7, 8, 9, 10, and 11, again supplementing them with other readings. A course following the entire text in order will cover the central issues in both meaning and language use.

We would like to thank Jessica Keiser, Jeff King, Jeff Pelletier, and Craige Roberts, who read and commented on chapters of the book, and Nick Allott, who read and commented helpfully on the entire book. Thanks too to our editor, Rosemary Crawley, and students in courses we have taught at Yale and Michigan.

We dedicate this book in gratitude to our teachers in both philosophy and linguistics, in the hope that it will improve and strengthen the close and fruitful relations that already bind the two subjects together.

0 Introduction

Modern semantics and pragmatics emerged from the work of philosophers and philosophically inclined mathematicians: Gottlob Frege, Bertrand Russell, Alfred Tarski, J. L. Austin, Peter Strawson, Willard van Orman Quine, Donald Davidson, Richard Montague, Paul Grice, and others. Many of the central ideas that now can be found in introductory textbooks of semantics and pragmatics were shaped in debates where language was seen merely as a way to make philosophical points about logic, epistemology, ontology, or ethics. Many of the participants in these debates would be puzzled to find themselves counted among the founding figures of branches of linguistics. For many of them, a systematic theoretical enterprise seeking to interpret the expressions of natural languages and to understand the conversational effects of uttering those expressions in a context would be unthinkable or even wrongheaded. Our survey of three crucial debates will give a sense of how philosophers and logicians – sometimes unwittingly – paved the road to scientific semantics and pragmatics.

0.1 Quine versus Carnap on Intensionality

Rudolf Carnap and Willard V. O. Quine were among the leading philosophers of the twentieth century. Carnap (who lived 1891–1970) was for a time a student of Frege's in Jena. He was influential in German and Austrian philosophy after the First World War, but moved to the US before the Second World War, teaching at Chicago University and then at UCLA. Quine (who lived 1908–2000), although he traveled widely, taught at Harvard for his entire career.

Both were logicians as well as philosophers, but their interests in logic were quite different. Quine contributed – in ways that now seem somewhat idiosyncratic – to logic and its systematic use in formalizing set theory and mathematics. Carnap sought to extend logical techniques that had been used to formalize mathematics to other domains, and especially to the physical sciences.

Both Carnap and Quine began with a syntactic approach to logic and language ("syntactic" in the logical sense, i.e. proof-theoretic), with works such as Carnap (1937) and Quine (1958). Carnap embraced Tarski's model-theoretic approach to semantics and sought to use it in his philosophical projects. Carnap (1956), for instance, is an extended and systematic attempt to apply these techniques to what he called "intensional" constructions.

Quine, on the other hand, although he was certainly aware of Tarski's ideas, avoided Tarski's semantic techniques in his logical work and rejected attempts to extend them to modal and psychological (that is, to intensional) languages. He regarded intensionality as problematic, and viewed semantic theories of intensionality with deep suspicion. As we will see, the debate between Quine and Carnap over intensionality is, in fact, only an aspect of a deeper difference of opinion concerning the nature of semantics.

The phenomenon of intensionality,[1] and its opposite, extensionality, have to do with the substitution of equals for equals. Carnap characterizes these notions in the following series of definitions:[2]

(i) A sentence ϕ is equivalent to a sentence ψ if and only if ϕ and ψ are either both true or both false. More generally, an expression η is equivalent to an expression η' if and only if η and η' have the same semantic value. In particular, if η and η' are referring expressions, they are equivalent if they refer to the same thing.

(ii) A syntactic constituent η in an environment ϕ is interchangeable with a phrase η' of the same syntactic type if and only if ϕ is equivalent to ϕ', where ϕ' is the result of replacing the constituent η in ϕ with η'.

(iii) The sentence ϕ is *extensional* with respect to a certain occurrence of the expression η in ϕ if and only if the occurrence is interchangeable with any expression equivalent to η.

(iv) Finally, the sentence ϕ is *intensional* with respect to an occurrence of the expression η in ϕ if and only if ϕ is not extensional with respect to this occurrence.

From the definition, you can see that intensionality is a semantic notion: it has to do with truth and reference. And it refers to a specific position in a sentence at which some component phrase occurs. To introduce some commonly used terminology, the component phrase occurs in the context of a sentence, and in this context it may or may not be intensional.

Borrowing linguistic notation for phrase structure, the structure of a noun phrase (an NP) occurring somewhere in an arbitrary sentence is this.

(0.1.1) $[X[\,Y]_{\mathrm{NP}}\,Z]_{\mathrm{S}}$.

In this diagram, X, Y, and Z represent stretches of syntactic material, and $[X \ldots Z]_{\mathrm{S}}$ is the context where the noun phrase Y appears.

[1] Intensionality is easily confused with intentionality. The latter notion was introduced by the philosopher and psychologist Franz Brentano and has to do with the "aboutness" of mental states. Although verbs having to do with mental states are in fact typically intensional, the two notions are different. Their relationship will be discussed in Chapter 5.

[2] The definitions are adapted from Carnap (1956: 14, 47–48). Notation has been modernized, and the definitions have been paraphrased to some extent, also to modernize them.

Where [Y'] is another noun phrase,

(0.1.2) $[X\,[\,Y'\,]_{\mathrm{NP}}\,Z]_{\mathrm{S}}$

will be the result of replacing Y with Y' in this context. It is this replacement we need to consider in testing for intensionality.

Let's confine ourselves to the case where the component phrase is either a name or a "definite description" – a definite noun phrase involving 'the'. (For philosophers, these are the paradigmatic cases.) And we'll assume that in our model, such phrases take *individuals* as values – these are elements of the model's domain.

Substituting equals for equals is a pretty fundamental principle of reasoning. If we are given two equations, such as

(0.1.3) $x = y - 4$
(0.1.4) $y = 2 \cdot x$

we automatically begin by substituting '$2 \cdot x$' for 'y' in (0.1.3), obtaining

(0.1.5) $x = (2 \cdot x) - 4$

and proceed, concluding that $x = 4$. This sort of reasoning is ubiquitous in mathematics and is so natural that we use it unthinkingly. Such reasoning is also commonplace in nonmathematical cases like (0.1.6–8):

(0.1.6) Jane is shorter than the tallest person in the room.
(0.1.7) Molly is the tallest person in the room.
(0.1.8) So Jane is shorter than Molly.

This means that any case of intensionality is also a violation of a plausible and fundamental principle of reasoning. But intensionality is not at all unusual, as the following two examples show.

(0.1.9) Jane might have been shorter than the tallest girl in the room.
(0.1.10) Jane (in fact) is the tallest girl in the room.
(0.1.11) ? So Jane might have been shorter than Jane.

(0.1.12) Fred suspects that Jane is the tallest girl in the room.
(0.1.13) Molly is the tallest girl in the room.
(0.1.14) ? So Fred suspects that Jane is Molly.

These examples illustrate two typical sorts of contexts that can precipitate intensionality: 'might' is a *modal verb*, and 'suspect' is a *psychological* one.

Sometimes we find ourselves taking anomalies for granted, without ever recognizing them as problematic. And sometimes difficulties that at first seem artificial and even superficial can turn out to be enormously challenging. The intensionality phenomenon is like this. We're familiar with examples like (0.1.9–11) and (0.1.12–14), and yet we happily use the rule of substitution of equals for equals, without noticing the incongruity. The difficulty only arises when we begin to think systematically about the semantics of languages that can have expressions like 'might' and 'suspect'. In fact, intensionality is the central problem of Frege (1892) and has haunted philosophy of language since then. But it hardly seems to have been taken seriously before the late nineteenth century.

The resulting quandary for semantic theory can be summed up like this. On the one hand, we have a plausible and fundamental principle of reasoning that moreover seems to be well motivated. If a sentence involves a referring expression, then it makes a claim about whatever thing that expression refers to. But then the truth of the sentence shouldn't depend on how we refer to this thing: that is, the sentence should be extensional. On the other hand, modals and psychological verbs provide straightforward examples of intensional contexts.

There are two responses to the problem of intensionality: (1) treat it as a challenge, as something that needs to be overcome by developing an improved semantic theory; (2) take it to indicate that the project of developing a semantics for any language capable of talking about modal or psychological matters is fundamentally misguided in some way. The first response is Carnap's; the second is Quine's.

As you might expect (especially if you knew how prolific and systematic a philosopher Carnap was), Carnap's reaction takes the form of an extended, articulated study of the semantics of intensionality: Carnap (1956), as well as shorter articles on related topics. Partly in response to Quine's criticism, Carnap also published methodological studies defending semantics as a legitimate area of inquiry. Quine too was a prolific writer, but his project is negative, and to make his point he doesn't have to produce an extended theory. So his contributions tend to be shorter, more targeted criticisms, although he did produce one extended work in the philosophy of language: Quine (1960).

There is no need here to go into the details of Carnap's solution to the problem of intensionality because it was the first systematic exercise in what is now known as possible worlds semantics. It is essentially the same as Richard Montague's solution, which is now the more or less standard approach to formal semantics in linguistics. We will return to this topic in Chapters 4 and 5.

From 1947 to the late 1970s, Quine produced a number of objections to the very idea of intensional semantics. The earliest of these revolve around *modal logic* – the logic of terms like 'must', 'may', and 'should'. The later objections are more general, and have to do with ontological and methodological considerations

To appreciate the background of Quine's earliest concerns, it is important to understand the use–mention distinction, the separation of object language from metalanguage, and the formalization of logical syntax.

In the twentieth century, formal logic evolved into the study of mathematical language and mathematical reasoning. Since logic is a branch of mathematics, logic itself must be among the subjects that logic can study. This reflective twist turned out to be crucial for some of the most important results in the field. Kurt Gödel's proof in Gödel (1931) that no consistent axiomatizable system of arithmetic could prove its own consistency and Alfred Tarski's proof in Tarski (1936) that no interpreted formal language can provide a definition of its true formulas both depend on the ability of logic to formalize itself. Part of Gödel's proof consists, for instance, in systematically showing how a formalized system of arithmetic can talk about its own formulas and proofs.

A logician dealing with a system of this sort is, of course, using language to talk about language. To introduce a technical term, the logician is using a *metalanguage* to theorize about an *object* language. The metalanguage will use expressions to name the formulas of the object language. But often these expressions will look a lot like the expressions they are supposed to name. It is easy to get confused about this sort of thing: to write '2 + 2=4', for instance, when what is meant is 'The formula '2 + 2 = 4' is provable'. But the former is *using* the formula to assert that the sum of 2 with itself is 4. The latter is *mentioning* the formula, saying that there is a proof of it in some axiomatic system.

As we said, it is easy to confuse use and mention. Such confusions are invited by the fact that, if quotation belongs to spoken language at all, it is almost always covert. And in written language, quotation marks serve many purposes, only one of which is to name the expression between the quotation marks. It is probably best to think of this use as a technical regimentation of everyday language, similar to the other regimentations that are found in mathematical language. We ourselves will use single quotes for use–mention, with a few exceptions. We will omit quotes in displayed examples, and – because quotes within quotes can be hard to parse, when we quote a sentence that itself involves quotation, we will use "corner quotes" for the outermost quotation, thus: ⌜the sentence 'Snow is white' is true⌝.

In the 1930s many logicians came to believe that the work of earlier thinkers had been flawed by carelessness about use and mention. Some philosophers even believed that use/mention confusions were a pervasive source of error in philosophical thinking. And Quine and other prominent contemporary logicians were somewhat obsessive about the use–mention distinction and the employment of various devices, and especially of quotation, to distinguish the two explicitly.

Some of Quine's earliest criticisms of modal logic seem to arise from the thought that it involves confusion of use and mention. If, for instance, the proper "analysis" of a modal claim like (0.1.15) is (0.1.16) – that is, if (0.1.16) is the correct explication of (0.1.15) – then modal statements contain covert quotation.

(0.1.15) 2 + 2 is necessarily equal to 4.
(0.1.16) The sentence '2 + 2 = 4' is provable from the axioms of arithmetic.

If so, then a logician who ignores the hidden quotation marks may be guilty of confusion. This suspicion is compounded by the fact that early work in modal logic, such as Lewis (1918), is indeed confused in just this way.

Quine correctly recognized that quotation creates environments that are logically peculiar and need special treatment. Certainly, covert quotation can produce intensional contexts. The following example is from Quine (1980):[3]

(0.1.17) Giorgione was so-called on account of his size.

(0.1.18) Giorgione was Barbarelli.

(0.1.19) ? Barbarelli was so-called on account of his size.

Quotation has many semantic oddities. In particular, it is opaque to quantification: (0.1.20) says that 2 has a square root, but (0.1.21) fails to claim the existence of anything, because putting quotation marks around '$x^2 = 2$' creates the name of an expression, in which 'x' is mentioned, not used. Compare (0.1.21), for instance, with $\exists x$['*six*' contains 'x'], which Quine (1980: 150) calls "a grotesque example."

(0.1.20) $\exists x\,[x^2 = 2]$.
(0.1.21) $\exists x$ ['$x^2 = 2$' is an equation].

Quine is careful to avoid saying that modal and other intensional constructions involve implicit quotation. Earlier, in the first edition of Carnap (1956), Carnap had proposed a quotational analysis of belief sentences, according to which belief is a relation between a person and a sentence. Alonzo Church criticized such analyses in Church (1950); Carnap accepted this criticism and modified his account. Quine was aware of this exchange and cites Church's paper in Quine (1980). Nevertheless, he believes that the analogy between quotation and intensionality is suggestive and in particular that "quantifying in" to an intensional context – binding a variable in an intensional context with a quantifier – is semantically problematic.

Quine asks what an example like (0.1.22) can mean.

(0.1.22) $\exists x$ [Necessarily, $x > 7$].

It seems to be saying that there is some number that necessarily is greater than 7. You might think that (0.1.22) is true, because 9, for instance, is a number, and because – as a matter of mathematical necessity – 9 is necessarily greater than 7. But, Quine (writing before the demotion of Pluto) asks what this number is. It can't be 9, because 9 is the number of the planets, and the number of the planets is *not* necessarily greater than 7. (Linguists may suspect

[3] The background for this example is that 'Giorgione' means, roughly, "Big George," and was a nickname for the painter Giorgio Barbarelli.

that there is a scope ambiguity in Quine's example: the adverb 'necessarily' may take wide or narrow scope with respect to negation. Quine frames his argument without seeming to notice the ambiguity. In this connection, see Stalnaker and Thomason [1968].)

Quine's point seems to be that quantification is *quantification over objects* and that an object is what it is and has the properties it does independently of how it is named. As a way of emphasizing this point, Quine uses the term 'referential opacity' instead of Carnap's 'intensional'.

It is possible to invent a formal system and yet to be confused about its semantics. Sometimes, perhaps, the confusion can be so acute that there is no sensible way to provide an interpretation of the formalism. In his early criticisms of intensionality, Quine seems to be saying that logical systems that combine modalities or other intensional operators with quantification and that allow formulas like $\exists x\phi$, where ϕ contains occurrences of x in intensional contexts, suffer from this sort of confusion.

Natural languages also allow this sort of "quantifying-in." (For instance, consider the following example, from a Manitoba Department of Corrections webpage: 'Anyone believed to be under the influence of alcohol or drugs will not be permitted to visit'.) If these criticisms are right, it would follow that taking language of this kind seriously and attempting to provide a semantic account of it is misguided. Doubts about quantifying-in can lead to skepticism about the viability of natural language semantics.

Over the years, Quine changed the focus of his criticisms, no longer insinuating that quantifying-in leads to semantic incoherence but claiming only that it leads to theories that are philosophically unacceptable. One line of argument, based on "semantic indeterminacy" – the underdetermination of semantic theories by linguistic evidence – is discussed in Chapter 3.

Another is ontological. Throughout his career, Quine had a preference for ontological parsimony, the idea that theories that postulate fewer kinds of things are preferable. This preference seems to have been motivated by a liking for *philosophical nominalism*, the position that denies the existence of "universals" and, more generally, of "abstract entities" or that at least (and this is Quine's position) treats these things with suspicion and seeks to minimize them.

Universals are what nominalized predicates purport to denote. Goodness, beauty, and triangularity are universals. Debates over the philosophical status of universals go back to ancient times. The category of *abstract entities* is somewhat vague, but includes sets, numbers, species, mathematical points, and other "nonconcrete" things that don't seem to be located in space or time.

Quine recognized, correctly, that a semantic theory of natural language would have to *reify* (to treat as existing) a host of things that philosophers with nominalist inclinations would find unacceptable. Anyone would find the question 'How many inhabitants of Ohio are there?' sensible, even if it might be difficult to answer exactly. But Quine thinks that if a theory were to admit *possible* objects (and this, it seems, is what a semantic theory of modal logic with quantifiers would have to do), it would have to treat questions like 'How many possible inhabitants of Ohio are there?' as legitimate.

In fact, it is far from obvious that accepting the legitimacy of quantifying into modal contexts entails accepting the existence of merely possible entities. 'There are at least three people who might be inhabitants of Ohio' quantifies over flesh and blood actual people, saying that at least three of them might live in Ohio. (Contrast this with 'Ohio might have at least three inhabitants', which does not quantify over actual people.) But Quine is correct in claiming that it is exceedingly hard to design a modal semantics that eschews ontological commitment to nonactual objects.

Rudolf Carnap and Alonzo Church opposed Quine's criticisms of semantics, taking the position that it is a science. Their point is that, like any science, semantics is entitled to make whatever assumptions are appropriate for its own needs, and that philosophical criticisms of these assumptions are beside the point. See Carnap (1950); Church (1951b).

Quine was a lifelong advocate of *naturalism* – of the view that science provides our best way of understanding things. If, as he seems to believe, scientific inquiry provides firmer ground than philosophical considerations, it is peculiar to find him rejecting semantics for philosophical reasons. Quine, then, seems to be treating semantics more like a philosophical than a scientific enterprise. As long as semantics is part of philosophy, Quine is merely indulging in the usual philosophical business of criticizing philosophical positions.

In fact, during much of the twentieth century, semantics was mainly a philosophical pursuit. But now it has become part of linguistics. With some justice, linguists are likely to feel indignant at philosophers who wish to tell them which parts of their subject are legitimate. Quine himself doesn't have much help to offer here; he seems to have little to say about what qualifies an area of inquiry as a science. But he might respond that it is up to linguists, if they wish to do semantics, to put it on a sound enough footing so that they will not find themselves committed to philosophical claims that philosophers can legitimately criticize.

On both sides in this debate, we can find points that are worth taking seriously. Certainly, Carnap and Church were right that a dedicated, scientific approach to semantics, based on ideas from logic, would be rewarding. Quine was right that such theorizing would make problematic assumptions. But in this respect, semantics doesn't seem to be unusual; the foundations of *any* science are philosophically problematic. In general, you would hope for a productive conversation between philosophers and scientists, in which on the one hand the philosophers respect the work of the scientists, and on the other hand the scientists can accept philosophical questions about foundations as legitimate and even interesting.

0.2 Russell versus Strawson on Referring

Bertrand Russell (who lived 1872–1970) was one of the most prolific and influential English-speaking philosophers in the first half of the twentieth century. With Alfred North Whitehead, he produced Whitehead and Russell (1925–1927), which develops a system of logic designed to avoid the logical paradoxes, and seeks to complete Frege's project of developing the mathematics of continuity from logical principles. (Volume I of the first edition of this work was published in 1910.)

Russell (1905), the landmark article with which we are concerned here, belongs to Russell's logical period. However, it was primarily intended as a contribution to philosophy, communicating an insight that, Russell felt, deflated the excesses of nineteenth-century German idealism. The paper was enormously influential, and precipitated a tradition – more or less successful – of "philosophical analysis."

Peter Strawson (who lived 1919–2006) belonged to a younger generation and was associated with a different style of philosophy becoming popular at Oxford – a style that tended to deprecate formal logic but was intensely interested in language. When he opted to tangle with Russell on his home ground in Strawson (1950), Strawson was making a bold and perhaps risky choice, but his paper, too, turned out to be quite influential.

Russell was concerned with what he called "denoting phrases." This term is not much used any more, either by philosophers or linguists. Russell doesn't define it, and what he intended has to be reconstructed from the examples he provides. These include, among other things, phrases headed by the indefinite article 'a' such as 'a man', and definite phrases like 'the present king of England' and 'Charles II's father'. Philosophers have coined the term "definite description" for NPs headed by 'the', possessive NPs, and perhaps some other definite NPs – but excluding proper names. Although the range of constructions that count as definite descriptions is somewhat vague, the term is still in general use in philosophy.

Surprisingly, Russell has nothing to say about proper names in Russell (1905), though he does turn to them in a later work, Russell (1918–1919: 524ff). Since there he extends his analysis of definite descriptions to include proper names, we should also think of these as denoting phrases. Russell contrasts denoting phrases with what in Russell (1918–1919: 201) he called "logically proper names." These may not be found in natural languages but according to Russell would occur in a logically perfect language.

Russell's insight can be put this way in more modern terms: in a language with variables and the universal quantifier – a language that supplies sentences of the form $\forall x\,\phi$ – we can define or "analyze" a wide variety of nominal constructions that superficially don't seem to be universal at all but rather appear to refer. He coined the term "denoting phrase" for the phrases that he thought could be analyzed in this way.

Indefinites can be defined in terms of the universal quantifier and negation. (0.2.23), for instance, is equivalent to (0.2.24); to work this out, notice that if I caught a fish, then it's false that everything I caught is *not* a fish. Conversely, if not everything I caught is not a fish, I caught a fish. Russell is appealing here to the logical equivalence (0.2.25).

(0.2.23) I caught a fish.

(0.2.24) It is not the case that everything I caught is not a fish.

(0.2.25) $\exists x\phi \leftrightarrow \neg\forall x\neg\phi$.

The main point of the paper, though, and what it is remembered for, is the idea that, using quantifiers, variables, and identity it's possible to analyze many definite constructions. Russell illustrates this with (0.2.26) and (0.2.27).

(0.2.26) The present King of France is bald.
(0.2.27) The father of Charles II was executed.

The analysis depends on the fact that *uniqueness* can be characterized using identity and the universal quantifier. To say, for instance, that Charles II had a unique father involves two things: (i) that Charles II had a father, and (ii) that he had no more than one father. But (ii) amounts to this: for all x and y, if x is a father of Charles II and y is a father of Charles II, then $x = y$. The indefinite 'a' in (ii) is inessential: at the risk of sounding archaic, Russell makes this clear by substituting 'begat' for 'is a father of'. Notice that (i) is an indefinite, which can in turn be analyzed using the universal quantifier. And (ii) involves only variables, the universal quantifier, and identity.

Putting these ideas together, we arrive at (0.2.28) as the analysis of 'Charles II had a unique father':

(0.2.28) (i) For some x, x begat Charles II, and (ii) for all y and z, if y and z begat Charles II, then $y = z$.

Part (i) of the analysis ensures that there is at least one begetter of Charles II, while part (ii) ensures that there is no more than one.

If now we want an analysis of (0.2.27), we merely have to add to (0.2.28) a clause saying that x was executed:

(0.2.29) (i) For some x, x begat Charles II, and (ii) for all y and z, if y and z begat Charles II, then $y = z$ and (iii) x was executed.

The logical version of (0.2.30) clarifies the structure of the entire analysis.

(0.2.30)
$$\begin{aligned}&\exists x[\text{Begat}(x, c)\wedge\\&\forall y\forall z[[\text{Begat}(y, c) \wedge [\text{Begat}(z, c)] \rightarrow y{=}z]\wedge\\&\text{Executed}(x)].\end{aligned}$$

Similarly, Russell's famous example about the king of France produces the following analysis and logical formalization.

(0.2.31) (i) For some x, x is a king of France, and (ii) for all y and z, if y and z are kings of France, then $y = z$ and (iii) x is bald.

(0.2.32) $\exists x$[King-of-France $(x) \wedge$
$\forall y \forall z$[King-of-France $(y) \wedge$ King-of-France $(z) \rightarrow y{=}z] \wedge$
Bald (x)].

If these analyses are successful, Russell has provided an account of the meaning of a fairly wide range of noun phrases using only a few semantic primitives: variables, the universal quantifier, and identity. The coverage even of noun phrases headed by 'the' is incomplete – Russell's theory leaves us in the dark, for instance, about how to interpret noun phrases like 'the kings of England', 'the water that was spilled', and generic uses of noun phrases like 'the snowshoe hare' (as in 'the snowshoe hare is white in the winter'). But the theory is economical and has many other virtues: in particular it provides plausible resolutions of an impressive list of semantic puzzles. Two of these are worth mentioning.

(i) Without having to postulate the reality of nonexistent entities, it explains how claims of nonexistence, such as 'The result of dividing 7 by 0 does not exist' can be meaningful and true.

(ii) It explains how George IV could have wished to know whether Sir Walter Scott was the author of *Waverley*, while at the same time George IV didn't wish to know whether Scott was Scott.

The first of these puzzles is resolved simply by performing the analysis. Suppose that to predicate existence of v is to say there is something to which v is identical, and that 'x is a result of dividing 7 by 0' is equivalent to '$0 \cdot x = 7$'. Then the analysis of 'The result of dividing 7 by 0 exists' will amount to this:

(0.2.33) There is an x such that (i) $0 \cdot x = 7$, and (ii) for all y and z, if $0 \cdot y = 7$ and $0 \cdot z = 7$ then $y{=}z$, and (iii) for some v, $v{=}x$.

This sentence is false, simply because its first clause is false: there is no x such that $0 \cdot x = 7$.

To say that the result of dividing 7 by 0 doesn't exist is to deny (0.2.33), so the nonexistence claim is true.

The second puzzle is somewhat complex. In particular, it involves the proper noun 'Scott', which according to Russell is not really a logically proper name, and should be analyzed as a covert description. But we can see how the solution works if we ignore this issue and treat 'Scott' as an individual constant.

Then, according to Russell's theory, 'Scott is the author of *Waverley*' and 'Scott is Scott' have quite different meanings. The first amounts to 'There is one and only one author x of *Waverley*, and x=Scott'. The second is a self-identity, 'Scott = Scott'. Since the meanings of the two are different, George IV could believe the second without believing the first, and could wish to know the first without wishing to know the second.

Feeling that denotation and denoting phrases were problematic, Russell provided analyses that assimilate them to complex quantifications. This is the source of the philosophical attractiveness of the theory, because reference and denotation are confusing in ways that quantifiers and identity are not. It is precisely this feature, however, that Strawson finds objectionable. He feels that the fundamental role of definite noun phrases is referential, and he attempts in Strawson (1950) to show this by paying attention to the circumstances under which these expressions are used.

Without distorting things too much, you could say that Strawson wants us to consider Russell's theory as a matter of linguistics, and to reexamine it in light of the linguistic evidence. But in 1950, linguists hadn't given much thought to semantic methodology. For Strawson, linguistic evidence had to do with constructed examples of usage and sensitivity to subtle nuances of meaning. By 1950, these techniques had become popular in the circle of philosophers growing around the philosopher J. L. Austin at Oxford. We will have more to say about these developments in Chapter 6.

Behind this dispute, and muddying it to some extent, there seems to be a fairly deep difference of opinion concerning the nature of logic. Russell thought of logic as closely related to mathematics. The clarity which logic shares with mathematics is due to its objectivity, and logic provides an improvement over less regimented and decontextualized forms of thought. Strawson, however, thought of logic as closely related to the way we ordinarily speak and think. The difference shows up when Strawson (1950: 21) says: "Russell's theory of descriptions . . . is still widely accepted among logicians as giving a correct account of the use of such expressions in ordinary language. I want to show, in the first place that this theory, so regarded, involves some fundamental mistakes." Russell, and most logicians, would not agree that logic is a theory of ordinary language usage.

If we were to pursue these fundamental differences here, we would lose touch with the core dispute between these two philosophers over definite descriptions. For our present purposes, we will pretend that their disagreement has to do with the meaning of expressions in natural (rather than logical) languages and not with their use. Other concerns that Strawson raises in his paper, and that raise larger issues, are discussed separately in Chapter 6 and in Chapters 4 and 7.

Instead of talking about "denoting phrases," Strawson begins by targeting phrases that have a "uniquely referring use." In presenting examples of such phrases, he produces a much more adequate inventory of linguistic definite noun phrases than Russell's: he includes demonstratives, singular pronouns, and 'the table', as well as 'the king of France'.

Strawson invites you to imagine that someone has said (0.2.34) to you, without, however, giving any other details about the imagined conversational circumstances.

(0.2.34) The King of France is wise.

This suggests an utterance that is more or less "out of the blue." He correctly points out that you'd be very unlikely to respond "That's untrue." And he believes that you'd resist being forced to say that the utterance was either true or untrue. Strawson concludes from evidence of this sort that nothing was said in uttering (0.2.34). Later authors, such as Strawson himself and van Fraassen (1966), have taken this to mean that the sentence (0.2.34) is, in this particular context, neither true nor false, and have shown how to develop a logical account of the phenomenon, using "truth-value gaps."

The dispute over nonreferring definite descriptions like (0.2.34) is this: Russell says they are false, while others, feeling that failures of reference are different from mere falsehoods, say that they involve a presupposition failure of some sort. Strawson's paper marks the beginning of interest in the phenomenon of presupposition, a topic about which we have learned a great deal since 1950.

Definite descriptions like 'the king of France' are not ideal for eliciting the intuitions that Strawson wished to mobilize. But another example of Strawson's makes his case more convincingly:

> Consider the sentence, 'The table is covered with books.' It is quite certain that in any normal use of this sentence, the expression 'the table' would be used to make a unique reference, i.e. to refer to some one table. It is a quite strict use of the definite article, in the sense in which Russell talks on p. 30 of *Principia Mathematica*, of using the article 'strictly, so as to imply uniqueness'. On the same page Russell says that a phrase of the form 'the so-and-so', used strictly, will only have an application in the event of there being one so-and-so and no more. Now it is obviously false that the phrase 'the table' in the sentence 'the table is covered with books', used normally, will 'only have an application in the event of there being one table and no more'. It is indeed tautologically true that, in such a use, the phrase will have an application only in the event of there being one table and no more which is being referred to, and that it will be understood to have an application only in the event of there being one table and no more which it is understood as being used to refer to. To use the sentence is not to assert, but it is (in the special sense discussed) to imply, that there is only one thing which is both of the kind specified (i.e. a table) and is being referred to by the speaker. (Strawson 1950: 332–33)

Despite appearances, it is not clear that there is a real conflict here. Russell would say that if 'The table is covered with books' is used to talk about a particular table that is indeed covered with books, then the *sentence* implies that there is just one table, and hence, it is false. Strawson would insist that under these circumstances (i) the *speaker* implies that there is a unique table he is referring to, and (ii) what he says about it is true. These claims are compatible.

Now the issue has shifted: Russell dismisses speaker implication (because it is psychological and his concern is logic), and Strawson claims that the notion of sentence implication is incoherent (because he thinks only uses of sentences have truth-values).

Here, both Russell and Strawson appear to be on weak ground. The idea that the sentence 'The table is covered with books' is false when used to refer to a particular table is highly unintuitive, but also it is implausible to say that, as well as referring to a table, a speaker is *also* somehow implying that he is referring to only one table.

As this example suggests, the phenomenon of the interpretation of definites is more complicated than either Russell or Strawson imagined. The subsequent enormous literature on this topic has borne this out: see, for instance, Ostertag (2002); Roberts (2002).

In the course of Strawson (1950), Russell is accused of a number of confusions, most of these having to do with neglect of the intimate connection between meaning and the use of an expression in a particular context. In Russell (1957), his reply to Strawson, Russell defends himself convincingly against these accusations and raises questions about the relevance of Strawson's evidence. At this point, the debate between the two begins to prefigure contemporary issues about the division of labor between semantics and pragmatics.

0.3 Ayer versus Geach on Ethical Statements

A. J. Ayer (who lived 1910–1989) taught philosophy at University College, London and Oxford. Ayer (1936) was an early work, which quickly became well known as an exposition of logical positivism. Ethics was not really Ayer's primary philosophical interest; he presents and defends views about ethical statements because of systematic considerations, which need to be understood in the context of empiricist tendencies in philosophy during the first half of the twentieth century.

From what we have already said about Carnap, Russell, and Quine, it should be evident that many philosophical contemporaries were enthusiastic advocates of various forms of empiricism. For some, this meant only that the empirical sciences and their methods are our primary source of knowledge; for others, it meant that anything contingently true, to be knowable, must rest on a foundation of empirical evidence. Logical positivism is an extreme and systematic expression of the second idea, holding that a declarative sentence is made true or false (and hence made meaningful) by two, and only two, factors: logic and empirical evidence. Logical positivism was in part a reaction to the enthusiastic and excessive metaphysics of the nineteenth century and was motivated by skeptical views about metaphysical claims. If such claims could be shown to be neither confirmable nor disconfirmable by a combination of logic and factual evidence they must be meaningless.

Ayer is concerned with ethical statements because examples like

(0.3.35) You were wrong to steal that money.

also seem to be independent of the totality of logic and empirical evidence; Ayer (1936: Chapter 6) is devoted to this topic. A disagreement between two people about (0.3.35) would typically begin with a debate about the relevant facts. But the debaters could eventually agree on all the facts, and use logic impeccably, and might still disagree about whether (0.3.35) is true. This aspect of ethical dispute, Ayer feels, rests on a confusion or misrepresentation of what is at stake when ethical claims are expressed and debated.

Ayer wants to say that statements about the rightness and wrongness of specific actions – and by extension, statements about generic rightness and wrongness – only appear to be stating anything over and above their factual core. Example (0.3.35), for instance, has no content over and above the claim that you stole the money. The contribution of 'wrong' to (0.3.35), Ayer thinks, is a matter of emotional coloring: it conveys disapproval. So, according to Ayer, (0.3.35) is equivalent to

(0.3.36) You stole that money. Shame on you!

and is comparable to overt expressions of disgust, like

(0.3.37) Ugh! Broccoli! (Said by a small boy at the dinner table.)

Ayer's formulation of the idea is unrefined and – most philosophers would agree – recklessly unqualified. But the philosophical position about ethical statements that he proposes, known as *expressivism*, is attractive in its own right as an ethical theory. It has been proposed and defended in much more detail and with more sophistication by later philosophers, including Charles Stevenson and Allan Gibbard. (See Stevenson [1944], Gibbard [1990].) The merits of expressivism remain an issue of contention among ethicists.

But the ethical issues are not really our concern here. Ayer is also making a *semantic* claim about the proper interpretation of ethical statements, but without pausing to consider how this claim could be reconciled with a general semantic account of how these statements interact with other constructions in the language.

Among other things, a semantic theory must account in a uniform and systematic way for the meaningful interactions of syntactic constituents. This means that it is not possible to make local and more or less ad hoc changes, without considering the systematic consequences – you must consider the impact of the change on the underlying system of semantic rules. In particular, you can't say, of two similar expressions, that one is somehow semantically defective and the other is not, because if the expressions are alike semantically, semantic rules must treat them alike.

This crucial point can be illustrated with the semantics of simple addition and division. The rule for interpreting $\alpha + \beta$, for instance, where α and β are numerical terms, is that $[\![\alpha+\beta]\!]$ (the denotation or semantic interpretation of $\alpha+\beta$) is the result of adding $[\![\alpha]\!]$ and $[\![\beta]\!]$: we take the denotations of the component terms and add these two numbers.

So far, so good. But suppose our arithmetical syntax sanctions division by zero, allowing terms like '$\frac{5}{0}$'. We have to treat these terms as anomalous; perhaps we say that such terms have no denotations. But if we stop there, our semantic rule for addition will be defective, because now it doesn't cover cases like '$\frac{5}{0}+3$', where one of the terms has no denotation.

We can, of course, revise the rule, and say that $\alpha+\beta$ denotes nothing if either α or β fails to denote, and that otherwise it denotes the sum of α and β. But this doesn't stop the flood of difficulties. What about '$\frac{7}{0}=6$'? The standard rule for identity is that $\alpha=\beta$ is true if and only if $[\![\alpha]\!]$ is identical to $[\![\beta]\!]$. We have to modify this rule, and the natural way to do that is to say that $\alpha=\beta$ is neither true nor false if either α or β fails to denote, and otherwise is true if and only if $[\![\alpha]\!]$ and $[\![\beta]\!]$ are the same. This restores the generality of the rule, but now we can no longer say that $\alpha=\alpha$ is logically valid, because '$\frac{2}{0}=\frac{2}{0}$' is untrue. This is embarrassing and unwelcome. And as we look further into the effects of admitting just one nonreferring term, we find other nasty consequences awaiting us. We will have to reconsider other standard logical validities, even things as innocuous as 'If ϕ then ϕ'.

The interconnectedness of semantic rules, and the surprisingly comprehensive consequences of small changes to semantic systems, have been well known to logicians and semanticists ever since Frege. This is the thought behind Peter Geach's critique of Ayer's proposal in Geach (1965). This criticism, and the difficulty it raises for expressivism and other similar theories, is commonly called the "Frege–Geach problem."

Geach's paper is actually quite general – it covers many topics, and the criticism of expressivism is bundled together with similar criticisms of other philosophical theories. But his argument against Ayer's expressivist account is quite simple: he invites us to consider ethical sentences when they occur as antecedents of conditionals. Examples like

(0.3.38) If stealing is wrong, so is robbery.
(0.3.39) If you should not steal, you should not rob.

are perfectly meaningful. But Ayer does not think the antecedents of (0.3.38) and (0.3.39), 'Stealing is wrong', and 'You should not steal', are truth-evaluable claims, thus making it difficult or impossible to say what the conditional sentences could mean.

Not only is it clear that (0.3.38) is meaningful, it participates in logically valid inferences just as a normal conditional would:

(0.3.40) If stealing is wrong, so is robbery. But stealing is wrong. Therefore robbery is wrong.

If the premises and conclusion are not truth-evaluable, as Ayer would have it, this inference couldn't be truth-preserving.

Geach puts his point like this; conditions for the assertion of a sentence can't account for its meaning, because when one sentence occurs as a constituent of a larger sentence, we require a meaning (not just assertion conditions) to determine the meaning of the containing sentence. The simple example of divisibility by 0 that we presented above shows that to address this problem it's necessary to modify an entire system of semantic rules and that even in relatively simple cases this can be challenging.

Even though Geach was a philosopher, his criticism has a distinctly linguistic flavor. Syntacticians and semanticists seldom think in terms of one example; in testing a theory, they habitually generate large sets of different but relevant examples. Also, they take very seriously the impact of a proposal on a theory, in the form of a system of rules. This is exactly what Geach is saying the expressivists must do to have a minimally acceptable theory.

The later history of expressivist ethical theories is actually a good example of how fruitful the interaction of linguistic considerations with philosophical theories can be. Expressivists have taken the Frege–Geach problem seriously, and some of the best subsequent work in the field has consisted of systematic and extended attempts to overcome the difficulties it raises.

PART I

Philosophy of Semantics

1 Frege and Tarski

1.1 Frege

Gottlob Frege (1848–1925) lived most of his life in Jena in quiet obscurity, working on an ambitious project aiming at a rigorous foundation for mathematics. He could have hardly predicted that a generation after his death he would be considered one of the most important logicians of all time, one of the central figures of analytic philosophy, and – most unexpectedly – one of the founders of modern semantics. For more information about Frege's life and work, see Kenny (2000).

Like many figures standing at the very beginning of a strikingly new intellectual tradition, Frege's insights into foundational issues were profound. The mathematical insights, for the most part, are not relevant to our purposes here. Many of the logical ideas have, with improvements and modifications, been incorporated into the material covered in introductory courses in symbolic or mathematical logic. Here, we'll concentrate on the ideas that are most closely connected to later developments in semantics. Even with this limitation, readers may bear in mind that, like all great thinkers, Frege and his work are complex. Explaining his ideas is not an easy task – soon exposition blends into scholarship and touches on matters of interpretation that can be controversial. We try here to avoid these matters, providing references for those who wish to pursue them.

1.1.1 Against Formalism and Psychologism

Like Plato, Frege thought that mathematics is a source of unalterable truths. In Frege (1953), an extended inquiry into the nature of numbers and arithmetic, he stresses that arithmetic is not sensitive to introspective evidence or to the empirical sciences. From this, he concluded that numbers cannot be either mental contents (ideas, images, concepts, etc.) or physical marks (ink marks, sound waves, pixels on a screen, etc.):

> Stricker himself states that the only idea he associates with the word 'hundred' is the symbol 100. Others may have the idea of the letter C or something else; does it not follow, therefore, that these mental pictures are, so far as concerns us and the essentials of our problem, completely

> immaterial and incidental – as incidental as chalk and blackboard, and indeed that they do not deserve to be called ideas of the number a hundred at all? ... A proposition may be thought, and again it may be true; let us never confuse these two things. We must remind ourselves, it seems, that a proposition no more ceases to be true when I cease to think of it than the sun ceases to exist when I shut my eyes. Otherwise, in proving Pythagoras' theorem we should be reduced to allowing for the phosphorous content of the human brain; and astronomers would hesitate to draw any conclusions about the distant past, for fear of being charged with anachronism – with reckoning twice two as four regardless of the fact that our idea of number is a product of evolution and has a history behind it.
>
> Mill always confuses the applications of an arithmetical proposition, which often are physical and do presuppose observed facts, with the pure mathematical proposition itself. The plus symbol can certainly look, in many applications, as though it corresponded to a process of heaping up; but that is not its meaning; for in other applications there can be no question of heaps or aggregates, or of the relationship between a physical body and its parts, as for example when we calculate about numbers or events. (Frege 1953: 6e)

If logic is to serve as a foundation for something that is quite separate from introspective or empirical facts, it must itself be equally free of these things. This freedom might be trivial because logic simply lacks a subject-matter. There is a long tradition in philosophy that sees logical truths as *empty*, saying nothing about what the world is like. But this is definitely not Frege's view – he thinks of logic as the most *general* inquiry. Thus conceived, logic must be associated with an ontology. Frege's ontology informs his thinking about the organization of a system of logic and the way in which its expressions must be understood. And since modern semantics took its inspiration from Frege's logical system, elements of the Fregean ontology are still recognizable in the type theory that most standard semantic theories employ. A less well-known version of intensional type theory, due to Alonzo Church, is directly based on Frege's ideas; see Church (1993).

1.1.2 Object and Function

For Frege, everything in existence belongs to one of two broad categories: it is either an object or a function. Frege thinks of functions as somehow incomplete – a metaphor that sits well with the idea that functions yield a value only when appropriate arguments are supplied. Rather than fleshing out the completeness metaphor, Frege chose to characterize objects by means of the sorts of expressions we use to refer to them: they are the things that can be picked out by singular nouns or noun phrases. This leads to trouble: Frege must insist that 'the function that assigns to every natural number its square' does not designate a function. (This is a version of the *concept horse* problem; cf. Frege [1979b].)

Frege allows functions to take other functions as arguments, so that his ontology gives rise to a hierarchy within the category of functions. This is a type hierarchy, but not quite the same as those that logicians use today.

Contemporary logic separates objects into a hierarchy of types, with a type of individuals at the bottom. This arrangement – the simple theory of types – is one of the generally accepted solutions to the Russell Paradox, a difficulty that undermined Frege's logical program after long years of hard work. See Church (1940); Kamareddine et al. (2004); Irvine and Deutsch (2014). Objects of higher type are formed by taking sets of individuals, sets of these sets, and so forth.

Nowadays, mathematicians do not consider the difference between a set and its characteristic function to be important, so that sets of individuals and functions that input individuals and output truth-values are more or less interchangeable. This is strikingly different from Frege's conception. Frege thinks of anything belonging to one of these higher types as an object, without making any type distinctions among them. On the other hand, functions do not count as objects for Frege: he thinks of the two as entirely distinct.

Frege's conception of a function is closely related to his discovery (which might well count as the most important single innovation in the history of logic) that quantifiers like ∀ ("for all") and ∃ ("for some") operate on what are now called *open expressions* – expressions containing free variables. Begin, for instance, with a numerical expression like this.

(1.1.1) $3^2 + 6{\cdot}3 + 1.$

We can, of course, evaluate this expression by carrying out the arithmetical operations:

(1.1.2) $3^2 + 6{\cdot}3 + 1 = 9 + 18 + 1 = 28.$

But suppose we need to carry out many similar calculations: say we're interested in a series of calculations beginning with (1.1.1), like this:

(1.1.3) $3^2 + 6{\cdot}3 + 1$ and $4^2 + 6{\cdot}4 + 1$ and $5^2 + 6{\cdot}5 + 1.$

We soon begin to realize a *pattern* here; we are taking the square of a number, adding that to the result of multiplying the number by 6, and then adding 1. Following mathematical practice, we depict the pattern by replacing '2' in (1.1.1) with the *variable* 'x'.

(1.1.4) $x^2 + 6{\cdot}x + 1.$

Example (1.1.4) pictures a *function*. Contemporary logicians think of such examples as having a *variable reference*; when the variable 'x' is assigned a number, (1.1.4) will refer to the result of applying the function to that number. Frege thought of (1.1.4) as having an indefinite reference. It corresponds to a function, which is something incomplete or *unsaturated*. Saturation is accomplished, and reference – say, reference to the number 28 – is achieved when a referring expression like '3' is substituted for 'x' in (1.1.4). This particular substitution produces the expression (1.1.1), which refers to the number 28.

At this point it will be helpful to introduce some notation: where β is an open expression and α is a closed expression, $\beta\,[^{\alpha}/x]$ is the result of substituting occurrences of α for all the occurrences of x in β. Using this notation, if β is (1.1.4) then $\beta\,[^{`3'}/x]$ is (1.1.1).

This allows us to state a fundamental principle about functions and reference: the reference of $\beta\,[^{\alpha}/x]$ is a function of the reference of α. Let's call this principle *referential functionality*. This means that $\beta\,[^{\alpha}/x]$ and $\beta\,[^{\alpha'}/x]$ must be coreferential (i.e., must have the same reference) if α and α' are coreferential. If we substitute '5' for x in (1.1.4), we get an expression that refers to the same thing (in fact, to 56) as the expression we get when we substitute '$2^2 + 1$' for x in (1.1.4). In mathematics, this is nothing more than the principle that substitutions of equals will be equal.

Now we come to an insight of Frege's that was at once remarkably fruitful and strikingly unintuitive: *sentences*, as well as expressions like '5' and '5 + 7', must be referring expressions. For one thing, sentences are as indispensable in mathematics as in natural languages; without sentences we can't say anything at all. (Ordinary speech does allow elliptical discourse, where a nonsentence can rely on context to communicate a complete thought. For example, one might say only "ridiculous" and thereby say something quite definite in a context where one is watching a political speech. But these sorts of examples play no role in mathematical discourse, which was Frege's main concern.)

But sentences like '5 + 7 = 12', contain no variables. Therefore, they must refer to objects. This conclusion follows from Frege's theoretical framework; nevertheless, we have no pretheoretic intuitions about sentences referring or about what they might refer to. At this point, then, Frege is free to stipulate what the references of sentences are, and systematic considerations force him to conclude that sentences refer to their truth-values.

Frege's views on this topic are a matter of scholarly controversy, but here is a version of the argument – sometimes called the *slingshot* – that many have subsequently attributed to him. Besides referential functionality, the argument requires only one further assumption: if two sentences are provably equivalent, then they have the same referent.

Let the referent of the sentence 'Snow is white' be the object o. The sentence '$\{x \mid x = 2 \wedge$ Snow is white$\} = \{x \mid x = 2\}$' is provably equivalent to 'Snow is white', and so, it too must refer to o. Since 'Snow is white' and 'Grass is green' are both true, '$\{x \mid x = 2 \wedge$ Snow is white$\}$' and '$\{x \mid x = 2 \wedge$ Grass is green$\}$' both refer to the same set: $\{x \mid x = 2\}$. (According to the *principle of extensionality* of set theory, sets are equal if and only if they have the same members, i.e. if the criteria for membership in the sets are equivalent.) But then, by the substitutivity of reference, '$\{x \mid x = 2 \wedge$ Grass is green$\} = \{x \mid x = 2\}$' also refers to o and, again by the assumption that provably equivalent sentences must have the same referent, so does 'Grass is green.'

The argument did not assume anything about either 'Snow is white' or 'Grass is green' except their truth, so it actually shows that all true sentences refer to the same thing. A parallel argument then shows that all false sentences must also refer to the same thing. (For more about this argument, see Church (1943), Davidson (1969), and Neale (2001), and the discussion in Section 1.2.6.) Frege calls the referent of true sentences *the True* and the referent of false ones *the False*. Using contemporary notation, we'll use '$\top$' and '$\bot$' for these.

If we don't follow Frege in lumping $\top$ and $\bot$ with the rest of the objects, we have a simple relationship between the extensional part of Montague's type theory and Frege's ontology. Montague has two basic types, objects (type e) and truth-values (type t). Functional types are then generated by the simple inductive rule: if α and β are types, so is $\langle\alpha,\beta\rangle$, the type that consists of functions that map entities of type α to entities of type β.

Besides contributing the ideas behind the ontology that underlies contemporary semantics, Frege is mostly famous among semanticists for drawing two important distinctions that helped to clarify our rough, intuitive conception of meaning. We now turn to these.

1.1.3 Force and Content

Frege's main program was to show that a large part of mathematics, including all of arithmetic, is part of logic. He tried to show that all arithmetical notions are definable in logic and that all arithmetical truths are derivable from those definitions using logic. It is in his pioneering 1879 work (Frege 1967) that the logical symbol '$\vdash$' makes its first appearance. While logicians now use it as a single sign for theoremhood, for Frege it was a complex sign for *judgments*.

The horizontal line within '$\vdash$' has a function similar to that of the orthographic period: it signifies that the group of symbols preceding it form a declarative sentence. Such sentences are true or false because they have "judgeable content." Judgment itself consists in mental assent to such a content, and the vertical line, when added to the horizontal, indicates such a cognitive assent. The overt expression of judgment is an act we call *assertion*.

Judging and asserting are acts. As such, they are performed by someone at a certain time and place, and obviously must be distinguished from the content that is being judged and asserted. The thought that there is no largest prime does not belong to any particular thinker or speaker and is true eternally. What made it hard for so many philosophers and linguists before (and even after) Frege to keep this straight was the idea that affirmative judgment is a matter of joining the ideas of subject and predicate, that the very act of forming truth-evaluable content is the same as the act of committing to its truth. Frege stresses that these acts are different: he calls the former the grasping of a thought and only the latter the judging that the thought grasped is true.

Frege uses the conditional 'If the accused was in Rome at the time of the deed, he did not commit the murder' to illustrate the need for a clean force–content distinction, Frege (1956: 375). He explains that in uttering this sentence, one is asserting neither that the accused was in Rome at the time of the deed nor that he committed the murder.

Frege also claims that the content of a yes–no question (e.g., 'Was the accused in Rome?') is the same as the content of the corresponding declarative, but takes a different approach to the contents of imperatives (e.g., 'Accused, be in Rome!'). His remarks on the topic were short and scattered; he did not develop a serious theory of speech acts and their relationship to sentential mood. But what he said was enough to highlight the need for such a theory.

1.1.4 Sense and Reference

Frege's central interest was mathematics; his life was devoted to developing a logic capable of providing a foundation for continuous mathematics, so that the results of calculus and the rest of analysis could be exhibited as theorems of logic. But the principles of logic apply in other areas than mathematics, and systematic considerations led Frege to consider logic in relation to languages more expressive than the formalisms used by mathematicians.

In perhaps his most famous paper, Frege (1892) grapples with a problem that arises at once in this broader context: the principle of referential functionality fails. (This is the same problem that Rudolf Carnap, Frege's student, labeled "the problem of intensionality.") Without giving a specific example, Frege begins with the thought that identity statements are often discoveries that couldn't be known without observation. From this thought, and his own first example, the following counterexample to referential functionality can be reconstructed.

(1.1.5) No empirical evidence is needed to find out that the fiery heavenly body that rose in the east this morning is identical to the fiery heavenly body that rose in the east yesterday morning.

Clearly, (1.1.5) is false; it refers to $\perp$; as Frege says, this identity was "one of the most fertile astronomical discoveries." On the other hand, (1.1.6) is obviously true; it takes no empirical evidence to know a self-identity.

(1.1.6) No empirical evidence is needed to find out that the fiery heavenly body that rose in the east this morning is identical to the fiery heavenly body that rose in the east this morning.

But in fact, the fiery heavenly body that rose in the east this morning is the sun and *is* identical to the fiery heavenly body that rose in the east yesterday morning. And we can obtain (1.1.6) by substituting 'the fiery heavenly body that rose in the east this morning' for 'the fiery heavenly body that rose in the east yesterday morning' in (1.1.5).

A simpler example, less faithful to Frege's text but frequently given to illustrate the point, may be helpful. The first planet seen in the evening, also called "the evening star," and the last planet seen in the morning, also called "the morning star," are one and the same thing: the planet Venus. This fact seems to have been one of the earliest astronomical discoveries. So we have:

(1.1.7) The morning star is identical to the evening star.

(1.1.8) The earliest astronomers knew that the morning star is identical to the morning star.

(1.1.9) The earliest astronomers knew that the morning star is identical to the evening star.

Example (1.1.7) is a true identity; (1.1.8) is (trivially) true; but (1.1.9), we can plausibly suppose, is false. Again, this is a counterexample to referential functionality.

If we recall that for Frege sentences refer to truth-values, we have even more stark examples of the same phenomenon.

(1.1.10) It is true that Columbus sailed from Spain, and true that Columbus didn't sail to India.

(1.1.11) Columbus believed that he sailed from Spain.

(1.1.12) Columbus believed that he didn't sail to India.

Examples (1.1.10) and (1.1.11) are true, but – since Columbus thought that he *had* sailed to India – (1.1.12) is false. But, according to Frege, 'Columbus sailed from Spain' and 'Columbus didn't sail to India' denote the same thing, $\top$. More generally, referential functionality for a language with 'believe', together with the idea that sentences refer to their truth-values, produces the absurd conclusion that anyone who believes anything true believes everything true.

Frege, the first to concentrate on mathematical language and mathematical proof as a central and paradigmatic challenge for logic, was also the first to discover that extending a logic from its original mathematical domain to wider areas of language and reasoning could prove to be problematic. The failure of referential functionality with which Frege (1892) is concerned is also a failure of a reference-based informal semantics that works well for mathematical language but not for languages containing *propositional attitudes* like 'believe'. The problem, in fact, is deep and pervasive. The consensus is that any systematic semantic theory must find a way to deal with this problem.

Frege solves the problem by bifurcating (or rather, *n*-furcating[1]) the fundamental relations between linguistic expressions and their semantic values. The content of an expression is broken into its reference (*Bedeutung*) and its sense (*Sinn*). The idea is that in certain contexts sentences refer not to truth-values but to beliefs. But what is a belief? Given what we have said about Frege's rejection of psychology as a basis for logic, he can't opt for a mental or cognitive account of the content of a mental state such as belief. Such a content must be something compatible with Frege's more platonist conception of logical ontology.

When we say that someone believes something – when, for instance, we say (1.1.11) – we have a sentence that refers to a believer (say, Columbus) and a belief (say the belief that Columbus sailed from Spain).

For Frege, such a content is the *sense* of a subordinate clause (for instance, the sense of 'Columbus sailed from Spain'). In general, he says that each expression of an (ideal) language must have a sense as well as a reference. (In Frege [1892] he allows for the possibility of nonreferring proper names in imperfect languages like German and English. These, he says, have a sense although they have no reference.) In simple cases (and this includes mathematical cases) the reference of a phrase depends only on the ordinary references of its constituents. But human languages exhibit more complex cases where the reference of a phrase may depend not on the ordinary reference but on the *secondary* reference of the constituent; this secondary reference is the (ordinary) sense. This device allows Frege to preserve the principle of referential functionality, by stipulating that sometimes – i.e. in some linguistic contexts – the reference is actually the secondary reference, namely the sense of a constituent.

The verb 'believe' is a secondary-reference inducing context. Thus, the reference of a sentence like (1.1.11) depends not on Columbus and the reference of 'Columbus sailed from Spain' (i.e., on Columbus and $\top$) but on Columbus and the *sense* of 'Columbus sailed from Spain'. Since the senses of 'Columbus sailed from Spain' and of 'Columbus didn't sail to India' are quite different, the inference from (1.1.10) and (1.1.11) to (1.1.12) is blocked, and belief is no longer trivialized.

Frege's solution to what is now called the "problem of intensionality," allows him to preserve referential functionality; he would say that the reference or truth-value of (1.1.11) depends on the references of its constituents. But (i) he associates a sense, as well as a reference, with each sentence; and (ii) he stipulates that in cases of indirect discourse the reference of a clause is its sense or secondary reference. Whether or not an ascription of belief like (1.1.11) is true or false will then depend on the believer and the sense, not the truth-value, of the subordinate clause.

[1] Frege's solution requires secondary senses, tertiary senses, and in general an infinite series of senses to deal with multiple embeddings.

Many contemporary solutions to this problem rely on a variant of Frege's idea. Frege's solution, however, is unsatisfactory or at least puzzling in two respects: the ontological puzzle of exactly what senses are and the technical puzzle created by the need for a hierarchy of senses.

It is clear what kind of thing Frege wants a sense to be – it must be something that is neither in space nor in time, and exists independently of human cognition. In other words, it would have the same ontological standing as that of numbers, according to Platonists. Accordingly, it is not an idea we have but something of which we can have an idea.

But it is not easy to say more about exactly what senses are. Avoiding psychological metaphors, Frege explains senses as modes or ways of referring. The idea is illustrated by Frege's example of the centroid of a triangle. The line joining the midpoint of one side of a triangle and the opposite vertex is called a *median*. A triangle has three medians, and any two of them will intersect at a point. A theorem of Euclidean geometry tells us that these midpoints are identical: the three medians all intersect at one point, the triangle's *centroid*.

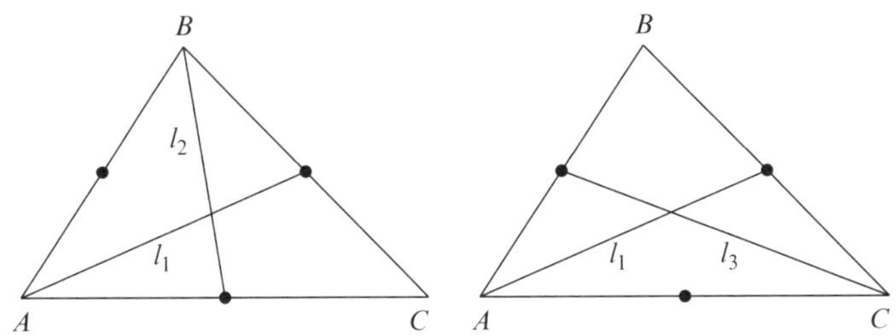

If we have a triangle ABC, then, with medians l_1, l_2 and l_3, the intersection of l_1 and l_2 will be the same as the intersection of l_1 with l_3: the references of (1.1.13) and (1.1.14) will be the same.

(1.1.13) The intersection of l_1 and l_2.
(1.1.14) The intersection of l_1 and l_3.

But the senses of these two expressions differ, because they use different procedures to locate the same point.

Frege also invokes the analogy of looking at an object through an optical instrument. Whether we observe the moon through a telescope or with the naked eye we see the same object, but by very different methods. If two observers use the same telescope to observe the moon, the moon itself is like the reference, the image of the moon in the lens is like the sense – it is not subjective, but the same for both observers. The patterns of activation in each observer's retinas are like the subjective mental impressions that accompany the reference.

Anyone who finds this analogy helpful will find it easy to see why concern with the traditional problems of philosophy can lead to an intensive interest in language and its semantics. The analogy assumes similarities, which might be deep and illuminating, between the semantics of linguistic expressions (accompanied by subjective ideas, mediated by an objective method of arriving at a reference) and perception (accompanied by subjective impressions, mediated by objective physical processes). If the analogy holds, semantics may illuminate epistemology and may even overlap with this traditional and central area of philosophy.

These explanations may be helpful but do not take us beyond an informal understanding of the semantics and its ontology. If we require, as Tarski did, that semantics should be a branch of mathematics, and if we want a semantics that can account for something like Fregean senses, we will have to do better than this.

A hierarchy of senses arises for Frege because a sentence like (1.1.11) must have a sense as well as a reference. Frege subscribed to a principle of sense functionality; the sense of a complex expression must be a function of the senses of its parts, rather than of their references. But in (1.1.11), the reference of 'Columbus sailed from Spain' is *secondary*; that is, it will be the sense of 'Columbus sailed from Spain'. So the sense of (1.1.11) must be the sense of this secondary reference. That is, it must depend on *the sense of the sense* of 'Columbus sailed from Spain'.

Without further elaboration of the theory, it is hard to tell whether this is a mere technicality or a deeper problem. Although Frege didn't provide the details, later logicians have, and it seems that although the theory can be worked out it is indeed quite complicated. (See Church [1951a]; Anderson [1977].)

1.2 Tarski

Alfred Tarski (1901–1983) was born in Poland, escaped Europe shortly before the Second World War, and for most of the remainder of his life taught at the University of California at Berkeley, making it for many years an unsurpassed center for research and education in mathematical logic. For more about Tarski's life and work, see Feferman and Feferman (2004).

Tarski was first and foremost a mathematician. He was interested in logic and semantics (or model theory) because of his conviction that here there was a promising new field of mathematics. Frege's interest in logic was also motivated by mathematical interests, but arose out a concern for rigor and detail that most mathematicians would have considered overdone and slightly obsessive. His impact on mainstream mathematics was indirect and was mediated by later figures such as David Hilbert, Paul Bernays, Thoralf Skolem, and Kurt Gödel. Tarski, on the other hand, felt that logic could have an impact on core areas of mathematics. At first he had to convince a mostly skeptical mathematical community of this, but eventually logic, set theory, and model theory were recognized by mathematicians as well-established subfields, and Tarski's ideas came to be seen as significant for other areas of mathematics.

1.2.1 Object Language and Metalanguage

Frege's logical successors gradually realized the importance of being more explicit about the study of mathematical language, transforming it into a branch of mathematics. Formalization became not just a matter of making mathematical proofs more rigorous but of developing a theory of proofs and the language in which they are framed. With Hilbert and Bernays (1934), *metamathematics* emerged as the mathematical study of mathematical theories: here are the beginnings not only of mathematical logic but of formal language theory and formal semantics.

Metamathematics involves at least two languages: an *object language*, the language under investigation (which typically would be a mathematical formalism) and the language in which the investigation is conducted, the *metalanguage*. At the outset, there may seem to be no reason why the object language and the metalanguage shouldn't be identical. And indeed, this is a genuine possibility as long as the topic is syntax (including proofs). But – as we will see – Tarski eliminated this possibility for semantic metalanguages.

Tarski and his contemporaries expected the object language to be *formalized*, to be explicitly and completely formulated. Because Tarski was concerned to make semantics mathematically respectable, the metalanguage could in principle be formalized, but usually, like most mathematical theories, it was left informal but precise. Eventually, a general consensus emerged that rigor could be achieved by assuming *set theory* as the background framework for semantics. This means that the ontology of the metatheory and its reasoning could be reconstructed in a set theoretic framework and that the axioms of set theory suffice to prove the basic results that are needed for semantic purposes.

1.2.2 What Should a Definition of Truth Accomplish?

Truth is central for Tarski, as it is for Frege, but Tarski narrows and sharpens the notion, as well as clarifying the theoretical setting in which it is to be approached. We have seen that, for Frege, the path from a sentence to its truth-value is mediated by a sense: a sentence ϕ has a sense p and this sense determines the truth-value. If (following the usual terminology) we call the sense of a sentence a *proposition*, Frege's framework allows us to speak (1) (indirectly) of the truth-value of a sentence and (2) (more directly) of the truth-value of a proposition.

It is indirect discourse, and in particular propositional attitudes like belief, that led Frege to say that senses (propositions) are associated with sentences.

For instance, (1.2.1) involves a proposition – the proposition that snow is white – and is true if that proposition is obvious and false otherwise.

(1.2.1) It is obvious that snow is white.

In the same way, (1.2.2) involves a (somewhat trivial) property of propositions.

(1.2.2) It is true that snow is white.

Mathematical languages and theories do not in general involve indirect discourse or intensionality. This enables Tarski to ignore senses and to conceptualize truth as a direct, unmediated relation between a sentence and a truth-value.

Tarski imposed three requirements on a satisfactory definition of truth for a given object language (which, he assumes, contains the resources of first-order logic and perhaps more). First, the definition should not have as a consequence a contradiction and "should observe the usual formal rules of definition," Tarski (1944: 68). This requirement includes adherence to classical logic and a ban on circular definitions. Tarski calls it *formal correctness*.

Second, Tarski required that the definition should be given in a metalanguage that does not contain undefined semantic terms, such as 'means', 'refers to', 'applies to' (Tarski, 1944: 68). If we want to use the definition to dispel lingering doubts about the coherence of the semantic enterprise – and there is no doubt that this was Tarski's chief motivation – this is a crucial desideratum.

Finally, we want the definition to cohere with our normal understanding of truth. Consider the sentence 'Snow is white'. Obviously, if this sentence is true, then snow is white, and if it is not true, then snow is not white. So, if our object language contains this sentence, an adequate definition of truth for it would have to entail

(1.2.3) 'Snow is white' is true if and only if snow is white.

We should want this for all the sentences of the object language. According to Tarski's Convention T, if α is a standard name in the metalanguage of a sentence ϕ of the object language L, then an adequate truth definition should produce all instances of (1.2.4):

(1.2.4) $T(\alpha) \leftrightarrow \phi$.

This is the requirement of *material adequacy*, Tarski (1944: 63).

Instances of Convention T may appear to be trivial and uninformative. But it is important to keep in mind that Tarski advanced (1.2.4) not as a definition of truth, but as a criterion of adequacy for a definition. And constructing a theory that conforms to Convention T turns out to be far from trivial. One intimation of this is Tarski's theorem on the undefinability of truth, proved in Tarski (1936); if T satisfies (1.2.4) for all formulas ϕ of L, then it can't be defined in L. An adequate semantic metalanguage must exceed the expressive capacity of the object language.

1.2.3 Defining Truth and Satisfaction

The ideas recorded in this section will be familiar to any reader who has taken an introductory course in symbolic logic or mathematical logic. But here, we will concentrate on the significance of the ideas for semantic theory.

Tarski's project begins with a formalized object language L, and is carried out in a suitable metalanguage ML. The formalization of L provides an explicit definition of the formulas, or more generally, of the "well-formed expressions" of L. The earliest attempts at formal syntax of which we are aware can be found in unpublished lectures of David Hilbert, given in 1917–1918 (Hilbert 1918) and involve an inductive or recursive definition that stipulates the simplest expressions of each syntactic type, as well as how simpler well-formed expressions can be assembled into more complex ones. This approach to "logical syntax" has persisted and is still in general use by logicians and computer scientists.

The inductive definition organizes the well-formed expressions into levels of complexity: the complexity of a basic well-formed expression is 0; if a maximally complex constituent of a complex expression is n, then the complexity of the entire expression is n + 1. This hierarchical organization is reflected in logical theory: most of the basic definitions and results of logic are obtained by induction on syntactic complexity: the result is stipulated for basic expressions, and then – assuming it holds up to complexity of level n – it is obtained for level n + 1.

Tarski's characterizations of truth follow this pattern; he defines truth by an induction on syntactic complexity. This is very close to saying that he assumes that truth is to be defined *compositionally*, and in fact he goes beyond this, assuming that the definition is *strongly compositional*. (For further discussion of these notions, see Section 2.2.)

Two approaches to truth can be found in Tarski's writings: (1) a *model-theoretic* definition of truth relative to a relational structure, and (2) an *absolute* or *translational* definition. The first approach is more useful in mathematical logic and in formal semantics; this is the definition that is reproduced in most logic texts. The second approach is influential in philosophy and in work on the Liar Paradox.

1.2.4 Relational Truth and Satisfaction

Tarski's languages are mathematical and include formalizations of number theory, abstract algebra, and set theory. Mathematical languages involve *mathematical structures*, and it is easily possible for a single language to be realized by many structures. Geometry provides a famous example: the language of geometry deals with points, lines, and their relations. Early geometers had in mind points and lines on a flat surface, but in the nineteenth century it was discovered that almost all the axioms of geometry were also true in other structures, such as the surface of a sphere.

It is this idea of truth in a structure that Tarski seeks to characterize. According to Tarski and Vaught (1956), a *relational structure* consists of a set of objects (or of *individuals*) and a set of relations over these objects. Relations can also be represented as sets: a one-place relation is a set of individuals, a two-place relation is a set of ordered pairs of individuals, etc.

We'll illustrate the idea with a simple first-order language equipped with a single two-place predicate letter R. Such a language might be used to develop a theory of ordering relations or of accessibility relations over worlds as in modal logic. Our language has only two *individual constants* or names, a and b. Like any first-order language, it has infinitely many *individual variables*, $x_1, x_2, \ldots$.

The syntax begins by listing the simplest expressions in each syntactic category. This is the *basis clause* – the lexicon – of the inductive definition.

(1.2.5) L_1 Syntax: Basis clause.

1. The set of terms is $\{a, b, x_1, x_2, \ldots\}$.
   a and b are constants, $x_1, x_2, \ldots$ are variables.
2. The only predicate letter is R (a two-place predicate letter).

Next, the *inductive clause* explains how complex phrases of each category can be formed out of simpler ones.

(1.2.6) L_1 Syntax: Inductive clause.

1. If α and β are terms then $R(\alpha,\beta)$ is an (atomic) formula.
2 If ϕ is a formula, then $\neg\phi$ is a (negative) formula.
3. If ϕ and ψ are formulas, then $(\phi \rightarrow \psi)$ is a (conditional) formula.
4. If ϕ is a formula and x is a variable, then $\forall x(\phi)$ is a (universal) formula.

The formulas are all and only those strings that can be generated by a finite sequence of applications of the clauses in (1.2.5) and (1.2.6), and whose final step is an application of one of the clauses of (1.2.6). Conjunction, disjunction, and existential quantification can be defined in this language.

An occurrence of x in a formula is said to be *bound* if it is in the scope of an occurrence of a quantifier $\forall x$. And an occurrence of x in a formula is said to be *free* if it is not bound. (The scope of an occurrence of a quantifier $\forall x$ within a formula is the formula occurrence that is contained in the matching parentheses immediately after the quantifier occurrence.) A formula like (1.2.8) with no free occurrences of variables is said to be a *sentence*; a formula like (1.2.7) with some free occurrences of variables is an *open formula*.

The syntax produces formulas such as these:

(1.2.7) $R(a, x_5)$

(1.2.8) $\forall x_1(\forall x_2(\forall x_3((R(x_1, x_2) \rightarrow (R(x_2, x_3) \rightarrow R(x_2, x_3))))))$

(1.2.9) $\forall x_1(\neg\forall x_2(\neg R(x_1, x_2)))$

Formula (1.2.7) says that two individuals are related: the first is the reference of the constant a and the second the reference of the variable x_5. Formula (1.2.8) says that the relation is transitive. Formula (1.2.9) says that everything is related to something.

Whether these formulas are true will depend on the relational structure. For instance, if the structure's domain is the set $\{1, 2, 3\}$, consisting of just three numbers, and its relation is *being less than*, then (1.2.8) is true and (1.2.9) is false. If the relation is *being different* (1.2.8) is false and (1.2.9) is true.

You would expect to proceed at this point with an inductive characterization of the conditions under which a formula is true in a relational structure. But in fact a direct attempt to do this fails, and repairing the failure introduces an idea that turns out to be of fundamental importance – not only for logic, but for linguistics.

The difficulty has to do with quantification. Take a simple universal formula like $\forall x_1(R(a, x_1))$. If the truth definition subscribes to strong compositionality, we must be able to say whether $\forall x_1(R(a, x_1))$ is true in terms of the truth of $R(a, x_1)$: in general, we must explain the truth of sentences in terms of the truth of open formulas.

But when is a formula like $R(a, x_1)$ true? There is a strong temptation, going back to Frege, to say it isn't true or false at all. But this would make it impossible to account for the truth of $\forall x_1(R(a, x_1))$. On the other hand, if we assume that variables refer like constants, then $R(a, x_1)$ will have a truth-value, but if $R(a, x_1)$ is true, this will not allow us to tell whether $\forall x_1(R(a, x_1))$ is true: the truth of $R(a, x_1)$ would only mean that the formula is true of (at least) one value of x_1, not that it is true of all values in the domain.

Tarski's solution to this problem turned out subsequently to be extremely fruitful. It is the basis, for instance, of algebraic approaches to logic such as *cylindrical algebras* and of *dynamic logic* (Ahmed 2005; Harel et al. 2000). And it is the idea behind the leading contemporary theory of indexicals; see Section 7.3.

The reference of a variable can be anything at all and is secured by indicating a reference, just as acts of pointing secure the reference of a demonstrative pronoun like 'that'. We can formalize a (simultaneous) reference-indication as an assignment of values to variables; a *variable assignment* (for a language L and a domain D) is a function g that assigns a member of D to each variable of L. If D is the set of nonnegative integers $\{0, 1, 2, \ldots\}$, and g is a variable assignment on D for L_1, then $g(x_1)$ and $g(x_2)$ are numbers – maybe $g(x_1) = 3$ and $g(x_5) = 0$.

Instead of inductively defining truth in a structure, Tarski defines *satisfaction*, which is a relation between a formula (which may or not be open) and a variable assignment. At the point in the induction where we wish to say whether or not $\forall x_1(R(a, x_1))$ is satisfied by assignment g, we will know *for all assignments* g′ whether g′ satisfies $R(a, x_1)$. This provides the needed information.

Recall that a relational structure for our language has two components: a domain D, which is simply a nonempty set, and a set R of ordered pairs of members of D. An *interpretation* I of the language in the structure assigns semantic values to basic expressions (except variables). The value of a constant depends on I. The value of a variable depends on a variable assignment g. So we must define the value of a term (an individual constant or variable) relative to *both* I and g. Recall, finally, that I(R) – the value of R – is a set of ordered pairs. These materials allow us to define the *reference* of a term, relative to an interpretation, as follows.

(1.2.10) Reference of terms of L_1, relative to interpretation I and variable assignment g:
$\mathrm{Ref}_{I,g}(a) = I(a)$, $\mathrm{Ref}_{I,g}(b) = I(b)$, and $\mathrm{Ref}_{I,g}(x_i) = g(x_i)$.

We can now define satisfaction for the formulas of our language, relative to a relational structure, an interpretation I and a variable assignment g on this structure. (Here we use the modern notation '$\models$' for satisfaction: '$I, g \models \phi$' means that I and g satisfy the formula ϕ.)

(1.2.11) Satisfaction for atomic formulas, relative to I and g:
$I, g \models R(\alpha, \beta)$ if $\langle \mathrm{Ref}_{I,g}(\alpha), \mathrm{Ref}_{I,g}(\beta)\rangle \in I(R)$.

(1.2.12) Satisfaction for complex formulas, relative to I and g:
1. $I, g \models \neg\phi$ if $I, g \not\models \phi)$
(i.e., if I doesn't satisfy ϕ).
2. $I, g \models (\phi \rightarrow \psi)$ if $I, g \not\models \phi$ or $I, g \models \psi$.
3. $I, g \models (\forall x(\phi))$ if for all variable assignments g′ that differ from g at most in the value assigned to x, $I, g' \models \phi$.

Clause 3 of this definition uses the idea of variables as pointers. $\forall x(\phi)$ is satisfied by I and g if ϕ remains satisfied, no matter how an individual is assigned to x.

In the special case of a sentence ϕ – a formula with no free variables, such as $R(a, b)$ or $\neg\forall x_1(R(x_1, a))$ – it turns out that satisfaction does not depend on the assignment: $I, g \models \phi$ for some g if and only if $I, g \models \phi$ for every g. This makes it possible for us to define – for sentences only – the simpler, nonrelational version of truth.

(1.2.13) Let ϕ be a sentence of L_1, i.e. a formula of L_1 containing no free variables. Then ϕ is true relative to I if and only if for every variable assignment g, $I, g \models (\phi, g)$.

Satisfaction, then, is a generalization of truth.

Since satisfaction rather than truth is needed for a compositional account, it looks as if this more general notion is more fundamental than truth – and likewise, sentences seem to be nothing more than formulas with the special invariance property mentioned in (1.2.13). Nevertheless, many logicians, including Tarski, have hesitated to exchange the more general notion of the satisfaction of open formulas for the less useful notion of the truth of closed formulas. Tarski, and many subsequent logic textbooks, treat free variables, satisfaction, and open formulas as a sort of necessary evil, a stepping stone to the definition of truth in (1.2.13) that can be forgotten once the recursive definition is in place. As we will see in Chapter 7, this parallels a prejudice that philosophers of language shared for many years about indexical sentences, as compared with what Quine called "eternal sentences."

Relational structures have advantages for linguistic purposes: they can be generalized. This can be useful in crafting suitable interpretations for linguistic constructions whose interpretation seems to need something other than individuals and simple set-theoretic constructions based on individuals. The addition of a domain of possible worlds is the most commonly used generalization of this sort. But relational structures can also be extended to deal with eventualities, plurals, and mass nouns. Linguists, who in general don't share the ontological concerns of some philosophers, are often happy to propose such extensions.

1.2.5 Absolute Truth and Satisfaction

In Tarski (1936), his earliest work on truth, Tarski develops an approach that dispenses with relational structures by supposing that the metalanguage is a *syntactic extension* of the object language. This means that every formula of L is also a formula of ML. That is less useful for mathematical purposes; many of the most important applications of logic in mathematics, such as the consistency and independence of the axiom of choice in set theory, work with truth in relational structures. But in this way Tarski was able to meet the second and third requirements he imposed on definitions of truth: his absolute definition of truth does not appeal to undefined semantic notions and it can derive instances of Convention T. (The ingredients of the relational definition of truth – relational structures, variable assignments, and interpretations – are not undefined in the presence of set theory. But for some purposes, one might want to take the notion of a set to be undefined.)

Since Tarskian truth applies to sentences, ML must contain an adequate syntax for L, including a standard name of each expression of L. How these names are constructed is not important, as long as they reflect the syntactic structure of the expressions that they name. This supposes that ML contains machinery for describing the syntactic structures of L – not a very demanding condition, because Gödel (1931) showed that a language with fairly minimal arithmetical resources will be capable of formulating the syntax of any language at all, including itself.

Finally, ML must be able to talk about truth in L. In the simplest case, this might be done by equipping ML with a one-place predicate letter *T*; but as we have seen, if there are quantifiers in L, we will need a two-place predicate letter *T* characterizing satisfaction – truth in L relative to a variable assignment.

These requirements allow the metalanguage not only to *use* formulas of the object language but to *mention* them. If, for instance,

(1.2.14) $5 + 7 = 12$

is a sentence of L, then it's also a sentence of ML. But furthermore, ML will have a standard name of '5 + 7 = 12', say

(1.2.15) $\ulcorner 5 + 7 = 12 \urcorner$.

Then

(1.2.16) $T(\ulcorner 5 + 7 = 12 \urcorner)$

will be a sentence of ML saying that (1.2.14) is true.

Assuming that L (and therefore, ML as well) have the resources of first-order logic (FOL), ML will be able to *combine* uses and mentions of L formulas, allowing hybrid formulas such as (1.2.17), which conjoins (1.2.14) – a claim about numbers in the language of L – with (1.2.16) – a claim in the ML about the truth of (1.2.14):

(1.2.17) $5 + 7 = 12 \wedge T(\ulcorner 5 + 7 = 12 \urcorner)$.

Tarski's Convention T involves such mixed use–mention formulas. (See (1.2.4), above.)

The problem of characterizing absolute truth then amounts to providing plausible axioms in ML that will entail all instances of Convention T. This can be done for first-order object languages by rehearsing the same inductive definition that we supplied in Section 1.2.4 for relational truth.

1.2.6 The Impact of Tarskian Semantics on Philosophy

Tarski's work on truth had an enormous impact on mathematical logic. But philosophers, as well as mathematicians, paid attention to it. Although philosophy was not his primary interest, Tarski was pleased about this and wrote a description of his approach to semantics with philosophers in mind (Tarski [1944]). This classic article is probably the best introduction to the topic for nonlogicians.

Rudolf Carnap, the most dedicated and talented advocate of formal approaches to philosophy in the first half of the twentieth century, began with only syntactic tools in Carnap (1934), but was converted to semantics soon afterwards. The results of this Tarski-inspired conversion, reported in

Carnap (1942), are a landmark in the history of philosophical semantics and point in the direction of later linguistic applications.

Carnap characterizes syntax, semantics, and pragmatics in a way that would satisfy most of our contemporaries: the difference between these three is a matter of abstraction from language use and users. Pragmatics doesn't abstract at all from users; semantics deals with expressions and designations, but abstracts from users. (For Carnap, 'designation' is more or less synonymous with the modern term 'semantic value'.) Finally, syntax abstracts from designations, leaving only language-internal relations among expressions.

Syntax, semantics, and pragmatics, of course, have to do with language, and Carnap's views about languages can be found in the first pages of Carnap (1934). He distinguishes "word-languages" (natural languages) from artificial symbolic languages. Both are languages, and both are legitimate objects of study, but word-languages are "unsystematic and logically imperfect." He isn't explicit about the nature of these imperfections, but shuns word-languages as improper, or at least hopeless, objects of study. In this respect, Carnap was no different from almost all the analytic philosophers of his time, and philosophical distaste for imagined imperfection was probably one of the main reasons for the gap between logical philosophy and linguistics that persisted into the 1960s and beyond.

The semantical project of Carnap (1942), then, deals only with formalized languages, including FOL and even type theory, and is mainly concerned to show that metalinguistic notions such as synonymy can be defined using a semantical apparatus. Unlike Tarski, Carnap embraces intensionality, allowing sentences to designate propositions – but without following Tarski in attempting to fit propositions into the ontology of set theory and without committing himself to an account of what propositions are.

Carnap characterizes the intensional part of his semantics as tentative, but Alonzo Church, in his review (Church [1943]) of Carnap (1942), demolishes the theory: using Carnap's principles, Church showed that any two true sentences must designate the same proposition if lambda abstraction is allowed in the language. Church concludes that there are fewer tenable alternatives in semantics than one would think; you could also conclude that it is harder to work out the logical details of a satisfactory intensional semantics than early theorists seem to have supposed. But Church's difficulties are answered in Carnap's mature work on intensionality (Carnap [1956]). This work is not only a technical advance but is a precursor of Montague's intensional logic and of the theories of intensionality currently favored by linguists.

Shortly afterwards, Pap (1958) appeared. This neglected classic of analytic philosophy deepens and develops Carnap's work in semantics, and places it in historical perspective.

1.3 Conclusion

Frege and Tarski are now figures of an increasingly distant past. But there is a direct chain from their ideas and work, through Carnap and Richard Montague, to the contemporary framework of formal semantics as practiced by linguists. Linguists have added something that was not appreciated by Frege, Tarski, or Carnap: respect for natural languages and a powerful arsenal of methods for dealing with semantic evidence. Linguists' confidence in the ultimate orderliness and underlying rationality of natural languages has proved to be far more rewarding than the skepticism of the logicians and philosophers discussed in this chapter. Nevertheless, the insights of these precursors remain valuable today.

2 Compositionality

2.1 What Follows from Productivity?

The main reason the interpretations of Frege's and Tarski's formal languages look like semantic theories to the contemporary linguist is that they are *compositional*: They specify the interpretation of complex expressions in terms of the interpretations of their simpler parts. The method has obvious advantages – we can prove that something holds for all expressions, provided we can show that it holds for the smallest expressions and that it continues to hold as they are combined into larger wholes.

But why should the languages we find (as opposed to the ones we construct) be compositional? The classic answer comes from the opening passage of the third essay of Frege's *Logical Investigations*:

> It is astonishing what language can do. With a few syllables it can express an incalculable number of thoughts, so that even a thought grasped by a terrestrial being for the very first time can be put into a form of words which will be understood by someone to whom the thought is entirely new. This would be impossible were we not able to distinguish parts in the thought corresponding to the parts of the sentence, so that the structure of the sentence serves as an image of the structure of the thought. (Frege 1984: 390)

The premise would be hard to dispute: Language can obviously be used to express many – in fact, probably infinitely many – thoughts by means of sentences, and those sentences can be understood by others, even when they hear them for the very first time. But the conclusion that sentences share a structure with the thought they express, which is sometimes called Frege's *parallelism thesis*, is a bold claim with perplexing consequences.

Let's say that a sentence is an adequate translation of another just in case the two express the same thought. Parallelism entails that if ϕ_1 is adequately translated as ϕ_2 then the two sentences have the very same structure – the structure of the thought they both express. Thus, for any two languages L_1 and L_2 if ϕ_1 is a sentence in L_1 then either there is a sentence ϕ_2 in L_2 with the exact same structure as ϕ_1, or there is a thought (to wit, the thought expressed by ϕ_1) that is inexpressible in L_2. This offers a difficult choice. Either we must be willing to say that the sentences of the artificially constructed language of first-order Peano Arithmetic conform to a Universal Grammar or that the peculiar syntax of, say, '$\forall x \exists y(y = x + 1)$' will make the exact thought this sentence expresses alien to natural languages.

Parallelism also makes it a mystery how definitions within a single language work. The point of a definition, one might think, is to bestow the meaning of a complex expression (the definiens) on a simple one (the definiendum). But if substituting a simple for a complex expression within a sentence inevitably changes the thought the sentence expresses, such an act of stipulation is impossible. In fact, there is a deep tension in Frege's discussion of definitions: he thinks definitions are epistemically fruitful (which pushes him towards the claim that definiendum and definiens have different senses) and logically eliminable (which pushes him in the opposite direction). How exactly Frege sought to resolve this conflict is a matter of extensive debate among historians of philosophy; see Bell (1987); Dummett (1988); Bell (1996); Bermúdez (2001); Horty (2009); Kemmerling (2011).

How could Frege's trifling premise yield such portentous conclusions? The answer is: it does not. The parallelism thesis holds that thoughts and sentences share a certain abstract structure. That sentences have structure is obvious, but the thesis that thoughts are structured in some nontrivial way is not. On standard semantic views, thought contents are propositions, and propositions are sets of possible worlds. Such sets have a structure imposed by the membership relation but that is not the sort of structure that could be identical to the syntactic structure of sentences. There are arguments – like the one based on the semantics of mental attitude ascriptions we saw in Section 1.1.4 – that could be used to make a case for structured propositions. But Frege's argument at the beginning of "Compound Thoughts" is not one of them. (For a more detailed and circumscribed version of the Fregean argument see Pagin [2003].)

This is not to say that Frege's argument is a complete failure, only that he overstated its conclusion. What we might quite reasonably infer from the fact that we can understand complex expressions we have never heard before – not just sentences but phrases or clauses as well – is that the meanings of those complex expressions are a function of the meanings of their simplest parts and the way those parts are put together.

Even this weaker conclusion might seem obviously false. Ask yourself what red trucks, red hair, red wine, red skin, red apples, red watermelons, red tomatoes, and red sunsets have in common. You might be inclined to say that what counts as redness in an F depends entirely on what F is, which seems to be a violation of compositionality. There isn't such a thing as the standard meaning of 'red' which, together with the meaning of *F*, could determine the meaning of 'red *F*'.

But this sort of argument rests on a confusion. Even if we grant that red trucks, red hair, red wine, etc. have nothing in common, it simply does not follow that the meanings of 'red truck', 'red hair', 'red wine' etc. have nothing in common. The meaning of 'red' could be, for example, a function from the meaning of *F* to the meaning of 'red *F*' for arbitrary *F*. This guarantees that there is a function from the meanings of 'red' and *F* to the meaning of 'red *F*': the function that takes a function and an argument and applies the first to the second.

Compositionality, then, is not trivially false. Still, why should we believe it? The most popular argument inspired by considerations with which Frege was concerned in the passage we quoted is this: if we can understand complex expressions we have never heard before, we must have some prior knowledge on the basis of which we can figure out what they mean.

Knowledge requirements are an old philosophical theme: In the *Meno* (80 d–e), Plato raises the question of how inquiry is possible. Either we know what something is or we don't. If we do, there is no need for search; if we don't, then we don't know what to search for. Plato's solution is that learning requires tacit knowledge: to be ignorant is to be temporarily unable to recall something that is already in our mind. The claim that knowledge that is already present must enable us to understand the meanings of novel sentences is similar.

Given the fact that speakers of wildly different background knowledge and intellectual powers tend to be more or less uniformly good at this task, we are very much constrained in what sort of prior knowledge we can plausibly posit. At least two sorts are definitely needed: syntactic and lexical. If, in processing a sentence, you lose track of the organization of constituents, you have also lost track of the meaning. "Garden-path sentences" like 'The horse ran past the barn fell' provide striking evidence for this: if you fail to realize that 'ran past the barn' is a relative clause, you can't arrive at a meaning. As for lexical knowledge, if you don't understand some of the words in a sentence, you may be able to guess at the meaning, and guess well – but this is conjecturing, not grasping the meaning.

The minimal assumption would be that these two kinds of prior knowledge are also sufficient: that the *syntactic* knowledge required for determining the complete structure of a complex expression and the *lexical* knowledge required for the interpretation of its ultimate constituents suffice to comprehend its meaning. But if this is so, the meaning of a complex expression must be a function of these two factors.

This is *the argument from productivity*. (It might have been better to call this the argument from understandability, but we will stick with the standard name.) Its conclusion can be stated as follows:

> *Compositionality*: There is a function that maps the complete structure and the meanings of the ultimate constituents of any complex expression onto the meaning of that expression.

While this seems reasonably clear, it actually needs a lot of clarification. We will attempt to provide this in the following seven comments.

1. Strength. The argument from productivity is rather convincing, but far from conclusive. It is neither a deduction nor an induction, rather, it is what Charles Sanders Peirce called an *abduction* – an argument to the best explanation. Such an argument is only as good as the explanation it evokes.

It is important to see that noncompositional languages are easy to imagine and that some of them would even be easy to learn. Here is an example. Suppose we stipulate that whenever it rains at the location of an utterance of the sentence 'Elephants are gray', the sentence shall mean on that occasion that Julius Caesar was murdered on the ides of March while retaining its usual meaning on all other occasions. Let's also stipulate that this is the *only* difference between English and our new language – *Rain English*. Accordingly, by stipulation, the meanings of 'elephants', 'are', and 'gray' as well as the structure of the complete sentence 'Elephants are gray' is the same in English and Rain English. It follows that Rain English is not compositional: the meaning of 'Elephants are gray' varies with the weather while its structure and the meanings of its constituents stay the same. Rain English is certainly learnable: we think you have all learned it already.

In concluding compositionality from productivity we make a bet that besides syntactic and lexical knowledge there isn't anything (like checking whether it's raining) that may be required to figure out the meanings of complex expressions. There is nothing odd about this: all abductive arguments in science involve similar bets.

2. Domain. The principle of compositionality quantifies over complex expressions but leaves the domain of quantification unspecified. If the domain comprises complex expressions of a single language, the principle says that there is a function that compositionally assigns meanings to complex expressions of that language. To conjecture that German or English is compositional is to assert the principle of compositionality with domains restricted to expressions of German or of English. But we can quantify over crosslinguistic domains as well. For example, if we take the domain to contain all the complex expressions of all natural languages, then the principle says that there is a function that compositionally assigns meanings to all the complex expressions of all the natural languages. Let's call this construal *crosslinguistic compositionality* of all natural languages. It is a strong thesis which does not follow from the claim that each natural language has its own compositional meaning-assignment function.

To see why, consider the English sentence 'Snow is white' and its German translation 'Schnee ist weiss'. Crosslinguistic comparisons of meaning and structure are difficult, but suppose that after careful consideration we establish the following conclusions: (i) the ultimate constituents of 'Snow is white' are 'snow', 'is', and 'white' and the ultimate constituents of 'Schnee ist weiss' are 'Schnee', 'ist', and 'weiss', (ii) 'snow' and 'Schnee' are synonyms, 'is' and 'ist' are synonyms, and 'white' and 'weiss' are synonyms, (iii) the complete structure of 'Snow is white' is identical to the complete structure of 'Schnee ist weiss', and yet, (iv) 'Snow is white' means something different from 'Schnee ist weiss'. Then we can conclude that natural languages are not compositional in the crosslinguistic sense mentioned above: there is no function that compositionally assigns meanings to the complex expressions of both English and German. And yet, for all we have established there may well be a compositional meaning assignment for English and another, different compositional meaning assignment for German.

The argument from productivity yields support for the claim that each natural language is compositional but not for crosslinguistic compositionality of all natural languages. One could try to argue that counterexamples to crosslinguistic compositionality, like the hypothetical example in the previous paragraph, are impossible because distinct natural languages cannot have simple expressions with the same meaning, or perhaps they cannot have complex expressions with the same complete structure. But these are rather implausible claims. Alternatively, one might claim that competent speakers of one language could understand a complex expression ϵ in an unknown language if they can be given a correlate ϵ in their own language that has the same structure as ϵ and has simple expressions that are pairwise synonymous with those in ϵ. This is reasonable but by no means obvious.

3. Syncategoremata. Compositionality does not rule out the possibility that some lexical items are *syncategorematic*: are assigned nothing whatsoever as their meanings, but contribute nevertheless to the meanings of phrases in which they occur.

The usual semantics of the language of propositional logic illustrates this somewhat subtle technical point. Usually logical constants like $\neg$ ('not') are not themselves interpreted directly by assigning them semantic values. Instead, semantic clauses specify the interpretation of complex expressions in which they occur as the main connective. This is precisely how we did things in Clause 1 of (1.2.12), where we defined satisfaction for a version of first-order logic.

On this way of arranging the semantic rules, although 'and' and 'or' occur in 'dogs bark and cats purr' and 'dogs bark or cats purr', respectively, they do not occur in them *as meaningful constituents*. Rather, they merely serve to mark the particular ways in which 'dogs bark' and 'cats purr' are combined. Nevertheless, the interpretations of these sentences are determined compositionally: there is a function that maps $[\![$'dogs bark'$]\!]$, $[\![$'cats purr'$]\!]$, and conjunctive structure to $[\![$'dogs bark $\wedge$ cats purr'$]\!]$, and maps $[\![$'dogs bark'$]\!]$, $[\![$'cats purr'$]\!]$, and disjunctive structure to $[\![$'dogs bark $\vee$ cats purr'$]\!]$.

There is a long tradition in philosophy of associating sycategorematicity with logicality. The idea is that what makes an expression logical is that it contributes to form, not content, and that this could be captured by treating such expressions syncategorematically. But this link is accidental at best. We could, in principle, treat any lexical item syncategorematically. For example, instead of assigning some semantic value to the word ‘black’, we could have a syntactic rule that says that if ϵ is a nominal then so is ‘black’ ϵ and a corresponding semantic rule that says that $[\![$‘black’ $\epsilon]\!] = \{x : x \in [\![\epsilon]\!] \wedge x \text{ is black}\}$.

Conversely, we could treat logical expressions categorematically. For example, we could say that ‘dogs bark ∧ cats purr’ and ‘dogs bark ∨ cats purr’ have the same syntactic structure, that their interpretation is the result of functional application of the interpretations of the main connective to the interpretations of the expressions it flanks, and that $[\![$‘∧’$]\!] = \lambda p \lambda q(p \wedge q)$ and $[\![$‘∨’$]\!] = \lambda p \lambda q(p \vee q)$.

In fact, in the presence of λ abstraction, syncategorematic expressions other than parentheses and commas are unnecessary. But the notion of syncategorematicity was invented by logicians who were thinking of a limited number of “categories” for classifying meanings, and who had no method of freely forming functional categories.

4. Idioms. Natural languages contain many idioms – complex expressions with meanings unpredictable from their makeup. Knowledge of lexical meanings and syntax won’t be enough to understand phrases like ‘a piece of cake’, ‘miss the boat’, ‘off the hook’, and thousands of others – Jackendoff (1997) estimates that the number of idioms in English is around twenty-five thousand. Sentences containing idioms will not necessarily be understood by otherwise competent speakers, and consequently they lie outside the scope of the argument from productivity. Nonetheless, idioms are not counterexamples to compositionality.

Granted, they do *look like* counterexamples. The expression ‘off the hook’ seems ambiguous: one of its meanings is idiomatic, the other not. Compositionality permits only two types of ambiguity: structural and lexical. (In fact, as standardly formulated, the principle of compositionality assumes that expressions have a single meaning and complex expressions have a single structure. Ambiguity is then understood as a matter of distinct expressions that share a phonological and/or orthographic representation.) Yet, neither of these sorts of ambiguity seems to be present in ‘off the hook’.

This conclusion can be avoided by positing a nonobvious structural ambiguity. The idiomatic reading, according to this account, has two components: an idiosyncratic syntactic rule and a correlated idiomatic semantic rule. The former combines the preposition ‘off’ with the phrase ‘the hook’; the latter interprets the result of this combination as $\{x : x$ has avoided some unpleasant situation$\}$. This will make a sentence like ‘Bill is off the hook’ structurally ambiguous. If it contains ‘the hook’ as a constituent, it means that Bill is no longer hanging on a curved piece of metal or plastic, if it contains ‘the hook’ as a non-constituent (because it was generated by the special syntactic rule associated with a semantic rule that treats the phrase syncategorematically), it means that Bill has avoided some unpleasant situation. Compositionality is not violated. This idea is complicated by the fact that many idioms allow for variations; for example, besides 'off the hook' we also have 'off the proverbial hook'. To capture this, we would need to build more flexibility into the idiosyncratic syntactic rule.

Of course, such a proposal can be resisted on syntactic grounds: one might insist that there is no independent reason to posit an unorthodox rule for combining 'off' and 'the hook', given that we already have a perfectly general way of creating phrases. On the other side of the ledger, we should note that 'off the hook' in its idiomatic meaning, is not used with the same flexibility as, say, 'off the airplane', which may justify the special treatment. In the end, to what extent semantic considerations should influence syntactic theory is a strategic theoretical question for linguistics, which cannot be assessed in isolation. The fate of compositionality is bound up with it. If introducing special syntactic rules on purely semantic grounds is disallowed, we will have to opt for the more moderate claim that natural languages are compositional – except for the finite number of noncompositional idioms they contain.

5. *Infinity.* The initial assumption of the argument from productivity – that we can understand complex expressions we have never heard before – is sometimes supported by the claim that people can understand an infinite array of complex expressions. This, in turn, can be supported by arguments like this one: (i) competent speakers of English can understand the English sentence 'Dogs bark' and (ii) if competent speakers of English can understand an English sentence ϕ, then they can also understand the English sentence ϕ' obtained from ϕ by prefixing it with 'I know that', (iii) ϕ' is longer than ϕ, and (iv) if ϕ' longer than ϕ then ϕ' is distinct from ϕ. While this is pretty persuasive, (ii) can be rejected by staunch opponents of infinity; see Pullum and Scholz (2010).

The thesis that natural languages contain infinitely many complex expressions has some plausibility. But the extra claim that all these expressions could be understood by competent English speakers is more controversial than the claim that we can understand complex expressions we have never heard before. Hence, it is not clear that the detour through infinity serves a useful dialectical purpose. Those who wish to provide support for the premise that we can understand complex expressions we have never heard before are better off appealing to examples like 'A_1 and A_2 and A_3 and A_4 went fishing'. It is uncontroversial that we can understand all such sentences whenever A_1, A_2, A_3, and A_4 are simple noun phrases we can understand, and equally uncontroversial that we have not heard all such sentences. Moreover, incorporating no more that twenty noun phrases in the conjoined subject creates far too many such sentences for it to be possible for human memory to store each meaning separately.

6. *Recursivity.* But suppose natural languages are indeed infinite and competent speakers could really understand all their expressions. What follows?

Presumably that there is some recursive way to specify the meanings of all the expressions of the language from the meanings of finitely many. Here is how Davidson (1965: 8) puts the point:

> When we regard the meaning of each sentence as a function of a finite number of features of the sentence, we have an insight not only into what there is to be learned; we also understand how an infinite aptitude can be encompassed by finite accomplishments. For suppose that the language lacks this feature; then no matter how many sentences a would-be speaker learns to produce and understand, there will remain others whose meanings are not given by the rules already mastered.

While this passage is often quoted in connection with compositionality, it actually argues for a different principle. A language could be recursive but not compositional: the recursion could be based on something in addition to syntactic structure and lexical meaning. Consider a compositional fragment of English that contains the sentence 'it is snowing' and modify the standard semantics by adding the proviso that whenever it snows every sentence in it means the conjunction of its standard meaning with the standard meaning of 'It is snowing'. If the standard semantics was recursive, so is the new one. Yet, the new interpretation is noncompositional: the meanings of sentences depend not just on their complete structure and the meanings of their ultimate parts, but also on whether it is snowing. As for the converse. if a language is compositional then there is a function that assigns meanings to its complex expressions solely on the basis of the meanings of its ultimate constituents and its complete structure. But nothing guarantees that this function is recursive.

7. Processing. According to the argument from productivity, we could understand a complex expression on the basis of our understanding its smallest parts and knowing how it is built from those parts. When the complex expression is novel, this is what we are supposed to be doing. But most of the expressions we hear are not novel, and the argument makes no claims about how we understand them. It may well be that we have all sorts of cognitive shortcuts in language processing – perhaps we store in memory a huge number of familiar phrases as units, and we never really work out their meaning in the bottom-up fashion we would have to resort to when the expression is still new to us. In other words, the argument from productivity makes no substantive psychological claim that could be translated into a prediction about the way we normally process complex expressions. And in particular, the standard assumption in psycholinguistics that processing time and syntactic complexity are directly correlated cannot be supported by an appeal to productivity.

Let's sum up. The principle of compositionality limits the factors upon which the meaning of a complex expression depends to just two: syntax and lexical semantics. This thesis is not to be confused with another one, according to which meaning can be recursively specified, even though both are usually supported by appeals to the productivity of understanding linguistic expressions. Compositionality is a modest thesis: it does not tell us how we actually process complex expressions, and it does not demand that we explicitly assign meanings to all lexical items. It is not easily proved or disproved – it cannot, for example, be deduced from the fact that we can learn the language, or refuted by the fact that the language contains idioms. Like any serious broad scientific hypothesis, it stands or falls with entire theories.

2.2 Substitutivity and Models of Meaning

Semantics is in the business of modeling meaning. Like all modeling, this involves choices about what to capture and what to ignore. Compositionality, or something like compositionality, is one of the key tools semanticists use in making these theoretical decisions.

How does semantic theory go about modeling meaning? Here is how David Lewis describes the key idea:

> In order to say what a meaning *is*, we may first ask what a meaning *does*, and then find something that does that. A meaning for a sentence is something that determines the conditions under which the sentence is true or false. It determines the truth-value of the sentence in various possible states of affairs, at various times, at various places, for various speakers, and so on ... Similarly, a meaning for a name is something that determines that thing, if any, the name names in various possible states of affairs, at various times, and so on ... Similarly, a meaning for a common noun is something that determines which (possible or actual) things, if any, that common noun applies to in various possible states of affairs, at various times, and so on. (Lewis 1970b: 22–23)

Of course, meaning does more than determine extension – just think of the contrast between 'and' and 'but'. Meaning also gives rise to various discourse effects, grounds many implications, and triggers diverse associations. But, at least initially, these aspects of meaning tend to be ignored in semantic theory.

The most important advantage of narrowing down the job description for meanings is that we can actually find something that is a natural fit. As Lewis (1970b: 23) goes on to say:

> What sort of things determine how something depends on something else? *Functions*, of course; functions in the most general set-theoretic sense, in which the domain of arguments and the range of values may consist of entities of any sort whatever, and in which it is not required that the function be specifiable by any simple rule. We have now found something to do at least part of what a meaning for a sentence, a name, a common noun does: a function which yields as output an appropriate extension when given as input a package of the various factors on which the extension may depend.

So, models of linguistic meaning – *semantic values* – are functions of some sort. While Lewis is explicit that the range of a semantic value contains extensions, he is noncommittal about what its domain looks like. It is supposed to include "packages" of factors on which the extension may depend, including a possible state of affairs, a time, a place, a speaker, and perhaps much else.

What exactly we include in these packages will depend on how closely we wish to model how meanings determine extensions. The crudest model, obviously, is the one where we ignore all variation and model meanings simply as constant functions. In this case the domain becomes superfluous, and we might as well assign extensions themselves to the expressions of the language we are interpreting. This way we get extensional semantics.

How do we tell when extensions are too crude as models for linguistic meanings? This is where compositionality enters the picture. Suppose the National Institute of Health conducts an extremely thorough survey to build a database of possible correlations of occupations and medical problems. To everyone's surprise, it turns out that all and only orthodontists are insomniacs, so the extensions of 'orthodontist' and 'insomniac' coincide. This means that in most cases one of these words can be substituted for the other *salva veritate*: if you see an orthodontist you see an insomniac, if you befriend a tall insomniac you befriend a tall orthodontist, and so on.

Now suppose on some exoplanet in a far-away galaxy, or at some forgotten time in ancient past, or in some bizarre possible world, there happens to be an orthodontist who sleeps every night like a baby. Then, substituting 'insomniac' for one of the occurrences of 'orthodontist' in 'Somewhere, there is an orthodontist who is not an orthodontist', or 'Once, there was an orthodontist who was not an orthodontist', or 'Possibly, there might be an orthodontist who is not an orthodontist' changes these false sentences into true ones. These are violations of compositionality. A function that maps the complete structure and the extensions of ultimate constituents of a complex expression to the extension of that expression would have to assign the same truth-values to sentences that differ from each other only in containing extensionally equivalent words in the exact same syntactic position. So, if we want to model meaning in languages containing expressions like 'somewhere', 'once', or 'possibly' and if we want to preserve compositionality, our semantic values cannot be extensions. Call this a *substitution argument* for richer semantic values.

Many would complain that this scenario is simply incoherent: if there is an orthodontist who is not an insomniac, no matter how far away, 'orthodontist' and 'insomniac' cannot have the same extension. Some would also say that the extensions must differ if there was a time when there was an orthodontist who was not an insomniac. And a few – notably, Lewis himself – would insist that the mere fact that there could be an orthodontist who is not an insomniac is enough to rule out the extensional equivalence of 'orthodontist' and 'insomniac'.

The attractiveness of these protests depends on your ontological convictions, on what you take to be *real*. The extension of 'orthodontist' contains all and only the real orthodontists – the pretend, the imaginary, the fake don't count. So, if you think (like most) that distant orthodontists are as real as proximal ones you will include them in the extension of 'orthodontist'. If you are convinced, (like some) that past orthodontists are just as real as present ones they too will be included. And if you believe (with Lewis) that merely possible orthodontists are real flesh-and-blood people who just happen to inhabit a different possible world, one that is spatiotemporally and causally isolated from ours, then these merely possible orthodontists cannot be excluded from the extension of 'orthodontist' either. On the other hand, if you are a *localist*, a *presentist*, and an *actualist* – if you think that nothing is real except for the actual here and now – you will not have any merely remote, past, or possible entities in the extension of any expression. The moral is that substitution arguments have metaphysical presuppositions.

Suppose you belong to the current metaphysical majority: you think spatially or temporally distant orthodontists are real, but modally distant ones are not. Then sentences containing 'somewhere' or 'once' are straightforward for you, but the ones containing 'possibly' still pose a compositionality problem. You need a semantic value that reflects the fact that the extensions of 'orthodontist' and 'insomniac' depend on a possible world. Intensions – functions from possible worlds to extensions – will do. 'Orthodontist' and 'insomniac' have different intensions, so the fact that 'Possibly, there is an orthodontist who is not an orthodontist' and 'Possibly, there is an orthodontist who is not an insomniac' have different intensions is not a problem. If we model meanings by intensions rather than extensions, we no longer have a violation of compositionality.

Do we need semantic values more fine-grained than intensions? Perhaps we do, assuming we have mental idioms in the language we seek to interpret. Here is a substitution argument to this effect. 'Sulphuric acid' and 'oil of vitriol' have the same intension – in every possible world they pick out a substance whose chemical composition is H_2SO_4 – and yet, it seems clear that 'Emily knows that sulphuric acid is widely used as a drain cleaner' and 'Emily knows that oil of vitriol is widely used as a drain cleaner' could diverge in truth-value. A natural way to react to the *hyperintensionality* of the complement of 'know' is to find the factor upon which the extensions of 'sulphuric acid' and 'oil of vitriol' depend and include them within the "packages" in the domain of the semantic values. We could say – following Frege – that the extensions are associated with different senses, or modes of presentation, and we could model these in a variety of ways. (One particularly elegant method uses conceptual covers; see Aloni [2001].)

But it is not clear that this is what we *should* do. One serious worry about introducing modes of presentation in the semantics is that they seem too fine-grained for the purposes of a theory of meaning. Take the words 'hardworking' and 'industrious' – as good an example of a synonymous pair as any. Using the same substitution method we can convince ourselves that their meanings should be modeled by different functions: Bob may well know that his neighbor is a hardworking accountant but not that he is an industrious accountant. The way in which Bob is presented with hardworking people and the way he is presented with industrious people is a matter of his *individual psychology* and it may be different even if 'hardworking' and 'industrious' mean the same thing in a *public language*. Fregean senses are, of course, public and non-psychological. But that is exactly why they would not help in explaining how the truth-values of 'Bob knows his neighbor is hardworking' and 'Bob knows his neighbor is industrious' can come apart.

Our initial assumption was that to be a meaning is to determine the conditions under which a sentence is true or false. The best thing might be to concede that this is incorrect, at least if we are considering languages that can be used to talk about mental states.

Are there other cases where we need semantic values more fine-grained than intensions? Lewis acknowledges that the truth-values of sentences may depend on the speaker, but when it comes to names or common nouns he does not mention this. This seems right – the extensions of 'I', 'my', 'we', 'our', and perhaps a handful of other words, as well as the extensions of most complex expressions that contain these as constituents are sensitive to who the speaker is, but the extensions of 'Gottlob Frege', 'Bertrand Russell', or the extensions of 'orthodontist' and 'insomniac' are not. Unlike place, time, and world-dependence, speaker dependence seems to have its source exclusively in a handful of highly specialized expressions.

While it is obvious that an extensional (or even intensional) semantics is inadequate for languages containing indexicals, it would be difficult to show this using a substitution argument. 'Somewhere/once, possibly, Obama is having breakfast' and 'Somewhere/once, possibly, I am having breakfast' cannot diverge in truth-value if the extensions of 'I' and 'Obama' coincide. There does not seem to be any expression in English that shifts the speaker in the ways in which 'somewhere', 'once', and 'possibly' shift the place, time, and world of utterance. (Imagine if 'As for some ballerina, I am having breakfast' meant that some ballerina is having breakfast; then 'as for some ballerina' would function as a speaker-shifter.) It could certainly happen that 'Obama knows Obama is having breakfast' is false while 'I know I am having breakfast' is true in a context where 'I' and 'Obama' have the same extension. Just imagine, following Perry (1977), that Obama becomes an amnesiac and does not remember who he is. But this sort of example may not be entirely convincing because it requires the use of an expression referring to a mental phenomenon.

Substitution arguments for enriching semantic values are often less restrictive than the ones we mentioned. Normally, a syntactic position within a complex expression is called extensional (intensional) just in case substituting any co-extensional (co-intensional) expressions in that position fails to change the extension (intension) of the complex expression. And when a syntactic position within a complex expression is shown to be nonextensional (nonintensional), the conclusion is drawn that a compositional semantics that covers the expression must be at least intensional (hyperintensional). It is important to see that this is a mistake.

The substitution arguments presented above involving the pairs 'orthodontist'/'dentist' and 'hard-working'/'industrious' rest on the following principle:

> *Substitutivity*: Substituting within a complex expression an ultimate constituent for a synonymous one does not change the meaning of the complex expression.

This principle is a trivial consequence of compositionality: if there is a function that maps the structure and the meanings of the ultimate constituents of a complex expression ϵ to the meaning of ϵ, then replacing one ultimate constituent with a synonymous constituent obviously can't affect the meaning of ϵ. But arguments involving substitution of arbitrary synonyms rest on a stronger principle, one that does not follow from the principle of compositionality.

> *Strong substitutivity*: Substituting within a complex expression a constituent for a synonymous one does not change the meaning of the complex expression.

Substituting a complex constituent for a simple one within some expression can change the structure of that expression, and since meaning in general does depend on structure, there is no guarantee that such a substitution will not affect meaning. Take, for example, the standard argument, due to Quine, that we could not have an extensional semantics for a language that contains modals. 'It is necessary that the number of planets is greater than seven' is false but 'It is necessary that eight is greater than seven' is true, even though 'the number of planets' and 'eight' have the same extension. (Quine uses 'nine' where we use 'eight' – he assumed that Pluto is a planet.) The argument rests on the assumption that definite descriptions have the same sort of extension as proper names, which proponents of quantificational accounts of definite descriptions (like the Russellian account) would reject. But even if we were to grant the assumption, the argument would still not go through: the difference in truth-value could be the result of the different syntactic structure of the two sentences.

It might be useful to illustrate the fact that strong substitutivity does not follow from compositionality with an example. Let N be a language whose expressions are the numerals in decimal notion. The lexical items are the digits **0, 1, 2, 3, 4, 5, 6, 7, 8, 9**; their meanings are the corresponding natural numbers. The sole syntactic rule is concatenation; it too receives the usual interpretation:

> Digits are numerals. If ν is a numeral and δ is a digit then so is $\nu\delta$.
> $[\![\nu\delta]\!] = 10[\![\nu]\!] + [\![\delta]\!]$.

N trivially satisfies both compositionality and strong substitutivity. But there are two simple ways of extending the language that will preserve only the former.

Let N^+ be an extension of N with the addition symbol. The complex expressions of N^+ consist of the numerals beyond **9** and of sums:

> If α and β are expressions then $(\alpha + \beta)$ is a sum.
> $[\![(\alpha + \beta)]\!] = [\![\alpha]\!] + [\![\beta]\!]$

N^+ is obviously still compositional but violates strong substitutivity: the numeral **4** and the sum **(1+3)** have the same meaning, yet if we substitute the latter for the former in **24**, we get **2(1+3)**, which is not even an expression of N^+.

This might be seen as a problem that calls for a simple reformulation of what counts as substitution. Let's say that replacing an expression with another within a larger expression counts as substitution only if it results in a syntactically well-formed expression. Clearly, if we start with a meaningful complex expression in N^+, substitute for one of its constituents a synonym, and get a syntactically well-formed complex expression, this expression can't have a new meaning. But in a further compositional extension of N^+ this can happen too. Let $N^{+,1^{st}}$ contain a function symbol which combined with an argument yields a complex expression whose meaning is the number picked out by the first digit of the argument:

> If α is an expression then $(1^{st}(\alpha))$ is an expression.
> $[\![(1^{st}(\alpha))]\!] = [\![\delta]\!]$ iff the first digit of α is δ.

$[\![(1^{st}(\alpha))]\!]$ is determined compositionally: the complete structure of α uniquely determines its first digit, the lexical semantics uniquely determines a meaning for this digit, which just is the meaning of $1^{st}(\alpha)$. Yet, substituting a synonym for another within a larger expression can yield an expression with a different meaning: while $[\![(1 + 3)]\!] = [\![(2 + 2)]\!]$, $[\![1^{st}(1 + 3)]\!] = 1 \neq 2 = [\![1^{st}(2 + 2)]\!]$.

Strong substitution follows from a principle that ensures not only that meaning is determined in a "bottom-up" fashion, but that this happens in a local manner:

> *Strong compositionality*: There is a function that maps the immediate structure and the meanings of the immediate constituents of any complex expression onto the meaning of that expression.

The immediate structure of an expression is the final step in its syntactic derivation; the immediate constituents are the expressions that are combined in this final step. Thus, according to strong constitutionality, if the final step in the syntactic derivation of 'Jack walks or Jill talks' is the combination of the clauses 'Jack walks' and 'Jill talks' via the connective 'or', then the meaning of this complex clause must be a function of the meanings of 'Jack walks', 'Jill talks', 'or', and the way these are combined. $N^{+,1^{st}}$ is not strongly compositional because '$1^{st}(1 + 3)$' and '$1^{st}(2 + 2)$' differ in meaning despite the fact that they have the same immediate structure (in both of them 1st is applied to an argument) and the meanings of their immediate constituents ('1+3' and '2+2', respectively) are also the same.

Strong compositionality enforces a tight correspondence between syntax and semantics. Clearly, it entails compositionality. The reason for this is that if we have a syntactic structure that satisfies strong compositionality, we can compose the local meaning functions together into a single function from the meanings of the lexical items to the meaning of the entire phrase. The converse, however, does not hold; the example of $N^{+,1^{st}}$ illustrates this.

Strong compositionality is what semanticists, following the work of Richard Montague, tend to assume in their work, and that is the principle most frequently called compositionality. (For a formal statement of the principle and for precise characterizations of its relationships to various other principles in the neighborhood, including principles of substitutivity, see Hodges [2001].) We avoided this assumption because strong compositionality is not supported by the argument from productivity. The idea that speakers could figure out the meanings of complex expressions in a bottom-up fashion has some plausibility, but the idea that they should be able to do so in a completely local manner, at each step disregarding everything but the meaning of the expressions they are combining, is nothing but speculation. There is no problem in assuming strong compositionality as a hypothesis, but if we do, we should be clear that we are working with an assumption that is supported only by the empirical success of strongly compositional theories.

To sum up, one of the main uses of compositionality in semantic theorizing is in constraining how fine-grained semantic values should be. We operate with the default assumption that extensions are a good model of meaning within a language fragment, unless adherence to compositionality forces us to opt for a function that encodes the dependence of extension on place, time, world, etc. We can show that compositionality is violated in a semantics by finding a pair of nonsynonymous complex expressions such that one can be obtained from the other by interchanging synonymous lexical constituents. Arguments that rely on arbitrary substitution of synonyms cannot show noncompositionality, only a violation of a stronger principle – one that is often assumed in semantics but cannot be supported by the usual considerations cited in favor of compositionality.

2.3 Context and Compositionality

Natural languages contain a number of expressions whose extension depends on the context in which they are used. The most obvious and least controversial examples are demonstratives, personal and possessive pronouns, and certain spatial and temporal words, like 'local', 'faraway', 'here', 'past', 'now', 'yesterday', etc. More controversially, tenses, modals, quantifiers, conditionals, gradable adjectives, and propositional attitude verbs are often viewed as having context-sensitive extensions. Some theorists – for example, Raffman (1996); Stanley and Szabó (2000); Rothschild and Segal (2009) – have claimed that this is true for all common nouns, all predicates, or even all vague expressions. In general, formal semantics tends to be generous in positing context-dependence.

At first glance, context-dependence is no threat to compositionality. Whether 'I was glad you were here yesterday' is true depends on who is speaking to whom, where and when, but the influence of the context can be anchored to four of the ultimate constituents of the sentence – 'I', 'you', 'here', and 'yesterday' through more or less clear rules. Once context settles what the extensions of these four words are, it has no further role to play. The extension of the sentence (in context) is a function of the extensions of its ultimate parts (in the same context) and the way those parts are combined.

There is a slight complication due to the fact that context can shift mid-sentence. Take the sentence 'It is more than 80°F here, but not here'. This seems like a contradiction, but it could be true if the speaker steps out of an overheated room after she utters the first occurrence of 'here' but before she utters the second. Still, all this requires is a slight modification in the statement of the principle:

> *Compositionality (with context)*: There is a function that maps the complete structure and the meanings of the ultimate constituents of any complex expression *in their respective contexts of utterance* onto the meaning of that expression *in its context of utterance*.

If the extension of the first occurrence of 'here' in its context of utterance is the location l_1 and the extension of the second occurrence of 'here' in its context utterance is l_2 then the extension of the sentence in its context of utterance is true iff it is more than 80°F in l_1 but not in l_2. The extension of the sentence depends on the context only insofar as the extensions of its ultimate constituents do.

Nonetheless, some philosophers feel that context-dependence raises a devastating challenge to compositionality. The point goes back at least to Searle (1978), and is foreshadowed in Wittgenstein (1953). Here is how Travis (1994: 171–172) has formulated it:

> As a commonplace example, consider the words 'The leaf is green', speaking of a given leaf, and its condition at a given time, used so as to mean what they do mean in English. How many distinct things might be said in words with all that true of them? Many. That emerges when we note that one might speak either truth or falsity in such words, if the leaf is the right way. Suppose a Japanese maple leaf, turned brown, was painted green for a decoration. In sorting leaves by colour, one might truly call this one green. In describing leaves to help identify their species,

> it might, for all the paint, be false to call it that. So words may have all the stipulated features while saying something true, but also while saying something false.

The claim is that the meaning of 'The leaf is green' fails to determine what the sentence says. For on both occasions the sentence means the same thing, and yet, on one occasion it is true and on the other it is false. And a true sentence cannot say the same thing as a false one.

Travis thinks this is an arbitrary example: similar context-shifting arguments can be constructed to argue that a great many sentences without any obvious kind of ambiguity or obviously indexical expressions can say different things in different contexts. 'Alice went to the gym' could say that Alice went into the gym or that she went near the gym; 'Bert didn't have fish for dinner' could say that he didn't eat fish for dinner or that he didn't order fish for dinner; 'Cecile destroyed her shoes' could say that she made them unsuitable to wear at formal occasions or that she made them unsuitable to wear at all; 'Dan owns a dangerous dog' could say that Dan owns a dog that attacks people or that Dan owns a dog that can infect people; 'Evelyn is a philosopher' could say that she is employed as a philosopher or that she has a contemplative mind, and so on. (These examples are from Cappelen and Lepore (2005). They are criticized in Szabó [2006].) There are literally hundreds of examples in the literature, which are supposed to show that what is said in a context by a declarative sentence is underdetermined by its meaning. Let's suppose some of these examples succeed. In fact, to keep things simple, let's suppose that Travis' original example is already a success. What are the consequences for compositionality?

Travis' example is supposed to show that content is not compositional. The burden of the argument rests on two claims: (1) that the content of 'The leaf is green' varies across contexts and (2) that the contents of 'the', 'leaf', 'is', and 'green' don't. Neither of these claims is obvious.

As for Claim (1), many have denied that 'The leaf is green' has a content that varies from context to context. One way to do this is to claim that the content is neither the proposition that the leaf is green on the outside nor the proposition that it is green on the inside, but rather, the *minimal proposition* that it is green *simpliciter*. Whether the minimal proposition is true or false in either of the contexts Travis describes is unclear. But perhaps that is no problem, since what speakers seek to convey is a different proposition in both cases, one that is specific with respect to the relevant part of the leaf that is supposed to be green.

Another line of thought is to say that the content is not a complete proposition, only an underspecified *propositional radical* or a *propositional skeleton* – something that can be enriched with extra content to arrive at the content of the speech act a speaker performs in context when she utters it. Thus, one can defend the compositionality of semantics by giving up the idea that semantics delivers robust truth-conditions (i.e. conditions competent speakers can normally recognize) or giving up the idea that it delivers truth-conditions at all.

Claim (2) is also far from obvious. It is one thing to point out that the four words in 'The leaf is green' are used on both occasions "in their usual meanings," and another to establish that these fixed meanings are their contents. Perhaps one of these four words – most likely, the adjective 'green' – is an indexical expression. In the context where we are sorting leaves for decoration, 'green' applies to a leaf painted green, in a context where we are concerned with biological classification, it does not.

Another option involves positing unpronounced ultimate constituents whose content involves variables. For example, there might be a variable in the sentence, sitting on its own leaf in the syntactic tree responsible for the variable content of the entire sentence. Either way, proponents of this response should try to find independent empirical evidence for their view and will need to find such evidence for each new Travis-like example. So if this is the way one tries to disarm the challenge to compositionality, one forfeits the hope for a general answer: compositionality of content survives as a hypothesis, but its continued survival may seem precarious. (See Collins [2007] and Szabó [2010] for arguments against and for this sort of strategy.)

But suppose we accept both Claims (1) and (2): What will the consequences be? We must then admit that the content of 'The leaf is green' depends not only on its complete structure and the contents of its ultimate constituents in the context of utterance but *in addition* on the context of utterance as well. What we get is a significantly weakened principle:

> *Weak compositionality (with context)*: There is a function that maps the complete structure of any complex expression, the meanings of the ultimate constituents of that expression in their respective contexts of utterance, *and the context of utterance* onto the meaning of that expression.

Weak compositionality permits context-dependence that is not anchored to the lexicon but emerges higher up on the syntactic tree. If the context dependence of a complex expression is unmoored in this way, then to understand it in context it is not enough to ascertain its structure and determine the contextually appropriate contents of its ultimate constituents.

In sum, Travis-style examples leave semanticists with three options. The first is to abandon the idea that semantic theories assign anything like the intuitive truth-conditions to declarative sentences. The second is to accept much more context-sensitivity at the lexical or phrasal level than what has traditionally been accepted. And the third is to substantially weaken compositionality, allowing the existence of context-sensitive expressions constructed entirely from context-insensitive parts. Which of the three is the best theoretical option is an open question at present.

2.4 Explaining Meaning

Compositionality is widely seen as one of the fundamental principles of semantics. A fundamental truth, one might think, is supposed to explain many others – this is what axioms in mathematics or laws of nature in physics do. And yet, there is no consensus about what, if anything, the principle of compositionality is supposed to explain.

According to the argument from productivity, compositionality is required by the best explanation of the fact that competent speakers of a language can understand many of its complex expressions when they hear them for the first time. Unfortunately, we don't *have* such an explanation; we just believe that, whatever the explanation will ultimately look like, it will rely, among other things, on compositionality. Moreover, even if we had an account of how people understand complex expressions they hear for the first time, it would not belong to linguistics proper, but to psychology. One might suspect that compositionality matters to semanticists because they care about the actual explanatory role that the principle plays within their own theories.

A theory of meaning should address at least two questions: *what* do the expressions of a language mean and *why* do they mean what they do. We might call a theory that addresses the first question *semantics* and a theory that addresses the second *metasemantics*. Philosophers tend to distinguish the two sharply and many believe that the latter is actually outside the scope of linguistics proper. David Lewis marks the division as follows (Lewis 1970b: 190):

> I distinguish two topics: first, the description of possible languages or grammars as abstract systems whereby symbols are associated with aspects of the world; and second the description of the psychological and sociological facts whereby a particular one of these abstract semantic systems is the one used by a person or population. Only confusion comes of mixing these two topics.

Since interesting possible languages are infinite, we can't just list all their expressions one by one and state what each means. We must resort to some recursive apparatus. But – as far as Lewis is concerned – the method of generating the infinite list has no explanatory value at all: any recursive method (compositional or otherwise) that gets the job done is as good as any other. The metasemantic question of why expressions mean what they do is settled by theories which interact only with the output of semantic theories, with the infinite pairing of expressions and meanings.

But while the distinction between the *what* and the *why* questions is important, the separation needn't be as strict as Lewis envisions. Maybe semantic theories are not *purely* descriptive. Here is an alternate way to think about semantics, due to Robert Stalnaker.

> A descriptive semantic theory is a theory that says what the semantics for the language is without saying what it is about the practice of using that language that explains why that semantics is the right one. A descriptive-semantic theory assigns semantic values to the expressions of the language, and explains how the semantic values of the complex expressions are a function of the semantic values of their parts. (Stalnaker 1997: 535)

Stalnaker agrees with Lewis that semantic theories should not try to explain why they provide the right interpretation for the expressions of the language in light of the linguistic practices of the community of speakers. That would be the task of a *metasemantic* theory. But, unlike Lewis, he thinks semantic theories do explain something: they tell us how the semantic values of complex expressions depend on the semantic values of their parts. Since semantic values model linguistic meaning, this amounts to an explanation of why complex expressions mean just what they do. The explanation is only partial: it says nothing about why lexical items mean what they do, but it does explain why complex expressions have their meanings. Phrases, clauses, and sentences mean what they do in virtue of the fact that their constituents mean what they do and the fact that they have been constructed from those constituents in a particular way.

On this sort of view, compositional semantic explanations rest on the assumption of explanatory priority of lexical meaning and syntax within a theory of meaning:

> *Explanatory compositionality*: Complex expressions have their meanings in virtue of the meanings of their ultimate constituents and in virtue of their complete structure.

This principle is stronger than compositionality – if X holds in virtue of Y and Z, then X functionally depends on Y and Z. The converse fails because explanatory primacy is asymmetric but functional dependence needn't be. There could be a one-to-one function between the meanings of complex expressions on the one hand and the meanings of their ultimate constituents and their complete structure on the other (as proponents of Fregean and Russellian structured meanings think), but explanations that go both ways would be circular. Explanatory compositionality commits us to seeing meaning as explicable in a *bottom-up* fashion.

Explanatory compositionality conflicts with what many philosophers believe. Frege famously declared that "it is enough if the sentence as a whole has meaning; thereby also its parts obtain their meanings" (Frege 1980a: Section 60). (The translation in the standard English edition is misleading – it renders the German "Satz" as "proposition," which in this context is out of place.) This is the *context principle*. It asserts the explanatory priority of sentences over their constituents and as such is in direct conflict with explanatory compositionality. Sentential priority has remained popular among many philosophers and has prevented them from seeing compositionality as an explanatory significant principle.

Why might one think that sentence meaning comes before word meaning in the order of explanation? One reason might be that lexicographers construct dictionary entries on the basis of corpus data, which consists largely (although not exclusively) of sentences. But this reason is not compelling: the meanings of certain sentences might give us evidence for ascribing meaning to a word, but they don't necessarily explain why the word has that meaning.

Here is a somewhat better reason: linguistic expressions get their meanings from the mental states they express or from the speech acts they are used to perform, and mental states and speech acts have propositional contents. From this, it follows that the linguistic expressions that have meanings in the first place must be the ones whose meanings are propositions, which – one might think – are the declarative sentences. The meanings of all other expressions must somehow derive from sentential meanings.

But there are two problems with this reasoning. First, there are all sorts of mental states and speech acts that are, at least prima facie, not propositional – we can see, hear, imagine, and think about, as well as mention, call attention to, or refer to objects without any necessary intervention of a full proposition. Even if we grant that linguistic expressions get their meanings from mental states and speech acts, it's not clear why mental states and speech acts with nonpropositional content could not be the source. Second, as we have seen in the previous section, the idea that declarative sentences have the very same content as beliefs or assertions is problematic. It is not clear that there are *any* linguistic expressions that can simply inherit the contents of mental states or speech acts. And if the relationship between mental and speech-act content, on the one hand, and linguistic meaning, on the other, is always more complex than simple identity, then it is no longer clear what is supposed to be so special about sentences from an explanatory point of view.

Suppose Stalnaker is right, and compositionality is an explanatory principle. What could be the source of its explanatory power? One possibility is that the dependence it states is *lawlike*, and hence, it supports the counterfactual claim that, had the meaning of a complex expression been different, then either the meaning of one of its ultimate constituents or its complete structure would differ as well. Compare this with physical laws: it is a law that a body near the surface of the Earth, subject only to its gravitational force, accelerates at approximately $9.81\frac{m}{s^2}$. So, had this body been accelerating at a different rate, then either it would not have been near the surface of the Earth, or it would have been subject to other forces as well.

Of course, even if we assume that natural languages are compositional, we can envision changes after which they would no longer be. To use an earlier example, if we stipulated that whenever it rains at the location of an utterance of the sentence 'Elephants are gray', the sentence shall mean on that occasion that Julius Caesar was murdered on the ides of March while retaining its usual meaning on all other occasions, the new language – Rain English – would no longer be compositional. So, even if compositionality is a law, it is certainly not a law of all possible languages. At best, it might be a law of all possible *human* languages – the sort of languages that normal human beings can acquire under normal social conditions as first languages. Rain English is plausibly not a possible human language in this sense: while it can be learned, competence with it is parasitic on prior competence with English. The claim that compositionality is best understood as a law of possible human languages is argued in Szabó (2000).

This sits well with a picture of linguistics as an empirical science in search of laws, just like physics, biology, psychology, or economics. The laws linguists seek to discover are not laws of languages in general (since there presumably are no such things) but, rather, laws of natural languages. Just like phonology or syntax, semantics is supposed to tell us what sorts of languages are compatible with our cognitive make-up.

There are, of course, many who would see this talk of laws as misplaced in the context of semantic theorizing. Indeed, it is often said that compositionality is simply a methodological assumption semanticists make and cherish because of the theoretical benefits it brings. Compositional theories have indeed been successful in providing interpretation for increasingly large fragments of natural languages, but if these theories explain nothing, we would still need an explanation for this success.

2.5 Conclusion

Standard semantic theories typically assume that the meanings of complex expressions are determined by their structure and the meanings of their constituents. The assumption is neither trivial (since it is easy to construct noncompositional languages we can learn) nor overly demanding (since it does not force us to see meaning as structured or interpretation as parsing).

Compositionality helps to set the appropriate level of abstraction for semantic values. If we are dealing with a fragment of a language suitable to discuss mathematics, we can model linguistic meanings extensionally. But if we have expressions that allow generalizations over places, times, or possibilities (and we don't believe in nonlocal places, nonpresent times, or nonactual worlds), compositionality will force us to adopt more abstract semantic values.

Compositionality is incompatible with the existence of complex expressions that are context sensitive without having some context-sensitive constituents. This too is a significant restriction on semantic theorizing: it locates interaction between context and interpretation exclusively at the level of lexical items and variables.

Adhering to the principle of compositionality forces us to think of semantics in a highly systematic way, linking semantic interpretation with syntactic structure. This makes it a fruitful hypothesis. But perhaps it is more than that: a generalization that holds across all possible human languages and has the force of a law.

3 Reference and Quantification

3.1 The Truth and Nothing but the Truth

Semantics is the theory of meaning, but 'meaning' is a dangerously amorphous word. Sometimes we are willing to say that 'example' and 'illustration' mean the same thing despite the fact that we would never call colored pictures in children's books examples or numbered sentences in linguistics articles illustrations. Other times we are very strict about such matters: we might even deny that 'ophthalmologist' and 'eye-doctor' mean the same thing on the grounds that we would never say that someone has received a medical degree in eye-doctoring. Judgments of synonymy are vague and capricious for a reason: word meanings are constantly negotiated on the fly. The more we care about a word, the less we are willing to cede control over its meaning to experts – just think of the debates about the meanings of 'life', 'liberty', or 'happiness'.

The notion of meaning that semanticists care about is technical. Semanticists are entitled to their technical terms like everyone else, but ultimately they too must situate their subject matter in the world we know by appealing to notions we understand. Most philosophers and linguists would agree that *truth* is a suitable notion for this clarificatory purpose. Some think it is the only one.

Here is how we could try to characterize the task of semantics in terms of truth alone. We start by focusing on declarative sentences. We make two assumptions about them: that many declarative sentences have the classical truth-values (i.e. true or false) and that if two of them differ in truth-value they must also differ in meaning. Let's call the conditions – actual or merely imaginary – under which a declarative sentence is true its truth-conditions. These two assumptions guarantee that truth-conditions capture one aspect of the meaning of many expressions. And to the extent that we see language primarily as a means for communication, communication as the transfer of information, and information as something inherently truth-apt, we are entitled to consider truth-conditions as the central aspect of linguistic meaning of these expressions.

As a third assumption, we adopt the principle we called "strong compositionality" in Section 2.2. Suppose the declarative sentences ϕ_1 and ϕ_2 differ from one another solely in that one has the expression η_1 as a constituent where the other has a different expression, η_2. If ϕ_1 and ϕ_2 differ in truth-conditions, and hence in meaning, then strong compositionality demands that the meanings of η_1 and η_2 should also differ. Thus, a theory that assigns truth-conditions to a large number of declarative sentences will also tell us something valuable about the meanings of words and phrases that these sentences have as their constituents.

Of course, while the three assumptions of truth-conditional semantics are widely accepted, there are many dissenters. We noted already in Section 2.2 that the usual considerations in favor of simple compositionality fail to support strong compositionality. A number of linguists and philosophers have claimed that declarative sentences can never be evaluated for truth or falsity outside of context, and consequently, in themselves they lack truth-conditions; see, for example, Searle (1978); Recanati (2002); Carston (2012). These views were mentioned in Section 2.3. The influential arguments in Chomsky (1986, 2000) can also be seen as supporting this claim; they will be briefly discussed in Section 12.4. And finally, a deep theoretical difficulty arises in reconciling two plausible ideas: that meaning determines truth-conditions and that understanding requires knowledge of meaning. This is the topic of Chapter 12.

Proponents of standard semantic theories accept all three assumptions and maintain that the job of semantic theories is to assign truth-conditions to the declarative sentences of a large fragment of a language in a strongly compositional fashion. This is done by giving *semantic values* to lexical items and pairing *semantic rules* with syntactic ones. Semantic values are what words and phrases contribute to the truth-conditions of declarative sentences, while semantic rules are the truth-conditional contribution of their syntactic structure.

Proponents of the most austere version of truth-conditional semantics make no assumptions beyond the three we mentioned. In particular, they do not assume that the terms 'semantic value' and 'semantic rule' correspond to anything in the actual workings of language. For them, semantic values and semantic rules are whatever gets the job done, and no more real than lines of latitude and longitude: they are representational devices introduced for the determination of facts. There are many alternative systems of geographic coordinates we could use to fix a position of a ship at sea and there are many equally good ways to pick semantic values and rules to fix the conditions under which declarative sentences would be true. We might like the ones we are used to, but nothing beyond convenience necessitates this choice. Those who favor the austere version of truth-conditional semantics seek to account for meaning in terms of truth, and nothing but the truth. In particular, they do not assume a pretheoretical notion of reference.

3.1.1 Davidson's Program

The classical program to design a theory of meaning resting exclusively on assignment of truth-conditions was initiated by Donald Davidson. He argued that a Tarski-style theory of truth for a language *can be viewed* as a theory of meaning for that language. Let's try to unpack the slogan.

Recall from 1.2.2 that Tarski proposed a criterion of *material adequacy* for any putative truth definition, a test that marks success in capturing what we intuitively mean by 'true sentence'. The criterion is that the definition must entail all instances of Convention T,

(3.1.1) $T(\alpha) \leftrightarrow \phi,$

where ϕ is a sentence of the object language and α a canonical name for that sentence in the metalanguage.

Convention T can only serve this role if its instances can be expressed, which means that the metalanguage must contain every sentence of the object language. But if the metalanguage is always an extension of the object language then we cannot, for example, define a truth-predicate for a language of arithmetic within a language of set theory, which is a considerable shortcoming. So, it is reasonable to relax this requirement: instead of demanding that within instances of the schema (3.1.1) ϕ should be *identical* to the sentence named by α, we merely require it to be a *translation* of that sentence. Call this the crosslinguistic version of Convention T. (Tarski (1944: 67) explicitly mentions this modification but ignores it in the rest of the paper.)

As a crosslinguistic schema, (3.1.1) concerns not one semantic notion but two: beside the overt reference to truth there is also covert reference to meaning. A sentence and its translations are synonymous, and so what the crosslinguistic version of Convention T demands is that $T(\alpha)$ should have the same truth-value as some sentence that means the same as α. Moreover, for the definition to be proper, it must be independent of the choice of translation. In other words, the crosslinguistic schema embodies the assumption that no sentence of the object language can have translations into the metalanguage that differ in truth-value. This assumption is only safe if we think that the meaning of a sentence must fully determine its truth-conditions.

According to one way of looking at Tarski's project, he took the notion of meaning (or at least the notion of sameness of meaning) for granted and showed how to give a theory of truth. Davidson contended that we should turn things around: take truth for granted (i.e. accept it as a primitive notion in our theory) and view the very same truth theory as a theory of meaning. In Davidson (1967: 309) he writes:

> What we require from a theory of meaning for a language L is that without appeal to any (further) semantical notions it place enough restrictions on the predicate 'is T' to entail all sentences got from schema T.

There are, of course, many sentences which lack coherent truth-conditions. Context-sensitive sentences (e.g. 'It is on the mat'), nondeclaratives (e.g. 'Is it on the mat?'), and performatives (e.g. 'I hereby confirm that the cat is on the mat') cannot easily be plugged into schema (3.1.1). And we don't want our theories of meaning to derive (3.1.2).

(3.1.2) Example (3.1.2) is not true.

(As usual, the number in (3.1.2) is a canonical name for the sentence that follows, so the sentence says of itself that it is not true.) If our theory of meaning derives the instance of the T-schema '(3.1.2) is true if and only if (3.1.2) is not true' then it is inconsistent. For more on this topic, see Section 13.2.

Davidson acknowledged these problems and made tentative proposals to meet them. (For a contemporary discussion of ways of handling these difficulties within a broadly Davidsonian framework, see Lepore and Ludwig [2007].) Whether the adjustments succeed is controversial. But even if they fail, the requirement that an adequate theory of meaning should derive all instances of schema T remains reasonable for a significant fragment of natural language free of indexicals, nondeclaratives, performatives, and devices that allow reference to expressions of the language. The more pressing question is this: can such a requirement by itself actually guarantee that the theory succeeds in identifying what the sentences within such a fragment mean? Davidson (2001: 80) has a negative answer to this:

> it is not my thesis that *all* we should demand of a semantic theory is that it meet the standard of Convention T. I shall suggest that theories satisfying Convention T are capable of explaining more than is often thought. But there may be choosing among such theories on the basis of further criteria; and of course there is much we want to know that lies outside.

For Davidson, the main explanatory task for a theory meaning is to account for the possibility of learning a language. A theory of meaning underlies competent speakers' ability to understand that language, and as such, it must be known to them. So, for one thing, it must be *compositional*, deriving the meanings of complex expressions from the meanings of their parts. Moreover, since he took meanings to be essentially public, Davidson also believed that there shouldn't be anything to this theory that cannot be made manifest in linguistic behavior. This leads to a further constraint: that the theory should be learnable through *radical interpretation*. A radical interpreter is someone who lacks any prior knowledge of the meanings of expressions in the language and gathers evidence exclusively from observing competent speakers' interaction with the environment.

Suppose that we accept all three of Davidson's requirements. Can a theory that (i) derives all instances of Convention T for a fragment of a natural language, (ii) does so in a compositional fashion, and (iii) is discoverable by radical interpreters serve as an adequate theory of meaning for the fragment?

The answer seems to be that it can't. For what if instead of (3.1.3) it derives (3.1.4)?

(3.1.3) 'Snow is white' is true if and only if snow is white.
(3.1.4) 'Snow is white' is true if and only if grass is green.

A clause like (3.1.3) is *interpretive* in the sense that the sentence on the right displays the meaning of the sentence on the left. While perfectly true, a clause like (3.1.4) is obviously not interpretive. If a theory of truth is to serve as a theory of meaning it should either not derive noninterpretive T-sentences at all, or if it does, it should specify some way of identifying the interpretive ones. But there is nothing in a truth theory that does that. This sort of objection was first raised in Foster (1976) and eventually came to be called *Foster's problem*.

Davidson (1967: 25–26) initially suggests that compositional theories would not derive clauses like (3.1.4). It's easy to see why Davidson thought this: the straightforward way for a truth theory to derive (3.1.4) is for it to contain clauses that say that 'snow' designates grass and 'is white' is satisfied by green things, but if we have such clauses we would presumably also derive false T-sentences as well. For example, if one of our clauses says that 'is green' is satisfied by green things, we can derive (3.1.5):

(3.1.5) 'Snow is green' is true if and only if grass is green.

And so, it might seem that Foster's problem will be avoided merely by insisting that the theory should derive only truths.

But this isn't so. As Foster pointed out, any compositional theory that entails (3.1.3) can easily be reformulated so that it entails (3.1.6):

(3.1.6) 'Snow is white' is true if and only if snow is white and grass is green.

(For example, instead of having an axiom that says that x satisfies 'is white' if and only if x is white, we could have one that says that x satisfies 'is white' if and only if x is white and grass is green.) Later, in Davidson (1967: fn.11), Davidson suggested that interpretive T-sentences are empirical laws and that this might allow us to distinguish them from noninterpretive T-sentences the theory derives. But, as Soames (1988) shows, this won't help either: while (3.1.6) is indeed an accidental truth, (3.1.7) is an empirical law, assuming that (3.1.3) is.

(3.1.7) 'Snow is white' is true if and only if snow is white and arithmetic is incomplete.

Where should we go from here? In the end, Davidson thought that the key to singling out interpretive theories is radical interpretation. Speakers not only know a truth theory for a language with which they are competent, they know that it is the sort of truth theory that can serve as a meaning theory. Hence, they must know that it is learnable on the basis of evidence available to radical interpreters. Axioms of the sort that allow us derive (3.1.6) or (3.1.7) do not belong to such a theory; see Davidson (1973: 139). (Davidson himself offers no detailed defense of this claim, but Heck [2007] attempts to make up for the lacuna.)

Whether or not this works, such a defense is viable only for those who accept radical intepretability as a constraint on theories of meaning. Most philosophers don't: it is far from clear that linguistic meaning must be public in the very strong sense Davidson assumes it is. People do learn natural languages: that's a fact. But it is an open question whether they could do that without relying on innate knowledge or insight into each other's mental states unmediated by observation.

3.1.2 The Inscrutability of Reference

Foster's problem arguably illustrates that without some constraint on the semantic values of words, there are too many ways to derive truth-conditions. The point can be further illustrated using a toy example.

Consider a toy language that contains just three proper names, 'Frege', 'Russell', and 'Tarski', and a single intransitive verb 'walks'. The only syntactic rule allows merging a noun and a verb; the correlated semantic rule says that the resulting sentence is true at a possible world w just in case the semantic value of the noun at w is a member of the semantic value of the verb at w. The obvious way to write the base clauses would be as follows:

$$[\![\text{`Frege'}]\!]^{w} = \text{Frege}$$
$$[\![\text{`Russell'}]\!]^{w} = \text{Russell}$$
$$[\![\text{`Tarski'}]\!]^{w} = \text{Tarski}$$
$$[\![\text{`walks'}]\!]^{w} = \{x : x \text{ walks in } w\}$$

But if all we are concerned about is getting the truth-conditions of sentences right, there are countless alternatives. For example, let π be a *proxy function* that maps Frege to Russell, Russell to Tarski, and Tarski to Frege. Also, assign to the proper names whatever the proxy function assigns to their ordinary semantic values. We can then use the inverse of π to define a semantic clause for the intransitive verb that cancels out the effect of π at the sentence level. (The inverse of π is the function π^{-1} that maps Frege to Tarski, Russell to Frege, and Tarski to Russell.)

$$[\![\text{`Frege'}]\!]^{w} = \pi(\text{Frege}) = \text{Russell}$$
$$[\![\text{`Russell'}]\!]^{w} = \pi(\text{Russell}) = \text{Tarski}$$
$$[\![\text{`Tarski'}]\!]^{w} = \pi(\text{Tarski}) = \text{Frege}$$
$$[\![\text{`walks'}]\!]^{w} = \{x : \pi^{-1}(x) \text{ walks in } w\}$$

On this interpretation, 'Frege walks' comes out as true at w just in case Frege's proxy is a member of the set of proxies of walkers in w – i.e. just in case Frege is a member of the set of walkers at w.

The idea of nonstandard re-interpretations of languages via proxy functions goes back to the concept of duality in abstract algebra, and was adapted to philosophical purposes in Quine (1992). Obviously, the technique can be generalized to larger languages and there are no constraints on π other than that it should be a one-to-one mapping. Proxies could be anything: shadows, addresses, numbers – we could even use words.

We might be inclined to say that on the standard interpretation the semantic values are the things the names *refer to*, while on the nonstandard interpretation they are something else – surrogates artificially concocted from the referent by means of the proxy function. But this is not what Quine says. On his view, the two interpretations are equally adequate: Frege has no more right to be called the referent of 'Frege' than Russell. What we take as semantic values of subsentential expressions is up to us – there are no empirical constraints on semantic theorizing beyond getting the truth-conditions of declarative sentences right.

This is the thesis of *inscrutability of reference*, introduced in Quine (1960) with the famous example of 'gavagai' – an imaginary word in an unknown language which is used in situations when rabbits are present. Yet, Quine argued, for all a field linguist could know it might refer to undetached rabbit parts, rather than rabbits.

What we are supposed to make of the alleged inscrutability is not entirely clear. Quine's own take was that we should conclude that ontology – philosophical theorizing about what exists – is inherently relative. There is no single, objectively correct way to take an inventory of the world. Donald Davidson, another proponent of inscrutability, thought this was a mistake: we cannot really make sense of people subscribing to alternative ontologies. Davidson (1979) took the moral to be that there is no objective fact about what language we speak. Either way, the consequences of inscrutability are fairly extreme.

Is there a way to reject the thesis? It seems perfectly obvious that 'Frege' refers to Frege, not someone else, and the idea is perplexing that a semantic theory of English that denies this could be called empirically adequate. What drove Quine to the inscrutability thesis was an austere form of empiricism. He was committed to the idea that the empirical basis of any theory consists of *observation sentences*. These are sentences of a language that linguistically competent and perceptually well-functioning speakers can come to agree on simply by witnessing a scenario. So, 'It's raining' or 'That's a cat' count as observation sentences but 'Men are mortal' or 'Two is a prime number' do not. If total evidence for a semantic theory is exhausted by the pattern of assents to and dissents from observation sentences, then, obviously, standard and nonstandard interpretations are evidentially on a par.

Davidson rejected the idea that there is a principled distinction between observation sentences and the rest, but he too believed that all evidence for or against a semantic theory comes from observable facts concerning the way speakers use their sentences – and this is enough for inscrutability. If we want to reject the thesis we need a more liberal view about what counts as evidence.

One option is to say that we have a priori evidence that 'Frege' refers to Frege simply because it is an instance of the schema ⌜'*N*' refers to *N*⌝, where *N* stands for a proper name. At first this sounds plausible, but empty names should give us pause. Should we say that we have a priori evidence that 'Santa Claus' refers to Santa Claus? If so, we also have a priori (albeit perhaps defeasible) evidence that there is someone (or something?) that is Santa Claus, which seems dubious. If not, we have to say that ⌜'Santa Claus' refers to Santa Claus⌝ is not an instance of our schema (i.e. that 'Santa Claus' is not a proper name), which seems equally dubious.

Another, perhaps slightly less costly option for resisting inscrutability is to appeal to simplicity. Certainly, a theory according to which, in normal cases, a particular use of a demonstrative pronoun refers to the object o the speaker demonstrates (usually by pointing, but often in some other way) is simpler than the one according to which it refers to some object o′ identified by first identifying o and then applying a proxy function. And, other things being equal, simpler theories are to be preferred to more complex ones. We need not take a stand on the thorny question of whether our reasons for preferring simpler theories are a priori or empirical – what matters is that simplicity counts. Simplicity is part of the reason we accept *any* theory, so there is no reason to discount it when it comes to semantics. Appeal to simplicity allows us to argue that some uses of some expressions refer much more determinately than Quine or Davidson would want to allow. And once inscrutability is given up for normal uses of demonstratives, we can leverage this to refute inscrutability for other expressions as well. We might insist, for example, that when someone introduces Frege by pointing at him and uttering 'Frege', then the word uttered must refer to the individual demonstrated.

3.1.3 The Irrelevance of Reference

Most semanticists don't believe that reference is inscrutable but are nonetheless unconcerned about the choice of semantic values for subsentential expressions. They might grant that we have good reasons to believe in objective facts of reference but they don't think these facts are relevant for natural language semantics. They might believe that Russell is not the referent of 'Frege' but insist that he, or any other artificial proxy of Frege, would serve to model the real referent within compositional derivations of truth-conditions. No theory should make assumptions beyond those it actually uses, and the assumption that semantic values are real-world referents is idle in semantic theorizing. Reference is not inscrutable, it is just beside the point.

It's hard to argue against a methodological stance such as this, but we can at least inquire into its motivations. If we provide semantics with a sufficiently narrow job description, the irrelevance of reference does follow. But why should semantics aim so low? The suggestion is that semantics should care about truth-conditions, compositionality, and nothing else. But truth-conditions hold no intrinsic interest for semantics – they matter because they cast some light on *meaning* – in particular, on the meanings of declarative sentences. If the semantic values of words and phrases are regarded as a more or less arbitrary way to derive the correct truth-conditions for declarative sentences, then the theory tells us very little about what words and phrases mean. After all, why should a semantic theory care only about a certain kind of linguistic expression and ignore all the rest?

It is equally mysterious why semanticists should care about compositionality if semantic values can be assigned at will to nonsentences. Zadrozny (1994) has shown that we can turn *any* assignment of semantic values into a compositional one by replacing the old semantic values with new ones from which they are uniformly recoverable; for a discussion of this and other triviality results, see Westerståhl (1998) and Dever (1999). The point can be illustrated with our toy language. Consider a third interpretation of the lexicon, one that employs the proxy function for the nouns but not for the verb:

$$[\![\text{`Frege'}]\!]^{w} = \pi(\text{Frege}) = \text{Russell}$$
$$[\![\text{`Russell'}]\!]^{w} = \pi(\text{Russell}) = \text{Tarski}$$
$$[\![\text{`Tarski'}]\!]^{w} = \pi(\text{Tarski}) = \text{Frege}$$
$$[\![\text{`walks'}]\!]^{w} = \{x : x \text{ walks in } w\}$$

This interpretation does not assign the same truth-conditions to sentences of our toy fragment as the previous two. But the problem can be fixed if we adjust the semantic rule: let's say that a combination of a noun with 'walks' is true at a world w not iff the semantic value o of the noun at w is a member of $[\![\text{`walks'}]\!]^{w}$, but rather iff $\pi^{-1}(o)$ is a member of $[\![\text{`walks'}]\!]^{w}$. With this rule, the interpretation is equivalent to the other two at the level of sentences, and it is no less compositional than they are.

Of course, specifying a compositional semantic rule for an arbitrary assignment of semantic values is harder if the language is more complex. But it can be done, as Zadrozny has shown. As Partee (1984) puts it:

> if the syntax is sufficiently unconstrained and the meanings sufficiently rich, there seems no doubt that natural languages can be described compositionally. Challenges to the principle generally involve either explicit or implicit arguments to the effect that it conflicts with other well-motivated constraints on syntax and/or on the mapping from syntax to meaning.

To give compositionality some teeth, we must constrain what we are willing to count as semantic values. If we assign truth-conditions to declarative sentences and are willing to grant the existence of some objective facts of reference it seems very natural, contra Quine and Davidson, to ask semantic theories to relate some expressions to their referents.

3.2 What is a Referring Expression?

Semantics textbooks usually tell us that referring expressions are pronouns, proper names, and definite descriptions. But bound or anaphoric pronouns, complex or descriptive proper names, and plural or mass definite descriptions are not always counted as referring expressions. To adjudicate the controversial cases we should try to go beyond a mere list and see what it is that referring expressions are supposed to have in common.

We begin with two thoughts.

(i) Some expressions refer, some don't. The French mathematician Urbain le Verrier made two famous predictions: on the basis of perturbations in the orbit of Uranus, in 1846 he posited the existence of the planet Neptune, and on the basis of the precession of Mercury's orbit, in 1859 he conjectured the existence of the planet Vulcan. He was right in the first case but not in the second, and so, the first name he coined refers while the second does not.

(ii) Some expressions are for referring, some are not. Although 'Vulcan' fails to refer, it is still a referring expression. Referring is its function in the language. (Here, of course, we are using 'function' in its nonmathematical sense.) In this respect 'Vulcan' resembles the word 'Neptune' and differs from the phrase 'orbits the Sun' or the sentence 'Neptune orbits the Sun'. The latter expressions have different functions (perhaps predicating and asserting), and consequently, they are not referring expressions.

Against (i), one might argue that 'Neptune' and 'Vulcan' are both names of mythological creatures and so, neither refers. But it is natural to assume that this is a case of ambiguity – when Le Verrier introduced these names he took inspiration from mythology, but he initiated new names. This is why dictionaries have separate entries for names of deities and names of planets. As for (ii), one might object that functions that remain forever unrealized are implausible and suspicious. But functions *are* sometimes forever unrealized: a task force could be set up to investigate a terrorist attack even if no such attack occurred. Similarly, a word can have the function of referring to a planet even if there is no such planet for it to refer to.

3.2.1 Standard Accounts

Given how natural our two minimal constraints seem, it may be surprising that they were rejected by both of the founders of modern semantics. According to Frege, all expressions refer; according to Tarski none do.

For Frege, semantic distinctions ultimately boil down to ontology. (Some interpreters also think that the ontological matters, in turn, boil down to syntactic and logical ones; cf. Wright [1983] and Hale [1987]. But this view is controversial.) The referent of 'Neptune' is an object (the cold, blue, gaseous planet), while the referent of 'orbits the Sun' is a concept (the function which maps an object to the True just in case it orbits the Sun). The sentence 'Neptune orbits the Sun' has a referent too – the truth-value we obtain if we apply the referent of 'orbits the Sun' to the referent of 'Neptune'.

For Tarski, semantic issues about reference reduce to syntax. To interpret 'Neptune' we need to give it an index, while to interpret 'orbits the Sun', we must fill its argument place with a variable (which also bears an index). When that is done both expressions become interpretable via satisfaction clauses: 'Neptune_1' is satisfied by a variable assignment g just in case $g(x_1)$ is Neptune, while 'x_2 orbits the Sun' is satisfied by g just in case $g(x_2)$ orbits the Sun. The sentence 'Neptune_1 orbits the Sun' has a satisfaction condition too – it is satisfied by a variable assignment g just in case g satisfies 'x_1 orbits the Sun'.

What about 'Vulcan'? Tarski has no problem with it – he already bit this bullet when he denied reference to 'Neptune'. He can say that 'Vulcan_3' is satisfied by a variable assignment g just in case $g(x_3)$ is Vulcan. Since nothing is Vulcan, 'Vulcan_3' is not satisfied by any variable assignment whatsoever. It follows that 'Vulcan_3 orbits the Sun' is false. Frege, on the other hand, certainly does have a problem – he assigned the commonsense referent to 'Neptune' but clearly he cannot do the same for 'Vulcan'.

Frege's official view is that we should forget about empty names: 'Vulcan' is not a bona fide linguistic expression, only a mock name (*Scheinname*). Regarding Schiller's play *Don Carlos*, which was loosely based on history, Frege (1979a: 130) writes:

> If [it] were to be regarded as a piece of history, then to a large extent the drama would be false. But a work of fiction is not meant to be taken seriously in this way at all: it is all play. Even the proper names in the drama, though they correspond to names of historical persons, are mock proper names.

But, in principle, Frege's semantic framework does make room for a more compromising view, even if Frege himself does not. Instead of banishing 'Vulcan' some of Frege's followers (among them Richard Montague) have provided it with a referent: the function F that assigns truth-values to any function G from objects to truth-values in such a way that F(G) is the True just in case G maps Vulcan to the True and everything else to the False. If we apply the referent of 'Vulcan' to the referent of 'orbits the Sun' we get the False, since the referent of 'orbits the Sun' does not map Vulcan to the True.

According to the ordinary pretheoretic notion of reference, 'Neptune' refers, 'Vulcan' does not, but (unlike 'orbits the Sun' or 'Neptune orbits the Sun') they are both referring expressions. Neither Frege nor Tarski employ such a notion in interpreting their respective formal languages. Still, could they define a recognizable notion of reference within their theories?

Let's start with Frege. To avoid confusion, henceforth when we speak of Frege's own notion of reference, we use his own term, *Bedeutung*. The question, then, is whether we can say what it is for an expression to refer or to be a referring expression in terms of Bedeutung. The natural suggestion is to say that expressions whose Bedeutung is an object refer. This would include 'Neptune' but not 'orbits the Sun'. In order to characterize referring expressions we might go along with the idea that the Bedeutung of an empty name is a higher-order function. Then we can define referring expressions as those expressions whose Bedeutung is an object or the function that assigns the True to all functions that assign the True to anything. This would guarantee that 'Vulcan' is a referring expression.

Unfortunately, this suggestion fails. Besides 'Vulcan', there are plenty of other expressions whose Bedeutung is this particular function – 'some planet inside the orbit of Mercury' and 'most planets made of gold' are good examples. Yet, we definitely don't want to say that all these are referring expressions. Moreover, the Bedeutung of 'Neptune orbits the Sun' is the True – an object on Frege's view. Yet, we don't want to say that 'Neptune orbits the Sun' refers.

In response to the first problem, semanticists sometimes posit a null-object – distinct from all objects we really think exist – and make this the Bedeutung of 'Vulcan'. While this seems nothing more than a technical trick, it certainly allows us to distinguish empty names from quantificational phrases and to deny that the latter are referring expressions. But there is a problem: if we can posit the null-object we can presumably name it too. Let's say we call it 'Nil'. This name poses a problem: on the one hand, we want to say that 'Vulcan' and 'Nil' have the same Bedeutung; on the other hand, we also want to say that 'Nil' refers but 'Vulcan' does not.

In response to the second problem, semanticists sometimes abandon Frege's austere ontology and allow truth-values to be neither objects nor functions. But this leads to the exact same problem as positing a null-object. If there are such things as truth-values, we should be able to introduce names for them. Frege himself employs 'True' and 'False' just this way. We'd like to say that 'Neptune orbits the Sun' and 'True' have the same Bedeutung and also maintain that the latter refers but the former does not.

Frege was well aware of a version of this problem. If there are such things as functions, we should be able to introduce names to refer to them. Let's stipulate that the name 'Horse' refers to the concept horse, i.e. the function that maps all horses to the True and everything else to the False. Then 'Horse' and 'horse' share a Bedeutung, yet the first refers to an object and the second does not. This is a formulation of what has come to be called the *concept horse problem*. Frege's own "solution" was to deny that we can introduce proper names like 'Horse'; perhaps one could say the same for 'Nil' and 'True' as well. But without resources to name most of the Bedeutungen, writing down

Fregean semantic clauses becomes a highly nontrivial task. Frege himself certainly did not succeed, and he knew it:

> By a kind of necessity of language, my expressions, taken literally, sometimes miss my thought; I mention an object, when what I intend is a concept. I fully realize that in such cases I was relying on the reader who would meet me half way – who does not begrudge a pinch of salt. (Frege 1960b: 193)

Contemporary semanticists have a less paradoxical way of saying essentially the same thing. They will point out that they are not really attempting to give a semantic theory for an entire natural language and insist that the proper names they use to refer to truth-values or functions are not part of the fragment under consideration. Those who use a type theoretic framework can say that the referring expressions are all and only those that belong to the semantic type e (i.e. all and only the ones whose Bedeutung is an object), but this will only work if they have decided to exclude expressions like 'True', 'Horse', or 'Vulcan' from the fragments they seek to interpret. It looks as if there is no straightforward way to explain what it is to refer or to be a referring expression in terms of Bedeutung.

Can we do better if we follow Tarski? Within the framework of a broadly Tarskian semantics, it would be natural to say that referring expressions are all and only those that bear indices, and among referring expressions, the ones that actually refer are all and only the ones that are satisfied by some variable assignment. In the formal languages Tarski considered, the index-bearing expressions are individual constants, variables, and nothing else. As long as we assign indices to 'Neptune' and 'Vulcan' but not to 'orbits the Sun' or 'Neptune orbits the Sun' this proposal delivers the right results.

But how are we to decide which expressions bear indices? In formal languages, indices are syncategorematic devices used to indicate interpretive dependencies. When we discover similar dependencies in natural languages, we might use the same sort of device to mark them. So, for example, the two true readings of 'Neptune orbits the Sun and it rotates around its axis' can be represented as 'Neptune$_5$ orbits the Sun$_8$ and it$_5$ rotates around its$_5$ axis' and 'Neptune$_5$ orbits the Sun$_8$ and it$_8$ rotates around its$_8$ axis', while the two false readings can be represented as 'Neptune$_5$ orbits the Sun$_8$ and it$_5$ rotates around its$_8$ axis' and 'Neptune$_5$ orbits the Sun$_8$ and it$_8$ rotates around its$_5$ axis'. However, if this sort of disambiguation is sufficient justification for positing indices, then they will show up on nonreferring expressions too. For example, we might use them to distinguish between 'Neptune [orbits the Sun but it also rotates around its axis]$_2$, and Vulcan [does too]$_2$' and 'Neptune orbits the Sun but it also [rotates around its axis]$_6$, and Vulcan [does too]$_6$'.

Of course, even if Tarski's own criterion fails there might be some other syntactic feature that characterizes all and only referring expressions. There are certainly robust distributional differences that allow us to distinguish proper names, intransitive verbs, and declarative sentences. Still, it is worrisome that, in terms of distribution, proper names are closer to common nouns than to pronouns, and definite descriptions are closer to indefinite descriptions than to indexicals. The category of referring expressions appears to be syntactically heterogeneous even within a single language, let alone crosslinguistically.

Quine (1948) coined the term 'Pegasize' for 'is identical to Pegasus' and later defended in detail the view that 'Pegasus' can be regimented as 'the thing that Pegasizes'. By the time he wrote *Word and Object*, Quine held the view that proper names themselves can be interpreted as predicates, so there is no need to use a morpheme to turn them into predicates. So let's stipulate that 'Neptunizes' is just an abbreviation for 'is identical to Neptune'. It follows that it is necessarily true that Neptune Neptunizes and necessarily false that anything else does. Neptunizing started about 4.6 billion years ago, and if everything goes well it will continue for a few more billion years. We could learn to speak this way.

'Neptune' and 'Neptunizes' concern (to use a neutral term) the exact same portion of reality, and yet the former is a referring expression and the latter isn't. There must be some difference in the way these two words relate to the planet which would account for the difference. For Frege, the difference is that 'Neptune' has the planet as its Bedeutung, while 'Neptunizes' picks out Neptune only indirectly by having a function as its Bedeutung that maps Neptune alone to the True. This is an explanation, even if it has the problems mentioned above. But to say, as Tarski does, that the difference is a matter of syntax – i.e. a matter of how 'Neptune' and 'Neptunizes' relate to other linguistic expressions – is no explanation at all. The syntactic difference might tell us that only one of these is a referring expression, but it would not tell us which one that is.

Let's sum up. We have an ordinary notion of reference, according to which 'Neptune' refers but 'Vulcan' does not, and according to which 'Neptune' and 'Vulcan' are referring expressions but 'orbits the Sun' and 'Neptune orbits the Sun' are not. Neither Frege nor Tarski have semantic theories which employ such a notion. Moreover, such a notion of reference does not even seem to be definable within semantic theories built exclusively on their ideas. We can do better if we follow Russell, as we will see in the next section.

3.2.2 Acquaintance, or Something like It

A name says a lot about its bearer. If a person is called 'Joshua Herschel', you can be pretty sure that he is Jewish; if a town is called 'Lake Placid', you can bet it is on a lake; and if a number is called '27', you know it equals two times ten plus seven. Nonetheless, we have a tendency to think that these are deviations from the ideal. A genuine, honest to God, proper name is supposed to be undefinable. One might define 'the present monarch of England' by saying in other words what it takes for someone to fit the condition of being the present monarch of England. (The definition is complicated but it has been laid down in the Bill of Rights 1689 and the Act of Settlement 1701.) But defining 'Elizabeth II' seems hopeless because the name places no substantive condition on its bearer. Of course this isn't entirely true – you can conclude that the bearer of 'Elizabeth II' is almost certainly female, probably from an English-speaking country, and likely related (by blood or otherwise) to another person named Elizabeth who was born before her. But, again, that is only because 'Elizabeth II' is not what Russell would call a *logically proper name*. Russell's idea is that logically proper names and only logically proper names are referring expressions, and all and only referring expressions actually refer.

What are logically proper names? They are mere tags – they attach to their bearers but remain silent about them. Pronouns might be the best examples. When a speaker uses a pronoun, she exploits some feature of the context presumed to be available to the hearer to pick out an item. I point at a book and I say, 'I should return this to the library'. It is the meaning of 'this' together with my pointing gesture that helps you to identify the item to be returned to the library. The meaning of 'this' tells you that the word refers to what is being demonstrated, and the demonstration shows what that thing is. But this information is not being used to describe the book as the demonstrated thing. Similarly, what helps you to identify the person who should return the book to the library is the meaning of 'I'. This, together with your awareness of who the speaker is, tells you that the word denotes the speaker. Again, the speaker is not being described as such, in fact, he is not being described at all. As Russell (1918–1919: 245) put it:

> the name itself is merely a means of pointing to a thing, and does not occur in what you are asserting, so that if one thing has two names, you make exactly the same assertion whichever of the two names you use.

What happens when a logically proper name fails to refer? Imagine overhearing someone next door uttering 'I should return this to the library'. In one sense you understand the utterance – you are a competent speaker of English, and you just heard a sentence with everyday words put together in a perfectly straightforward way. Yet, in another sense you have no idea what (if anything) was said. You need to find out what needs to be returned to the library and by whom in order to assess the claim. Russell would say that what you lack is an immediate awareness of these things. He called this immediate awareness *acquaintance*.

The ordinary notion of acquaintance is a matter of degree: knowing more and more about someone makes you better and better acquainted with the person. But, Russell insisted, knowing more and more facts about a thing never gets you all the way to knowing the thing itself. There is a qualitative difference between knowing that something or other is such-and-such, and knowing of a thing that it is such-and-such – to get to the latter from the former you need acquaintance. And when you have acquaintance you cannot be mistaken about the existence or identity of the thing you are acquainted with. For Russell, to be acquainted with x and a distinct y and to assert that x or y does not exist or that x is identical to y is to assert a contradiction. Not surprisingly, Russell declared that the only objects we are acquainted with are the self (not to be confused with a flesh-and-blood human being) and our sense data (not to be confused with external objects). We know bodies – including our own – only by description as the thing, whatever it is, that causes our experiences. Anything that can be presented to us in more than one way, anything towards which we can have more than one perspective, is automatically unsuitable for acquaintance.

Acquaintance in Russell's sense is hard to come by. But perhaps we could keep half of the idea – that of a relation that enables us to be in immediate epistemic contact with something – and relax the requirement that this closeness should put us in a position to discern the thing from everything else. When it comes to physical objects, acquaintance might be just perception. If you touch, taste, see, smell, or hear something, the thing must exist but you can certainly perceive one thing as if it was two, or two things as if they were one. Perception does not reveal the nature of what is perceived – which is why it can reach beyond ourselves and our sense-data. When Le Verrier finally observed Neptune, he became acquainted not with the surface of the planet, or the light reflected from the planet, or the image of the planet on the lens of the telescope, or his own sense-data – he perceived the planet itself. Let's grant that this was acquaintance enough.

Imagine that you hear for the first time about Neptune from a friend. As you learn the name you also form the intention to use it to refer to whatever your friend used it to refer to. The intention needn't be specific – you don't have to explicitly think to yourself that you wish to align your use of the name with that of your friend. It is more like having a standing disposition to follow the linguistic practice of your community and the fact that you take your friend to be a member of the community who is competent with the name. We can think of these intentions as establishing an epistemic link between you and your friend: if she is acquainted with Neptune, and hence is able to use 'Neptune' to refer to it, you inherit this ability from her. If your friend is not acquainted with Neptune, she too refers to it on account of having picked up the name from someone else. Since picking up the name requires some sort of interaction between the source and the recipient, this chain of transmission is causal. It leads back to someone who actually saw the planet. That person was aware of the referent, and this awareness spread from person to person all the way to you through chains of transmission sustained by referential intentions.

Something is a referring expression, according to this liberalized Russellian view, if its uses are linked by an appropriate causal chain to someone who has perceived the referent. Philosophers have devoted much attention to the workings of this process; see Evans (1983); Boër and Lycan (1986); Kvart (1993). But no matter how far we stretch the notion of acquaintance it will surely never reach a nonexistent thing, such as Vulcan. So, what sort of expression could 'Vulcan' be?

According to Russell, it abbreviates a definite description, say, 'the planet responsible for the precession of Mercury's orbit'. And Russell must say the same thing about uses of demonstratives that designate unperceived things. Imagine that you are blindfolded and you are supposed to pick one among three items placed in front of you – one to the right, one to the left, and one in front. You point to the left and and say 'I choose that one'. On a Russellian view, your use of the demonstrative is proxy for a description, say, 'the item I am pointing at', and hence, it did not refer.

This theory has proved to be a promising start for a serious semantics for singular definite descriptions; for more details see Neale (1990). According to these theories, descriptions are not referring expressions, and, of course, neither are expressions that are used to abbreviate definite descriptions. Whenever there is a unique object that satisfies '*F*' we can say that 'the *F*' *designates* that object, even though it does not refer to it.

Accordingly, followers of Russell are in a position to meet our first requirement: they can say that 'Neptune' refers but 'Vulcan' does not. Can they guarantee that 'orbits the Sun' and 'Neptune orbits the Sun' are not referring expressions? Like Frege, Russell seeks to explain the distinctions among names, predicates, and sentences in ontological terms – except that he relies on different categories: particulars and universals rather than objects and functions. The main difference between the two is that Russell's insistence that reference requires acquaintance gives him an *epistemological* handle on the ontological distinction Frege lacks.

Acquaintance with particulars is a different sort of relation than acquaintance with universals. The former requires perceptual awareness, the latter conceptual apprehension. Like other empiricists, Russell (1912: Chapter 10) claims that we come to the latter by means of the former:

> When we see a white patch, we are acquainted, in the first instance, with the particular patch; but by seeing many white patches, we easily learn to abstract the whiteness which they all have in common, and in learning to do this we are learning to be acquainted with whiteness. A similar process will make us acquainted with any other universal of the same sort. … I see successively a number of sense-data in which one part is to the left of another; I perceive, as in the case of different white patches, that all these sense-data have something in common, and by abstraction I find that what they have in common is a certain relation between their parts, namely the relation which I call 'being to the left of'. In this way I become acquainted with the universal relation.

This model of how we could come to be acquainted with the property of being a horse is intuitively compelling. But it fails when it comes to the property of being a unicorn; since there aren't any particular unicorns, there is nothing to abstract from. Following Plato, Russell would say that unicornhood exists despite being uninstantiated. Following Aristotle, one might complain that his official story fails to explain how we can come to refer to uninstantiated universals.

Russell's adherence to Platonism is based on a link he envisioned between understanding and acquaintance. He called this the *Principle of Acquaintance*, (Russell 1910–1911: 117): "Every proposition which we can understand must be composed wholly of constituents with which we are acquainted." This principle can explain why the sentence 'I should return that to the library' overheard from next door should be incomprehensible to perfectly competent speakers of English: 'I' and 'that' are logically proper names, and, if the hearer is not acquainted with their referents, she is in no position to grasp the proposition the sentence expresses. And, given Russell's tight conception of acquaintance, one cannot be acquainted with something at a time when one is not experiencing it. Yet there is no similar incomprehensibility when it comes to a sentence like 'There is a unicorn in the garden'. This sentence is readily understandable, which by the Principle of Acquaintance entails that a competent speaker is acquainted with the property of being a unicorn – the propositional ingredient contributed by 'unicorn'. The natural conclusion to draw is that acquaintance with universals is more or less automatic, at least as far as mature thinkers are concerned.

Even though Russell's semantics is like Frege's in being based on a simple binary ontological distinction, it can avoid the concept horse problem. The problem for Frege was that since he wanted to say that proper names can only refer to objects, he had to deny that we can introduce proper names for functions, which forced him to deny that 'horse' and ⌜the function to which 'horse' refers⌝ corefer – despite the fact that this is exactly what his semantics says. Russell holds that proper names can only refer to particulars, so he has to deny that we can introduce a proper name for a universal. But, first, he can certainly admit that 'horse' and ⌜the universal to which 'horse' refers⌝ designate the same thing – the former by referring to it, the latter by denoting it. Moreover, Russell can give a principled reason for denying the possibility of introducing a proper name for a universal. He can say that understanding such a proper name would require us to be acquainted with a universal in the way we are acquainted with particulars, i.e. perceptually – which is impossible.

Let's sum up. We can liberalize Russell's notion of acquaintance to allow acquaintance with everyday objects, not just with our sense data and ourselves, and can extend it to allow acquaintance with things with which others are acquainted, as long as they stand in the right sort of causal and epistemic relations to us. Acquaintance comes in two forms: acquaintance with particulars and acquaintance with universals. Referring expressions are those that refer to a particular. And so, 'Neptune' is a referring expression, while 'orbits the Sun' and 'Neptune orbits the Sun' are not – they refer, but not to a particular. We cannot really say that 'Vulcan' is a referring expression (and so, we must admit that we cannot fully satisfy our second minimal requirement), but we can say that it shares an important function with referring expressions – to designate a particular. But it fails to perform this function – the definite description it stands for describes nothing at all.

Nevertheless, there remains a problem. Consider again Le Verrier when he conjectured the existence of a planet responsible for the perturbations in the orbit of Uranus and introduced the name 'Neptune'. At this time Le Verrier was not acquainted with Neptune, and, consequently, the name 'Neptune' can only be an abbreviation for a description. What description? Presumably the one Le Verrier himself would use to explain what he means by the word – i.e. 'the planet responsible for the perturbations in the orbit of Uranus'. After Johann Galle confirmed Le Verrier's prediction by spotting Neptune through a telescope, he at least became acquainted with the planet, and perhaps through his discovery subsequent users also can be credited with some sort of extended acquaintance. This means that the name 'Neptune', originally a disguised description, at some point changed its semantic character and became a referring expression. 'Vulcan' cannot make this transition, so it remains a proxy for 'the planet responsible for the precession of the orbit of Mercury'.

So far so good. But now consider a different way things could have turned out. Suppose as a result of a collision with a giant meteor, Mars ends up on an orbit closest to the Sun and becomes responsible for the precession of the orbit of Mercury. (Einstein showed that general relativity can explain the precession of Mercury. Still, perhaps if the orbit of Mars had been different, it could have been the dominant factor in accounting for Mercury's precession.) Since such a cosmic cataclysm seems possible, we can conclude that, contrary to fact, the planet responsible for the precession of Mercury could be Mars. Now, if Russell were right that 'Vulcan' abbreviates the description 'the planet responsible for the precession of Mercury' we could also conclude that Vulcan could be Mars. But this seems wrong. And of course, the same problem applies to 'Neptune'. Imagine some cosmic cataclysm after Le Verrier introduced 'Neptune' but before Galle made his observation. Neptune is blown to smithereens, but Jupiter is knocked out of its orbit in such a way that it becomes responsible for the perturbations in the orbit of Uranus. Again, Russell's theory predicts that Jupiter could be Neptune – but it couldn't.

The problem is that ordinary proper names, whether they are empty or not, are modally and temporally *rigid*: they designate the same thing at all possible worlds and at all times if they designate anything. The natural response to this observation is to rigidify the description that a name like 'Neptune' initially abbreviates. Instead of saying that when Le Verrier introduced the name at time t in world w it abbreviated the description 'the planet responsible for the perturbations in the orbit of Uranus', we will say that it abbreviated the description 'the planet responsible for the perturbations in the orbit of Uranus at t in w'. This guarantees rigidity. One might object that ordinary speakers don't know what possible worlds are and have no idea when a name was introduced in the language, so they couldn't possibly use those names as abbreviations for these sorts of descriptions. But people use abbreviations all the time without knowing how to unpack them. Just as a proper name can refer in my mouth to whatever it refers to in my linguistic community, perhaps it can also go proxy for whatever description it matches in my linguistic community.

This last suggestion is fairly heretical. The idea that proper names abbreviate definite descriptions has always been understood to mean that the description is something a competent user of the name could in principle spell out. That is why this view is thought to be vulnerable to Kripke's Feynman objection. Kripke's point is that ordinary speakers successfully refer to Richard Feynman even if they could not tell him apart from Murray Gell-Mann, and even if the only thing they know about Feynman is that he is a physicist. But perhaps the right moral to draw from the Feynman objection is not that the descriptivism is false, but rather that names can go proxy for descriptions only experts could identify. There do seem to be clear examples of this phenomenon: one could refer to NATO without knowing that the acronym abbreviates 'North Atlantic Treaty Organization'. Perhaps the case is not that different when it comes to 'Feynman' or 'Neptune'.

The liberalized Russellian view meets the minimal conditions we formulated in Section 3.2. Unlike theories that follow the footsteps of Frege or Tarski, this view can draw distinctions between referring expressions and the rest, and between referring expressions that refer and the rest. It does this by making substantive metaphysical and epistemological assumptions: that there is a fundamental distinction between particulars and universals and that, as a result, we cannot be conceptually acquainted with the former or perceptually acquainted with the latter.

The philosophical literature has many able critics of the view that reference requires any sort of acquaintance between competent users of a referring expression and its referent. For a book-length attack on epistemic and causal conditions on reference, see Hawthorne and Manley (2012). Saul Kripke, who in *Naming and Necessity* introduced the idea that proper names refer in virtue of a chain of transmission ultimately going back to an "initial baptism," did not require that those who initiate the use of a name should be perceptually aware of its referent. On his view, Le Verrier (or anyone else who formulates the description 'the planet responsible for the perturbations in Uranus' orbit') could refer to Neptune by the name 'Neptune' before the discovery of the planet. Giving up on acquaintance is liberating – one can now easily explain how we can apparently refer to our future grandchildren or to the square root of two. But those who abandon acquaintance still have to say something about what distinguishes referring expressions from the rest. And that is not an easy task.

3.3 What Is a Quantifier?

Russell (1905: 479) argues that the function of definite descriptions is to *denote*. Denoting, like referring, is a notion of aboutness, but it is supposed to be significantly less demanding:

> By a 'denoting phrase' I mean a phrase such as any one of the following: a man, some man, any man, every man, all men, the present King of England, the present King of France, the center of mass of the solar system at the first instant of the twentieth century, the revolution of the earth round the sun, the revolution of the sun round the earth. Thus a phrase is denoting solely in virtue of its form. We may distinguish three cases: (1) A phrase may be denoting, and yet not denote anything; e.g., 'the present King of France'. (2) A phrase may denote one definite object; e.g., 'the present King of England' denotes a certain man. (3) A phrase may denote ambiguously; e.g. 'a man' denotes not many men, but an ambiguous man.

What is supposed to be denoted by 'some man', 'any man', 'every man', and 'all men'? Clearly not a definite object. We might say that they don't denote anything, but if so, they don't just happen to lack a denotation, like 'the present king of France'. Russell most likely thought that just like 'a man', they denote an ambiguous man – whatever that might be.

It is quite puzzling that Russell invokes such obscure and misleading language here. Quine (1981) describes *On Denoting* as one of the milestones of empiricism, a work that helped us avoid ascribing some sort of being or second-class existence to the present king of France. Such praise is diminished if we really have to believe in the existence of ambiguous present French senators just because there are 348 perfectly unambiguous members of the French senate at present. Perhaps a more charitable way of reading Russell's "ambiguous men" would be to take him to be saying that 'a man' does not *collectively* denote many men but *distributively* denotes each of them. But if that's what he means, Russell would have to hold that the (ambiguous) denotations of 'a man' and 'every man' are identical.

Luckily, Russell is able to specify the meanings of sentences containing his denoting phrases without mentioning denotation. He says that a sentence of the form *C*(*a man*) amounts to 'It is sometimes true of x that x is human and $C(x)$', and a sentence of the form *C*(*all men*) amounts to 'It is always true of x that if x is human then $C(x)$'. The interpretation of definite descriptions is more complex but follows the same format: a sentence of the form *C*(*the man*) amounts to 'It is sometimes true of x that $C(x)$ and it is always true of

y that if y is human and $C(y)$ then $x = y$'. (We have simplified Russell's own formulations here by avoiding reference to propositional functions.)

This, and the fact that Russell himself avoided talk of denotation in some of his later expositions of the theory of descriptions, led most semanticists to the idea that Russell considered 'a(n)' and 'the' along with 'some', 'any', 'every', and 'all', as well as 'everything', 'something', and 'nothing' to be *quantifiers*. To say today that one holds a Russellian view of descriptions is to say that one is committed to the idea that descriptions (or at least singular-count descriptions) are quantifiers, and sentences (at least some of the declarative ones) in which they occur have the truth-conditions that Russell's own theory ascribes to them. (Merely agreeing with Russell about truth-conditions is not enough; Glanzberg [2007] gives a referential semantics for definite descriptions that preserves the Russellian truth-conditions.) But this just pushes the question one step back: what exactly makes an expression a quantifier?

3.3.1 Standard Accounts

Russell, as we have seen, gives examples in lieu of a theory. But Russell (1918–1919: 221) emphasizes that, unlike names or predicates, quantifiers are *incomplete symbols* – they have "absolutely no meaning whatsoever in isolation but merely acquire one in a context." Russell's syncategorematic interpretation of quantifiers makes them bearers of scope, and this ultimately allows Russell to solve the puzzles with which he is concerned. This is how, for instance, he explains how 'The present king of France is bald or the present king of France is not bald' could seem true while neither of its disjuncts does. But, of course, quantifiers are not the only scope-bearing expressions and there are many other ways to treat scope. Scope cannot be the defining characteristic of quantifiers and neither can syncategorematicity.

One thing that Russell does not stress, but is nonetheless striking, is that all the expressions on his list save 'the' have universal or existential force. Moreover, the meaning of sentences containing the definite article is specified as a conjunction with one existential and one universal conjunct. So, perhaps we could say that quantifiers are those expressions that can be defined using the standard resources of logic: $=$, $\neg$, $\vee$, and $\exists$. But since natural languages contain quantifiers whose semantic clauses cannot be formulated in first-order logic – 'more than half of' is a well-known example, but there are many others – we can improve this idea by including higher-order existential quantifiers as well. That way we won't leave out anything logicians would want to call a quantifier.

Nonetheless, such a characterization would still be inadequate: it would exclude some nonlogical quantifiers (like 'many'), and it would include some nonquantificational logical expressions (like 'and'). Further refinements might help with these problems. One might, for example, insist that the vagueness of 'many' is a matter of mere context-sensitivity, and in any given context 'many' can be translated as a precise logical expression. (This is objectionable: it seems plausible that no logical expression is vague.) And in response to the second problem, one might say that what sets apart quantifiers from other operators is that they bind variables. (This too is suspect: combinatorial logics seems to be able to express quantification without the use of variables.) To tie the notion of a quantifier to logic and syntax requires controversial theoretical decisions about vagueness and variables. It would be better to get a grip on what quantifiers are without making such commitments.

This criticism applies to the standard definition of quantifiers within formal semantics as well. Generalized quantifier theory, developed originally by Mostowski (1957) and Lindström (1996), and fully developed in Peters and Westerståhl (2006) identifies quantifiers either as all the expressions that belong to specific semantic types, or as logical expressions within those types. (Logicality is captured by certain invariance conditions.) If the logicality requirement is adopted, the status of vague expressions as quantifiers is in doubt, but if it is dropped, the definition becomes too permissive. The determiners 'every', 'this', and 'Russell's' are plausibly all of type $\langle\langle e,t\rangle,\langle\langle e,t\rangle,t\rangle\rangle$, and yet, only the first is a quantifier. Moreover, the demand that quantifiers occur only in some semantic types and not others remains a bare stipulation – we are left without any real explanation of why 'some' counts as a quantifier while 'or' does not.

3.3.2 Generalizing over Instances

Let's try a different route. It is natural to think that quantified sentences express generalizations over their instances. Instances are usually thought of as expressions obtained by swapping a proper name for a quantifier; generalizations over instances are sentences whose truth-value depends only on how many true and false instances it has. So, the instances of 'I have something in my pocket' are 'I have η in my pocket', where η is a proper name, and the sentence counts as a generalization over its instances because it is true just in case it has at least one true instance.

Substitutional clauses for the universal and existential quantifiers within the language of first-order logic L can be given as follows:

$$[\![\forall x F(x)]\!]^M = \top \text{ iff for every name } \eta \in L, [\![F(\eta)]\!]^M = \top$$
$$[\![\exists x F(x)]\!]^M = \top \text{ iff for some name } \eta \in L, [\![F(\eta)]\!]^M = \top$$

For these to deliver the intuitively correct truth-conditions, we need to stipulate that everything in the model has a name. If we add quantifiers like 'exactly two', we need to assume that everything in the model has exactly one name. Since this is unrealistic (especially if the model has infinitely many elements), substitutional accounts of quantification have largely fallen out of favor.

What has replaced them are objectual accounts. According to these, 'I have something in my pocket' is true just in case 'I have x in my pocket' is true of some object. The objectual clauses for the universal and existential quantifiers are these:

$[\![\forall x F(x)]\!]^{M,g} = \top$ iff for every object $a \in M$, $[\![F(x)]\!]^{M,g'} = \top$,
where $g'(x) = a$ and otherwise g' is like g.
$[\![\exists x F(x)]\!]^{M,g} = \top$ iff for some object $a \in M$, $[\![F(x)]\!]^{M,g'} = \top$,
where $g'(x) = a$ and otherwise g' is like g.

Objectual clauses cut out the middle men – names that must be paired with objects in a one-to-one fashion – and look directly to the objects in specifying truth-conditions. But this does not necessarily mean that objectual quantification is not generalization over instances. It all depends on what instances are supposed to be.

Consider again the sentence 'I have something in my pocket'. It would be natural to say that one can produce an instance of this sentence by pointing at an object and uttering 'I have that in my pocket'. We should consider all possible demonstrations whether or not we could actually perform them. Instances don't have to be modeled by conjuring a name for the demonstrated object – pairing the demonstrative sentence with the demonstratum will do equally well. When the language is that of first-order logic, we can stipulate the interpretation of instances as follows:

$[\![\langle F(x), a\rangle]\!]^{M,g} = \top$ iff $a \in M$ and $[\![F(x)]\!]^{M,g'} = \top$,
where $g'(x) = a$ and otherwise g' is like g.

We can restate these clauses in terms of generalizations over instances. What we get is this: a universally quantified formula is true just in case all its instances are, and an existentially quantified formula is true just in case some of its instances are.

The syntax of the language of first-order logic is quite different from what we find in natural languages. In English, for example, you typically cannot put a quantifier in front of a sentence and get another sentence. English has no variables, and while it has pronouns, which are in many ways analogous to variables, there is no need to use a pronoun to express quantification. It is certainly possible that English sentences have an underlying level of representation where quantifiers move out of argument position and leave a co-indexed trace behind, as May (1977) and many others following him have argued. But this should not be taken for granted just to identify the instances of quantified sentences.

We need three assumptions. First, let's suppose that for any quantifier Q there is a demonstrative expression D^Q which can be substituted for it. Second, let's posit that demonstrative phrases are referring expressions and that they refer to whatever they are used to demonstrate as long as that thing satisfies their complement. Otherwise, the reference remains undefined. Finally, let's say that if an expression contains an undefined constituent it too is undefined. (The last two assumptions guarantee that if 'I have [that coin]$_1$ in my pocket' receives no truth-value when nothing is demonstrated or when the demonstratum is not a coin.)

Now we can define and interpret instances of quantified sentences. We allow contexts to assign values to indices; also, we will index demonstrative expressions. If the quantifier Q takes widest scope in the sentence ϕ, then instances of ϕ are ordered pairs $\langle\phi', \mathrm{a}\rangle$, where ϕ' is the result of substituting D^Q for Q in ϕ, and a qualifies as a semantic value of D^Q. Then we can say that an instance $\langle\phi', \mathrm{a}\rangle$ of $[D^Q]_i$ is true relative to the context c just in case $[\![\phi']\!]$ is true relative to a context c′ which differs from c only in assigning a as semantic value to index *i*.

We do not need a detailed syntax and semantics of quantification in natural languages, but we do need some minimal assumptions about these things. Consider, for example, the sentence 'Two coins are in my pocket and they are hard to get'. The sentence is ambiguous: in its dominant reading the pronoun 'they' is bound by 'two coins' but there is another reading where the pronoun is used to pick out coins in general, or perhaps coins of a certain type. This difference is usually indicated by indexing.

(3.3.8) [Two coins]$_i$ are in my pocket and [they]$_i$ are hard to get.
(3.3.9) [Two coins]$_i$ are in my pocket and [they]$_j$ are hard to get.

After appropriate number adjustments, the first components of the instances of these sentences with respect to 'two' are:

(3.3.10) [That coin]$_i$ is in my pocket and [it]$_i$ is hard to get.
(3.3.11) [That coin]$_i$ is in my pocket and [they]$_j$ are hard to get.

In (3.3.8) the co-indexing marks a binding relation, in (3.3.9) an anaphoric relation. It is crucial that the semantics should ensure that anaphors are coevaluated with their antecedents relative to every context. This is what justifies the use we made of indices in characterizing instances.

Examples (3.3.8) and (3.3.9) express generalizations over their instances with respect to 'two'. If the second component of an instance is my office key, the instance is undefined; if the second component of an instance is a coin on the table, it is false. Both (3.3.8) and (3.3.9) are true just in case they have two true instances with respect to 'two', and otherwise they are false. Thus, 'two' occurs in both of these sentences as a quantifier. Now, consider the instances of 'Two coins are in my pocket' with respect to the occurrence of 'two coins'. These are pairs of the form ⟨'That is in my pocket', a⟩, where a is some entity or other. Whether the sentence is true cannot be determined just on the basis of counting true and false instances – we would also need to know whether objects that are the second components of the instances are coins or not. So, 'two coins' does not occur in the sentence as a quantifier.

The idea that quantifiers are used to express generalizations over instances has a number of advantages. It is broadly applicable to formal and natural languages. (The account as stated applies to count quantifiers only, but it could be extended to mass as well.) It is cast in ordinary terms and – setting aside the precise definition of instances – it stays close to an intuitive idea.

It explains why 'and' is not a quantifier: conjunctions don't have instances, and so they cannot express generalizations over them. It leaves room for vague quantifiers – generalization over instances can be vague. The truth-value of 'Jack used many coins to pay for coffee' needn't be determinate, but in any given context the sentence could not change its truth-value as long as the number of true and false instances with respect to 'many' remains the same. So, it counts as a generalization.

This view of quantifiers makes some predictions which seem salutary. Consider the sentence 'Jack used my coins to pay for the coffee'. Whether this sentence is true depends on which coins are mine, and so, its truth-value *can* change in a given context even if the number of coins Jack used to pay for the coffee and the number of coins he did not use to pay for coffee remains the same. The conclusion is that 'my' is not a quantifier. However, according to generalized quantifier theory, the semantic type of 'my' is $\langle\langle e, t\rangle, \langle\langle e, t\rangle, t\rangle\rangle$, just like the semantic type of 'every' or 'some', and so 'my' counts as a quantifier, albeit not a logical one. Perhaps it is more natural to think it is not a quantifier at all.

The situation is even more interesting when it comes to 'only'. Whether 'Jack used only coins to pay for coffee' is true depends on whether he also used something else, say, a dollar bill. So, the sentence can change its truth-value within a fixed context even if we hold the number of coins Jack used to pay for coffee and the number of coins he did not use to pay for coffee fixed. It follows that, on the definition proposed here, 'only' is not a quantifier. In generalized quantifier theory, this conclusion may be reached through a syntactic argument which shows that 'only' is not a determiner, and hence, it should not receive the type $\langle\langle e, t\rangle, \langle\langle e, t\rangle, t\rangle\rangle$. But what if we had a real determiner that works as 'only' seems to in this sentence? Following Barwise and Cooper (1981) some have conjectured that natural languages only contain conservative quantifiers, and if 'only' is a quantifier it is not a conservative one. But a quantifier absent from natural languages is still a quantifier. Better to say that 'only' is not a quantifier at all, because while a sentence like 'Jack used only coins to pay for coffee' expresses a generalization, it does not express a generalization over its instances.

3.4 Conclusion

Semanticists typically define referring expressions and quantifiers in a parochial way: either by simply listing them or by identifying them in terms of their syntactic distribution or semantic type. This would be acceptable if the semantic values of subsentential expressions had nothing over and above an instrumental role in semantics, as Quine and Davidson thought. We have argued that their reasons for denying that there is anything objective about the semantics of words and phrases are not conclusive, and that if there are objective facts about how subsentential expressions relate to the world, semantics should take those into account. To go beyond mere stipulation, one needs to say something about what referring expressions and quantifiers are for, what their function is within the language.

The function of referring expressions is, of course, to refer. Not all expressions have this function (e.g. verb phrases and sentences don't) and the ones that do don't all succeed in fulfilling it (e.g. names introduced as a result of a mistake don't). The standard semantic frameworks, whether they are inspired by Frege or Tarski, don't have the resources to define the category of referring expressions in a satisfactory manner. We examined an approach inspired by Russell, according to which referring expressions designate particulars with which the speaker or someone in the chain of transmission leading to the speaker must be acquainted. This sort of approach does meet the minimal requirements, but it does so by taking on significant and controversial metaphysical and epistemic commitments.

The function of quantifiers, we have suggested, is to express generalizations over instances. This definition (combined with a suitable notion of instance) matches our intuitive classification to a considerable degree: it gets the core cases right, and it makes sensible predictions elsewhere (e.g. it implies that 'only' is not a quantifier). It also captures the notion that quantification is secondary to reference, in the sense that truth-conditions for quantified sentences can be given in terms of referential instances.

4 Tense and Modality

4.1 Time, Modality, and Linguistics

The philosophy of time is just about as old as philosophy itself. It is still a vigorous area of inquiry but now – after Einstein's theory of relativity – is often known as "philosophy of space and time" and usually (but not always) is pursued by philosophers of science. Many of the issues gathered together under this topic have little to do with language and linguistics.

In this chapter, we will try to identify themes that bear on modeling time for semantic purposes and on the interpretation of the tense and aspectual systems of natural languages. We will be concerned with the ontological requirements associated with these enterprises and with philosophical problems that might somehow reappear as problems for temporal semantics. Several times in this chapter, we will cite a philosophical puzzle about time and ask whether it raises difficulties for interpreting the tense and aspectual systems of natural languages.

This makes for a highly skewed and partial discussion of the philosophy of time. For readers interested in the general topic, there are many references, including van Fraassen (1970); Sklar (1976); Poidevin and MacBeath (1993); Markosian et al. (2016).

The philosophy of modality is comparatively recent, and was inspired by the same logical and philosophical developments that make linguistic semantics possible. There is more mutuality of interest here, so, although our discussion of the topic is brief, it gives a more complete picture of the philosophical issues.

4.2 Time and Existence

Ontology appears as a motif in the oldest recorded philosophical reflections about time, in the fifth century BCE. The Eleatic philosophers, including Parmenides of Elea and Zeno of Elea, argued that time and change are illusory, a conclusion that contributes to an austere ontology denying not only times but any sort of multiplicity. This makes a wonderfully simple theory, but of course it departs entirely from common sense. Eleatic philosophy thus provides an early instance of a dubious philosophical position derived by a process of pure reasoning, adhering to the conclusions come what may.

Four of Zeno's arguments against the existence of motion have survived; the best known of these are the Bisection and the Achilles Paradoxes. (See Huggett [2010].) In subsequent discussions of Zeno's paradoxes, these arguments are usually treated separately. According to the Bisection Paradox, for instance, you can never get from point A to point B because first you have to get to the midpoint A_1, then to the midpoint A_2 of A and A_1, and so on; hence you have to visit infinitely many points. The Achilles is similar, except that it produces infinitely many times that Achilles (a famous runner) would have to visit in order to catch a tortoise with a head start. These paradoxes can be solved by pointing out that, according to scientific theories, both time and space are continuous – infinitely many times are available in which to visit infinitely many points, and vice versa.

But in an insightful and convincing analysis of Zeno's four arguments, Vlastos (1966) argues that Zeno's "paradoxes" together form a larger argument that (1) assumes the existence of space and time and (2) arrives at a contradiction by asking whether time is continuous and whether space is continuous and deriving a contradiction from each of the four cases. The four-part argument, then, is meant to show that time, as well as space, is illusory, and piecemeal criticisms of the four arguments are misguided.

The Bisection deals with the case in which space is continuous and time is discrete, and the Achilles with the case in which space is discrete and time is continuous. The least discussed of Zeno's arguments may be the most interesting: the Moving Arrow. If Vlastos is right, this is the case that should worry us most, because it addresses continuous time and space – and this, of course, has been the accepted physical theory of both since the seventeenth century. According to the Arrow, at any moment of time a flying arrow traverses no distance; therefore it never moves. The difficulty for physically minded contemporaries, then, is this: if time is decomposed into a continuum of instantaneous moments, it is hard to see how genuine change can arise. At any instant there can be no change, because change requires at the very least two times. But to say that at any instant there is no change is to say there is never any change, and so change must be impossible.

Physics addresses change (in the form of velocity) by first and primarily defining it over *intervals* of time and, second, defining velocity at an instant t by taking the limit of velocity over smaller and smaller intervals that contain t. This works beautifully for the physics of motion but not at all well as a philosophical explanation of change. It is puzzling how, if *instants* are the basic units of time, then the fundamental account of change should be in terms of change over *intervals*. And this may help to explain why time and change have remained as perennial problems of philosophy, regardless of progress in the physics of space, time, and motion. Also, many philosophers have felt a dissonance between the decontextualized scientific accounts of time and our subjective, conscious experience of time and change. (McTaggart's puzzle, which we discuss in Section 4.5.1, is an example.) For more about this history see, for instance, Poidevin (2015).

In logical and semantic theories the continuous doesn't prevail: it isn't uncommon to model time discretely. Discrete times are commonly used in dynamical systems – in modeling games, for instance, and the execution of computer programs – and this preference is inherited by dynamic approaches to semantics. Zeno's arguments, of course, do not affect these theories directly; the Achilles and the Stade, for instance, don't raise problems for dynamic logic. But there are related foundational and philosophical concerns.

Problems arise, for instance, if a discrete control system is situated in a continuous environment. When such a controller (a digital computer or a nervous system) is coupled with sensory and motor systems, we have a large continuous physical system consisting of two interacting parts – a mind and an environment. What justifies singling out the mind and treating it as discrete, and how can we characterize the interaction between the discrete and continuous components? As far as we know, there is no general answer to this question. A special case of this foundational problem arises in linguistic theories, where the semantics of tense is continuous as in Montague (1974), and this is combined with a discrete dynamic semantics or pragmatics. Although combinations of this sort raise philosophical and technical questions, few if any moderns would think of concluding, like the Eleatics, that time is therefore unreal.

Philosophical concerns about the nature of change do seem to translate into semantic problems about progressive aspect. As we said, Richard Montague treated times as continuous. Furthermore, he proposed an account of progressive aspect that depended on topological properties of patterns of the instantaneous truth and falsity of sentences. If 'The door be open' is true over an open interval of time, on this theory, then 'The door is opening' is true at any instant in this interval. As Barbara Partee pointed out, this falls prey to the "imperfective paradox" – it implies that if the door is closing it will close; see Bennett and Partee (1982). Montague's idea looks very natural in light of physical notions of change, which seek to account for change in terms of patterns of instantaneous states. But it seems that these notions do not work so well for semantic purposes. The later approach to the semantics of aspect beginning with Parsons (1990) treats events rather than instants as basic, and on the whole is much more successful.

The problems raised by Zeno and other ancient philosophers begin a long tradition of philosophical reflection on time and change. From a distance, they still haunt contemporary philosophical thinking about the nature of time, and many philosophical views about time conflict with common sense. Although it takes a philosophical extremist to deny the reality of time, as Zeno did, we will see that a similar view about possible worlds is actually popular among contemporary philosophers. Whether or not it challenges common sense to do away with possible worlds, the philosophers who deny their existence do seem to be questioning a device that is widely and more or less uncritically used in linguistic semantics.

4.3 Events and Temporal Structure

Suppose we grant, along with just about everyone, that time exists. What, then, is time, and what are times? For linguists, the following closely related question is especially relevant: how should times be represented in the models that are used to interpret natural languages? This section will discuss philosophical work that bears on this issue.

According to Aristotle (*Physics* 4, 219^{a}13–220^{a}25), time is the measure of change. It is natural to develop this thought into the idea that changes – and events – are more fundamental than times. And this suggests a temporal ontology that begins with events and processes and somehow constructs times from these more basic units. This idea was turned into a formal theory in work that began with Russell (1914).

In this and later studies, Bertrand Russell developed a qualitative theory of time based on relations among events. Russell's ideas have informed an extensive literature and have been refined and corrected by many later authors, most notably Hans Kamp and Steven K. Thomason. See Kamp (1979); S. K. Thomason (1984, 1989).

As physics has developed, and especially as it has investigated phenomena beyond ordinary experience (very large or small scales, large velocities, high energies, the very remote past), the picture it paints distances itself more and more from common sense. Russell, writing after the discovery of Special Relativity but before Quantum Mechanics, was concerned with this difference, which since then has only worsened.

Lecture IV of Russell (1914) is entitled "The World of Physics and the World of Sense." Concerning time, Russell has this to say:

> It is to be observed that we cannot give what may be called absolute dates, but only dates determined by events. We cannot point to a time itself, but only to some event occurring at that time. There is therefore no reason in experience to suppose that there are times as opposed to events: the events, ordered by the relations of simultaneity and succession, are all that experience provides. Hence, unless we are to introduce superfluous metaphysical entities, we must, in defining what mathematical physics can regard as an instant, proceed by means of some construction which assumes nothing beyond events and their temporal relations. (Russell 1914: 117)

Whether or not our experience of time is a better guide to what time is actually like than physical theories, it is reasonable to think that human experience has shaped the structures that are at stake in representing the meanings of temporal expressions in natural languages. The mathematical project that grew out of Russell's idea is therefore of linguistic interest.

In S. K. Thomason (1984, 1989), Steven K. Thomason produces an improved version of Russell's project; we summarize the main ideas here.

Qualitative approaches to time begin with a set of happenings. Following the customary philosophical terminology, we'll call these "events," understanding that all that is meant by this is that events can be temporally extended. Events are not meant to presuppose any independent notion of time or times: indeed, moments of time are to be constructed from events.

An *event structure* consists of a set of events together with three relations over them: $<$ ("wholly precedes"), $<_0$ ("begins before"), and $<_1$ ("ends before"). It is this relational, and apparently nonquantitative basis, that makes the theory qualitative.

Before Davidson-style formalisms became generally used in formal semantics, temporal structures consisting of intervals were popular. Interval structures contain less information than event structures. The set of intervals generated by a linear set of "instants" is an event structure, but event structures are more general than interval structures because different events can co-occur, i.e. can correspond to the same set of instants.

The basic axioms for event structures produce something like a linear ordering, and additional axioms can yield denseness and continuity. Crucially, there is a way to recover instants from event structures. The idea (which according to Whitrow (1980) is due to Arthur G. Walker) is that an instant corresponds to a division of events into disjoint Past, Present, and Future sets, so that an instant will be a triple ⟨P, C, F⟩ of sets of events. P and F must be nonempty, while C may or may not be empty. Every event in P must wholly precede every event in F. C consists of the events in neither P nor F. And finally, every event in C overlaps with some event in P and some event in F.

The last condition ensures that the set C representing the present is clustered around a division between past and present events. If, for instance, our set of events is the set of open intervals of real numbers, C will consist of all open intervals containing r, where r is some fixed real number. Constraints on event structures will determine the structure of the instants that are derived from them; S. K. Thomason (1984) shows what conditions are needed, for instance, to make these instants isomorphic to the real continuum.

This construction shows that event structures are not only consistent with punctual time structures but provide a definition of these structures as ordered triples of sets of events.

Under the influence of Arthur Prior's work in tense logic, early formal semantics based its treatment of temporal constructions on an ontology of temporal instants. But for many reasons, and not merely because of the need to account for progressive aspect, more recent approaches have added eventualities. See, for instance, Higginbotham et al. (2000); Tenny and Pustejovsky (2000); van Lambalgen and Hamm (2005). Typically, these theories include both events and instants in their ontologies, and make no claims about which is fundamental. But S. K. Thomason (1984) shows that plausible assumptions about events make it possible to define instants in terms of events. So it would be more economical for such theories of time to begin with events, and to derive times from these using Walker's construction or one like it.

Prior's theory took a flexible approach toward punctual temporal structures: It assumed a set of instants along with an ordering relation. A temporal logic could involve very weak assumptions about the ordering relation, or could make very strong and specific assumptions. This flexibility can be preserved in the event-based approach: An event structure consists of a set of events along with several relations, and again, very weak or quite specific assumptions can be made about these relations. There is a striking resemblance between this treatment of time and *mereological* theories of the part–whole relation; see, for instance, Casati and Varzi (1999). In natural languages, these are reflected in similarities between temporal constructions on the one hand, and plurals and mass nouns on the other. For more on this topic, see Schein (1993); Lasersohn (1995); Landman (2000).

Early attempts to correct Montague's problems with progressive aspect, including Bennett and Partee (1982) and Dowty (1979) used *interval-based* temporal structures, where intervals are simply pairs of instantaneous times. This is only a modest generalization of punctual structures. Eventualities invite a more radical view of the basic units of times; these units are individuals that can have many characteristics over and above the stretches of time they occupy. They can stand in causal relations, can have parts, can have agents, and can differ in the kinds of changes they represent. This approach is now commonly referred to as "neo-Davidsonian semantics"; see Lasersohn (2006) for further information and references.

The origins of this picture of time in philosophy actually go back to Aristotle's metaphysics. Aristotle's ideas were revived in the twentieth century by philosophers who were influenced by Aristotle but who also were well aware of their relevance to linguistics.

4.4 Eventualities, Potentiality, and Actuality

Confronting a changing world, we are naturally atuned to the likely outcomes that are contained in what we experience, and the threats and opportunities that they offer. This habit of thought is deeply embedded in our common sense reasoning and language.

Again, we find the beginnings of philosophical reflection on this topic in Aristotle, for whom the distinction between ἐνέργεια (actuality) and δύναμις (potentiality) was fundamental. Aristotle deploys this distinction throughout his work, using it to address various philosophical problems. And the task of explicating it is prominent in his metaphysics.

Aristotle's most sustained discussion of the topic is in Book θ of the *Metaphysics*. The actuality of a thing is a realization of its capacity, either as an artifact (in which case the realization is caused externally, by an artisan) or as a natural entity (in which case the cause is internal). Aristotle's examples include the capacity of wood to become a table, of a person to learn to play the flute, and of a seed to grow into a plant.

Potentiality and actuality connect to another idea of Aristotle's: that processes can tend towards a τέλος (a goal, a purpose, or, more loosely, a culmination). When this happens, the goal serves to explain the entire process. Aristotle grants that there are mechanical or "efficient" causes but thinks that purposes or "final" causes are equally legitimate and often provide deeper and more appropriate explanations.

This certainly works for the kinds of examples that are most prominent in Aristotle's work. The purpose in the mind of the artist – an intended shape or form, say, of a woman's body – can explain the steps that take place as a slab of marble is made into a statue better than anything else. In the case of a growing tree, the shape or form of the mature plant similarly explains the process of maturation, though now the pattern is internal. Instead of gravity, Aristotle invokes a perpetual goal of celestial bodies to perfect themselves by moving in circles to explain celestial dynamics. And it is the nature of earth (one of Aristotle's four elements) to tend to move towards the center of things. This explains why terrestrial bodies will fall if they're unsupported.

We can do little more than speculate about the extent to which these ideas were rooted in the aspectual system of ancient Greek. (Like English, Greek aspect distinguishes ongoing processes from completed processes that have achieved a goal.) It might be better to say that commonsense dynamical notions involving teleology inform not only Aristotle's metaphysics but the aspectual systems of many languages, including Greek.

Recognition of the connection of teleological metaphysics to the semantics of aspect only began to emerge well into the twentieth century, when philosophers who were thoroughly acquainted with Aristotle became especially interested in the workings of language.

Linguists mentioning the philosophical origins of event types frequently refer to Zeno Vendler, occasionally to Anthony Kenny, never to Gilbert Ryle. But the ideas presented in Ryle (1949) influenced both Kenny and Vendler, and were incorporated in a far-reaching (if somewhat misguided) philosophical project. Ryle, who taught at Oxford from 1925 to 1968, combined the keen interest in language usage he shared with many of his Oxford colleagues with a desire to debunk the philosophical ideas about the mind that, he thinks, originate with Descartes. Ryle suggests a much more modest conception: People, of course, perform actions, many of them informed by thought. Nevertheless, there is no separate "thinking substance," enjoying its own peculiar states and performing its own characteristic mental actions.

If Ryle could demonstrate this thesis, it would certainly show that serious misconceptions inform many traditional philosophical questions, including the mind–body and free will problems. The appeal of these misconceptions, he thinks, lies in specious misunderstandings of the meanings of words. He appeals to linguistic considerations in explaining these misunderstandings and in making his anti-Cartesian case.

We would say, adopting the term that is now used for happenings in general, that Ryle is using linguistic evidence to distinguish two kinds of eventualities: *episodes* and *achievements*. Episodes are true over a span of time, and are associated with adverbial phrases like 'for a while'. Achievements are punctual, and are the outcomes of episodes: where looking for a book would be an episode, finding the book would be an achievement.

Ryle wants to persuade us that knowledge, for instance, is not a state of a separate mental entity, of a mind. Indeed, it isn't a state at all, but an achievement – the successful completion of an episode. The idea is that knowledge stands to inquiry as finding stands to looking. A person looks, say, for a set of keys. When the search is successful, we describe the episode by saying she has found the keys. The suggestion, then, is that knowing something is merely a way of indicating that an episode of inquiry has ended happily.

To this suggestion, Ryle adds another: Philosophers are deceived by language into thinking that a culminated episode of inquiry must be something that is somehow much more impressive. Since, unlike the inquiry, the knowledge isn't observable, philosophers conclude it must attach to an occult, unobservable sort of thing: the mind.

These reflections concentrate on the acquisition of knowledge. Working from the other end, Ryle deploys arguments that involve the practical use of knowledge, and these use the category of *dispositions*. Dispositional concepts and terms have to do with the potentialities and tendencies of things. As such, they are conceptually connected with conditionals. That a glass will break if it's dropped is evidence that the glass is fragile. Conversely, if a glass is fragile, we expect it to break if it's dropped. Ryle appears to assume, without arguing for it, that episodes (like the breaking of a glass) are somehow primary and that the meaning of a dispositional term is more or less exhausted by noting that it allows us to infer the occurrence of certain episodes under certain conditions. Granting that these conditions may be more determinate and easy to enumerate (as with 'fragile') or less (as with 'hard'), Ryle is happy to classify many presumptive mental states as dispositions. This not only demotes their status, making them secondary to the episodes to which they point through conditionals, but makes it easier to say that in speaking of "mental states" we are talking not about hidden properties of a mind but about conditional properties of a person.

Here too, it is suggested that language has tempted philosophers to draw unwarranted metaphysical conclusions from quite ordinary ways of speaking about quite everyday things.

Ryle's ideas are not popular today. He was not a behaviorist, but his views have a similar impact on the legitimacy of mentalist theories. Cognitive science as we now know it didn't exist in his time, but if Ryle had been right about the mind, the entire field and not just philosophy of mind would be misconceived.

But when a building is condemned and abandoned, the builder's tools may still be useful. Ryle's distinction between episodes and achievements influenced later work in philosophy and is the contemporary inspiration for later work in philosophy and linguistics on *Aktionsarten* or *aspectual types*. And in drawing attention to dispositions, he was prefiguring an area of inquiry in which philosophy and linguistics are closely entangled.

If Ryle's use of *Aktionsarten* in philosophy is less than successful, in the work of Anthony Kenny and Zeno Vendler their philosophical impact is less easy to discern.

Neither Vendler nor Kenny could be called ordinary language philosophers, but, like Austin and unlike Ryle, they concentrate on linguistic analysis almost entirely for its own sake, and remain willing to postpone the larger philosophical consequences. Their work on aspect and *Aktionsarten* in Vendler (1957) and Kenny (1963) might well be called "informal semantics," and could as easily be classified as linguistics as philosophy.

Aristotle remains the best example of a philosopher who has integrated ideas about aspect into a philosophical system. In our time, the scientific side of Aristotle's approach is discredited, for the most part with good reason. Biologists, for instance, prefer mechanistic to teleological explanations. But Aristotle's work still has merit as a systematic explication of commonsense forms of thought that find their expression in natural languages. For more on this topic see, for instance, Code (1995), Cohen (2014).

4.5 Observer-Dependent Temporality

4.5.1 Subjective and Objective Conceptions of Time and McTaggart's Argument

Arguments against the reality of time did not die with Zeno. The most powerful recent example is due to John McTaggart, an early twentieth-century British idealist. (Idealism was a philosophical position that dominated the nineteenth century. In at least one sense of the word, idealism claims that there is nothing apart from minds and their ideas. An idealist like McTaggart will hold that, while there may be temporal arrangements of ideas, these do not correspond to any temporal relations among external things.)

McTaggart begins by drawing a plausible and well-motivated distinction between two ways to think about time and then claims that these two conceptions are inconsistent. Times, McTaggart says, can be ordered in two different ways: The first ordering he calls the "A-series," the second the "B-series." The A-series uses terms like 'today' and 'tomorrow', and so is dependent on a changing temporal standpoint. The B-series uses terms like 'before' and 'after' and is temporally decontextualized. An account of time (like the decontextualized theories found in the natural sciences) that omits the A-series is fundamentally incomplete, according to McTaggart, who thinks that change is inconceivable without the A-series. But the A-series and its associated concepts are inconsistent, McTaggart claims, because, for instance, (1) no time can be both future and past and (2) any given time *is* both future and past.

At this point, the argument looks specious: You would want to say that a time that is future will be past or that a time that is future from one perspective is also past from a different perspective. McTaggart anticipates these objections: He says that using tense to say that an event will be past is to say that in the future it *is* past, and that this is either circular or leads to a regress because explaining the tensed verb 'is' in the explanation of 'moment M is past' will require a secondary A-series. Similarly, to introduce a perspective is to invoke a secondary present.

These arguments look fallacious, but philosophers haven't found it easy to agree on where to locate the problem. See, for instance, (Dummett, 1960; Prior, 1967: 1–9; Mellor, 1981; Rochelle, 1998). Nevertheless, perhaps we can say that the weakest point in the argument is McTaggart's claim to have found a vicious regress in the explication of A-series concepts. Arthur Prior provides a convincing dissolution of McTaggart's regress in Prior (1968a); see also Ludlow (1999: 107–108).

For our purposes, though, it might be more useful to consider what the impact might be on the standard theories of tense in formal semantics, which developed out of early work in tense logic, such as Prior (1967). These theories explain the present tense form of a sentence ϕ[+pres] at t in terms of the truth of tenseless ϕ at t. If McTaggart is right, this is unworkable, and it might be more honest to prefer a tensed metalanguage to the standard approach. (In fact, in his later work, Prior seems to recommend something like this. See Prior and Fine [1977].)

A tensed metalanguage, however, would not only deviate from normal practice in formal semantics but would be problematic in fundamental respects. We expect scientific theories to be observer-independent. Formal semantics, like the rest of linguistics, is supposed to be a science. Furthermore, linguistic theories are meant to explain linguistic phenomena and to answer linguistic questions. Even if, for instance, McTaggart has shown that a tenseless semantic metalanguage cannot provide a philosophical analysis of the object language, this doesn't mean that such a metalanguage is inadequate as a linguistic theory.

4.5.2 Interactions with Propositional Attitudes

If we set aside metaphysical considerations, we may ask whether decontextualized theories of tense can address the relevant linguistic evidence. The question is this: Do McTaggart's worries, or something similar to them, resurface when a semantic theory of tense is confronted with linguistic evidence?

In fact, it seems that they do. The relevant evidence has to do with the interaction of tense and propositional attitudes. In Prior (1959), Arthur Prior considers the case of someone who has forgotten the date, but who, "in a dateless haze" says on June 15, 1954, "Thank goodness that's over!" To add detail, suppose this person is recalling yesterday's visit to the dentist and impulsively expresses her relief that the episode is over. This is not at all the same as thinking you're glad that the visit ended before June 15, 1954. Moreover, the confused person who believes on June 15 that today is June 14, does not believe that June 15 is June 14.

But the standard theories of tense found in formal semantics predict this incorrect pattern of beliefs. These theories treat thinking at time t that the visit is over as a relation between an agent and the set of worlds in which the visit occurred prior to t. If t = June 15, 1954, then this is the same as the set of worlds in which the visit occurred prior to June 15, 1954. Since, according to the standard theory, belief is a relation between an agent and a set of worlds, the beliefs must be the same.

It's important to understand that this is not the same as the intensional puzzles that inspired Frege's distinction between sense and reference. Standard theories that use possible worlds to deal with intensionality nevertheless generate Prior's problem. And the usual examples of intensionality have nothing in particular to do with context or perspective. But context and perspective are crucial for the interpretation of 'now'.

This breakdown seems to raise doubts about the adequacy of the entire framework – it begins to look as if propositional attitudes are inextricably entangled with observer dependence. Perhaps, then, the ideas of philosophers like McTaggart can be translated into linguistic reasons for rejecting an approach to tense based on a metalanguage using only B-series concepts.

Before questions such as these arose in formal semantics, they were canvassed in the philosophical attempts to provide a general analysis of speaker-dependent, or "egocentric," or "indexical" expressions. We will discuss this topic in more detail in Chapter 7; here, we only need to sketch the views of Hans Reichenbach.

Reichenbach (1947) presents an analysis of indexical expressions; the idea is to account for them in terms of a demonstrative reference to the linguistic token produced in an utterance. (See Section 7.2 for more on token reflexives.) When in Prior's lost-in-time example, a speaker says 'I believe that today is June 15', thereby producing an utterance u, the token-reflexive analysis would be 'Speaker(u) believes at Time(u) that Day(Time(u)) is June 14'. This is not equivalent to the corresponding analysis of 'I believe that June 15 is June 14', for the same reason that 'I believe that the number of US states is greater than 48' is not the same as 'I believe that 50 is greater than 48'.

The adequacy of Reichenbach's analysis has been much debated in the subsequent philosophical literature – see, for instance, Kaplan (1989), Crimmins (1995), Ludlow (1999) and Garcia-Carpintero (2000). Predelli (2006) is a recent discussion of the issues.

The leading alternative to the token-reflexive account relativizes the interpretation of an expression to an abstract representation of the relevant features of the context. If, for instance, we are only interested in the indexical word 'now', the context would simply be a time. The intension or proposition $[\![\phi]\!]^t$ assigned to a sentence ϕ will then depend on t.

When Reichenbach's idea is compared to this alternative, it is difficult to find linguistic evidence in favor of either approach because the desired features of context can usually be extracted from the location (in time, space, and a given possible world) of an uttered token. (There are, of course, anomalous cases like that of the professor who leaves a message on her answering machine saying 'I'm sorry I'm not here now to take your call'; but perhaps these can be resolved by a better account of what is meant by "a token" and so are not conclusive.) Therefore, a chief point of contention in the debate is the legitimacy of the shift from the interpretation of sentences – whether these are thought or uttered – to the interpretation of tokenings or perhaps of utterance events.

But perhaps we were premature to say that the sentences-in-context approach is comparable in adequacy to Reichenbach's token-reflexive theory. We pointed out that the former approach, even though it is generally accepted in textbook formal semantics, fails to account for the interaction of context-sensitivity and propositional attitudes, showing that it gives an incorrect account of the person who, on June 14, believes that it's June 15. If the story ends here, it looks as if the less popular token-reflexive theory provides a more adequate account, even if it is awkward and implausible in some respects. (See the discussion of Reichenbach's theory in Section 7.2.)

Prior's lost-in-time problem arises when the objects of belief, or propositions, are insensitive to perspective. This is illustrated by theories such as Montague's that represent propositions as sets of possible worlds. When times are taken into consideration, this means that a proposition amounts to a function from times and worlds to truth-values. But the proposition expressed by 'Today is June 14' on June 15 would be the function that returns $\top$ at w and t iff June 14 is June 15 at t in w. This is the contradictory proposition that is uniformly false and is not a worthy object of belief. If we identify Montagovian propositions with objects of belief, we create a version of Prior's problem.

Fortunately, a quite natural extension of the standard framework seems to solve the difficulty. We build perspective into propositions and represent them in a more general way, as sets of *centered worlds*. These are simply worlds associated with a time location, i.e. ordered pairs consisting of a world and a time. This is, of course, a generalization of the simpler idea that propositions are sets of worlds, because we can identify perspective-free propositions with centered propositions p that are time-independent: that satisfy the condition that if $\langle w, t\rangle \in p$ for some t, then $\langle w, t'\rangle \in p$ for all t.

To see why Prior's problem doesn't arise in this more general setting, imagine a person who thinks, on June 15, that it's June 14. This person believes a centered proposition consisting of the pairs $\langle w, t\rangle$ such that t occurs on June 14. This proposition is not at all the same as the necessarily false proposition that June 15 is June 14.

This approach to the interaction of propositional attitudes with context dependence was suggested by David Lewis in Lewis (1979a). Lewis prefers a formalization that depends on counterpart theory. (This is David Lewis' approach to quantification and modality. See Lewis [1968].) But he also mentions centered worlds, attributing the idea to Quine (1969). If you neglect the aspects of his counterpart theory that differ from Montague's simpler account of individuals in quantified modal logic, Lewis' idea is equivalent to the one presented here.

In the literature on centered worlds, time is only one of the many aspects of self-location that are incorporated in these worlds. (Spatial self-location is similar: Imagine someone who, without knowing who she is, says to herself "It's dark here.") But temporal self-location is an important case and illustrates the general ideas well.

This is not the end of the story. The interactions between tense and intensionality are complex and challenging, for linguists as well as philosophers. For more information on this topic, see Salmon (1986); Ninan (2013).

4.6 Time in Philosophy and Linguistics

From the very beginning, philosophers have found time to be profoundly problematic. Although, for the most part, the natural sciences have managed to insulate themselves from these problems, perhaps linguists can't afford to disregard them so blithely. The philosophical problems arise, for the most part, in articulating our commonsense conception of time, and it is this conception that we would expect to inform the meanings of temporal expressions.

Any science, to qualify as such, must find a workable way to keep philosophy at arm's length. For linguistics and in particular, for semantics, this means finding a way of distinguishing linguistic problems from those that can be left to the philosophers. When Aristotle asks, for instance, "Does the present that appears to limit the past and the future always remain one and the same or is it always different and different?" (*Physics* 4, $21^{a}8$–9), he seems to be raising a question that linguists can safely ignore; the language used to state the question, in Greek and English, is highly technical, and the problem, as it stands, does not seem to challenge the adequacy of a semantics for either language.

However, we have seen that McTaggart's argument can be converted into properly semantic issues having to do with the interaction of tense and, more generally, of context, with propositional attitudes. And his regress arguments raise legitimate issues about what is required of semantic explanations.

The regress issue may turn out to be no more than a worry about semantic metalanguages. Tarski showed conclusively in Tarski (1936) that a hierarchy of semantic metalanguages is inevitable. Later work on the formalization of truth has shown that there are ways to repackage this result, but this does not seem to have eliminated the need for a hierarchy of some sort. Mathematical logicians have learned to live with this fact, and linguists who use logical methods do not need to be embarrassed by a hierarchy of metalanguages if this is all there is to McTaggart's point. Moreover, there are convincing philosophical responses to McTaggart's regress, such as the one Prior offers in Prior (1968a).

As for the more centrally linguistic philosophical issues, we argued that there is an attractive response available to formal semanticists. Using centered worlds to enrich the representation of propositions, we are able to maintain a natural extension of the standard semantic theory that is free of subjectivity and that appears to deal with the most pressing difficulties.

4.7 Possibility and Possible Worlds

Possible worlds played an important part in the philosophy of the seventeenth-century philosopher Leibniz. It was not until the second half of the twentieth century, however, that they caught on as a working component of philosophical theory and became a topic of active metaphysical debate.

The popularity of possible worlds in philosophical circles, and the habit that other disciplines (aside from formal semantics) have of avoiding the term, suggest that philosophers own the intellectual property rights to this concept. But that would be a mistake. Under various names, possible worlds have been prominent in many areas of science for centuries. Until relatively recently, most of the scientific applications have been to do with probability.

4.7.1 Possibilities, Propositions, and Probability

The origins of probability in the seventeenth century were closely connected with combinatorics. Determining the likelihood of an outcome is a two-step process: first, generate the possibilities as combinations of factors and then calculate in what proportion of these possibilities the outcome occurs. If you flip two fair coins, there are two variables, tracking whether the coins turn up heads or tails. That produces four possibilities. At least one of the coins turns up heads in three out of these four "worlds." So the probability that at least one coin will turn up heads is $\frac{3}{4}$.

Very gradually, the theory of probability became more abstract, passing through the theories of phase space developed by physicists in the late nineteenth century to Kolmogorov's idea of a sample space, in which the possibilities are unanalyzed points and their basis in combinatorics disappears entirely.

Phase spaces provide a good example of how the idea works in practice. The phase space of a physical system is determined by associating values to each of the physical variables that constitute the system. If, for instance, the system consists of 1000 particles, each with a position p and momentum m, then the points of phase space will be triples $\langle \mathrm{n}, \mathrm{p}, \mathrm{m} \rangle$, where p is a triple of reals, m is a real number, and $1 \leq \mathrm{n} \leq 1000$. A possible world, then, will correspond to a legitimate combination of value assignments to each of the variables. But what counts as legitimate? To determine this, we can refer to physical laws. We certainly want to require that positions and momenta are nonnegative and that no two particles can occupy the same position. We may want to impose relativistic constraints.

Consider a simpler example: Suppose that we have a closed box whose empty weight is 1. The box contains three balls a, b, and c, and the weight of the box and balls is 6. Each ball has a weight of 1, 2, or 3. What is the probability that two balls have weight 1? In this example a possible state of the system – or a possible world – is a function Lb from $\{\mathrm{a}, \mathrm{b}, \mathrm{c}\}$ to $\{1, 2, 3\}$, satisfying the condition that $\mathrm{Lb(a)} + \mathrm{Lb(b)} + \mathrm{Lb(c)} = 5$.

First, we determine the number of worlds. If $\mathrm{Lb(a)} = 1$, then Lb(b) can be 1, 2, or 3. We can calculate the weight of the third ball from the weight of the second, so there are three worlds in which $\mathrm{Lb(a)} = 1$: Call them w_{113}, w_{122}, and w_{131}. If $\mathrm{Lb(a)} = 2$, then Lb(b) can be 1 or 2, so there are two worlds where $\mathrm{Lb(a)} = 2$: Call them w_{212} and w_{221}. And there is only one world where $\mathrm{Lb(a)} = 3$: Call it w_{311}. So we have six worlds in all. Assuming the worlds to be equally likely, we can calculate the probability that two balls have weight 1 by counting the worlds where this proposition is true and dividing by 6. Since there are three of these worlds, w_{113}, w_{131}, and w_{311}, the probability is $\frac{1}{2}$.

Typically, probabilities are assigned directly to sets of states without deploying a language. But it can be instructive to think about the probability $P(\phi)$ of a formula ϕ. An appropriate language for the balls-in-a-box domain has atomic formulas $Lb(x, \mathrm{n})$, where $x \in \{a, b, c\}$; and $\mathrm{n} \in \{1, 2, 3\}$; $Lb(a, 2)$ means, for instance, that the weight of ball a is 2 units. Formulas are built up using the boolean operators $\wedge$, $\vee$, and $\neg$. The formula

$$(Lb(a, 1) \wedge Lb(b, 1)) \vee (Lb(a, 1) \wedge Lb(c, 1)) \vee (Lb(b, 1) \wedge Lb(c, 1))$$

says – somewhat awkwardly – that at least two balls have weight 1.

The disjuncts of this formula are pairwise inconsistent, so its probability is the sum of the probabilities of its disjuncts. (Here, we use one of Kolmogorov's probability axioms. See Kolmogorov [1956].) What about $Lb(a,1) \wedge Lb(b,1)$? This formula is true in just one world, w_{113}, so $P(Lb(a,1) \wedge Lb(b,1)) = \frac{1}{6}$. On the other hand, $P(Lb(a,1)) = \frac{1}{2}$ and $P(Lb(b,1)) = \frac{1}{2}$.

Here, we have two formulas with probability $\frac{1}{2}$, and the probability of their conjunction is $\frac{1}{6}$. This is an intermediate case: There also are two extreme cases. In one of these, one conjunct entails the other, and the joint probability (the probability of the conjunction) is the minimum of the probabilities of the conjuncts. In the other extreme case, the formulas are inconsistent and the probability of the conjunction is 0.

We can, of course, calculate the truth-value of a conjunctive formula from the truth-values of its components. But we have seen that the situation is very different with probabilities; the values of $P(\phi)$ and $P(\psi)$ impose only very weak constraints on $P(\phi \wedge \psi)$. In fact, to calculate a joint probability we need to understand how the conjuncts are related statistically. If they are *independent*, we can multiply their probabilities. If not, we have to do an ad hoc calculation based on their relationship, and the joint probability can be anywhere between 0 and the probability of the less likely conjunct.

Because of this feature of joint probabilities, the assignment of probabilities to formulas is not strongly compositional: $P(\phi \wedge \psi)$ is not determined as a function of $P(\phi)$ and $P(\psi)$. This is why languages and formulas are generally neglected in the theory of probability, and instead probabilities are attached to subsets of the sample space, or sets of possible worlds. (More precisely, probabilities attach to *measurable* sets of possible worlds.) If we do, however, wish to work with a language, we must invoke a set W of worlds (the sample space), and a probability measure μ taking measurable sets of worlds into values in the interval $[0, 1]$. We then interpret a formula ϕ in two steps: First we assign a (measurable) set of worlds $[\![\phi]\!]$ to ϕ. If we are working with a boolean language, this can be done using strong compositionality: The crucial identity is $[\![\phi \wedge \psi]\!] = [\![\phi]\!] \cap [\![\psi]\!]$. The probability of an arbitrary formula ϕ is then obtained by taking $\mu([\![\phi]\!])$.

The idea behind this picture replicates the usual semantics of the intensional constructions more familiar to linguists. If we add a possibility operator $\Diamond$ to a boolean language, then $\Diamond(\phi \wedge \psi)$ is not truth-functionally dependent on its components ϕ and ψ. We therefore appeal to a set of possible worlds and strong compositionality to assign sets of worlds to formulas, calling these sets "propositions." Again, $[\![\phi \wedge \psi]\!] = [\![\phi]\!] \cap [\![\psi]\!]$. And $[\![\Diamond\phi]\!]$ is $\{w \mid wRu \text{ for some } u \in [\![\phi]\!]\}$, where R is a relation over W.

This simple example provides machinery that can be applied successfully to a large variety of intensional constructions. In the twentieth century, philosophical logicians demonstrated this by producing an extended body of work showing how to apply the idea to tense, necessity, deontic, epistemic, and conditional constructions. Most of this work took place between 1950 and 1980, and involved, among others, Rudolf Carnap, Arthur Prior, Stig Kanger, Saul Kripke, Jaakko Hintikka, Ruth Marcus, David Lewis, Richard Montague, and Robert Stalnaker.

4.7.2 The Modal Logicians

Although most of the formal work on possible worlds semantics began with a rather limited application in mind – the interpretation of a modal necessity operator, corresponding roughly to the English 'necessarily' – several logically minded philosophers realized at an early stage that it might have wider applications. Rudolf Carnap, Jaakko Hintikka, and Arthur Prior were influential in this process. Carnap (1956: 124–133, Sections 29–30) noticed that possible worlds could serve many of the earlier purposes of Frege's earlier distinction between sense and reference. (We can agree, for instance, with Frege that the reference of a sentence is a truth-value and go on to say that its sense is a function from possibilities to truth-values.) Hintikka (1962) argued that possible worlds could provide a theory of propositional attitudes like 'know' and 'believe', and, beginning in the 1950s, Arthur Prior explored their application to the logic of time. These philosophers were aware of Quine's foundational concerns about intensionality, which we discussed in Section 0.1. They felt that these concerns raise technical problems that require logical solutions. And indeed, it's unusually difficult in Quine's earlier writings on intensionality to disentangle philosophical objections from technical challenges.

By the late 1960s, work on possible worlds semantics was well enough advanced, and extensive enough in its applications, for Richard Montague to claim that it was capable of supporting a general approach to intensionality in natural languages. Montague's "proper treatment" of intensional constructions in explicitly propositional cases (for instance, sentential 'that' complements) uses operators over sets of worlds. Other constructions, such as intensional transitive verbs, are explicated by other types that Montague's intensional logic makes available: This logic in effect makes it possible to form arbitrary functional types out of individuals, truth-values, and possible worlds. Montague himself didn't treat possible worlds as a primitive type. But Gallin (1975) shows that Montague's more indirect approach to intensionality is equivalent to a logic with primitive possible worlds.

4.7.3 Philosophy of Possible Worlds

It is standard practice not only in formal semantics but in physics and many other sciences to make use of possible worlds. If realism is the default position concerning scientific ontology, you might expect philosophers to agree that there are many possible worlds, only one of which – the one that matters in determining the truth-values of contingent propositions – is actual. But few philosophers are willing to take for granted the apparent assumptions of the sciences of the possible, perhaps because they see possible worlds as belonging to philosophy and because they see a path from naive realism about possible worlds to metaphysical assumptions that seem extreme. Their status has been, and no doubt will continue to be, a matter of debate among philosophers.

The initial positions in this debate are more or less similar to the corresponding positions concerning the nature of probabilities. (1) If probabilities are subjective and merely quantify our ignorance, then hypothetical possibilities are merely a mathematical convenience that doesn't correspond to any reality, even though it provides a calculus that is useful for reasoning about degrees of ignorance. (2) Or probabilities are distributions over a set of many possible worlds, which objectively have the same reality as the actual world. In philosophy, this second idea is associated with David Lewis; in physics it is associated with the Everett-Wheeler interpretation of quantum mechanics; see Wallace (2012).

Whether we think possibilities are real or not, we are welcome to think of them combinatorially. One chooses a set of variables and then defines a possible world as an assignment of a value to each of these variables, perhaps adding conditions on which assignments are legitimate. This suggests that we can look at possibilities as realizable combinations of real parts. If the combinatorial principles are objective truths, then they yield what we may reasonably call real possibilities; if they reflect nothing beyond the workings of our cognition then they don't.

The two unrefined positions, then, correspond to the archetypical positions that are available in any debate on philosophical ontology: nominalism and realism. The nominalist says that possibilities are convenient but nonexistent fictions. The realist says they are as real as anything that is posited by a correct theory: Possibilities exist (perhaps as part of a multiverse), even though almost all of them are unactualized. But, of course, the prevailing philosophical views tend to be more nuanced. One idea treats possible worlds as fictions, but offers a sophisticated account of how fictions can be theoretically useful; see, for instance, Yablo (1996). According to another popular account, possible worlds are real, but are not what the naive realist thinks they are. Perhaps possible worlds – quite unlike the actual world – are abstract entities of some sort. See Stalnaker (2012) for an extended version of this idea. The differences between David Lewis' realist position and accounts like Stalnaker's do not impact the use of possible worlds in formal semantics – both make sets of "worlds" available that will serve the linguistic purposes equally well. The leading issue between Lewis – the archetypical realist – and philosophers like Stalnaker is metaphysical and has to do with the status of actuality. According to Lewis, all worlds, including our actual one, are on a par, and, for the inhabitants of other possible worlds, those worlds are just as actual for them as ours is for us; Lewis (1970a) paints a vivid picture of this idea.

We saw that combinatorial techniques are important if we wish in practice to come to grips with what possible worlds are like. This doesn't mean that we must identify possible worlds with combinations – in fact, all the metaphysical positions on the status of possible worlds can be combined with combinatorial techniques for constructing possibilities.

Scientists tend to be casual, naive realists about the subject matter of their sciences. Physicists gladly assume that electrons and even forces are real, and mathematicians, perhaps less gladly, make the same assumptions about sets and numbers. If these assumptions are questioned, they can be dismissed or referred to the philosophers.

No doubt, this makes it easier for scientists to concentrate on the business of their disciplines. But this option isn't available to philosophers. Therefore, although many contemporary philosophers happily theorize about possible worlds, very few of them join Lewis in extreme realism about possibilities.

Debate about the ontological status of possible worlds has a metaphysical flavor – participants in the debate don't appeal to linguistic arguments. For linguistic purposes, these issues may be relatively remote. And in fact, as with the philosophy of probability, where the various philosophical positions are all constrained by the need to preserve the mathematical theory, the metaphysics of possible worlds is obliged to be consistent with the many applications of possible worlds theory in areas such as linguistics.

But a closely related debate on the interaction between individuals and possible worlds relates more directly to linguistic concerns, because it affects the interpretation of sentences where quantifiers and modalities interact. A sentence like

(4.7.1) Some famous novelists might have died in infancy

depends on *individuation* or *cross-world-identification*. It involves choosing someone who in this world is a famous novelist – say, Jane Austen – and finding another world in which she (the same person) died in infancy.

Lewis treats individuals as world-bound – individuals belong to only one world. To interpret sentences like (4.7.1), he invokes a *counterpart* relation: (4.7.1) would be true, for instance, if a counterpart of Jane Austen belonging to another world died in infancy. Lewis' counterpart relation is unconstrained: Nothing would prevent Jane Austen from having several counterparts in the same world, or no counterpart at all. For details of counterpart theory, see Lewis (1968).

Lewis' opponents, on the other hand, tend to treat individuals simply as belonging at once to many worlds. For these philosophers, the idea of an individual with many "counterparts" in another world is ruled out.

This issue depends, at least to some extent, on linguistic evidence about patterns of validity. It seems as if neither Lewis' entirely unconstrained approach nor the tightly constrained theories of his opponents is entirely right. Gibbard (1975) and Gupta (1980) argue that criteria of individuation are associated with common nouns, and that different nouns may carry different criteria. This idea, although it's important and seems plausible, seems to have had little or no influence on linguistic semantics.

4.7.4 Possible Worlds and the Requirements of Formal Semantics

In works of Montague's, such as Montague (1974), and in subsequent work in formal semantics, possible worlds are invoked, but very little is said about them. In fact, all we are told is that there is a nonempty set of possible worlds, and it is hard to imagine how less could be said than this. This is not only compatible with most philosophical views about possible worlds but compatible with just about anything one might want to say about them.

We might well wish, however, to be more ambitious about the semantic requirements of a modal term like 'might'. We might want a series of sentences such as the following to be true or, at least, the series to be consistent with the meaning postulates in our linguistic semantics.

(4.7.2.a.) There is something that is larger than exactly one thing, but that might be larger than exactly two things.

(4.7.2.b.) There is something that is larger than exactly two things, but that might be larger than exactly three things.

(4.7.2.c.) There is something that is larger than exactly three things, but that might be larger than exactly four things.

...

To make all these sentences true, we will need a different possibility for each of them – an infinite series of distinct worlds. Even though linguists may not need to say what possible worlds are, or even to care what they are, natural intuitions about possibility seem to demand a great many of them. The conclusion seems to be that, to satisfy the needs of intuitions such as these, linguists will need a set of possible worlds that is compatible with the combinatorial account and that is based on principles of combination that are quite liberal.

Other scientific domains that appeal to possibilities are no different in this respect. A game theorist who wishes to model a player's knowledge about a hidden card might want to satisfy a series of sentences like this. (For many similar examples, and for applications of possible worlds semantics in nonlinguistic domains, see Fagin et al. [1995].)

(4.7.3.a.) That card might be an ace.

(4.7.3.b.) That card might be a king.

(4.7.3.c.) That card might be a jack.

...

These ideas seem almost inevitable. They are likely to cause no discomfort to many philosophers, and certainly should not trouble linguists. They provide a sound basis for the theory of modals that is generally accepted by formal semanticists, as explained in Kratzer (2012); Portner (2009).

4.8 Possibilia

Philosophical issues about possibility become even more vexed when one considers not only the status of possible worlds but of individuals as they enter into various possibilities. A sentence like

(4.8.4) There could have been a person over twelve feet tall.

requires a possible world in which (4.8.5) is true (at some time).

(4.8.5) Someone is over twelve feet tall.

If no one (no actual person) could have grown to be over twelve feet tall, to make (4.8.5) true, we need a world containing someone who doesn't exist in the actual world.

At this point, we are straining the reasonable capacities of a combinatorial account of possible worlds. We are no longer imagining different qualities that actual things might have but introducing entirely new things into the mix.

But with wide scope on the existential quantifier, as in (4.8.6), we have a very different situation.

(4.8.6) There is a person who might be over twelve feet tall.

This requires there to be an actual person (perhaps someone well over ten feet tall, who underwent hormone therapy as a young teenager) such that, in some possible world, *that very person* is over twelve feet tall.

These two examples show that – as Quine suspected – additional philosophical complications can arise when quantifiers are combined with modalities; see Quine (1953b).

Example (4.8.4) shows that we somehow need to allow possible worlds to be inhabited by individuals that don't actually exist. At the very least, this would have to involve careful rethinking of what possible worlds are.

Example (4.8.6) raises the problem of individuation that we alluded to in Section 4.7.3. It seems to require us to find some deep trait in an existing individual that makes it what it is, enabling us to identify it in different circumstances. In fact, we frequently indulge in counterfactual reidentifications, as in this example:

(4.8.7) If Nixon hadn't resigned, <u>he</u> would have been impeached and removed from office.

But this becomes increasingly more problematic as the possibilities become more and more remote:

(4.8.8) If Nixon had been the youngest of three triplets, he would not have had political ambitions.

This is the philosophical problem of *essentialism*. Philosophers have had a great deal to say about this problem; see, for instance, Kaplan (1969); Plantinga (1974); Mackie (2006). But it is hard to see how it intersects with concerns that are directly linguistic.

A related issue, however, does have linguistic overtones. This concerns objects of the progressive verbs of creation. Parsons (1990) mentions a sign in Hawaii indicating "the house that Jack London was building." The sign indicates an empty foundation. But how can an empty foundation be a house?

The status of the objects of verbs of creation is controversial; some theorists feel they can be analyzed as wide-scope modals, along the lines of (4.8.5), others feel they are genuine wide-scope existentials. This issue has linguistic overtones because it turns on a large suite of natural language examples; see Szabó (2004).

4.9 Conditionals

A conditional sentence, like:

(4.9.9) If it snowed last night the roads are slippery

contains two sentential clauses: a subordinate or conditional clause ('it snowed last night') and a main clause ('the roads are slippery'). Traditional grammarians use 'apodosis' for the subordinate and 'protasis' for the main clause, and many linguists adopt this terminology. Logicians and many philosophers, thinking not so much of the grammar but of formalizations like

(4.9.10) $P \rightarrow Q$,

call the subordinate clause the "antecedent" and the main clause the "consequent." Since our discussion here will track the philosophical tradition, we'll use the second terminology.

Modern concern about the meaning of 'if' begins in reaction to the so-called "material conditional," the idea that a conditional is true if and only if the antecedent is false or the consequent is true. This account of a conditional's truth conditions makes for a simple theory that actually fits mathematically minded practice and reasoning well. But it is highly unintuitive with respect to commonsense reasoning with conditionals and commonsense intuitions about their truth conditions.

Some early authors seemed to think of the "material conditional" as an actual sense of 'if'. Rather than encouraging that idea, we will speak of the *material theory*.

The conditions under which people would think a conditional is false clash with the conditions (antecedent true, consequent false) for the falsity of the material conditional. You can be persuaded, for instance, that (4.9.9) is false if you're told that the local winter road maintenance is highly efficient and effective and the roads are hardly ever slippery after a snowstorm. You do *not* say "I agree, but that doesn't show that (4.9.9) is false; we need to find out whether it snowed last night."

The idea that a conditional with a false antecedent can be false is even more compelling with subjunctive conditionals, like

(4.9.11) If it had snowed last night, the roads would have been slippery.

For a long time, examples such as these were called "counterfactual conditionals," because it was thought that they actually *imply* the falsity of the antecedent. But Anderson (1951), disproved this idea; Anderson imagines a doctor looking at a patient and saying "if he had taken arsenic, he would be exhibiting just these symptoms."

The philosophically minded logicians who worried about these discrepancies were, unlike Russell, those who were willing to take ordinary language and commonsense reasoning somewhat seriously. Philosophers of science found other reasons for concern when they tried to explain the uses of 'if' in scientific theories. Among other things, such theories support subjunctive conditionals, like these:

(4.9.12) If this sugar lump were put in water it would dissolve.
(4.9.13) If this weight were dropped it would hit the ground in 2.23 seconds.

Two broad strategies are available to philosophers who wish to improve on the material theory. They can say that the theory gives a correct account of the meaning of 'if' but not of its use. Or they can offer an alternative theory of the meaning of 'if'. These strategies can be mixed: Perhaps conditionals are ambiguous, and the material theory fits one meaning, but a different theory is needed for the other.

Paul Grice's views are perhaps the most extreme example of the first approach. We will see in Chapter 9 how he proposes to make a case for this idea. David Lewis has a more moderate view. According to him, *indicative* conditionals are explained by the material theory, but other conditionals, and especially those conditionals that are explicitly subjunctive, require a different theory with different truth-conditions.

Those who proposed alternative theories of the meaning of (at least some) conditionals sought at first to provide philosophical *analyses*: to give something like a definition, in a privileged language or in terms that are somehow philosophically satisfactory – and that, in particular, do not themselves involve conditionals. (The tradition of philosophical analysis has a long history in philosophy and has meant different things at different times; for more on this topic, see Beaney [2016].) The search for a satisfactory analysis of subjunctive or counterfactual conditionals was intensive for a long while, especially in the 1940s; this work is documented well in Schneider (1953). But Goodman (1955) showed persuasively that the prospects for providing a satisfactory analysis were dismal. These attempts typically begin with a background theory, then add to this the condition expressed by the antecedent, then add certain "background conditions" from the current state of affairs: The conditional is then said to be true if the consequent is a logical consequence of the resulting body of claims.

The chief difficulty here is to say what background conditions should be carried over. To some extent, Goodman's argument recollects Quine's concern that intensional terms such as 'meaning', 'synonymy', 'analyticity', and 'definition' cannot be explained in extensional terms; Goodman shows that conditional notions seem to be needed to explain what should count as a background condition. But Goodman's circle is more disturbing than Quine's, because analyses are not supposed to be circular. Moreover, Goodman shows that the attempt to characterize background conditions creates many challenging secondary difficulties. Goodman's challenge made the search for an analysis much less popular.

A logical approach to conditionals is not the same as an analysis. If fully developed, it would consist of a formalized language, rules of proof, and a model theory. Those who take this approach use a formal language with some arrow-like notation for the conditional: for instance, '$P \dashv Q$', '$P \Box\!\!\rightarrow Q$', or '$P > Q$'. Rules of proof will certainly not require an analysis, and a model theory, though it must provide truth conditions, can avoid many of the requirements associated with an analysis.

Tarski's account of quantification, which was discussed in Section 1.2.4, illustrates this point well. A model consists, among other things, of a domain D – which is simply a nonempty set – and of an assignment of a subset E of D to a one-place predicate letter P. The formula $\exists x P(x)$ is true in a model if E is a nonempty set. This provides truth-conditions for existential formulas – conditions which are relativized to a domain D – but it avoids anything like an analysis of existence.

Clarence I. Lewis offered the first alternative to the material conditional. He felt that what the material theory lacked was the ingredient of *necessity*; his proposal amounts to the following formalization:

(4.9.14) $\Box(\neg P \vee Q)$,

Using Lewis' symbol for his "strict conditional," this is $P \dashv Q$.

In other words, a conditional says that *necessarily* either the antecedent is false or the consequent is true. Of course, this idea requires a logic that makes $\Box$, or necessity, available. C. I. Lewis was in fact a pioneer of modern modal logic.

It's helpful at this point to return to attempts to analyze the conditional. Behind these attempts is the idea that conditionals involve two components: necessity (an appeal to laws of some sort) and background conditions, which are contingent matters of fact. C. I. Lewis' account appeals to the first of these elements but neglects the second. This leads to several apparent defects. The most important is that the strict theory validates *strengthening of the antecedent*. For instance, (4.9.12) and (4.9.13) would imply these – apparently unacceptable – two consequences.

(4.9.15) If I put this lump of sugar in water that is sugar-saturated it will dissolve.

(4.9.16) If this weight were dropped while equipped with a parachute it would hit the ground in 2.23 seconds.

If we think of strict conditionals in terms of possible worlds semantics – an innovation that was introduced after C. I. Lewis' earlier work – we can state the problem this way. According to Lewis, (4.9.12) is true if in *every possibility* in which the sugar is put in water, it dissolves. But the possibility in which it's put in saturated sugar solution is, however remote, still a possibility. C. I. Lewis' theory neglects the factual component of "counterfactuals," the background conditions.

Introducing quite a different line of thought, during the early 1960s, Alan Anderson and Nuel Belnap proposed a logical approach to conditionals motivated by the idea that the antecedent of a true conditional should be relevant to its consequent. The striking characteristic of the family of logics they proposed is that *ex falso quodlibet*,

(4.9.17) $(P \wedge \neg P) \rightarrow Q$,

is invalid. This idea, developed in Anderson and Belnap (1975), led to a subsequent tradition of *relevance logic* or *paraconsistent logic* that is still alive. But, though some relevance logicians suggested at first that their theory might account for commonsense conditionals, they never insisted on this suggestion or elaborated it, and relevance logic has generally been applied to mathematical theories and to the logical paradoxes.

The two most influential logical approaches to conditionals were developed somewhat later, at about the same time (in spite of the differences in publication date), and quite independently, by Robert Stalnaker and David Lewis. (See Stalnaker [1968]; Lewis [1973].) Both theories rely on possible worlds semantics, and both make room for background conditions by restricting attention to worlds that are "close" to the actual world. And both impose formal conditions on the closeness relation. Neither theory depends on an analysis (in the traditional sense) of closeness, but both Stalnaker and Lewis have a great deal to say about how this relation is to be understood. Even though their informal explanations of the theory somehow involve conditionals or related notions, Goodman's criticism of circularity has lost its sting; what they do for conditionals is no more circular than what Tarski does for negation. (Recall that in (4.9.12), negation is used in the satisfaction clause for negative formulas.)

Even if these logical theories do not solve the philosophical problem of conditionals, they can certainly claim to have solved a closely related logical problem, providing a solution that illuminates the philosophical issues.

We will not rehearse the technical details of Stalnaker's and Lewis' models; for readers interested in these details, Nute (1984) and Arlo-Costa and Egré (2016) would be a good beginning. But we do wish to stress two important differences. (1) Lewis retains the idea that conditionals involve an element of necessity, while Stalnaker abandons it. (2) Lewis endorses the material theory of indicative conditionals, reserving his account only for conditionals with a "counterfactual" flavor, while Stalnaker proposes that 'if' is not ambiguous and that the effects of subjunctive mood are pragmatic, so that there are no logical differences between indicative and subjunctive conditionals. For both these reasons, Stalnaker's theory is more ambitious than Lewis'.

For Stalnaker, conditionals are wholly contingent – as contingent as any simple nonconditional sentence like 'Nairobi is the capital of Kenya'. But unlike such sentences, their truth-conditions are "counter"-factual, depending on the "counter-facts" of a single nonactual possible world. This feature is incorporated in Stalnaker's theory by postulating that (unless the antecedent is impossible, true at no worlds at all) there is a unique closest world in which the antecedent is true. This uniqueness constraint validates *conditional excluded middle*,

(4.9.18) $(P > Q) \vee (P > \neg Q)$,

and allows Stalnaker to say that the negation of a conditional is the conditional negation. (Stalnaker uses '>' for the conditional.) For instance, the negation of (4.9.9) is simply

(4.9.19) If it snowed last night the roads aren't slippery.

For Stalnaker, then, the only necessity that attaches to an asserted conditional is pragmatic. If, for instance, the conditional is the conclusion of an argument, it will inherit whatever necessity the argument confers on it. But this necessity will not be part of its meaning.

The difficulty in maintaining, as Stalnaker does, that there is one logic for conditionals is that some inferences appear to be valid for indicative conditionals that are not valid for subjunctives. For instance, (4.9.20) looks like a good inference, and (4.9.21) looks terrible.

(4.9.20) My daughter drove my car away or someone stole it.
So if my daughter didn't drive my car away, someone stole it.

(4.9.21) My daughter drove my car away or someone stole it.
So if my daughter hadn't driven my car away, someone would have stolen it.

To solve this problem, Stalnaker appeals to a pragmatic theory of indicative mood, as well as a notion of the *pragmatic validity* of an inference. See Stalnaker (1970).

For David Lewis, however, the truth of a conditional corresponds in general to the uniform truth of the consequent in a multiplicity of close possibilities in which the antecedent is true. So – at least in some cases – there will be an inherent necessity in the meaning of a conditional. Of the two theories, Lewis' is better known and more popular among linguists, largely because of the work of Angelika Kratzer; see Kratzer (2012), as well as Portner (2009).

The differences between the two theories plays out in many matters of linguistic interest. For Lewis the relation between a subjunctive conditional and the modal 'might' reveals the internal modality of the conditional. For instance, (4.9.22) means (roughly) that in some closest worlds where 'It snowed last night' is false, the roads weren't slippery, and it is simply the negation of (4.9.23).

(4.9.22) If it hadn't snowed last night the roads might not have been slippery.
(4.9.23) If it hadn't snowed last night the roads would (still) have been slippery.

For Stalnaker, however, (4.9.22) is to be interpreted using strong compositionality, just as an unconditional sentence like (4.9.24) must be strongly compositional:

(4.9.24) The roads might not have been slippery.

Perhaps, for instance, (4.9.22) means that (4.9.24) is true in the closest world in which 'It didn't snow last night' is true.

Many traditional areas of philosophy (e.g., the free will problem, rational choice, and causality) involve conditionals. Here, philosophical inquiry depends on how the meanings of commonsense conditionals are to be understood. Work in these areas was hampered for a time due not only to uneasiness about Goodman's skeptical results but to weakness of informed intuitions about the truth or falsity of the relevant conditionals. Stalnaker's and Lewis' logical theories produced a sense of liberation and renewed interest in such questions.

Philosophers have, of course, questioned and sought to improve the Stalnaker and Lewis theories. But the confidence these theories inspired has had, and continues to have, a considerable impact on philosophy. And the study of conditionals offers a natural opportunity for cooperation between philosophers and linguists.

4.10 Beyond Extensions

Natural languages contain expressions that seem to refer to times (e.g. 'yesterday', 'last Monday', etc.) and expressions that seem to quantify over them (e.g. 'most Thursdays', 'every second', etc.). It would thus be hard to imagine a semantics for natural language without entities representing times in our models.

When it comes to possible worlds, the situation is less clear. We do talk about things like the world of *Sherlock Holmes*, but whatever such a thing might be, it seems neither possible (due to inconsistencies in Conan Doyle's story) nor in fact to be a world (due to the fact that Conan Doyle's story does not specify in full detail a way things could be). What convinced most semanticists that it makes sense to add possible worlds to our semantic theories is the fact that modal adverbs like 'possibly' and 'probably' and auxiliaries like 'can' or 'ought' appear to have quantificational force and that (at least in some of their uses) the adjective 'actual' and the adverb 'actually' appear to single out the actual world.

So, let's grant that we want times and worlds in our semantic theories. The question is what role they should play. Consider

(4.10.25) Cicero denounced someone.

There is a sense in which (4.10.25) is about the past. In many standard semantic theories, this is assimilated either to the sense in which (4.10.25) is about Cicero or to the sense in which it is about everyone. That is, many standard semantic theories take it that (4.10.25) contains a referring expression whose semantic value is a time. The referring expression is either free (evaluated by the context of utterance) or bound (within the scope of some covert quantifier):

(4.10.26) Cicero denounce someone at t.
(4.10.27) For some t before n, Cicero denounce someone at t.

The first is a *referential* semantics for the past tense, the second is a *quantificational* semantics (with the referential element n picking out the time of utterance.)

These two options are available for modality as well. (Here, a is an indexical that refers to the world of utterance.)

(4.10.28) Cicero may denounce someone.

(4.10.29) Cicero denounce someone at w.

(4.10.30) For some w accessible from a, Cicero denounce someone at w.

The referential and quantificational approaches can even be combined: One might say that the interpretation of sentences without tense and modals contains a free variable for times and worlds, that this variable can be bound by a quantifier, and, if it isn't, it can be either evaluated directly by the context or be subject to some sort of default closure.

This sort of semantics is extensional – it does not introduce indices relative to which (4.10.25) or (4.10.28) are evaluated. The alternative is, of course, to go intensional. Then we can say that there is no expression in (4.10.25) that picks out a time and no expression in (4.10.28) that picks out a world.

How should semanticists choose between extensional and intensional theories of tense and modals? One possibility is simply to appeal to tradition: Logicians who have designed formal languages overwhelmingly chose the intensional route, so the conservative choice is just to follow them. However, in this case, logicians are motivated by considerations that aren't necessarily relevant for natural language semantics. If you add quantifiers to a nonquantificational language, you have to rewrite all of its syntax and semantics. Adding operators is a much less disruptive form of expansion, and, as a consequence, it will be much easier to generalize the logical results you have from the old language to the new one. It is not clear why this consideration should move semanticists.

A more fruitful way to approach the choice between extensional and intensional theories might be to ask how similar tense and modals are to pronouns. For suppose we are all in agreement that pronouns do not force us to introduce intensions into our semantics – then, if tense and modals are like pronouns we should treat them extensionally. Interestingly, the similarities are quite robust. In the case of tenses, this was pointed out in Partee (1973); Stone (1997) generalized her observations to include modals.

Pronouns, tenses and modals all give rise to three distinctive uses: deictic, anaphoric, and bound:

Deictic:

(i) He is a fraud.
(ii) I left the stove on.
(iii) You would make me feel loved.

Each of these sentences is to be interpreted in a context where an explicit or implicit demonstration took place: in (i) to a person, in (ii) to a past time (when the speaker left the stove on), and in (iii) to a possible world (which is as similar to the actual one as it can be, given that the item the speaker and hearer are looking at was purchased by the addressee for the speaker).

Anaphoric:

(i) He is a fraud and he doesn't care.
(ii) I left the stove on and you did not warn me.
(iii) If you had bought me flowers you would have made me feel loved.

In the preferred interpretations of (i), (ii), and (iii), the person who doesn't care must be the person who is a fraud, the time when the addressee failed to warn the speaker is the time when she left the stove on, and the world where the addressee was made to feel loved is the world where the speaker bought him flowers.

Bound:

(i) No politician will admit that he is a fraud.
(ii) When I go to work, I leave the stove on.
(iii) If you give a man flowers, you make him feel loved.

The preferred interpretations of (i), (ii), and (iii), involve binding: for no politician x will admit that x is a fraud, for every time t when I go to work I leave the stove on at t, for every possible world w where you give a man flowers you make him feel loved at w.

The similarities suggest that our default attitude should be to treat all these cases alike in the semantics. Given that pronouns are hardly ever treated intensionally, this seems to be a reason to choose a uniform extensional semantics. But are there reasons why we may need to ultimately reject the default?

One reason to go beyond extensions is *syntactic*. Natural language semantics traditionally seeks to stay close to actual syntax – ideally interpreting complex expressions in a strictly compositional fashion without positing some extra level of representation. And there might be purely syntactic reasons for thinking that sentences do not contain hidden variables referring to times or possible worlds. If so, we might decide that despite the similarities of interpretation, pronouns should be handled extensionally, but tense and/or modals should be given an intensional semantics.

There are considerations tied to *communication*. While having an empirically adequate semantic theory for a large fragment of a natural language is no small feat, we should always keep in mind how such a theory would embed in a larger explanatory enterprise. What we ultimately want to understand is how human beings manage to coordinate their actions by making articulate noises and images. A theory that performs this task will undoubtedly use contents that are more fine-grained than mere extensions. In particular, it will most likely posit that typically when a speaker makes a linguistic utterance, she thereby conveys a proposition to the addressee. It would unify the explanatory apparatus considerably if semantics assigned these more fine-grained contents (e.g. sets of possible worlds, sets of centered worlds, structured propositions) to declarative sentences.

4.11 Conclusion

As logicians see them, time and modality are closely related; both involve operators over sets of possibilities that may be ordered in various ways. (See Rini and Cresswell [2012] for a book-length treatment of this theme.) Tenses and modals both create intensional contexts and provide a showcase for possible worlds semantics. The logic of modality and tense is highly developed. Even though they disagree about the status of possible worlds and past and future times, philosophers agree that they provide a successful theory of futurity, necessity, and related concepts about as much as they agree on anything. Using times and worlds, linguists have developed highly successful theories of tense and modality.

These similarities between times and modalities were not recognized or exploited in the philosophical tradition, although philosophical thinking about the nature of both time and necessity has a long history. Our discussion of these matters in this chapter was selective and included philosophical work on events and aspectual types, puzzles about the subjectivity of time, and recent philosophical debates concerning possible worlds.

The work that began with the study of necessity in Carnap (1956) and culminated in Montague's account of intensionality in Montague (1974) exhibits real progress in the development of technically sophisticated solutions to the problems of intensionality that were raised in Frege (1892). In the final form of this work, intensions are realized as functions from possible worlds to items of an arbitrary type. This means that the intension of an expression can be captured by lambda abstraction from the pattern of its extensions, and unifies the treatment of intensionality with the general apparatus of type theory and lambda abstraction. The older distinction between *de dicto* and *de re* uses of referring expressions can be captured as a matter of scope distinctions. Types are readily available for intensional transitive verbs. The overall picture is elegant and easy to work with.

However, this picture of the semantics of intensionality depends on assimilating intensional phenomena of all kinds, including propositional attitudes, to the constructions – modals and tenses – which seem to be well suited to an interpretation based on possible worlds. As we will point out in Section 5.3.3, this assimilation is problematic in some ways.

5 Intentionality

5.1 Mental Phenomena

Even if there is no entity distinct from the body that we could call the mind, mental and bodily phenomena are different – if not in fact, then at least in how we think of them. If a particular state of your brain is identical to your experience of reading this sentence, it would still be the case that what makes that state physical and what makes it mental are not the same. One of the primary tasks of philosophy is to account for this distinction. This is the *mind–body problem.*

5.1.1 Consciousness as the Mark of the Mental

Consciousness is uncontroversially a sufficient condition for mentality, but to accept it as necessary saddles one with strange views. It led Descartes to the claim that we must perpetually think as long as we exist, and hence, that we cannot really be knocked unconscious or sleep without dreaming:

> As to the fact that there can be nothing in the mind, in so far as it is a thinking thing, of which it is not aware, this seems to me to be self-evident ... In view of this I do not doubt that the mind begins to think as soon as it is implanted in the body of an infant, and that it is immediately aware of its thoughts, even though it does not remember this afterwards because the impressions of these thoughts do not remain in the memory. (Cottingham et al. 1984, 2: 171–172)

Also, if mental phenomena are conscious by their very nature, then the apparent stability of our beliefs and desires is a mystery. Right now I think that Paris is a great city and I wish to be there, but as soon as I cease to have Paris in mind, my belief and desire cease to be conscious and, according to the Cartesian view, cease to exist. Later on, when I come to think that Paris is a great city and wish to be there again, my temporarily extinguished belief and desire come back again. This is perfectly coherent, but not what we tend to think.

One might suggest that even if there are mental phenomena we are not actually aware of, they still must be potentially accessible to consciousness.

But to identify the mental with what could become conscious extends the scope of the mind too far. There are cognitive techniques that enable people to become conscious of a great variety of bodily phenomena most of us don't have subjective awareness of. And even if we currently cannot be conscious of the level of our blood pressure or the phases of our digestion, it is not clear that future discoveries in medicine couldn't change this fact.

5.1.2 Intentionality as the Mark of the Mental

The idea that *intentionality*, not consciousness, is the mark of the mental was first suggested by the German philosopher and psychologist Franz Brentano. In the first volume of his *Psychology from an Empirical Standpoint* he writes:

> Every mental phenomenon is characterized by what the Scholastics of the Middle Ages called the intentional (or mental) inexistence of an object, and what we might call, though not wholly unambiguously, reference to a content, direction toward an object (which is not to be understood here as meaning a thing), or immanent objectivity. Every mental phenomenon includes something as object within itself, although they do not all do so in the same way. In presentation something is presented, in judgment something is affirmed or denied, in love loved, in hate hated, in desire desired, and so on. (Brentano 1995: 88)

According to Brentano, when I think of Paris my thought has Paris "within itself." Unfortunately, "directedness toward an object" is a metaphor and "intentional inexistence," "reference to a content," and "immanent objectivity" are pieces of philosophical jargon that are hard to detach from the medieval background. Posterity came to see the notion of *representation* as the best way to elucidate intentionality, and the thesis that what is distinctive of mental phenomena is that they represent has come to be called *Brentano's thesis*. To represent is to represent something in some way. What is represented is the *intentional object* of the representation, and the way it is represented is its *intentional content*. So, when I am thinking of Paris, the intentional object of my thought is the city itself, and the intentional content is the way the Boulevard St. Michel looked to me one sunny afternoon.

There is no question that many of the paradigm examples of mental states are intentional: A thought is always a thought *about* something; a wish is always a wish *for* something; a fear is always a fear *of* something; and so on. Critics of Brentano's thesis often point to mental states that don't seem to be directed at anything: bodily sensations (e.g. feeling pain, feeling an itch, feeling dizzy, etc.) and moods (e.g. being anxious, being happy, being depressed etc.). But it's not obvious that these are genuine counterexamples. (See Sections 2 and 3 of Crane [1998] for a detailed defense of Brentano's thesis against the putative counterexamples from bodily sensations and moods.)

Bodily sensations lack an external object, but they do seem to have an internal one. We can distinguish between the feeling of a pain and pain itself – that which is felt. The latter, one might think, is just a state of a certain part of the body where the former is felt. There is such a thing as nonlocalized pain, but that is just a pain felt at a vague region of the body, not a disembodied pain. (The thesis that bodily sensations are sensations of one's own body is defended in Armstrong [1968].)

When it comes to moods, it is harder to argue that they are directed at something. Anxiety often feels to be about nothing in particular, which may be exactly what differentiates it from fear. On the other hand, it is also less clear that anxiety is a mental state of its own. To experience anxiety may be nothing more than to have intentional states in a certain way: thinking anxious thoughts, wishing anxious wishes, hoping anxious hopes, and so on. (See Sartre [1971].)

So, intentionality is a much more promising necessary condition for mentality than consciousness. Unfortunately, as a sufficient condition it is a non-starter. Nonmental representations are abundant – the words in front of you are a good example. Brentano's thesis must be qualified by identifying a characteristic that distinguishes mental representations from the rest.

It's a time-honored idea that mental representations are special because they are necessarily *private*. You can think, wish, or fear what I do, but you can't have my own thought, wish, or fear. By contrast, we can both look at the very same map, read the very same sentence, or be puzzled by the very same sign at the airport. But nothing seems to be incoherent about either collective mental states or private representations. We often talk about what corporations or the government think, want, or intend to do. Such talk may be nonliteral but that is far from obvious. We also seem to have representations inside our bodies that are not directly accessible to others – a retinal image is a good example. Moreover, even if a heroic philosophical argument were to convince us that mental representations are essentially private and nonmental representations are essentially public, the characterization would remain disappointingly nonexplanatory: If mental representations are essentially private, there must be something special that makes them available to a single subject only. To preserve the spirit of Brentano's thesis we should aim for a characterization of the mental as a distinctive *type* of intentionality.

In *De Doctrina Christiana*, Augustine drew an important distinction between two kinds of representations – natural and conventional:

> Natural signs are those which, apart from any intention or desire of using them as signs, do yet lead to the knowledge of something else … Conventional signs, on the other hand, are those which living beings mutually exchange in order to show, as well as they can, the feelings of their minds, or their perceptions, or their thoughts. (Augustine of Hippo 1995: 57)

Conventional representations, though nonmental, can derive a sort of intentionality from the mental. The mechanism is complex and not particularly well understood but it is generally accepted that without minds there could not be any conventional signs. Putnam (1981) illustrated this insight with the example of accidental sand-marks. Imagine that an ant traces a line in the sand that looks just like a drawing of Winston Churchill. That would be a remarkable coincidence. So much so that you might suspect that there is something funny going on: maybe someone has put sugar on the sand to lure the ants onto a particular path, or maybe the ant really is intelligent. But if you know that nothing like this took place, that it is pure coincidence that the ant moved the particular way it did, you would be inclined to say that, while the line looks like a portrait of Churchill, in fact, it isn't that. In order for a line to constitute a drawing, someone must think of it in a certain way. The drawing represents because of those thoughts, but the thoughts represent on their own account.

Thinking of Winston Churchill does not seem to be an exception – it seems that mental states in general represent their objects nonderivatively. One could, in principle imagine or remember Churchill without anyone ever having done that before. And while I couldn't imagine or remember Anna Karenina without having read or at least heard of the novel, Tolstoy could and did.

Natural signs also represent nonderivatively: tracks would indicate the shape of animal feet, growth rings would indicate the age of trees, and reflections on the surface of a lake would indicate the clouds above even if nothing else represented the objects they do. These things represent in virtue of a certain causal link which ensures that features of the sign covary with features of what is signified. And exactly because of the causal link, there is a sense in which natural signs cannot misrepresent. If there is smoke but no fire, the smoke did not lie – rather, it turns out that this particular smoke wasn't a sign for fire. Perhaps it was a sign for something else, say, dry ice. Or perhaps it wasn't a sign for anything.

Mental representations are *nontransparent* – they can misrepresent. This is obvious when it comes to imagination or belief because these sorts of representations can be false. But there are mental states that cannot: perception and knowledge being prime examples. If I see that you are holding a glass then you are, and if I know that you drank your martini then you did. Nonetheless, perception and knowledge can also involve misrepresentation. When I see that you are holding a glass, I may present this fact incorrectly (say, as you holding the glass with just three fingers, when in fact you are holding it in your palm). And when I know that you drank your martini I may still misrepresent this fact (for example, I may think of the martini as a cocktail that contains vodka, when in fact it contains gin). This does not seem to have an analogue among natural signs.

Nontransparency is reflected in the way in which we talk of mental phenomena. If I see that you are holding a glass, and the glass is in fact expensive, it does not follow that I see that you are holding an expensive glass. And even if I know that you drank your martini, the fact that martini is in fact your favorite cocktail does not guarantee that I know that you drank your favorite cocktail. If 'see' and 'know' were extensional verbs, these inferences would hold – it would not matter how the glass in your hand or the martini in the glass is described in the perception and knowledge reports. And when it comes to natural signs, the description is indeed immaterial: If a blush is a sign of your embarrassment, and your embarrassment is in fact embarrassment for having drunk my martini, then the blush is *ipso facto* a sign of your embarrassment for having drunk my martini. Of course, I may recognize that your blush is a sign of your embarrassment without recognizing that it is a sign of your embarrassment for having drunk my martini, but that's because recognition is a mental state.

There is a tradition in philosophy, going back to Chisholm (1957) and Quine (1960) that seeks to define intentional phenomena in terms of intensional language. But this is not what is proposed here – the correlation between intentionality and intensionality is imperfect. We talk of certain intentional phenomena (e.g. images in a mirror) extensionally, and we talk of certain nonintentional phenomena intensionally. Dispositions illustrate this last point: For instance, a gas in a closed container heats if and only if its pressure increases. But its disposition to press harder on the container and its disposition to heat are not the same.

To say that there is something that sets mental representations apart from all the representations we can find in nature may sound like a tacit endorsement of dualism – the philosophical doctrine according to which mind and matter are ontologically distinct categories. It is not. The idea that there is something in virtue of which some representations count as mental does not mean that this thing must be a characteristic that transcends materiality. But it does mean that materialists have work to do: They must show how something wholly material is capable of the sort of nontransparency mental phenomena display. This is the problem of *naturalizing* the intentionality displayed by mental phenomena. There are two influential projects of this sort: *informational* (Dretske 1980, 1981, 1995), and *teleosemantic* (Millikan 1984, 1993, 2005).

So, here is the amended version of Brentano's thesis: nonderivative nontransparent intentionality is the mark of the mental. It is a serious proposal about the nature of the mind. It is philosophically controversial. Pains – mental states that seem not to be directed at anything in particular – must not only be seen as representing a state in the body, but as potentially misrepresenting it. If there are self-representing states (some think conscious states are like this), then thinking of such a state is a derivative mental state. If there are mental states that by their nature must represent with full accuracy (some think imagination is like that) then these mental states are transparent.

Our examination of Brentano's thesis clarifies why mental phenomena are central for the philosophy of language. Beliefs, desires, and hopes share an important characteristic with linguistic expressions: They are representations, and as such, they have a semantics. Moreover, mental representations are prior to linguistic ones: There cannot be any language without thought. And finally, the feature that distinguishes mental representations from the sorts of representations that can exist in a mindless world – nontransparency – seems often to be marked in natural languages by intensionality.

5.2 Unreality

If mental phenomena are intentional, then they must invariably be directed at an object. And yet, it seems clear that many of them are not directed at anything real. When Ponce de Leon was searching for the fountain of youth, he was certainly searching for something, and yet, what he was searching for was not a real thing. This sounds so obvious that it takes a minute to realize how close it is to outright contradiction. How can we make sense of this?

Unreality is sometimes seen as *the* central problem of intentionality, but it is important to remember that there are representations whose objects must be real – undoctored photographs are a good example. So, the problem of unreality is somewhat narrower than the problem of intentionality. Still, the capacity to represent what is unreal is what makes certain intentional states particularly interesting. It is also what makes the semantics of their ascriptions particularly puzzling.

Consider the intentional object of Ponce's search – what he was searching for. What sort of thing is it? There are three possible answers. The first is that it is a fountain whose water makes those who drink it young again. This is certainly how Ponce himself would have characterized the object of his search. We can agree with him, adding that unfortunately the sought-after object does not exist. Unbeknownst to him, Ponce was looking for a *nonexistent object*.

The second option is that the intentional object of Ponce's search is nothing at all. On this view, being an intentional object is not an ontological category, and saying that Ponce was searching for something does not amount to saying that he bore a relation to some extraordinary thing. It's just saying that he was engaged in a search and characterizing the search as being directed in the-fountain-of-youth*ish* way. Unbeknownst to him, Ponce was not looking for something that could be found at all, but rather for *no object*.

The third possibility seeks a middle ground between these extremes. There is an object Ponce is seeking, but it is an imaginary object. Imaginary fountains do exist, but they aren't fountains – they are a completely different thing. Of course, Ponce would dispute the claim that what he is searching for is an imaginary thing, but that's exactly where his mistake lies. Unbeknownst to him, Ponce was not looking for something that could be found in time and space but rather for an *abstract object*.

5.2.1 The Nonexistent Object View

The classic objection against the nonexistent object view is that it requires a distinction between what there is and what exists – a distinction that is hard to make sense of. Here is Alexius Meinong (1981: 20), doing his best:

> the *Sosein* ["suchness"] of an object is not affected by its *Nichtsein* ["non-being"]. The fact is sufficiently important to be explicitly formulated as the principle of the independence of *Sosein* from *Sein* ["being"] ...the principle applies, not only to Objects which do not exist in fact, but also to objects which could not exist because they are impossible. Not only is the much heralded gold mountain made of gold, but the round square is as surely round as it is square.

If the round square is round then something is round – the round square has *Sosein*, even though the round square is impossible, and hence, has no *Sein*. The main problem with the distinction between what there is and what exists, as Hume (1978: 66–67) famously put it, is that "[t]o reflect on any thing simply, and to reflect on it as existent, are nothing different from each other." Think of a fountain. What do you have to add to your thought, if you want to think of an existing fountain? It seems that nothing is amiss – thinking of a fountain is *ipso facto* thinking of an existing fountain.

Despite its popularity, the Humean objection to Meinong is not entirely convincing. Imagine being in Rome, standing right in front of the Trevi Fountain and thinking to yourself: "This fountain does not exist." This is an odd thought, no doubt. It is untrue, maybe even necessarily so. Still, it does not appear to be a contradiction. Maybe you think you are dreaming, or you have been reliably informed by your psychiatrist that you are susceptible to fountain hallucinations. In either case, you might be tempted to think: "This fountain does not exist." Yet, no matter what wild skeptical hypothesis you are considering, you would not be tempted to think: "This existing fountain does not exist." Unlike the former thought, this is definitely contradictory.

There is another problem with positing nonexistent objects: counting. How many moons does the Earth have? One, we think. Except that Frédéric Petit, the director of the Toulouse Observatory, in 1846 announced that he had discovered a second moon in an elliptical orbit around Earth. He was wrong, but he was undoubtedly searching for such a moon, and decades later Jules Verne was thinking of it when he discussed it in his novel *Around the Moon*. If the intentional objects of searches, thoughts, and discussions are nonexistent entities then the Earth has at least two moons. And, of course, we cannot stop here. Besides Petit's moon, there are dozens of others that have been claimed to exist but proved not to. On the nonexistent entity view, all these scientific mistakes and outright frauds had moons of the Earth as their intentional objects. Which would mean that Earth has lots of moons, albeit only one that exists.

A similar counting objection can be raised against David Lewis' view, that merely possible individuals are just like actual ones, except that they inhabit worlds that are spatiotemporally isolated from ours. If Lewis (1986) is right, the Earth has infinitely many moons, but only one that is actual; these other moons orbit some counterpart of the Earth, but this does not change the fact that they are the Earth's moons. Lewis has a response: He says that when we count, we tend to restrict our attention to the actual, and when we say 'The Earth has just one moon' we quantify restrictedly. Analogously, Meinongeans can insist that counting and quantification normally deal only with what exists. But not always – when in *Jeopardy!* you are asked about the number of the Horsemen of the Apocalypse your answer should be four, even if you don't believe a word of the story in the Book of Revelations.

5.2.2 The No Object View

Accepting nonexistent entities is more than what most of us are willing to do. We want to believe that Ponce de Leon was searching for the fountain of youth without having to add something strange to our ontology. This is what the no entity view of intentionality promises: To believe that Ponce de Leon was searching for the Fountain of Youth, you must believe in the existence of Ponce, his search, and nothing more.

Our language insists on providing intensional verbs with a direct object, even when there is nothing to which it refers. But perhaps language is ontologically misguiding. This is a thought that many philosophers have found attractive. Here is the classic statement about why we should not posit meanings willy-nilly just because we speak as if there were such things:

> I feel no reluctance toward refusing to admit meanings, for I do not thereby deny that words and statements are meaningful. McX [this is Quine's imaginary Meinongean opponent] and I may agree to the letter in our classification of linguistic forms into the meaningful and the meaningless, even though McX construes meaningfulness as the having (in some sense of 'having') of some abstract entity which he calls a meaning, whereas I do not. I remain free to maintain that the fact that a given linguistic utterance is meaningful (or significant, as I prefer to say so as not to invite hypostasis of meanings as entities) is an ultimate and irreducible matter of fact; or, I may undertake to analyze it in terms directly of what

> people do in the presence of the linguistic utterance in question and other utterances similar to it. (Quine 1948: 11)

Quine is happy to say that words have meanings but refuses to believe that there are meanings. He suggests that we should regard talk of having meaning as a convenient proxy for the ontologically more apt talk of meaningfulness. Thus, we could take ⌜The German sentence 'Schnee ist weiss' means something⌝ simply as another way of saying that the German sentence 'Schnee ist weiss' is meaningful. ⌜The German sentence 'Schnee ist weiss' means what the English sentence 'Snow is white' does⌝ stands for ⌜The German sentence 'Schnee ist weiss' and the English sentence 'Snow is white' are synonyms⌝ and ⌜The German sentence 'Schnee ist weiss' means that snow is white⌝ allows us to say something we would have a hard time to express without apparent commitment to meanings. We might approximate it by the imaginary sentence ⌜The German sentence 'Schnee ist weiss' means snow-is-white*ly*⌝. To say *what* the sentence means would be just to say *how* it is meaningful. For Quine, what goes for word meanings goes also for what Ponce was searching for.

This view is rather unorthodox when it comes to syntax and semantics: The direct objects of 'mean' or 'search for' are not adverbs, but they are being interpreted as such. That does not bother someone like Quine, who is altogether skeptical of semantics for natural languages. For him (as for Frege or Tarski before him) English (or German or Polish) is not the proper medium for doing serious scientific inquiry. We have to *regiment* sentences of the vernacular into a formal language and we should only be concerned with explaining inferences within that language. Regimentation is not a mechanical translation and needn't preserve meaning – it is just a process of replacing a murky formulation with a clear one, which counts as adequate if it fits our theoretical needs.

5.2.3 The Abstract Object View

For philosophers who care about ontology and don't care about semantics, the no object view of intentionality is a natural fit. For linguists who are concerned primarily with semantics and willing to work with whatever ontology is most convenient, the nonexistent object view is unbeatable. Many of us, however, are somewhere in the middle. This explains why the most popular approach to intentionality is the abstract object view. If intensional objects are abstracta then their existence is unproblematic for everyone, except for die-hard nominalists. And if they can be the semantic values of the expressions in the complements of the verbs we use to describe intentional phenomena, we get a fairly intuitive semantics as well.

The version of this view most familiar to semanticists is due to Richard Montague. According to his theory, the complement of 'search for' is an entity of type $\langle s, \langle\langle e, t\rangle, t\rangle\rangle$. (Actually, in the original version of Montague

[1974], an entity of type $\langle s, \langle\langle s, \langle , e, t\rangle\rangle, t\rangle\rangle\rangle$. We follow most formal semanticists who have simplified the type-assignment somewhat.) This is a function from possible worlds to sets of sets of objects.

Accordingly, the intentional object of Ponce's search is an abstract entity – the function that assigns to each possible world the set of those sets that contain the fountain of youth in that world as a member. Of course, Ponce himself would never say that what he is searching for is an abstract entity of this sort. But, perhaps, that's exactly where he is mistaken.

There is a well-known problem with Montague's proposal: It makes intentional objects insufficiently fine-grained. If Sally is searching for the largest negative rational number and Molly is searching for the smallest positive rational number, they are definitely not looking for the same thing. And yet, given the fact that there is no possible world with either a largest negative rational number or a smallest positive rational number, the intentional objects of their searches are identical on Montague's account. Non-mathematical examples are also possible. Sally may want a glass of water but not a glass of H_2O, even though necessarily, a glass of water is a glass of H_2O. Also Sally may draw a unicorn but not a griffin. But, if Kripke (1972: 156–158) is right, neither unicorns nor griffins could have existed.

One standard reaction to the problem holds that the semantic values of noun phrases which will play the role of intentional objects should be structured in a way that mirrors their syntax. Such a proposal was made in Lewis (1970b), following a suggestion in Carnap (1956). If semantic values of linguistic expressions are trees mirroring syntactic structure with nodes that are decorated with a category label and an intension then ⟦'the smallest positive rational number'⟧ ≠ ⟦'the largest negative rational number'⟧ simply because ⟦'smallest'⟧ ≠ ⟦'largest'⟧. But such a maneuver will not solve the problem of coarse-grainedness for syntactically simple expressions: We still would like to say that it could be that ⟦'Some people envy Cicero'⟧ ≠ ⟦'Some people envy Tully'⟧ even though ⟦'Cicero'⟧ = ⟦'Tully'⟧.

A different approach to the problem is to opt for more fine-grained entities in the type theory employed by the semantics. Thomason (1980) replaces the basic type **t** standing for truth-values with that of **p** standing for propositions, which are taken to be *sui generis* entities, not functions from possible worlds to truth-values. This means that if we want to say what the truth-conditions of a declarative sentence are, we cannot just assign a proposition to it; we have to say in addition under what conditions that proposition is true. While this makes the semantics more complex, it also has a benefit: We do not have to deal with intensions at all; we can say that the semantic type of an intransitive verb is $\langle e, p\rangle$, the semantic type of a transitive verb is $\langle e, \langle e, p\rangle\rangle$, the semantic type of a noun phrase is $\langle\langle e, p\rangle, p\rangle$. If propositions are individuated finely, so are these functions, and hence, they can be seen as adequately modeling fine-grained properties, binary relations, and properties of properties. If we assume that the proposition that Cicero is Cicero is distinct from the proposition that Cicero is Tully, then the theory distinguishes the property of being Cicero and the property of being Tully as well as the property of being a property Cicero has and the property of being a property Tully has. In other words, following Montague's semantics with Thomason's revision, we can have $[\![\text{'Cicero'}]\!] \neq [\![\text{'Tully'}]\!]$ despite the fact that for all possible worlds w, $[\![\text{'Cicero'}]\!]^w = [\![\text{'Tully'}]\!]^w$.

As for the abstract object view of intentionality, the main sticking point tends to be its sheer prima facie implausibility. Ponce de Leon was not a genius, but he surely did not mistake an abstract object for a concrete one when he was looking for the fountain of youth! The criticism is sometimes dismissed by saying that semantic values should not be confused with the real things they are supposed to model. This is a fine response as long as we are only concerned with semantics. But now we are asking not about the truth-conditions of 'Ponce de Leon was searching for the fountain of youth', but about what it is that Ponce was searching for. We were entertaining the possibility that the answer to the latter question can be guided by an answer to the former, i.e. that the semantic value of the complement of the verb *just is* the intentional object of the search. So the complaint that the semantic value does not seem to be the right kind of thing to be the object of Ponce's search is legitimate.

What can be said in response to this complaint? We could start by suggesting that we should be less deferential to common sense in this area. What would the proverbial man on the street say about the object of Ponce's search? He might say that it is a fountain which somehow fails to exist and consequently is nothing at all. But a fountain that is nothing at all *is* a contradiction. Even though our inquiry begins with common sense, it seems that it can't end there.

The next step is to recognize that there is, in fact, something reasonable we could say about the fountain of youth. It makes sense to characterize it as an imaginary fountain – an object that exists but is not really a fountain. When challenged about the nature of this object we should resist the temptation to say that it is an idea in Ponce's head. That idea *represents* an imaginary fountain, but it is not *identical to* an imaginary fountain. Instead, we might say that the imaginary fountain is an abstract entity, perhaps a property of properties. People might say that Ponce is searching for an imaginary fountain and deny that he is searching for a property of properties, but this is in many ways similar to saying that Cicero was an orator and denying that Tully was. We don't think of imaginary fountains as abstract but that does not mean they aren't abstract.

However, the abstract entity view is not out of the woods yet. Had Ponce de Leon found what he was looking for, he would certainly have found a real fountain. But if the object of his search was not a real fountain, how can his search succeed just because he finds something other than the object he was looking for?

This objection is based on an equivocation. There are, in fact two kinds of searches (just as there are two kinds of fears, wants, imaginings, etc.). Some searches are *specific*, aimed at finding a particular thing; success in such a search requires that one find the very thing one was looking for. If Ponce is looking for his misplaced sword and finds one just like it, he might think that he has found what he was looking for, but he would be wrong. But there are other kinds of searches as well. *Nonspecific* searches are aimed at finding something or other that fits a certain description. If Ponce is simply looking for a sword – when, as Quine (1956: 185) would put it, he seeks relief from mere swordlessness – we say that he found what he was looking for whenever he found something with the requisite characteristics. Finding what one is looking for requires identity between the object sought and the object found only in the case of a specific search. For nonspecific searches the requirement is different: What one finds must fit the description associated with what was sought.

Ponce's search for the fountain of youth was nonspecific. And the fact that the latter entailment holds may be used to explain why it is infelicitous to deny that Ponce was searching for a particular fountain. Granted, nothing short of the fountain of youth itself could provide specific success-conditions for Ponce's search – but there is no such thing. So Ponce is merely trying to find something that matches a description – a fountain whose water makes one young again. He might think that there is a particular fountain he seeks to find, but we know better. Whatever he says, as a matter of fact, finding anything with the right characteristics would amount to him succeeding in his search. But if Ponce's search was nonspecific, it is no surprise that he could have found what he was looking for without finding the very thing that was the intentional object of his search.

Let's sum up. We can draw a unicorn, wish for a unicorn, search for a unicorn, and even owe a unicorn if we lost the right kind of bet. The intentional object of these mental processes and states could be a concrete but nonexistent thing, nothing at all, or an abstract but existing thing. There does not seem to be a knock-down objection against any of these views. But the first is ontologically excessive and the second linguistically revisionary. The main objection to the abstract object view is that it relates those who draw, wish, seek, or owe a unicorn to the wrong kind of thing. We have suggested that this objection can be answered.

5.3 Propositions

Beliefs can be called true or false without the slightest sign of linguistic impropriety. In this regard, they are somewhat exceptional among mental phenomena. It sounds odd to call an experience of heat, a feeling of joy, or a hope for rain true or false. And while we might call knowledge true, we would never call it false. Convictions, presumptions, suspicions, are all assessed for truth or falsity, but they are – arguably – just qualified beliefs. A conviction is a firmly held belief, a presumption is belief based on admittedly insufficient evidence, a suspicion is a timid presumption.

Some of what we believe, we express in speech. When we do so we purport to assert just what we believe. In fact, such a match is regarded as a mark of sincere and honest self-expression, as we all learned from Horton: "I meant what I said, and I said what I meant. An elephant's faithful one-hundred percent" (Seuss 1940). What Horton meant is that he would babysit Mayzie's egg come what may, which is precisely what he believed. So, if he said what he meant then he said (asserted) what he believed. The match between what he meant and what he said entails a match between what he believed and what he asserted. It is quite natural, then, to think that the intentional objects of belief are also the intentional objects of assertion.

What philosophers nowadays call *propositions* are the things we believe and assert. Like beliefs and assertions, propositions themselves invite truth-evaluation: We say not only that Columbus' belief that he had sailed to India is false but also that the proposition that Columbus sailed to India is false. Moreover, Columbus' belief is false because the proposition he believes is false, not the other way around. And so, it seems natural to think that beliefs have their truth-values in virtue of having a proposition as their object that is true or false. This is the sense in which propositions are the *primary bearers of truth-value*: Whatever else has a truth-value (a belief, a sentence, a theory, a story, etc.) inherits it from a proposition.

Beliefs and assertions appear to be individuated by their objects: You and I share a belief just in case what you believe and what I believe are the same. (Of course, when we believe the same thing we still have different belief *tokens*; it's the belief *types* that are identical when their objects coincide.) For most mental states, this is emphatically not the case: The fact that you and I desire, fear, or regret the same thing is normally not enough to conclude that we have the same desire, fear, or regret. If you and I both want a cake, but I want to eat it and you want to smash it in my face, it would be bizarre to say that we have the same desire. If you and I both are afraid of snakes, but my horror is that they might suffocate me and yours is that they might bite you, we don't quite have the same fear. And if we both regret our fight last night because we both think we could have won the argument if only we tried a bit harder, then my regret isn't yours and yours isn't mine. To be (type-) identical, mental states must not only represent the same thing, they must represent it in the same way. In other words, mental representations are individuated in terms of their contents, not their objects. And because beliefs *are* individuated in terms of their objects, it is natural to think that their objects are also their contents. This is what accounts for the widespread practice of talking interchangeably of the propositional object and the propositional content of beliefs. But we will not indulge this habit: We regard the claim that the intentional object and the intentional content of beliefs are the same as substantive.

5.3.1 Beyond the Minimal Characterization

There are other things that are sometimes taken to be definitional of propositions but are best treated as substantive theses. For example, it is often said that propositions are the meanings of indexical-free declarative sentences. Since Searle (1978), this claim has been subject to vigorous criticism. The putative counterexamples involve sentences that do not contain any overt indexical element, and a pair of situations where they are uttered to make assertions with apparently different truth-values. (We touched upon this controversy already, in Section 2.3.) Which (if any) of the dozens of standard examples are convincing is debated and so is the claim that the conclusion we should draw from them is that the meaning of the relevant sentences is not a proposition. Given the complexity of the issues, it would be a mistake to make it a matter of definition that propositions are what indexical-free declarative sentences mean.

It is also often said that propositions are what 'that'-clauses refer to – or more cautiously, since clauses don't seem to be referring expressions, what 'that'-clauses designate. But 'that'-clauses don't seem to designate one kind of thing: Sometimes they pick out events (as in 'It makes me happy that you came'), sometimes they stand for facts (as in 'I regret that you could not come'), and sometimes they designate neither (as in 'It is possible that the class will be canceled'). Of course, these appearances might be deceptive: Perhaps propositions can make one happy (which would mean, presumably, that they have causal powers), and perhaps facts are just true propositions. But these metaphysical views are sufficiently idiosyncratic that we should not assume them without argument. Certainly, we can provide a uniform semantics for 'that'-clauses, but that does not mean that they must all attach to something that can also be the object of belief and assertion and the primary bearer of truth and falsity.

It is also typically assumed that propositions are the contents of a great many mental states besides belief: They are often taken to be what we know, hope, or fear, and perhaps also what we see, imagine, or admire. The stated reason for this claim is often nothing more than the fact that the relevant verbs can take a 'that'-clause as their direct object – which is a feeble argument. Apparently, the things we know are facts, the things we hope are states of affairs, and the things we fear are possibilities. When we substitute 'the proposition that so-and-so' for 'that so-and-so' in the relevant ascriptions of mental states, we get sentences that are peculiar (as in 'Jill knows that it will rain' versus 'Jill knows the proposition that it will rain') or downright anomalous (as in 'Jack hopes that it will rain' versus 'Jack hopes the proposition that it will rain.') For a discussion of these substitution problems see King (2002) and Moltmann (2003).

Also, many mental verbs take a noun phrase as direct object: We can say that we want a cookie, that we expect a delay, that we hear a dog. How could the intentional object be a proposition in these examples? In some of these cases there is an argument for hidden clausal structure. 'Sue will want a cookie on Sunday' can report either a desire on (say) Saturday for a cookie on Sunday, or a desire on Sunday for a cookie right then. This is well accounted for if we think that the structure of the sentence is something like ['Sue'['will want'[PRO 'to have a cookie on Sunday']]] and that the prepositional phrase can modify either the overt 'want' or the covert 'have'. But there is no analogous argument for hidden structure in 'Sue will expect a delay' or in 'Sue will hear a dog'. The thesis that these sentences also relate Sue to some proposition is defended in den Dikken et al. (1996) and Larson (2002); for arguments that intensional transitive verbs always take clausal complements, see den Dikken et al. (1996). For objections to this view, see Forbes (2006) and Szabó (2005b).

The term 'propositional attitude' is ubiquitous in philosophy, but it is never defined precisely. Whether there are any mental phenomena besides belief whose intentional objects are propositions is by no means obvious. In fact, 'proposition' itself is best understood as a technical term of philosophy. Its meaning has changed over the ages, and today there are only three things that are generally agreed to be definitive: that propositions are the objects of belief, that they are the objects of assertion, and that they are the primary bearers of truth-value. Everything else is up for debate.

5.3.2 Are There Propositions?

Champions of propositions often write as if there was an easy and decisive argument in favor of positing them. This rests on the observation that there are certain inferences whose validity seems best explained if we assume that singular belief-ascriptions and indirect reports involve a binary relation between a person and a proposition. For versions of this argument, see Horwich (1990); Higginbotham (1991); Schiffer (1996); Bealer (1998).

Here is such an argument:

(1) Jack believes that the moon is made of green cheese, and so does Jill; therefore there is something Jack and Jill both believe – to wit, that the moon is made of green cheese.

(2) Jack said that the moon is made of green cheese, and Jill believes everything Jack said; therefore Jill believes that the moon is made of green cheese.

(3) Jack believes that the moon is made of green cheese, it is false that the moon is made of green cheese; therefore, Jack believes something false.

We should be skeptical. If this was enough to establish the existence of propositions, we should believe in stranger things as well – like the fountain of youth:

(1′) Ponce de Leon was searching for the fountain of youth, and so was Alexander the Great; therefore there is something Ponce de

Leon and Alexander the Great were both searching for – to wit, the fountain of youth.

(2′) Alexander the Great was longing for the fountain of youth, and Ponce de Leon was searching for everything Alexander the Great was longing for; therefore Ponce de Leon was searching for the fountain of youth.

(3′) Ponce de Leon was searching for the fountain of youth, the fountain of youth is famous; therefore, Ponce de Leon was searching for something famous.

It is hard to account for intentional objects. And the task is not noticeably easier if we restrict our attention to the intentional objects of belief and assertion. (See Elbourne [2011: Chapter 4] for a similar point.) A Meinongean view about the intentional object of Jack's belief that the moon is made of green cheese treats this object as a nonexistent fact. A Quinean view says that it is nothing at all: *What* Jack believes is simply a matter of *how* he believes. This isn't to say that we should shun propositions: As we suggested in Section 5.3.1, when it comes to intentional objects, the most promising balance between ontology and semantics is probably the abstract entity view. But saying this is a far cry from claiming that the existence of propositions is a trivial matter.

Just what sort of abstract entity a proposition might be will be explored in the next section. But before turning to that, let's illustrate what philosophers who don't believe in propositions might say about ascriptions of belief and assertion.

One option is to say that belief and assertion are not relations to one thing but to many. Bertrand Russell held this sort of view for a while, after he abandoned his early theory of propositions; see Russell (1910). When Othello believes that Desdemona loves Cassio there is a relation that holds between the subject of the belief, Othello, and its objects, Desdemona, loving, and Cassio. The three objects do not constitute a single thing, since Desdemona does not love Cassio. We could say that Othello's belief is true just in case its objects make up a fact; otherwise it is false.

McGrath (2008) raises the following objection: When Othello believes that Desdemona loves Cassio, he also believes the proposition that Desdemona loves Cassio. Even if the former belief is a four-place relation between Othello on the one hand and Desdemona, loving, and Cassio on the other, the latter must still be a two-place relation between Othello and a proposition. But proponents of the multiple relation view would be no more compelled to infer the existence of a single entity from the presence of a 'the'-phrase than they are from the presence of a 'that'-clause. They could say that when Othello believes the proposition that Desdemona loves Cassio, he stands in the belief relation to the semantic values of 'the', 'proposition', 'that', 'Desdemona', 'loves', and 'Cassio' – whatever exactly those semantic values might be. On the other hand, the multiple relations view leads to a semantic theory of 'believe' that is – to say the least – awkward. What about 'Othello believes that Desdemona loves Cassio and that Cassio hates Roderigo'? Is this a three- or a four-place relation? And how is it connected semantically to 'Othello believes that Desdemona loves Cassio and believes that Cassio hates Roderigo'?

The multiple relations view of belief denies that beliefs have a single intentional object. One might preserve this intuition and still do away with propositions by insisting that the intentional object of a belief is a sentence. So, when we say that Galileo believed that the Earth moves, we say that he stood in the belief relation to the sentence 'The Earth moves'. This, of course, sounds odd: How could Galileo believe a sentence he does not even understand? The natural response (first given in Supplement C of Carnap [1956]) is that for the truth of 'Galileo believed that the Earth moves' it is enough if he believed another sentence that bears some relation (Carnap called it 'B') to the English sentence 'The Earth moves'. A more refined version of this view was presented in Davidson (1968), who argued that the logical form of 'Galileo said that the Earth moves' is something like 'Galileo said that. The Earth moves' – where the 'that' refers to the utterance of the sentence that follows. What is required for the truth of the report is only that Galileo made some other utterance that stands in the "samesaying" relation to the ascriber's utterance.

The idea that the complementizer and the demonstrative 'that' are the same word has little plausibility. (Their translations differ in most languages and they sound different even in English.) But the core idea of the *paratactic view* – that the complement clause in indirect reports and belief-ascriptions is not used but mentioned in order to give an exemplar of the sort of utterance Galileo made – is intriguing. Of course, a proponent of the account should try to tell us something informative about what it takes for utterances to samesay without falling back on the idea that they must say the same *thing* or, in other words, must express the same proposition. But this is a general problem that philosophical attempts to do away with abstract entities face, not something specific to the paratactic view. Nominalists often say that what red things have in common is not that they instantiate the universal redness, but rather that they all resemble each other in a certain respect. Then they are pressed to explain what resemblance in that respect consists in without falling back on talking about universal redness.

You can find linguists and philosophers who will tell you that it's trivial that propositions exist, and others who will tell you that it's obvious that they don't. The moral of this section is simple: Don't trust them.

5.3.3 What Are Propositions?

Let's suppose, then, with the majority of philosophers of language, that propositions do exist. What sort of thing could they be?

Fregean Propositions

While propositions in more or less our sense have been widely discussed since the Stoics and especially in medieval philosophy, today the standard reference point for philosophers is Frege's account. (For information about the history of propositions, see the classic trilogy Nuchelmans [1973, 1980, 1983].) Frege called propositions *Gedanken*, a term normally translated as "Thoughts," but distinguished them sharply from both the mental states we ordinarily call thoughts and their physical realizations in the brain.

Frege did not identify Thoughts with the meanings of indexical-free declarative sentences: He allowed that certain aspects of sentence meaning make no difference to truth-value, and he believed that Thoughts comprise only those aspects of sentence meaning that are relevant for truth. So, for example, the Fregean Thought expressed by 'Alfred has still not come' – the sense of this sentence – is the same as the one expressed by 'Alfred has not come'. The presence of 'still' merely hints that Alfred's arrival is expected. If Alfred's coming is not in fact expected, the Thought that Alfred has still not come is true all the same, as long as Alfred has not come. (See Frege [1956].)

The example illustrates the fact that while Thoughts are supposed to have a structure that *more or less* mirrors the syntax of sentences that express them, the qualification is crucial. The truth predicate provides an even more dramatic illustration of Frege's view that sentence structure and propositional structure can be quite different. According to a central doctrine of Frege's, predicating truth of a Thought adds nothing to it. It follows, for instance, that the Thoughts expressed by the sentences 'Two is a prime number', 'It is true that two is a prime number', and 'It is true that it is true that two is a prime number' are all identical.

Frege held that within the complement of certain mental verb phrases 'that'-clauses refer to Thoughts. But he did not think 'that'-clauses invariably refer to Thoughts: He claimed that such clauses following 'command', 'ask', or 'forbid' refer to commands or requests, and that while these things are "at the same level as" Thoughts, they differ from them on account of not being true or false.

Metaphysically, Thoughts are timeless, unchanging entities that inhabit a realm distinct both from the external and the internal world. What distinguishes them from physical entities is that (like mental entities) they are in principle insensible; what sets them apart from mental entities is that (like physical entities) they are in principle public. The influence of Thoughts on the physical world is mediated by their influence on the mental world of thinkers: They impact the minds of those who grasp them, and this influences their outward behavior.

> When a thought is grasped, it at first only brings about changes in the inner world of the one who grasps it; yet it remains untouched in the core of its essence, for the changes it undergoes affect only inessential properties. There is lacking here something we observe everywhere in physical

> processes – reciprocal action. Thoughts are not wholly unactual but their actuality is quite different from the actuality of things. And their action is brought about by a performance of the thinker; without this they would be inactive, at least as far as we can see. And yet the thinker does not create them but must take them as they are. They can be true without being grasped by a thinker; and they are not wholly unactual even then, at least if they could be grasped and so brought into action. (Frege 1956: 311).

Fregean Thoughts are much like Plato's Forms. This is no surprise, given that the two ontologies were both fashioned from reflecting on mathematical examples. When it comes to isosceles triangles, prime numbers, or sets of ordered pairs, it is natural to say that they exist neither in space nor in time, and that they exert no causal influence on anything. The radical Platonic-Fregean suggestion is that this sort of realm extends far beyond the scope of mathematics.

Some philosophers – the nominalists – reject the existence of Thoughts because they eschew all abstract entities. But Thoughts have at least two features that make them much more problematic than mathematical entities. The first is *falsehood*. When we have false beliefs, make false assertions, or write false sentences, their falsehood is supposed to be explainable in terms of the propositions believed, asserted, or meant. If propositions are Fregean Thoughts then they exist eternally and necessarily, and are quite independent of beliefs, assertions, and sentences. Yet, some insist, in a world without minds, there simply wouldn't be such a thing as falsehood. In such a world, there could be planets and stars, electrons and photons, mountains and trees, even numbers and functions, but nothing that is false about tracks, growth rings, and reflections on the surface of a lake. (Recall that this was the reason given in Section 5.1 for the claim that only mental phenomena have nonderivative nontransparent intentionality.) There would perhaps be facts, including all the facts of mathematics, and the existence of facts might even encourage us to say that truth wouldn't be entirely absent. It is, after all, fairly natural to think that the truth that $2+2=4$ is nothing other than the fact that $2+2=4$. But what about the falsehood that $2+2=5$? Such a thing seems to have no place in a world devoid of mental phenomena. And in fact, Russell (1910) repudiates his early commitment to propositions in part because he saw no way to make sense of mind-independent falsehood.

The other problematic feature of Thoughts is their *identity*. We feel much more confident about an obscure mathematical entity when it has impeccably clear identity-conditions. Sets, for instance, are identical iff they have the same members, and functions are identical iff they have the same domains and assign the same values to each member of their domains. Frege defended his Thoughts by providing a sensible identity-condition: He says Thoughts are identical just in case no one could believe one without the other. (This follows from a remark in Frege [1906].) How clear one finds this condition will depend on how comfortable one is with the intensional idiom in theoretical contexts. But even for those of us who do not insist on extensionality in stating identity-conditions, Frege's identity-condition for propositions might be problematic. Propositions are supposed to be the primary bearers of truth-value, but how could they explain the truth or falsity of beliefs if propositions themselves are individuated in terms of beliefs?

Russellian Propositions

The problem of identity goes away if we abandon the Fregean conception of propositions in favor of the more this-worldly Russellian picture. As Russell famously put it in a letter to Frege: "in spite of all its snowfields Mont Blanc itself is a component part of what is actually asserted in the proposition 'Mont Blanc is more than 4,000 metres high' " (Frege 1980b: 169).

Mont Blanc itself can be identified without appeals to possible beliefs about Mont Blanc, and hopefully the same can be said of the other component of the proposition – the property of being more than 4000 meters high. If so, the proposition itself could have perfectly mind-independent identity-conditions.

The downside of this belief-independent conception is that Russellian propositions end up being more coarse-grained than Fregean Thoughts. Recall Frege's puzzle, that someone could believe that Hesperus is Hesperus without believing that Hesperus is Phosphorus. If the proposition that Hesperus is Phosphorus is to be built up from the planet Venus (twice over!) and the relation of identity, it is unclear how it could differ from the proposition that Hesperus is Hesperus. This leaves defenders of Russellian propositions with three options: (i) deny that one could believe that Hesperus is Hesperus without believing that Hesperus is Phosphorus, and explain the contrary appearance as a pragmatic illusion; (ii) abandon the idea that beliefs are individuated by their propositional contents; or (iii) acknowledge further (unarticulated) constituents within these propositions. For representative examples of these strategies, see Salmon (1986); Braun (1998); Soames (2002). Each alternative surrenders something of the appealing simplicity and straightforwardness of the Russellian idea.

In its original form, Russell's view of propositions fares no better than its Fregean cousin when it comes to the problem of falsehood. If falsehood is essentially a matter of representation, the question for the Russellian is how a collection of objects, properties, and relations which don't represent anything can make up something that does. This is sometimes called the problem of the *unity of the proposition*. The term is somewhat misleading: for any entity that has parts, there is a question about what exactly holds the parts together. What makes the many one? For the solar system the answer to this question is gravity, for a novel it is authorial intent, for a set it is membership, and so on. For a structured proposition it is structure. So the hard question for a Russellian is how structure can give rise to intentionality.

One option, explored by King (2007) is to say that propositions represent in virtue of a structure that they inherit from sentences. Without sentences there wouldn't be propositions either. For King, the relation that holds between Socrates and running in virtue of which they make up the proposition that Socrates runs is the relation that holds between an object o and a property P just in case there is a language L, a context c and lexical items *a* and *b* of L such that *a* and *b* occur at the left and right terminal nodes (respectively) of the sentential relation R that in L encodes ascription, o is the semantic value of *a* in c, and P is the semantic value of *b* in c. That this complex relation holds between Socrates and running is attested by the English sentence 'Socrates runs' (or the German sentence 'Sokrates rennt', or the Latin sentence 'Socrates currit', or the Hungarian sentence 'Szokratész fut', etc.) For King, the proposition that Socrates runs is just a fact – but not the fact that Socrates has the property of running, but rather the fact that he stands in this more elaborate relation to the property of running – which he does even if he does not run.

The view elaborated by Soames (2010) is also committed to the idea that propositions represent in virtue of their structure, but does not tie this structure to natural languages. For Soames, it is acts of predication – acts of ascribing a property to an object – that are essentially representational. Predication is a cognitive event that can take place in individual minds, and it does not presuppose any sort of linguistic vehicle. Predication events come in types and the proposition that Socrates runs is one such cognitive event type. Propositions are true or false because their instances are. This sort of inheritance is seen as metaphysically commonplace: What makes the Audi A4 a comfortable car is that particular tokens of this type are comfortable; what makes the Coke bottle iconic is that individual Coke bottles have this property; what makes Psycho a terrifying movie is that its screenings tend to terrify people; and so on.

On King's and Soames' views, whether a world without minds would have falsehoods depends on whether it would have interpreted natural languages or cognitive event types, respectively. Assuming a non-Platonic view of languages and types, either view delivers an answer to the problem of falsehood. The fact that the radius of the Earth was approximately 4000 miles was around for a long time, but the false proposition that the radius of the Earth is approximately 3000 miles (or, for that matter, the true proposition that the radius of the Earth is approximately 4000 miles) is much younger.

But a puzzle remains here. Let's assume that the proposition that the radius of the Earth is approximately 4000 miles did not exist a billion years ago. Still, we all agree that it was true a billion years ago that the radius of the Earth is approximately 4000 miles. What is it that was true then? Surely, the proposition that the radius of the Earth is approximately 4000 miles. But how can a proposition be true at a time when it does not even exist?

The puzzle arises for modality as much as it does for time. Let's assume that the proposition that the radius of the Earth is approximately 4000 miles does not exist in some possible world, where the radius of the Earth is approximately 4000 miles. How could that be? Wouldn't this mean that in this world the proposition that the radius of the Earth is approximately 4000 miles is true, even though the proposition does not even exist?

One might try to answer this objection by following Adams (1981) in distinguishing between two ways in which a proposition can be true with respect to a world. On the one hand, a proposition could be true *in* a world, in which case it had better exist within that world. On the other hand, a proposition might not be part of the world and nonetheless be true *at* that world. One might support the need for this distinction by considering the proposition that there are many possible worlds, which is true at the actual world, but – one might think – not in the actual world. The actual world cannot contain other possible worlds as parts. And, of course, one could use similar arguments in support of the idea that we need a distinction between truth at a time and truth in a time as well. Once these distinctions are made, we can say that the proposition that the radius of the Earth is approximately 4000 miles can be true at times when it does not exist, even if it cannot be true in those times.

Opponents of the distinction will insist that the intuition that the proposition that there are many possible worlds is not true in the actual world rests on a certain controversial view about what possible worlds are. If, as Lewis (1986) contends, they are concrete particulars like the actual world, it is certainly true that they cannot be parts of the actual world – which is why Lewis says that they are spatiotemporally disconnected from our world. But if they are abstract entities of some sort – say, maximal consistent states of affairs, as Plantinga (1974) thinks, or properties, as Stalnaker (1976) does – then there is no real obstacle to placing them within the actual world. (Of course, to say that other possible worlds actually exist does not, on these views, entail that they are actual – saying *that* would be a contradiction.) And similarly, the plausibility of a distinction between truth at a time and truth in a time seems to presuppose that we are realists about past and present times.

In the end, whether we can make the existence of propositions a contingent and transient matter depends on other issues in the metaphysics of modality and time.

Carnapian Propositions

Most philosophers who believe in propositions subscribe to broadly Fregean or Russellian views. Most linguists who specialize in formal semantics subscribe to neither: They tend to assume the Carnapian view that propositions are simply sets of possible worlds. What makes sets of possible worlds apt candidates for the role of propositions is that their connection with truth is clear: a proposition is true just in case it contains the actual world as a member. What makes them less than ideal is that it is hard to believe that this claim is literally true. Is the entire world (including Mont Blanc with all its snowfields) really a *member* of what I believe when I believe that it will rain tomorrow in New Haven? Is a set even the sort of thing that can be literally true or false? It seems more plausible to think that propositions – whatever they might be in the final analysis – can be modeled, at least for certain theoretical purposes, as sets of possible worlds. No one will quarrel with that. The disagreement is only whether they can play the definitive roles of propositions – being the primary bearers of truth-value and being the intentional objects of belief and assertion.

Let's start with logic. Logical truths are true in virtue of their form, so whatever is logically true must have logical form. Sets of possible worlds won't do. But a proponent of coarse-grained propositions needn't despair: She could follow Tarski and declare that logic does not deal directly with propositions.

Consider the English sentence 'It is raining or it is not raining' and let's grant that it is a logical truth. To account for this status, we need a theory that associates a logical form with this sentence. Such a theory would arguably go beyond syntax and semantics: Besides specifying that the structure of the sentence (at a certain level of abstraction) is ⟦'It is raining' $\vee\neg$ 'It is raining'⟧ and saying what ⟦'It is raining'⟧, ⟦$\vee$⟧, and ⟦$\neg$⟧ are, we also need to know that the last two are logical constants, and hence, their interpretation stays fixed across models. Once we have all this, we can explain why 'It is raining or it is not raining' is a logical truth: The sentence comes out true in all models, which is to say, it remains true under all reinterpretations of its nonlogical expressions. But of course, one might then ask why it is that the sentence is true under any particular one of those interpretations. It is only at this point that propositions enter the explanation. We can say that 'It is raining or it is not raining' is true in a given model M_1 because the sentence expresses relative to M_1 the proposition that elephants are gray or elephants are not gray, and, as a matter of fact, elephants are gray; it is true in another model M_2 because the sentence expresses relative to M_2 the proposition that penguins can fly or penguins cannot fly, and, as a matter of fact, penguins cannot fly; and so on. Propositions can certainly play *this* explanatory role, even if they are as coarse-grained as sets of possible worlds.

What about the role propositions play in psychology? Could propositions be course-grained within theories where they are playing the role of intentional objects of belief and assertion? Following Hintikka (1962), we might analyze belief and assertion as relations that subjects bear to sets of possible worlds. Let's call the set of possible worlds compatible with x's beliefs x's *doxastic alternatives*; then for a to believe a set of possible worlds p is for p to be a subset of a's doxastic alternatives. Assertion could be analyzed in the same vein: If the set of possible worlds compatible with x's assertions are x's *assertive alternatives* then for a to assert a set of possible worlds p is for p to be a subset of a's assertive alternatives. And there is a straightforward way to turn these analyses into semantic clauses for belief ascriptions and indirect speech reports:

$[\![B_a\phi]\!]^w = \top$ iff $[\![\phi]\!]^{w'} = \top$ for all w′ compatible with what a believes in w.
$[\![A_a\phi]\!]^w = \top$ iff $[\![\phi]\!]^{w'} = \top$ for all w′ compatible with what a asserts in w.

But these analyses suffer from a well-known problem. They entail that everyone believes (asserts) everything necessitated by anything they believe (assert). This sounds obviously false: The mere fact that I believe that it is raining should not count as a reason for concluding that I believe all mathematical truths. This is called the problem of *logical omniscience*, which is misleading both because it's not really about logic (the set of worlds where there is water in my glass is a subset of the set of worlds where there is hydrogen in my glass, but the entailment is not logical) and because it's not really about knowledge (but rather, about anything analyzed as a relation between a subject and a set of worlds). Alas, we are stuck with the name.

In response to the problem of logical omniscience, it is standard to say that the analysis doesn't apply to belief as such, but to something like implicit commitment. (In the case of assertion, the relevant speech act might be the expression of such a commitment.) This, of course, is no help in our present context: Propositions are supposed to be what we believe and assert, not what we are implicitly committed to.

There are three main lines of response to the problem of logical omniscience. (We use belief to present them; they all generalize to assertion.) The first is concessive: If sets of possible worlds are too coarse-grained let's add impossible worlds to our ontology. Then we could explain why Jack might believe that 2 is a prime number without believing that 544 is divisible by 17 – an impossible world where 2 is a prime number and 544 is not divisible by 17 might be among Jack's doxastic alternatives. Hintikka (1975) elaborates such a view, and for those who favor logical solutions there are other alternatives; for a survey of the literature on this topic, see Halpern and Pucella (2007).

The second response gives up the intuitively compelling idea that beliefs are individuated by their objects. What Jack believes when he believes that 2 is a prime number is the very same thing as what he believes when he believes that 544 is divisible by 17, but those beliefs are nonetheless different. They are believed in different ways. This view could be coupled with a semantics for belief ascriptions that follows a suggestion in Carnap (1956), and is elaborated in slightly different ways in Lewis (1970b) and Cresswell (1985). The idea is that the semantic value of a 'that'-clause is an entity that is the result of taking the syntactic structure of the clause and replacing the lexical items on its terminal nodes with their intensions. This will guarantee that [\!['that 2 is a prime number']\!] ≠ [\!['that 544 is divisible by 17']\!], and so there is a possible world where 'Jack believes that 2 is a prime number' is true while 'Jack believes that 544 is divisible by 17' is false.

The third option is to bite the bullet: If Jack believes that 2 is a prime number he also believes that 544 is divisible by 17. The reason this does not seem to be the case has to do with the way we use language. In a normal context we interpret 'Jack believes that 544 is divisible by 17' metalinguistically, i.e. roughly as ascribing to Jack the belief that the referent of '544' is divisible by the referent of '17.' And of course there are possible worlds where this does not hold and some of them may well be among Jack's doxastic alternatives. A proposal along these lines was developed in Stalnaker (1991).

Unsurprisingly, all three of these proposals have their drawbacks. It is somewhat surprising, though, that the issues and arguments concerning them are similar to those Russellians used to deal with Frege's puzzle. Introducing impossible worlds is a way to make propositions more fine-grained while keeping the basic architecture of the account of propositions the same. This is analogous to what Russellians do when they introduce unarticulated constituents. Introducing structured meanings is a way of indicating in the semantics that the same proposition can be believed in different ways, which is another Russellian strategy. And, of course, the option of biting the bullet and explaining away recalcitrant intuitions by appeal to contextual effects on the interpretation of belief-ascriptions is also familiar from Russellian discussions.

5.4 Conclusion

Philosophers' concern with linguistic meaning owes much to their interest in a broader phenomenon – intentionality. Intentionality is a necessary condition for mentality and nonderivative nontransparent intentionality might be the very essence of the mind.

Intentional states and processes often have unreal objects – while we cannot talk *to* Santa Claus we can certainly talk *about* him. How can we make sense of this fact? There are three options: We can say that when we talk about Santa our talk is about a nonexistent person, about nobody, or about a nonperson. While none of these options can be conclusively ruled out, the first seems ontologically excessive and the second linguistically revisionary. The most popular view is the third. This option identifies intentional objects with abstract entities of some sort. It too has puzzling aspects but we have shown how the most pressing objections against it can be answered.

The most popular intentional objects are propositions – the objects of belief and assertion and the primary bearers of truth-value. We have argued that, contrary to widespread belief, the existence of propositions is no more certain than the existence of the intentional object of a search for Santa Claus. There is no question that in our theory of communication we should model what is believed and what is asserted, and it is quite plausible that whatever models we use for this will make their appearance in our semantic theories as well. But it is not clear that when we believe or assert something there must be a thing such that we are believing or asserting it.

Those who believe in propositions are still divided when it comes to their nature. None of the views are perfect. According to the Carnapian view, propositions are sets of possible worlds. The main disadvantage of this view is that it follows that there is only one necessary proposition. According to the Russellian view, propositions are complexes built from intentional objects (things we can think about). The main disadvantage of this view is that it entails that many propositions exist only temporarily and contingently. According to the Fregean view, propositions are complexes built from intentional contents (ways we can think about things). The main disadvantage of this view is that we are hazy about the constituents of Fregean propositions.

PART II

Philosophy of Pragmatics

6 Austin and Grice

6.1 Austin

John Langshaw Austin (lived 1911–1960) was the center of a group of philosophers at Oxford (including Gilbert Ryle, James Opie Urmson, Geoffrey James Warnock, and Peter Strawson) who felt that linguistic usage could be a guide to good philosophy. The circle of philosophy originating from this center is known as "ordinary language philosophy."

This school is a form of commonsense philosophy. Like David Hume and later empiricists, Austin and his colleagues were skeptical about the claims and methods of speculative metaphysicians. Unlike the empiricists, however, the ordinary language philosophers trusted everyday, unreflective forms of thought rather than science. They believed that linguistic usage, if it is examined with sensitivity and care, could shed light on these forms of thought.

6.1.1 Ordinary Language

The methods that Austin and his associates developed prefigured the techniques used by contemporary linguistic semanticists: in particular, they developed methods for constructing realistic linguistic examples designed to illuminate features of meaning. In Austin (1956–1957), for instance, we find the recommendation that, rather than theorizing about ethical matters, we should look carefully at the way we use language in situations where ethical concerns are in play. To illustrate the commonsense distinctions we make in this arena, he constructs a minimal pair involving the difference between 'by accident' and 'by mistake':

> You have a donkey, so have I, and they graze in the same field. The day comes when I conceive a dislike for mine. I go to shoot it, draw a bead on it, fire: the brute falls in its tracks. I inspect the victim, and find to my horror that it is your donkey. I appear on your doorstep with the remains and say – what? "I say, old sport, I'm awfully sorry, &c., I've shot your donkey by accident"? Or "by mistake"? Then again, I go to shoot my donkey as before, draw a bead on it, fire – but as I do so the beasts move, and to my horror yours falls. Again the scene on the doorstep – what do I say? "By mistake"? Or "by accident"? (Austin 1956–1957: 11)

Linguists generalize from examples, and use their generalizations to test theories. Austin and his associates were willing to draw cautious generalizations and to use them to make suggestions of philosophical interest, but – unlike linguists – were reluctant to commit themselves to frameworks or theories. The impact of their work was therefore largely negative, raising difficulties for those more willing to commit themselves to systematic philosophical views.

Towards the beginning of Austin (1956–1957), there is a brief and eloquent endorsement, intended for philosophers, of the virtues of paying attention to language. Austin feels, for one thing, that carefully examining what we would say under certain conditions is important because "words are our tools ... and we should use clean tools." For another, the distinctions incorporated in the meanings of the words we use reflect a long process of discovering what features and distinctions are worthwhile – these are likely to be better, Austin thinks, than what "we can think up in our armchairs of an afternoon" (Austin 1956–1957: 7–8).

This passage reveals another difference between Austin and contemporary semanticists. Although Austin cited *sentences* as examples, and often provided stage directions for them, his examples were intended to shed light on the meanings of *words*. Unlike many modern linguists, he avoided asking how these meanings contribute to the meanings of larger expressions.

How does Austin extract philosophically relevant material from his investigations of usage? We'll mention three instances: from these, it will be clear that the relevance to philosophy is not at all trivial: insights into usage can undermine entire philosophical positions.

1. Volition. A long-standing tradition, taken for granted by many philosophers, assumed that human actions can be accompanied by a kind of mental impetus, consisting of an act of will or volition. Acts that have this component are *voluntary*; those that do not are *involuntary*. Like most of his philosophical points, the criticism of this in Austin (1956–1957: 15–16) is indirect: he makes a linguistic observation, and leaves it to the reader to draw the philosophical conclusion.

He begins by saying that words have a typical or expected range of application and that qualifications are not only unneeded but anomalous in the normal cases. Consider someone who, preoccupied with her daily tasks and not thinking much about what she is doing, gets up from a chair. We would not say "She tried to get up from her chair" or "She managed to get up from her chair."

Imagining himself sitting in a chair in the normal way, Austin says, quite correctly and uncontroversially, "it will not do to say either that I sat in it intentionally or that I did not sit in it intentionally." He then goes on to imagine a quite normal, pre-bedtime incident in which he yawns, and says "I yawn, but do not yawn involuntarily (or voluntarily), nor yet deliberately.

To yawn in any such peculiar way is just not to yawn." Austin moves quietly here from *what we would say* about sitting in a chair to *matters of fact* about whether yawning before bedtime is voluntary. The transition is worth noting.

Elsewhere, in Austin (1956), Austin concludes from the fact that 'I can if I choose' is equivalent to 'I can' that this is not a causal conditional. Again, there is an implicit conclusion here, similar to the one that Gilbert Ryle draws explicitly: To think of the will as a mental faculty that somehow causes actions is to be misled by language. But, unlike Ryle, Austin declines to develop a philosophical position from this thought.

2. Sense-data. Phenomenalism is an epistemological position according to which the foundation of any empirical statement consists in "raw" evidence, or sense-data.

The main support for phenomenalism is the *argument from illusion*, which goes, roughly, as follows. Macbeth says that he sees a dagger, but there is in fact no dagger in front of him – he is under an illusion. While his visual experience is not of a real dagger, he characterizes it as an experience of seeing something. It is tempting to say that this something – the intentional object of Macbeth's illusory experience – must be a special sort of nonphysical object, available to him alone. If we call this object a *sense-datum*, we can conclude that at least sometimes visual experiences are experiences of sense-data.

But illusions and veridical perceptions are subjectively indistinguishable and they can even "fade into" each other. They must have something in common and it is natural to conclude that this something is the sense datum. In other words, when we see, we always see sense-data – although in veridical perception we see a physical object as well. But now it looks as if sense-data are the evidence for the conclusions we draw about the physical world; physical objects and their characteristics are not perceived, but are inferred from direct perception – perception of sense-data. We now have an infallible basis for our beliefs. Although the beliefs can be mistaken, we are never wrong about what we sense.

Phenomenalism is certainly far removed from colloquial ways of talking about perception. (Austin 1950: 124) invokes the ridiculous example of someone looking into the pantry, finding a loaf of bread, and saying "Hmm – all the signs of bread." In Austin (1962b) his criticism goes far deeper than this. Austin insists that the argument from illusion ignores two crucial distinctions marked by ordinary language. One is the distinction between how things *seem* and how they *look*. It we are aware of the fact that a stick is in water we would agree that it looks bent, but we might not say that it seems bent. The way the stick looks is a matter of experience, but it isn't really subjective – it can be captured in a drawing or a photograph. Not so for the way the stick seems – that is subjective, but it isn't really a matter of experience. Rather, it is a perceptual judgment. The difference is subtle but it helps Austin to resist the idea that we must posit sense-data to account for the contents of subjective experience. On the one hand, we have the contents of objective experience (the ways physical objects look to perceivers), and, on the other hand, we have the contents of subjective judgments (the ways the world is taken to be by perceivers).

But then, what does Macbeth see when it seems to him that he sees a dagger? Austin's view is that he does not see anything. Moreover, he isn't even subject to an *illusion* – he is a victim of a *delusion* or *hallucination*. This is the other distinction ignored by the sense-datum theorist. Illusions are misperceptions: their intentional objects are ordinary physical things and their intentional contents present them as being different from the way they really are. Delusions and hallucinations might be subjectively indistinguishable from illusions, but our language equips us with a distinction between the two sorts of experiences. This allows us to resist the claim that both must have an intentional object.

3. Knowledge. The standard view in philosophy has always been that knowledge is a certain kind of true belief: one that has some feature – being justified, being formed in a reliable way, being based on evidence, being caused by a corresponding fact, etc. – which elevates it above a lucky guess. Knowledge certainly *entails* belief but that does not mean it *is* a belief. (After all, knowledge also entails truth, and it isn't a kind of truth.) Austin argues that knowledge is an apprehension of reality that has more in common with perception than with belief.

The evidence, again, comes form ordinary language. Austin (1946) points out that knowledge and belief claims are questioned in very different ways. You might naturally ask *how* I know what I claim to know, but asking *why* I know does not count as a challenge. For belief, it's the other way around: 'Why do you believe this?' is the standard way to challenge a belief claim. But 'How do you believe this?' sounds odd. Moreover, if I'm unable to explain how I know something you might conclude that I *don't*, while if I can't say why I believe something you might conclude that I *shouldn't*. According to Austin, these differences in the use of 'know' and 'believe' are due to differences between knowledge and belief. We should have reasons for what we believe but not for what we know; we do have proofs (albeit ones we are often unable to state) for what we know but not for what we believe.

Austin (1946: 98–101) also drew an intriguing analogy between saying 'I promise' and saying 'I know.' First, he notes a parallel constraint: If you promise something you cannot add that you have no intention to do it, just as you cannot add that you are not certain after you have said you know it. Second, he observes that when you say 'I shall do *A*' you imply that you at least hope to do it (and if you have been "strictly brought up," that you fully intend to do it) and when you say '*S* is *P*' you imply that you believe that S is P (and, if you have been "strictly brought up," that you are quite sure S is P).

Finally, Austin thinks that when these claims are strengthened to 'I promise that I shall *A*' and 'I know that *S* is *P*' you take a "new plunge": You are not reporting your intention or belief but performing a social act authorizing others to do and say certain things.

6.1.2 Statements and Truth

For Frege, truth is a property of propositions (and, for him, these are the senses of sentences); for Tarski, it is a property of sentences (which he takes to belong to particular languages). Austin thought neither of these ideas conforms to our ordinary and natural characterization of things as true:

> For we never say 'The meaning (or sense) of this sentence (or of these words) is true': what we do say is what the judge or jury says, namely that 'The words taken in this sense, or if we assign to them such and such a meaning, or so interpreted or understood, are true.' Words and sentences are indeed said to be true, the former often, the latter rarely. But only in certain senses. Words as discussed by philologists, or by lexicographers, grammarians, linguists, phoneticians, printers, critics (stylistic or textual) and so on, are not true or false: they are wrongly formed, or ambiguous or defective or untranslatable or unpronounceable or mis-spelled or archaistic or corrupt or whatnot. Sentences in similar contexts are elliptic or involved or alliterative or ungrammatical. We may, however, genuinely say 'His closing words were very true' or 'The third sentence on page 5 of his speech is quite false': but here 'words' and 'sentence' refer, as is shown by the demonstratives (possessive pronouns, temporal verbs, definite descriptions, &c.), which in this usage consistently accompany them, to the words or sentence *as used by a certain person on a certain occasion*. That is, they refer (as does 'Many a true word spoken in jest') to *statements*. (Austin 1950: 119)

This passage is vintage Austin: Rather than addressing a philosophical issue directly, it addresses the proper use of English, making points that seem at best distantly related. But on reflection, there is a real insight here. Propositional and sentential truth are decontextualized, while ordinary truth does not seem to be. Austin is decades ahead of linguists and philosophers in identifying a host of devices – possessive pronouns, temporal verbs, definite descriptions – as "demonstratives," i.e. as expressions whose interpretation is linked via some overt or tacit indication to the context of utterance. To interpret 'His closing words were very true' we must figure out whose words are said to be true on what occasion; to interpret 'The third sentence on page 5 of his speech is quite false' we must know which article, memo, or book is at issue. This observation is then promoted to the bold and intriguing claim that truth can only be properly attributed to particular uses of linguistic expressions – to statements.

The claim is bold because, for instance, ⌜'Snow is white' is true⌝ seems to be a perfectly natural ascription of truth. About this, Austin would presumably say two things: that such a sentence would hardly ever be used outside of the context of a philosophy paper and that when it is used it might be understood to be a truncated version of the generic claim that the sentence 'Snow is white' is normally used to make a true statement.

'Statement' (or the currently more popular term 'assertion') is ambiguous. When someone makes a statement, (i) an act is performed (his stating of something) and (ii) the act will have an intentional object (what was stated). When Austin talks about statements, he usually means the former – the *speech act*. To avoid misunderstanding, we might call the object of the speech act a proposition. (Austin himself avoided the term 'proposition' – no doubt because its ordinary use does not match the way philosophers use it.)

It is *conventions* that make it possible to use words to make claims about the world. Austin's main insight is that we need two different types of conventions: *descriptive conventions* correlating linguistic expressions with types of things, and *demonstrative conventions* linking speech acts with particular things. Given these, he defines the truth of a statement as follows, (Austin, 1950: 122). "A statement is said to be true when the historic state of affairs to which it is correlated by the demonstrative conventions (the one to which it "refers") is of a type with which the sentence used in making it is correlated by the descriptive conventions."

Suppose I were to utter the sentence (6.1.1) thereby making a statement:

(6.1.1) The cat is on the mat.

According to Austin, the statement (6.1.1) is true when the state of affairs my statement is about is a cat-on-the-mat type state of affairs. What type of state of affairs is that? This is precisely what a semantic theory for English is supposed to tell us – it associates a set of states of affairs with every declarative sentence in the language. (We can think of the set of states of affairs as a representation of the truth-conditions of the sentence.) When is a statement about a particular state of affairs? That is what a theory of demonstrations might tell us – it identifies a state of affairs as the focus of attention at any given time during a conversation. (We might think of this as the topic the conversation is about at that time.) On this view, there is no truth without convention:

> A picture, a copy, a replica, a photograph – these are never true in so far as they are reproductions, produced by natural or mechanical means: a reproduction can be accurate or lifelike (true to the original), as a gramophone recording or a transcription may be, but not true (of) as a record of proceedings can be. In the same way a (natural) sign of something can be infallible or unreliable but only an (artificial) sign for something can be right or wrong. (Austin 1950: 126)

Austin cautiously agreed to classify his views on truth as a form of correspondence theory: it portrays truth as a relation between what is being stated (a proposition) and the thing that is being stated of (a state of affairs). But it is quite different from the classic correspondence theory of truth, according to which truth consists of a correlation between proposition and fact. In particular, on Austin's view, the correspondence is not a one-to-one relation: Propositions are typically true of many states of affairs.

Austin's views on truth raise two fundamental challenges to semantics. The first and most immediate of these is the suggestion that the truth or falsity of a declarative sentence without overt indexicality (such as the sentence 'The cat is on the mat') still depends on the context. Austin uses context-sensitivity of this recalcitrant sort to argue against the idea that truth-conditions can be seen as an important aspect of the meanings of a large class of sentences. The second challenge is this: If ascriptions of truth are acts of classification, perhaps these ascriptions are subjective and relative to the purposes of speakers. Austin highlights our reluctance to call the statements that might be made by uttering 'France is hexagonal', 'Belfast is north of London', or 'Beethoven was a drunkard' either true or false. Such statements simply are *rough*: On many occasions they are in fact neither true nor false.

Later, the first challenge was sharpened by the *radical contextualists*, who argue that no sentence (with the possible exception of ones drawn from pure mathematics or theoretical physics) has a context-independent meaning that determines its truth-conditions. The second, was strengthened by the *expressivists*, who claim that many expressions (including predicates of personal taste, slurs, epistemic modals) lack descriptive meaning and the sentences in which they occur are not truth-evaluable.

6.1.3 Speech Acts

Austin's most important contribution to the philosophy of language was his pioneering work on speech acts, culminating in Austin (1962a), which was published posthumously. The term 'speech act' is not his; it originates in Searle (1969), which refines, systematizes, extends, and modifies Austin's ideas.

Uttering meaningful words is, of course, an act. But the performance of this act normally constitutes another – an assertion, a query, a request, a bet, a warning, etc. These are speech acts.

Austin begins with a distinction between *constatives* and *performatives*. The basic idea is simple and can be illustrated with a version of Austin's own famous example:

(6.1.2) I named this ship *The Donald.*
(6.1.3) I name this ship *The Donald.*

You can ask me what I did yesterday, and, if I respond uttering (6.1.2), I describe what I did, thus making a constative utterance. But when I pronounced (6.1.3) yesterday, as I smashed a bottle against the side of the ship, I was not describing my action – I was performing it. My utterance *was* the naming – a performative utterance.

In some ways the example is misleading. It is tempting to think that Austin has in mind a semantic distinction: There is something about the combination of the first-person pronoun, the simple present, and the use of the verb 'name' that encodes the information that (6.1.3) is a sentence that can only be used in performative utterances. But this is not so, as the following examples show.

(6.1.4) If I name this ship *The Donald*, it should be painted orange.

(6.1.5) Here is my plan: I name this ship *The Donald*, and then we promptly sink it.

Example (6.1.3) can even be used unembedded to describe what one is doing: You might narrate the video footage of what you did earlier.

Performatives are a challenge for truth-conditional semantics for two reasons. The less important of these is that they provide a much more forceful illustration of Austin's claim that many utterances are not truth-evaluable than the constatives he mentions in his work on truth. It may be foolish or misplaced to ask whether a particular utterance of 'Belfast is north of London' was true – but it isn't entirely misguided and out of line. We might deal with such a question by saying "It depends" and asking for further clarification. On the other hand, to ask whether a ceremonial utterance of (6.1.3) is true is to betray a serious misunderstanding, calling for correction rather than clarification.

Defenders of truth-conditions can point to sentences like (6.1.4) and (6.1.5) to support the idea that we *should* assign truth-conditions to (6.1.3). How else are we to account for the fact that (6.1.3) and (6.1.4) entail that the ship should be painted orange, or that (6.1.3) and (6.1.5) entail that my plan is at least partially realized? Maybe we should just embrace the claim that if the naming was successful then (6.1.3) was true as uttered, even if the utterance itself was not the sort of thing that could be called true.

The deeper challenge performatives pose for truth-conditional semantics is that, even if we do decide to assign truth-conditions to sentences like (6.1.3), these truth-conditions seem detached from the ordinary use of these sentences. How is knowing the truth-conditions supposed to help the audience to understand what it is that I am doing when I utter this sentence?

It is natural here to question Austin's claim that performative utterances are doings *instead of* sayings. Perhaps, a successful performative is doing *by means of* saying. If so, perhaps performatives all work the same way: when successful, they bring it about that they are true. When I sincerely utter 'I apologize for being late', I make it the case that it is true that I apologized for being late, and, when I sincerely utter 'I promise that it won't happen again', I bring it about that it is true that I promised that it won't happen again, and, when you sincerely utter 'I bet you will be late next week again', you make it true that you bet I will be late next week again. Of course, I can also make the apology by saying "Sorry," or make the promise by saying

"This won't happen again," and you can make the bet by saying "Twenty bucks you will be late next week again." But in many cases context provides enough information for the hearer to fill in the details.

Lewis (1975) makes a similar proposal for permission and commands. When someone performs an act of permission, uttering 'You can jump', perhaps she is simply uttering a sentence that is true just in case the addressee jumps in some normatively accessible possible world. What makes the utterance performative is that there is an extra rule ensuring that when the sentence is addressed to someone over whom the speaker has authority, at least some world where the addressee jumps becomes normatively accessible from the actual one. Similarly, 'You must jump' is true if and only if in all possible worlds normatively accessible from the actual one, the addressee jumps, and when the sentence is addressed to someone over whom the speaker has authority an extra rule ensures that all normatively accessible worlds are ones where the addressee does jump. The extra rules make it explicit how the utterance changes the facts to guarantee its own truth.

Despite its promise, it is far from clear that this strategy can work in general. Greetings and insults are speech acts, and while it might be that in uttering 'How are you doing?' or 'You are an idiot', speakers make it the case that it is true that the addressee was greeted or insulted, the truth-conditions of the sentence seem irrelevant to what kind of greeting or insult is made. In Chapter 10 we will return to the topic of speech acts and their relationship to semantics.

6.2 Grice

Paul Grice (lived 1913–1988) was an associate of Austin's at Oxford, relocating in the later years of his career to the University of California at Berkeley.

Two strands in Grice's philosophy helped to launch the field of pragmatics as we know it today: his work on "non-natural meaning" or *speaker meaning*, and his later recognition and explanation of the phenomenon of *conversational implicature*.

6.2.1 Speaker Meaning

Grice published ideas about what we now call "speaker meaning" in Grice (1957). These ideas belong to a tradition beginning with Charles S. Peirce's theory of signs; see Atkin (2013). This train of thought is radically different from the one that derives from Frege and Tarski. Grice regards meaning as something that agents create by their communicating actions and that is rooted in their intentions and beliefs. He offers an analysis of speaker meaning that characterizes it as a peculiar sort of communicative intention. We will have more to say about this analysis later, in Sections 9.2.2 and 11.2.

When language is used to communicate – when, for instance, Hamlet says "Mother, you have my father much offended," there is a speaker meaning: Hamlet has a communicative intention to convey the thought that his mother has greatly offended his *biological* father. But the words he uses, assembled to make a sentence, have at least two literal meanings: that Hamlet's mother has greatly offended his biological father, and that she has greatly offended his stepfather. To understand Hamlet's intended meaning – the speaker meaning – Hamlet's mother must disambiguate the sentence and choose the correct literal meaning. (Grice calls this literal meaning the "meaning in the favored sense.")

Neither the Peircian tradition of speaker meaning nor the Tarskian tradition of compositionally derived sentence meaning gives a complete picture of what happens when speakers use language, because speakers are *both* publicizing their communicative intentions *and* exploiting the conventional meanings of linguistic items.

We need syntax and compositional semantic rules to explain how sentences are associated with one or more conventional linguistic meanings. We need an account of what the speaker means in order (at least) to characterize what it means for a disambiguation to "capture the correct meaning" of an utterance. But this is only part of the story: Speaker meaning and linguistic meaning can diverge, so that the identification of speaker meaning is not merely a matter of selecting one of the literal meanings of a sentence in a given context. Speakers can manage, when they use a sentence, to convey more than the literal content of the disambiguated sentence and, occasionally, something that is quite different. And they can manage to mean things without using language at all.

6.2.2 Conversationally Implicated Meaning

This brings us to the second strand of Grice's work, presented in his 1967 William James Lectures on the topic of "Logic and Conversation." This later work also had a striking impact on subsequent philosophy of language and on the emerging field of linguistic pragmatics. The entire lectures were only published many years later in Grice (1989b), but copies of a typescript were widely circulated earlier than this.

In part, Grice's William James Lectures are a carefully considered reaction – not to judgments about what we would say – but to the philosophical conclusions that Austin draws from them. Grice sets about in these lectures to attack the popular sentiment among ordinary language philosophers that logical theory was inappropriate and beside the point in accounting for the workings of natural languages. Perhaps, in the end, Grice (1989a) is not entirely successful in making a case for the strong thesis he wishes to defend: that standard logical theories of 'and', 'or', and 'if', if properly understood, furnish a correct account of their literal meanings in English. But along the way he makes many points of enduring importance and introduces a remarkably sophisticated and fruitful way of thinking about linguistic usage and the meaning of linguistic expressions. In retrospect, Grice's undermining of the prevailing idea that "formal" and "natural" languages were fundamentally different helped to remove the leading impediment to the employment of Tarski's methods in linguistic semantics.

In the first lecture, entitled "Prolegomena," Grice lists many cases where some philosophers (Grice calls them "A-philosophers," where 'A', presumably, stands for 'Austin-inspired') have drawn conclusions from linguistic usage. In each case, the A-philosopher intimates (as Grice points out, the conclusion is often not explicit) that, when it would be anomalous to use an expression, the anomalous utterance would then be untrue.

He illustrates the point with 'try'. When someone sets out in the normal way to accomplish something, succeeding routinely and without any difficulty, the question is this: Did that person try to do it? If a woman goes into a bank and effortlessly cashes a check, did she try to cash it?

A-philosophers would begin by agreeing that it would be peculiar and misleading to describe what she did by saying "She tried to cash a check." One A-philosopher might end with this fact about usage. Another A-philosopher might go further, insinuating that it is a philosophical error to suppose that an everyday action can be separated into two parts: a mental component of "trying" and a bodily realization of the action. Yet another A-philosopher might conclude that since the usage is anomalous, the claim that she tried to cash the check is false or perhaps neither true nor false.

Austin frequently emphasized that there are many different ways in which an utterance may be infelicitous. Grice departs from him and from A-philosophers in general, in no longer seeing truth as an exclusive characteristic of felicitous utterances; he thinks we should allow that utterances can be anomalous but nonetheless true. And he suggests tests for diagnosing when this happens.

Ordinarily, when we say that someone has implied something, we mean something quite different from what logicians have in mind. Logical implication is a matter of entailment – a sentence ϕ entails a sentence ψ if there is no way that ϕ can be true without ψ also being true. More technically, this means that every model that satisfies ϕ also satisfies ψ. But when someone implies something – when, for instance, an employee implies by what he says that he will show up for work, this is usually understood to be something that is *not* entailed.

Suppose the employee calls his boss early in the morning and says "Sorry, I got up late; I won't be on time for work." In saying this, the employee implies that he will show up for work and that he will not be on time because he got up late. Usually, he means both of these things, and his boss will understand that they are meant. But they are not entailed. If in fact the employee did wake up late, but this happened a thousand miles away in Las Vegas, what he said is true: He did wake up late, and he will not be at work at all.

Grice called things that are implied in this way, without being literally said, "conversational implicatures." He developed a theory of how they arise as side-effects of rational conversation and proposed tests for distinguishing them from entailments. For instance, Grice applies his *cancelability test* for conversational implicature to the check-cashing example.

We'll illustrate the test with an example that is slightly more elaborate than Grice's. Suppose the bank hires customer-satisfaction consultants to investigate the quality of their service and how to improve it. The consultants watch customer activity from a hidden location, identifying the goals of people entering the bank and tracking them to see how well they are served. The customers want many things: Some want to make deposits, some want to open accounts, some want to take out a loan, some want to cash a check. The consultants are watching a woman at the teller's window, unsure of what she's doing. As she leaves, one consultant turns to the other and says: "Did you catch what she was up to?" The other replies, "She was trying to cash a check. And she did cash it. Write her down as a satisfied customer." Somehow, the anomaly has disappeared. If the woman herself says to a friend after the transaction, "I was trying to cash a check," this would be deviant. Grice's point is that it hardly makes sense to say that what the woman said was untrue but that what the consultant said was true, when they said the same thing.

This example shows that the incongruity of the "suspect utterance" depends on the context. In some circumstances, to say "She was trying to cash a check" would be anomalous and misleading because of the false suggestion that she had some difficulty in doing so or was unlikely to succeed in cashing the check. In other circumstances, this utterance would not carry this suggestion.

Grice's "Prolegomenon" lecture points in two directions. It looks backward to the origins of Grice's pragmatic theory in his misgivings about basing philosophical conclusions on linguistic usage. And it looks forward to a systematic theory of how an utterance can be misleading, of how it can convey information that is not part of the literal meaning, of the meaning "in the favored sense."

In fact, the first appearance (in very rough form) of Grice's theory of conversational implicature is in Grice (1961), which defends phenomenalism against the criticisms of Austin and other ordinary language philosophers that were described in Section 6.1.1.

Investigating how a "suspect condition" can be associated with an utterance without being part of the literal meaning of an utterance leads Grice to develop an elaborate theory. The suspect conditions, Grice will say, are *conversationally implicated*, and this reflects a pervasive feature of conversational reasoning. The details are discussed in Chapter 9. Grice, then, followed a path from philosophy to linguistics. Misgivings that originally were distinctively philosophical led eventually to a theory of usage that is, if not entirely linguistic, at least an inquiry into rational discourse.

The rest of Grice (1989b) covers a lot of territory, with many digressions. But, by introducing the idea of conversational implicature, Grice makes a convincing case that speakers understand that utterances can be true even while they are inappropriate or somehow misleading. He believes that general principles of rationality can help to understand many conversational implicatures and that a theory of the phenomenon can be based on this idea. We will have much more to say about this in Chapter 9.

Beginning with doubts about some of the conclusions drawn by the ordinary language philosophers, Grice found himself investigating the nature of certain "implications" they had noticed. This led him to develop a pragmatic theory that is more linguistic than philosophical and, finally, to use the theory to draw new and important philosophical conclusions. This is a striking example of a project that interleaves philosophy and linguistics.

6.2.3 Grice and Austin

The largely autobiographical Grice (1986) is a valuable source of information about Grice's association with Austin. There, Grice speaks of Austin with great affection and respect. On page 59, he explains why he adopted a different approach to philosophy and language:

> These affectionate remembrances no doubt prompt the question why I should have turned away from his style of philosophy. Well, as I have already indicated, in a certain sense I never have turned away, in that I continue to believe that a more or less detailed study of the way we talk, in this or that region of discourse, is an indispensable foundation for much of the most fundamental kind of philosophizing … [That collecting linguistic data] is impossible without hypotheses set in at least embryonic theory, is a proposition which would, I suspect, have met general, though not universal assent; the trouble began when one asked, if one ever did ask, what sort of theory this underlying theory should be.

Grice goes on to say that his theorizing was guided and influenced by the work of Quine and Chomsky. This is somewhat surprising, because his philosophical views were strikingly different from Quine's, and specific influences from Chomsky or other linguistic theorists are indetectable in his published work. But apparently, it was not so much the content of Quine's and Chomsky's views that influenced Grice as the idea that rigorous theorizing about language was possible and could be rewarding.

6.3 Conclusion

Austin, in inviting philosophers to take seriously the facts about what we would say in specific circumstances, made a case for the importance of linguistic evidence for philosophers. But the (often implicit) consequences for philosophical theory were somewhat equivocal. In trying to sort out these consequences more thoroughly, Grice showed that we need to develop a linguistic theory. At each step, the interconnections between philosophy and linguistics become richer and more complex. The field of linguistic pragmatics owes a great deal to the work of these two Oxford philosophers.

7 Context and Content

7.1 Stage Directions and Senses

When languages are used (and this includes programming languages as well as natural languages), context is vitally important. The content of a sentence can change systematically with context, as in the following three examples.

(7.1.1) It's getting light outside. [*Very long pause*] It's totally dark outside.

(7.1.2) [*Jill speaks:*] I'm leaving! [*Jack speaks:*] I'm staying!

(7.1.3) [*Witness 1 points at Witness 2 and speaks:*] He's lying! [*Witness 1 then points at Witness 3 and speaks:*] He's telling the truth!

Each of these examples would be a contradiction if it were not for the stage directions, which indicate changes in the context.

Contextual effects such as these challenge the Fregean picture of meaning – and other pictures as well, perhaps. If each meaningful expression, and in particular each sentence, expresses a sense, and the sense, in connection with the facts, fixes a reference, then what is the sense of a sentence like (7.1.4)?

(7.1.4) I'm leaving.

Sentences are linguistic items and, as such, are common property of a linguistic community. When Jill uses (7.1.4), the sense of her utterance is that Jill is leaving. But if we say that the *sentence* (7.1.4) has the same sense as the sentence 'Jill is leaving', what are we to say about the same sentence if Jack appropriates it? In Jack's mouth, the sentence has quite a different sense, with entirely different truth conditions.

On the other hand, we can't say that the sense of (7.1.4) is that whoever is speaking is leaving, because of examples like these.

(7.1.5) [*Jack speaks:*] If Jill were speaking I would be leaving.

(7.1.6) [*Jack speaks:*] If Jill were speaking the speaker would be leaving.

(7.1.5) is false (because Jack is staying) and (7.1.6) is true (because Jill is leaving). But, assuming strong compositionality, if 'I am leaving' and 'The speaker is leaving' had the same sense, we would expect (7.1.5) and (7.1.6) to have the same sense and so to be alike in truth-value.

7.2 The Problem of Indexicals before 1967

Frege turned his attention to present tense and words like 'today', 'here', 'there', and 'I' in Frege (1956), first published in 1918. He acknowledges that these show that "the mere wording, which can be grasped by writing or the gramophone does not suffice for the expression of the thought" (1956: 296). He then attempts to explain how contextual effects fit into his framework. The relevant passages are difficult – experts continue to differ on their interpretation; see Perry (1977); Evans (1981); May (2006).

Contextual effects were, on the whole, neglected in logic and philosophy of language until 1940, when Bertrand Russell devoted a chapter of Russell (1940) to what we now call "indexicals." (This term was coined by the American philosopher Charles Sanders Peirce.) At the same time, other logically minded philosophers were becoming interested in these expressions: Russell mentions unpublished work of Hans Reichenbach on the same topic, which he says is similar to his own ideas. A few years later, in 1945–1955, work on the topic from several quite different points of view began to appear; most probably, these publications were delayed by the Second World War.

At this point, three quite different approaches began to emerge: (1) an analytic and metalinguistic approach, (2) a usage-based approach, more or less closely associated with the British ordinary language tradition, and (3) an attempt to fit indexicals into a logical framework, in the spirit of Tarski.

Russell (1940) undertakes a large-scale philosophical project: It is a quite general attempt to base an empiricist epistemology and metaphysics on logic and language. He imagines an ideal language that matches the world picture of phenomenalism – the view that immediate experiences are epistemologically fundamental, that all knowledge is ultimately justified by immediate sense impressions. In this language, proper names would refer to such experiences, located in space and time and endowed with phenomenal qualities. Russell devotes a chapter to indexicals, which he calls "egocentric words," because they might provide counterexamples to this theory of proper names.

Among the egocentric words, Russell includes 'this', 'that', 'I', 'you', 'here', 'then', 'past', 'present', 'future'. He asks whether anything that can be said could be said without the use of such terms. Russell takes this issue seriously: Recall that his theory of descriptions answers an analogous question for the words 'the' and 'a(n)'. He claims that eliminating these articles would not result in loss of expressive power in a language that can express universal quantification and identity. But in the case of egocentric words, he is more cautious, saying that it is not easy to tell whether they are dispensable in principle.

Declaring that 'this' is the paradigmatic and fundamental egocentric word, Russell notes some of its peculiar properties: (1) It doesn't seem to be definable without appeal to other egocentric words; (2) it doesn't involve any property of "thisness" (it has no descriptive content); (3) it seems to apply to different objects, but it isn't ambiguous; (4) it seems to have a single, constant meaning, but this meaning can't be its designation; (5) it is neither a proper name nor a description. These observations set the stage for the subsequent philosophical discussion; linguists would probably agree with all of them.

Russell then appeals to a relation between a language user and the object which 'this' denotes on a particular occasion. So far, this is very like contemporary accounts of indexicals, according to which they are related to a reference by a context of use. But Russell then explains the relation in terms of a direct causal chain between the object and a verbal response using 'this'. If, indicating a slice of cake, I say 'This is what I want', the piece of cake serves as a causal stimulus and is part of the causal complex that produces the linguistic response. This account cannot work in general: There are many examples in which there is no plausible causal link between the reference of 'this' and the speaker: Someone might say "the center of the earth is molten iron and this is not a place anyone will ever visit."

Still, most contemporaries might agree at least that the interpretation of indexicals will involve something like an occasion of use and that there is a close connection between salience on that occasion and the referent of 'this'. So the relational character of indexicals is not only striking but was stressed very early in the literature on the topic. It's somewhat surprising, then, that it seems to have caused so much subsequent confusion.

Hans Reichenbach was a thoroughgoing empiricist with strong interests in philosophy of science. The account of indexicals to which Russell was referring was published in Reichenbach (1947: 284–287). This book was written at a time when introductions to logic were not narrowly devoted to the technical side of logic but often served to develop and exhibit what we would now think of as a much wider philosophical program. Reichenbach conceives of logic as a very general discipline, devoted to the analysis of language. This conception would seem to include linguistics as well as logic, but Reichenbach's logic text shows little or no interest in most linguistic topics.

What he seems instead to have had in mind would now be classified as "philosophical logic," and has to do with how to use formal logic as a philosophical instrument. Chapter 7 of Reichenbach (1947), "Analysis of Conversational Language," is devoted to a miscellaneous collection of topics, including proper names and descriptions, tense, and certain indexicals. The analysis of tense in terms of speech point, event point, and reference point that occurs in this chapter is well known to linguists and often cited, though the token-reflexive account of indexicals is largely ignored, despite the fact that Reichenbach evidently thought of his account of tense as an application of the token-reflexive theory.

A *type* stands to a *token* as something general stands to an instantiation of it. Species are types, and individual animals are tokens. Letters are types, and inscriptions of letters are tokens. This terminology, as applied to language, seems to go back to Charles Sanders Peirce; see Peirce (1906: 506), It was later incorporated in the American semiotic tradition, which was positivist, behaviorist, and – on the linguistic side – structuralist. For background, see Morris (1946).

In philosophy, the distinction itself is invoked for many purposes, has metaphysical overtones, and raises philosophical problems: for a general discussion, see Bromberger (1992); Szabó (2005a); Wetzel (2014).

Reichenbach's idea is that, although the denotation of an indexical like first-person 'I' is variable and so can't be associated uniquely with the type – that is, with the pronoun as an item in the English lexicon – it can nevertheless be associated with its tokens. These would be specific sounds or inscriptions, occurring in specific locations in space and time. Reichenbach gives no linguistic reasons for employing tokens in the interpretation of indexicals. He simply says that it's easy to see that indexicals can be defined with reference to tokens: that 'I', for instance, "means the same as 'the person who utters this token'" (Reichenbach 1947: 284).

Reichenbach chose to invoke tokens in his analysis for philosophical reasons. Tokens seem to him like a good choice because they are tangible or audible things and so provide an empirical foundation for the analysis. The philosophical prejudice that is in play here is very similar to the one that leads Russell to think of more or less direct causal chains. Reichenbach recognizes that indexicals are relational, seeks for a relatum, finds it in the token that is produced when an utterance is made, and (stretching the pretheoretic notion of reference almost out of shape) imagines that indexicals actually refer to these tokens. When Jill says 'I am leaving', she is referring to the very token she produces in the act of speaking, and describing herself by means of this reference.

It is harder to find counterexamples to the token-reflexive analysis than to a stimulus-response theory like Russell's, but Hector-Neri Castañeda pointed out (Castañeda 1969) that whereas (7.2.7) is only contingently false, Reichenbach's analysis (7.2.8) of this sentence couldn't possibly be true. (Suppose that Jill hesitates, and then says "I am leaving." Noting her hesitation, Jack then remarks, truly, "She might not have said anything.")

(7.2.7) I am uttering nothing.
(7.2.8) The person uttering this token is uttering nothing.

In 1967, it may have been hard to tell whether examples like Castañeda's could be shrugged off; their theoretical importance became clearer ten years later, with Hans Kamp's logic of indexical 'now'.

Russell and Reichenbach represent the formal and logical approach to language, which, as we've seen, was accompanied at this time with a strong dose of logical positivism and empiricism, and which took for granted a profound distinction between formal and natural languages. Postwar philosophers at Oxford, inspired mainly by J. L. Austin, made a new start, scrapping the philosophical frameworks of the previous generation and approaching philosophical issues with the idea that fresh insights would emerge from listening carefully to linguistic usage. An approach to indexicality emerged from this work. Although Austin and Peter Strawson differed on many important points, what they had to say about indexicals was quite similar and influenced the way a subsequent generation of philosophers approached the issues.

The logical positivists approached indexicality as a syntactic problem – that is, as a problem having to do with words and sentences. This was partly a philosophical bias – linguistic tokens are solid, empirical items, and linguistic types are solid, empirical ways of classifying these items – but it was partly logical, as well. Metalinguistic techniques were flourishing at the time, due to the influence of logicians such as Hilbert, Gödel, and Tarski and philosophers such as Carnap; see, for instance, Carnap (1934); Kleene (1952). Logically minded philosophers readily adopted these techniques.

In Section 6.1.2, we discussed how Austin turned away from this, taking truth to apply primarily to statements. Both Austin and Peter Strawson lay great stress on the fact that the same statement can be made on different occasions and illustrate the point with indexicals. For instance, you and I make the same statement when I say 'It is mine' and, agreeing with me, you then say 'It is yours'.

Both philosophers begin with usage, or the utterance of a linguistic item. Under the right conditions, when someone utters certain words, a statement will be made and something will be stated: A content will be associated with the utterance. But for Austin, it is acts of stating – illocutionary act types – that are the primary bearer of truth or falsity.

The illocutionary act of stating something can serve much the same purposes as Reichenbach's linguistic tokens. In fact, if we confine ourselves to spoken language, the associated utterance will involve a linguistic token, which will be produced by an agent at a specific time and place. So if we wish to account for the meaning of first-person 'I', or any of Russell's "egocentric words," we get much the same result whether, like Reichenbach, we appeal to the token or we appeal to an utterance or to an illocutionary act.

Nevertheless, invoking the utterance is less artificial and more plausible. When someone points at a cat and says "The cat is on the mat," we can all agree that an illocutionary act occurred, though many of us may doubt that the speaker referred to a sentence token. In this respect, statements seem to provide a better basis for explaining indexicals than tokens. On the other hand, indexicals can occur in questions and imperatives. These are not statements, and now the token-reflexive story begins to look better, unless statements are replaced with the more general category of sentence uses. And it isn't clear how to reconcile either story with a compositional semantics for languages with indexicals. Nevertheless, some of the technical problems associated with Austin's theory of truth can be addressed. Barwise and Etchemendy (1987) provides a logically rigorous version of the Austinian approach that is strikingly different from Tarski's account.

Strawson (1952: 3, 212) makes points about indexicals that are similar to the ones he uses to criticize Russell in Strawson (1950), but here Strawson is more systematic in deploying the apparatus of statements: He says that sentences themselves can't stand in logical relations like inconsistency, but statements can. Strawson seems unwilling here to invoke propositions, relying instead on uses of sentences to make true or false statements. As Strawson recognizes, this raises problems for notions such as logical entailment: It must be wrong even to say that 'I am hungry' (to take Russell's example) entails 'I am hungry', because two uses of the sentence could be involved here, and the first use may make a true statement while the second makes a false one. To define entailment, Strawson (1952: 212) has to resort to counterfactual uses:

> If at some time, at some place, in the mouth of some speaker, the utterance of *S* results or would result in a true statement, then the utterance of *S′* at that time, at that place, in the mouth of that speaker, would result in a true statement.

A dedicated empiricist would have problems with such a definition. And mathematical logicians should have other concerns. Logical entailment is fundamental in logic, and – since mathematical logic is interested in proving theorems about logical systems, such as semantic completeness theorems – it is crucial to have a mathematically precise definition. If Strawson is right, and the presence of indexicals forces us to revise the usual definition of entailment as he suggests, it would also undermine mathematical logic. We do not find counterfactuals in rigorous mathematical theories, and – though counterfactuals about the statements of a hypothetical speaker may be acceptable in a philosophical analysis – they do not seem to provide a basis for doing rigorous mathematics. According to many philosophers, however, counterfactuals are important in the natural sciences.

Therefore it's somewhat surprising to find formally minded philosophers agreeing with Strawson about the impact on logic of indexicality. Yehoshua Bar-Hillel was heavily influenced by Carnap and was squarely in the formal language tradition. Nevertheless, in Bar-Hillel (1954), he finds Strawson's approach superior to Reichenbach's and agrees with Strawson that when indexicals influence the truth-value of a sentence we can't call the sentence true or false, though we can say that a token of the sentence in a context of utterance, or a statement, has a truth-value.

Although the notion of a context of utterance seems to originate with Bar-Hillel, he didn't seem to appreciate its significance. Like Strawson, he thinks that indexical phenomena challenge the logical idea that entailment is a relation between indexical sentences. In Bar-Hillel (1963: 88–89), he says "Logical relations hold primarily between statements, derivatively between the non-indexical (context-dependent) sentences that can be used to make them, but not at all, in any nontrivial sense, between indexical sentences (whereas with respect to formalized language-systems, logical relations hold ... between ... the sentences)."

In the 1950s, then, although formal and informal language enthusiasts diverged on many points, they agreed that natural languages and the artificial languages of logicians differed in fundamental respects, citing indexicals as an important source of these differences. The striking title of Montague (1970) – "English as a Formal Language" – was not only addressed to linguists but to philosophers and logicians such as Strawson and Bar-Hillel. Montague regarded the differences between natural languages and the formal languages of logicians as a challenge to be overcome. In this as well as other papers, he presents a technical solution to the problem of how to define entailment for sentences containing indexicals.

However, the idea behind this solution did not originate with Montague. It was mentioned much earlier in Quine (1940: 43). There (unhappily, conflating ambiguity and indexicality), Quine says:

> In general, the trustworthiness of logical analysis and inference depends on our not giving one and the same expression different interpretations in the course of reasoning ... Insofar as the interpretation of ambiguous expressions depends on circumstances of the argument as a whole – speaker, hearer, scene, date, and underlying problem and purpose – the fallacy of equivocation is not to be feared ... [the interpretation of terms of ambiguous reference] is indifferent to the logical soundness of the argument, provided merely that it stays the same throughout the space of the argument.

And twelve years later, commenting on Strawson's claim that formal logic can't deal with indexicals, Quine (1953a: 441) repeats the point, adding that "Formal logic would be a pretty idle luxury if its applicability were limited thus severely."

Here we find the crucial insight that informs the approach to indexicals in contemporary formal semantics: In evaluating inferences (and so, in characterizing inferences) indexicals are not problematic *as long as their interpretation is held fixed.*

But it was E. J. Lemmon who made the point most clearly. Speaking in Lemmon (1966: 228) of the flaw in the reasoning of theorists like Strawson, Lemmon says:

> It is as though one were to say that we cannot speak of a gate as having a definite colour, because the same gate may have different colours at different times. The proper consequence ... is that, if we wish to speak of sentences as true or false, then this talk should be *relative to context of utterance,* just as talk of the colour of a gate is relative to date.

Lemmon has an excellent point: It does seem as if those who concluded that indexical sentences can't be true or false because their truth-values depend on context either didn't see the availability of the relational account of truth or thought it wasn't appropriate. If indeed truth is a relation between a context and a sentence, this actually *legitimizes* speaking of a sentence as true or false, as long as it's clear what context we have in mind. Lemmon's clear thinking about the issues doesn't stop there: His article is still a valuable resource for readers who want to sort out the differences between statements and propositions.

7.3 Variables and Open Formulas

The language of first-order logic (FOL) exhibits two kinds of simple referring expressions: *constants* and *free variables*. (In the rest of this section, where we talk simply about "variables," we mean free variables.) In this respect, FOL reproduces ordinary mathematical usage: In Equation (7.3.9), for instance,

(7.3.9) $x^2 - x = 6$

'6' is a constant – a fixed name of a certain number – and 'x' is a variable.

Informally and very inaccurately, people often say that variables refer to arbitrary or unknown numbers. But it's much better to say that when we use a variable like 'x' in a formula, we're interested in the pattern of behavior as 'x' takes on various temporary and provisional references. Like demonstrative pronouns, variables serve as shiftable pointers to their references. As the pointer shifts, the content of linguistic phrases containing these demonstrative items will change, and, if the phrase is a sentence, its truth-value may change. For instance, when we say that Equation (7.3.9) has two roots, −2 and 3, we mean that it is true when and only when 'x' points at −2 or 3. And to know that this is so, we need to know the entire pattern of truth-values of the formula for values of 'x'.

Mathematicians often explicitly set and reset the values of variables: For instance, you might write an equation like (7.3.9) on the blackboard and say "Let x be 3" and then, after some calculations, say "Now, let x be −2." There is a close parallel between this mathematical usage and demonstrative uses of pronouns. When a salesman compares two automobiles by pointing at one of them and using 'it' to describe its features, then pointing at the other and repurposing the same pronoun, 'it', for the second automobile, he is manipulating the context to make it clear how the reference shifts: Pointing performs the same task as the mathematician's more explicit "let x be."

Philosophers like Bar-Hillel coupled indexicals with other supposedly suspicious and problematic features, like vagueness, that were thought to distinguish natural from formal languages. One can only do this, however, by refusing to notice that free variables – which do occur in many formal languages – are in fact indexicals, at least in formal languages that, like programming languages, are actually used for practical purposes. Neglecting this fact was made easier by a strong tradition in logic of treating free variables and "open formulas" as second-class citizens.

We explained in Section 1.2.3 how Tarski was forced to assign temporary values to variables in order to produce a compositional definition of generalized truth, or satisfaction, but that he refused to give first-class status to open formulas. Tarski's prejudice seems to be similar to the idea of Strawson's (that relational truth can't really be truth) that was criticized so effectively by Lemmon. As we will see, overcoming this prejudice was crucial to securing a viable semantic theory of indexicals. This story begins with temporal indexicals, and especially 'now'.

7.4 Indexicals and Time

Lemmon (1966) is not often cited, but the approach he advocates there – treating the truth-in-a-context of a sentence as primary – is vitally important. This approach can, and usually does, recruit propositions, as well as sentences. To illustrate how sentences, contexts, propositions, and truth-values work according to this picture, we repeat Example (7.1.1):

(7.4.10) It's getting light outside. [*Very long pause*] It's totally dark outside.

Suppose the first sentence is uttered at a time t_1 in the morning, and the second is uttered at a time t_2 after sunset on the same day. And suppose they are both uttered in the same place so that we needn't worry about the indexicality of 'outside'.

The first sentence expresses the proposition that it's getting light outside at t_1, and (say) is true because it's getting light outside at t_1. The second expresses the proposition that it's getting dark outside at t_2 and (say) is true because it's getting dark outside at t_2. Both sentences are true in the contexts that anchor them but are true for very different reasons, because the associated propositions are different. For those who do not feel that statements are needed to explain propositions, this approach eliminates the need to appeal to statements in accounting for indexicals – or indeed, for any semantic purpose. Few contemporary philosophers of language still invoke statements in this way.

Philosophers like Lemmon left the notion of a context of utterance informal, but that too began to change – and again the epicenter of the change is southern California. At the same time, with the discovery that indexicals raise peculiarly logical problems, the topic takes on a logical flavor.

Scott (1970), written and privately distributed in 1968, emerged from conversations among Dana Scott and others, including Richard Montague and David Kaplan, and contains a number of recommendations concerning how to think about modal logic. Discussing indexicality, and especially tense, Scott begins with possible worlds. The values of expressions in a modal logic depend in general on possible worlds. We can think of these values as occupying points in a one-dimensional space consisting of the worlds. (The logical role of possible worlds, as a parameter of satisfaction, is very similar to the role of variable assignments in first-order logic. But the similarities weren't exploited until the development of "correspondence theory." See Blackburn et al. (2001: Chapter 2.)

Scott recommends making this space many-dimensional, with worlds as only one coordinate. Among the other coordinates he suggests are *time*, *place*, and *agent*. This appears to mark the beginning of the theories of indexicals that later emerged at UCLA in the writings of Richard Montague, Hans Kamp, David Kaplan, David Lewis, and Max Cresswell.

Scott's idea implies that indexical contexts should be modeled as points in a many-dimensional space – that is, as n-tuples of objects. The dimensions correspond to the type of the object – whether, for instance, it is a time, a place, a world, or an individual of some kind. On the one hand, Scott creates a bundle of values designed to provide exactly what is required to interpret whatever indexicals occur in the language. On the other, when a sentence is uttered in a real situation, a much more robust notion of context is available. We then have all the salient features of the real situation in which the utterance is made. Usually, a speaker is readily identifiable in such a situation, and so the right "anemic" context or n-tuple will have that speaker as the value of 'I'.

There is no fundamental conflict here; the thin-blooded notion is useful for logical purposes, and the full-blooded one (which is closer to the ordinary, pretheoretical notion of context) is useful for pragmatic purposes. We will have more to say about this in Chapter 8.

By the late 1960s, logical theories of tense were well developed, with most of the credit going to Arthur Prior; see Prior (1967). Prior treated ⟨Fut⟩ ("true at some future time") and ⟨Past⟩ ("true at some past time") as modal operators, and his satisfaction conditions were relativized to times, as in the following condition for future tense:

(7.4.11) $[\![\langle\text{Fut}\rangle\, \phi]\!]^{t} = \top$ if and only if for some $t' > t$, $[\![\phi]\!]^{t'} = \top$.

Combining the semantic theories of two relatively well understood phenomena can lead to unexpected problems because of unanticipated interactions between the two. Hans Kamp seems to have been the first who discovered that this happens when indexicals are combined with tense operators. In Prior (1968b), which deals with the same difficulty, Prior mentions an unpublished document circulated in 1967 by Hans Kamp, presenting a problem that arises in logics containing an indexical [Now] operator as well as tense operators. The same document also seems to have been mentioned in early versions of Montague (1968). A later version of Kamp's early manuscript was published as Kamp (1971).

The difficulty that Kamp noticed is this: In standard tense and modal logics, if a formula ϕ is a logical theorem, then so is $\Box\phi$, where $\Box$ is any necessity operator. In tense logic, these would include the operators [Fut] (true at all future times) and [Past] (true in all past times). A theorem of a logical system must be valid; in possible worlds semantics this means that it must be true at every world of any model. But if ϕ is true at all worlds, then $\Box\phi$ will be true at any world – and, of course, the same goes for times.

However, there will be counterexamples to this rule when the indexical 'now' ("true at the present moment") is added to a language with tense and modal operators. For instance, (7.4.12) seems to be a logical truth. It can't be false, because at any time t, [Now]ϕ is true at t if and only if ϕ is true at t.

(7.4.12) $[\text{Now}]\phi \rightarrow \phi$

On the other hand, (7.4.13) should *not* be a logical truth.

(7.4.13) [Fut]([Now]It's-Raining → It's-Raining)

Example (7.4.13) amounts to this: For any future time t', if it's raining now then it's raining at t' – that is, if it's raining now it will always be raining. This is presumably false. The problem is that on the one hand (7.4.13) is a necessitation of a logical truth but is false, while on the other hand the necessitation rule is valid.

This dilemma is neither artificial nor superficial. In fact, it raises fundamental issues about the interaction of indexicals with tense operators. And the problem arises with conditionals and modal operators as well.

Kamp (1971) diagnoses the difficulty by noticing that, in a tense logic with indexicals, formulas are evaluated using a single temporal parameter: $[\![\phi]\!]^t$ is the truth-value of the formula ϕ at time t. However, this temporal parameter is playing two distinct roles: (1) It fixes the interpretation of indexical operators like [Now] and (2) it serves as a variable parameter in interpreting tenses. For instance, the time parameter is shifted in interpreting a sentence like [Fut]'It's-Raining': $[\![$[Fut]'It's-Raining'$]\!]^t = \top$ if and only if $[\![$'It's-Raining'$]\!]^{t'} = \top$ for some $t' > t$. Truth of a formula at t is checked by referring to the truth of a simpler formula at other times t'.

Kamp's solution is to separate these two roles: He develops a *double indexing* approach. Instead of interpreting a temporal formula ϕ at one time only, $[\![\phi]\!]^t$, he interprets such a formula at two times, $[\![\phi]\!]^{t_1,t_2}$. The first time, t_1, is the *indexical anchor* and fixes the interpretation of temporal indexicals. The second time, t_2, is a *tense shifter* which is shifted systematically in determining the satisfaction conditions of temporal modalities. When a temporal modality such as ⟨Fut⟩ is interpreted at $\langle t_1, t_2\rangle$, t_1 is held constant (because 'now' is fixed by the time of utterance) and t_2 is shifted. When [Now]ϕ is interpreted at $\langle t_1, t_2\rangle$, we forget t_2 and reset the tense shifter to t_1.

This produces the following semantic rules for future tense and 'now'.

(7.4.14) $[\![[\text{Now}]\phi]\!]^{t_1,t_2} = \top$ if and only if $[\![\phi]\!]^{t_1,t_1} = \top$.
(7.4.15) $[\![\langle\text{Fut}\rangle\phi]\!]^{t_1,t_2} = \top$ if and only if for some $t'_2 > t_2$, $[\![\phi]\!]^{t_1,t'_2} = \top$.

When an utterance is made, both the indexical anchor and the tense shifter are equal to the time of the utterance: If a pair of times $\langle t_1, t_2\rangle$

can be associated with an utterance, t_1 and t_2 must be the same. (Here, Kamp is making assumptions about genre – there are uses of 'now' involving "historical present" when the anchor is not the same as the time of the utterance.) This explains why (7.4.12) is logically true; it is true at every index $\langle t, t\rangle$; every utterance of 'If it's raining now, then it's raining' is true. Example (7.4.13), on the other hand, is invalid: in determining whether [Fut]([Now]'It's-Raining' → 'It's-Raining') is true at $\langle t, t\rangle$, we must evaluate [Now]'It's-Raining' → 'It's-Raining' at indices $\langle t, t'\rangle$ where t' is in the future: $t < t'$. Although the semantic evaluation of a formula always begins with a pair or identical times, the process of interpreting the formula can take us to nonidentical pairs.

Kamp's ideas introduce a new and somewhat startling logical category of *contingent logical truths*. This category arises quite naturally out of the interaction of indexicals and modalities, although logicians and philosophers had assumed up to this time that logical truths were paradigmatic necessities. (In fact, the logical positivists had claimed that all necessities either were logical truths or could be obtained from logical truths by expanding them using definitions.) This assumption seems to have been a leading cause of the confusion one finds in the earlier work on indexicals.

7.5 Generalizing Indexical Semantics

Richard Montague mentions indexicals in several of his papers devoted to the formalization of natural languages. But his most extensive discussion of the topic is in Montague (1968). Evidently Montague regarded that paper as a definitive statement of his views on pragmatics, but in fact most of it is devoted to what we would now call formal semantics. The pragmatic component consists in explicitly relativizing semantic values to contexts of use and so is confined to indexical expressions. What Montague says about indexicals is based on Scott (1970) and Kamp's double indexing. He models contexts of utterance as indices or points of reference, noting that what is incorporated in these indices will depend on the indexical constructions afforded by the language: For instance, a language equipped with first- and second-person pronouns and proximal and distal demonstratives would require indices with four components. Kamp's use of a pair of temporal indices can then be generalized; only certain indices can correspond to utterances, and relativizing validity to these indices can account for certain "pragmatic validities": Montague's example is the Cartesian 'I exist'.

A later paper, Kaplan (1978), generalizes Kamp's double indexing idea to include 'I' and 'here', and modals, as well as tenses. At the same time, Kaplan introduces a distinction between *character* and *content* that helps to illuminate the difference between anchoring parameters and the time- and world-shifting parameters used in the satisfaction clauses for tense and modal operators.

In a language with ⟨Fut⟩ , [Must], 'I', 'here', and 'now', a sentence ϕ must be interpreted relative to anchoring parameters p, l, and t, (where p is a person, l a location, and t a time), and shifting parameters w and t. Bundling the anchors together in a unit $c = \langle p, l, t\rangle$, we evaluate formulas with respect to c, w, and t: $[\![\phi]\!]^{c,w,t}$ is the truth-value of ϕ relative to context c, world w and time t.

An *index* is a triple $\langle c, w, t_2\rangle$ consisting of a context c, a world w, and a time t_2. An index $\langle\langle p, l, t_1\rangle, w, t_2\rangle$ is *initial* if $t_1 = t_2$ and p is located at l in w, and logical truths are formulas that are true at all initial indices. This adds new constraints to Kamp's idea of a combination of parameters at which an utterance could occur: In particular, it requires that in the world of utterance, the speaker is spatially located at the position designated by 'here' and temporally located at the position designated by 'now'. (Of course, there are narrative contexts where spatial location is dislocated from the utterance location.)

This theory makes (7.5.16) a logical truth, without at the same time making (7.5.17) logically valid. (This example is more felicitous if [Must], the operator associated with the modal 'must', is interpreted causally rather than epistemically. So it would be better to read the operator as "must have been.")

(7.5.16) I am here now.
(7.5.17) [Must]I am here now.

The essential point is that a valid formula is one that is true at all initial indices. It follows directly from the definition of initiality that (7.5.16) is true at all such indices. On the other hand, (7.5.17) fails to be valid because the semantic rule for [Must] requires evaluating 'I am here now' at other worlds w′ than the initial world w. This involves indices $\langle\langle p, l, t_1\rangle, w', t_2\rangle$ – which in general will not be initial.

In a language without indexicals but with modalities or other constructions interpreted in terms of possible worlds, it takes two steps to get from a sentence ϕ to a truth-value. (1) Compositional semantic rules assign ϕ a function from possible worlds to truth-values: This is the *intension* $[\![\phi]\!]$ of ϕ. (2) Having fixed a possible world w, we obtain the truth-value of ϕ in w by applying the function $[\![\phi]\!]$ to the world w. This truth-value is $[\![\phi]\!]^{w}$.

Kaplan elaborates this interpretive process by proposing a *three*-stage procedure for languages with indexicals. (1) Compositional semantics assigns ϕ a *character* $[\![\phi]\!]$, which is a function from contexts to *contents*. In technical presentations, Kaplan identifies these contents with intensions, so that $[\![\phi]\!]$ will be a function which inputs contexts and outputs intensions; elsewhere, and especially when he is being more philosophical, he identifies the contents of declarative sentences with Russellian propositions. (2) We obtain a content from a character by applying the character to a context. If we simplify by ignoring times and places, and consider only the indexical 'I', then a context will simply be a person, and the character [['I am awake']] of 'I am awake' will be a function that inputs a person p and outputs a content. Because Kaplan thinks of contents as functions that input possible worlds, and in particular of sentential contents as functions that output truth-values, this content will be a function $[\![$'I am awake'$]\!]^p$ from possible worlds to truth-values. Finally, this content (3) will return $\top$ when it is applied to w if p is awake in w, and $\bot$ if p is not awake in w.

An issue about how to package the interpretation of indexical expressions separates Kaplan and Stalnaker on the one hand from David Lewis on the other. Lewis (1981) argues against Kaplan's breakdown of the transition from sentences-in-context to truth-values, proposing a framework that goes directly from a bundle of parameters and a sentence to a truth-value. For Stalnaker's reasons for preferring Kaplan's approach, see Stalnaker (2014: 19–24).

7.6 Looking Further

Kaplan's work has been very influential in philosophical circles, because – besides solving technical problems – it provides a framework for thinking about meaning-in-context and its relation to truth and reference. This framework in fact is an elegant and attractive alternative to the Fregean picture – for which indexicals are problematic. (But see Forbes [1989] for a detailed discussion of how Frege's approach might be modified to accommodate indexicals, as well as a comparison to Kaplan's approach.)

Kaplan's framework, however, is not entirely without problems. It relies on possible worlds semantics and on the idea that sentence contents are sets of possible worlds – although it may be relatively easy to separate Kaplan's approach from the idea that intensions are based on possible worlds. Also a large subsequent literature wrestles with whether in fact the framework can account correctly for the interactions of indexicals with propositional attitudes.

This issue is closely related to the puzzle about being "lost in time" that was raised in Prior (1959) and that is discussed in Section 4.5.2. But it concentrates on the first-person pronoun. Here, the analog of being lost in time is radical amnesia – ignorance of one's own identity. This train of thought begins with work of Hector-Neri Castañeda's such as Castañeda (1966). Subsequent work on this topic includes Richard (1990); Perry (1993); Stalnaker (2008); Cappelen and Dever (2013).

'I', 'here', and 'now', of course, are not the only expressions whose content depends systematically on contextual parameters. The expressions 'right-left', 'foreign', 'beyond', 'come', and 'go' depend in various ways on orientation.

Mainly because of Lewis (1979c) and other writings of Lewis on this topic, philosophers have become excited about the possibility that attributing indexicality to words like 'know' and 'flat' would provide a new line of attack on some of the difficult and perennial problems of philosophy, and especially on problems having to do with skepticism. The word 'know', for instance, might depend on a set of presumed alternatives and 'flat' on presumed standards of precision. Unfortunately, the linguistic evidence about these cases is not nearly as clearcut as the evidence about, say, 'I'. For more about these issues, see Preyer and Peter (2005); Rysiew (2016). The philosophical debate on the context-sensitivity of knowledge is inconclusive; see, for instance, DeRose (1992); Preyer and Peter (2005).

The idea of relating adjectives to standards of precision has been in play since Kamp (1975), which shows how to use this idea to derive the interpretation of comparative adjectives from their absolute forms. For more recent work on the topic, see Kennedy (2007). Scalar approaches to precision have become more popular than Kamp's qualitative approach, but this issue hasn't been settled definitively. A more serious difficulty is that any theory along these lines soon runs into paradoxes of vagueness, and especially the sorites paradox. We will return to this topic in Chapter 13.

Some philosophers have argued that most adjectives and perhaps many other lexical items are indexicals. For example, in some contexts 'red' can mean "red on the outside" and in others "red on the inside." In such cases, if they are indeed to be treated like indexicals, it is much more difficult to package the relevant contexts. For more on this topic, see Szabó (2001); Stanley (2005); Hawthorne (2007); Rothschild and Segal (2009). This work adds an essential element to the problem by concentrating on formalizing the reasoning that is involved in lexical interpretation. See, for instance, Pustejovsky (1995); Pustejovsky and Boguraev (1997).

Many uses of context are less related to indexicals than to the evolving informational situation of a conversation. Stalnaker (2014: Chapter 1) provides an extended explanation and comparison of these two conceptions of context. We will discuss this issue in Section 9.1.

7.7 Conclusion

To take a sentence out of context is not only to risk misinterpretation – to risk distortion of the content – but often to lose the content entirely. If you find an unsigned, undated, unexpected note on your windshield saying simply "I'll be back in an hour," you have a sentence, but hardly any idea of what to make of it, of what the content is.

The interrelationship of context and content emerged in the first half of the twentieth century as a surprisingly perplexing challenge for theorists. Workable solutions to the problem were slow to emerge, but by 1970 an approach had appeared that could be adapted to the purposes of formal semantics. As usual, these developments left a residue of unresolved philosophical problems.

8 Common Ground and Conversational Update

8.1 Conversation and Cooperative Activity

Paul Grice's groundbreaking work in pragmatics was entitled "Logic and *Conversation*" rather than "Logic and *Language*." Examples of implicature – the central topic of Grice's lectures – can be found in lectures, radio broadcasts, newspapers, and novels. But Grice assumes that face-to-face conversational exchange is the central source of the pragmatic effects in which he is interested. Subsequent work in pragmatics follows Grice in assuming the primacy of conversation. Even though many linguists, and almost all philosophers, use constructed examples in their pragmatic work, rather than annotated transcriptions of actual conversations, their examples are usually intended to illustrate conversational phenomena.

There are many differences between conversation and other genres; for instance, participants in a face-to-face conversation have access to intonational cues, body language, and facial expressions. But perhaps the most important difference is that conversation is a coordinated group activity.

People have a general sense of how these activities should work, whether or not language is involved. Two children building a snowman have a shared sense of what goal is to be achieved and what the stages in achieving it should be like. They understand that a large snowball is needed at first, perhaps too large for either child to manage alone. So when one child starts to roll a snowball, the other may begin to help. The other tasks may be performed separately or together, without a word being said – but relying, of course, on close monitoring of collaborators' activities and on a general willingness to be helpful when it's perceived that help is required.

In this example, the activity is structured by a quite definite shared sense of the desired outcome, but cooperative activity can take place when the goal is less definite. Improvisational music, for instance, and unstructured children's play are like this.

Generalizing a bit, we can see that (1) cooperative group activity needn't involve language, but (2) does involve expectations about what sorts of contributions are appropriate, (3) may be more or less regimented, and (4) often requires constant monitoring of collaborators' actions and intentions. Of course, conversation makes use of language – but aside from this, it may not differ strikingly from other collaborative activities.

Occasionally, people wonder how conversation can be fundamentally cooperative, when sometimes the purposes of the participants can conflict, as in political debates or cross-examination of a hostile witness. This worry can be addressed by appealing to competitive games. Even though the purposes of two chess players conflict, the players must cooperate at least to the extent of following the rules of the game. Similarly, for hostile conversations to be conversations at all, the participants need at least to try to coordinate on what is communicated: When a speaker uses a referring expression, for instance, it needs to be worded so that the hearer can work out the intended referent. And when at a given stage of the conversation an issue is salient, relevant, and unresolved, speakers are normally expected to address that issue.

Actually, conversation isn't quite like chess. Pragmatic theorists agree that conversation is rule governed, but the rules are not entirely explicit and can be manipulated in hostile conversations. Here is a plausible rule, that applies quite generally: If a direct question is asked at one turn in a conversation, the next turn should be an attempt to answer or at least to address the question. But this rule is regularly violated in hostile interviews.

In adversarial interactions, it may not be easy to draw the line between conversation and the animal noises that accompany intimidation displays or fighting. But this doesn't mean that conversation has no rules – it means only that the rules aren't regimented and explicit, so they can break down gradually before adversarial conversations descend into inarticulate hostility. And without assuming that there are genuine rules of conversation, it is hard to see how we could have a theory of conversation at all.

Grice sought to ground his explanations of conversational implicature in the rationality of the participants and on what he called "the cooperative principle" (Grice 1989b: 26):

> Make your conversation such as is required, at the stage at which it occurs, by the accepted purpose or direction of the talk exchange in which you are engaged.

This very general and value-laden formulation gives no specific guidance about what would be appropriate at any given point in a conversation. Except for "adjacency pairs" like 'Thank you / You're welcome', there will be many sensible ways to continue a conversation, and the boundaries between cooperative and uncooperative responses may be difficult to draw.

However, Grice is introducing a new and important thought when he speaks of "the accepted purpose of the talk exchange." In Grice (1957), he seeks to explain meaning in terms of the purposes of the speaker; this is the notion of "speaker meaning" that we mentioned in Section 6.2. Also, of course, at any stage of the conversation, the participants will have their private purposes and beliefs. But it is quite different to speak of *the conversation itself* as having its own purposes. If conversations have a purpose, it must be some purpose peculiar to this activity that the participants share. Although Grice doesn't develop this idea, others have suggested that in this peculiar sense we may also speak of shared conversational goals and assumptions. This leads us to the idea of *common ground.*

8.2 The Idea of Common Ground

When an agent plans, and acts on those plans, the process will be shaped by intentions, desires, and beliefs. These attitudes, of course, change as the activity evolves. A desire may create a goal, an intention may then emerge from planning to achieve that goal, and both the desire and the intention will vanish when the plan is successfully executed.

These agent attitudes can be modeled in various ways. Decision theory uses numerical values – it treats beliefs, for instance, as subjective probabilities, which are real numbers, and it uses probabilities and numerical utilities to calculate an optimal action; see, for instance, Jeffrey (1983). Some artificial intelligence theorists model attitudes using possible worlds and use planning and scheduling algorithms to arrive at actions. See, for instance, Wooldridge (2000).

Agents bring their attitudes to group activities. Each player in a poker game will have her own beliefs, desires, and intentions, and these will evolve as the game is played. Group participation requires more complex beliefs: beliefs having to do with other agents' intentions and beliefs. Nevertheless, it's natural to characterize group activities in terms of the evolving attitudes and actions of the individual members of the group. Philosophers disagree about whether all group actions and perhaps even all group attitudes can be explained as constellations of individual actions and attitudes; see Tuomela (1995). But the reductionist attitude towards group actions and attitudes remains standard, in philosophy and pragmatics.

In some games, we can see an element that to some extent transcends patterns of individual attitudes. If some cards in a poker game are dealt face up and others face down, the game relies on a difference between *public* and *private* information. Every player is aware of public information and aware that every player is aware of it. (This is actually the beginning of a series that in principle can be continued indefinitely. We will return to this complication below, in Section 8.6.)

It might be useful to think of the public information that is available at each stage of a conversation as a "cognitive state" of the conversation itself, different from the states of the participants. Similarly, it often makes sense to ascribe goals to a conversation. But what actually drives a conversation, of course, is what the participants *think* is public. And sometimes – for instance, when a misunderstanding has occurred – participants may differ in their opinions as to what is public. Most pragmatic theorists would acknowledge the difference between what is public and what a participant considers to be public, but often it can be safely ignored. Participants in a conversation use a variety of mechanisms to maintain "grounding," or identity between what is public and what is perceived to be public. The idea is that conversations are usually well run, and in a well-managed conversation there will be no such difference. And when there are such misunderstandings, they are likely to be insignificant.

There is plenty of evidence that speakers track the difference between what is public and what is private in the course of a conversation. Consider the following exchange.

LADY CROOM What have you done to me!
NOAKES Everything is satisfactory, I assure you. A little behind, to be sure, but my dam will be repaired within the month—
LADY CROOM (*Banging on the table*)
Hush!
(*In the silence, the steam engine thumps in the distance.*)
Can you hear, Mr. Noakes?
NOAKES (*Pleased and proud*) The improved Newcomen steam pump – the only one in England!
LADY CROOM That is what I object to. If everybody had his own I would bear my portion of the agony without complaint. But to have been singled out by the only Newcomen steam engine in England, this is hard sir, this is not to be borne.
(Stoppard 1993: 85)

In this conversation between Lady Croom and her landscaper, the phrasing is shaped by what is taken to be public at each stage of the conversation. Some of these things are in the environment (and this is one reason why stage directions are necessary to make the dialog intelligible to readers), and some are established in the course of the conversation. At the very beginning, the noise of the steam pump is there in the background, but – because it's a familiar background sound – Lady Croom can't assume that Noakes is aware of it, the sound isn't public. So it would be far less felicitous for her to say "Can you hear?" without first calling for silence. Similarly, Noakes shouldn't say "The improved Newcomen steam pump" without some assurance that the reference will be salient – presumably, this is accomplished by the pause. And Lady Croom can't say "his own" (using an ellipsis rather than "his own Newcomen steam pump") until Noakes has publicly established Newcomen steam pumps as the topic.

Making something in the environment salient to facilitate referring to it and using something that the conversation has just made public and salient to support ellipsis are ways in which conversants recognize the difference between what is public and what is not. In fact, the inventory of ways in which public information can influence conversation is rather large and open-ended. But it begins with presupposition.

8.3 Common Ground and Presupposition

Before 1966, many authors alluded to presupposition, but it would be hard to find anything like an explicit theory. Frege, for instance, not only recognized the phenomenon, but, in Frege (1960b) and Frege (1956), as well as in writings that remained unpublished during his lifetime, he had insightful things to say about how to classify the linguistic phenomena. (See Horn [2007] for an extended discussion of Frege's views on this topic.)

Peter Strawson criticized Russell's theory of definite descriptions by claiming, among other things, in Strawson (1950) that by uttering the sentence 'The present king of France is bald' the speaker does not say, but *presupposes* that there is a king of France. (This was mentioned in Section 0.2.) The theories that emerged about fifteen years later concentrate on the existential presuppositions associated with definite descriptions, and it is only somewhat later than this, when linguists became interested in presupposition, that it was generally realized how widespread the phenomenon is.

Van Fraassen (1966) provides a logical formulation of the distinction on which Strawson's criticism depends. The idea behind van Fraassen's *semantic* account of presupposition is this:

(8.3.1) ϕ presupposes ψ if (1) ψ is true in all models in which ϕ is true and (2) ψ is true in all models in which ϕ is false.

In classical logic, every sentence is true or false, so this definition would be trivial: Anything that is presupposed would have to be a logical truth, true in all models. So van Fraassen's proposal involves a modification of classical logic to allow the possibility of *truth-value gaps*. Because it is based on patterns of truth and falsity, this is a semantic theory. We will not go into the details of van Fraassen's theory, which involves *supervaluations*. Supervaluations are no longer favored as accounts of presupposition because nowadays pragmatic theories are widely used. But supervaluations are useful for other purposes, such as vagueness.

Shortly later, in 1967, Paul Grice delivered the William James Lectures at Harvard University, on the topic of "Logic and Conversation." Although he doesn't have much to say in those lectures about presupposition, the materials for a theory are there, and this theory is developed in some detail in Grice (1981). There, he uses his ideas about implicature to defend Russell's theory of definite descriptions.

Grice's strategy in the William James Lectures assumes that what logic textbooks tell us about truth conditions is correct. He assumes, for instance, that every sentence is true or false and that 'If ϕ then ψ' is equivalent to 'Not-ϕ or ψ'. He seeks to explain apparent differences between these truth conditions and usage by deploying pragmatic machinery. For definite descriptions, this would suggest (1) assuming that Russell's theory provides the correct truth conditions and (2) invoking conversational implicature to explain apparent presuppositions. This account of presupposition is *pragmatic* because, unlike van Fraassen's theory, it depends on the thoughts that normally accompany the utterance of a sentence rather than on its truth or falsity.

In fact, for pragmatic accounts of presupposition, it is speakers as they are uttering sentences rather than sentences themselves that are the fundamental bearers of presuppositions. So if a pragmatic theorist wishes to account for the presuppositions of sentences and for words that are "presupposition triggers," she must somehow define this in terms of features of speakers and their utterances, at the time of utterance. One way to do this proceeds in two steps. First, generalize (8.3.1) by exchanging logical implication for a relation of *support*:

(8.3.2) ϕ presupposes ψ if ϕ supports ψ and Not-ϕ supports ψ.

Second, explain "supports" as a general inferential relation that could be logical implication but could also be characterized pragmatically. Grice's idea, for instance, is that ϕ supports ψ if either ϕ logically implies ψ, or an utterance of ϕ would usually implicate ψ. (Many contemporary pragmatic theorists would not agree with this treatment of presupposition in terms of a "support" relation, but it provides a useful way of comparing van Fraassen's semantic with Grice's pragmatic theory.)

We can illustrate Grice's idea with Russell's original example, (8.3.3):

(8.3.3) The present king of France is bald.

Russell's analysis, according to Grice, treats (8.3.3) as a conjunction of three components:

(8.3.4) There is a king of France.

(8.3.5) There is at most one king of France.

(8.3.6) Every king of France is bald.

For Russell, all three of these are logically implied by (8.3.3), so – assuming that logical implication is a form of Support – they are all supported by (8.3.3). However, Grice suggests that someone will usually utter (8.3.3) only when (8.3.4) and (8.3.5) are "common knowledge," or at least are considered to be noncontroversial. (Grice seems to use "common ground" for what is either common knowledge or uncontroversial. Here, the issue of *accommodation* becomes relevant, although Grice himself has little to say about it. For more about accommodation, see Section 8.7.)

The contrast between at-issue and not-at-issue content was created later to characterize the contrast that Grice has in mind here. As far as we know, the first appearance of the distinction is in Karttunen and Peters (1979); Potts (2005) and Simons et al. (2010) provide later accounts. The idea is that the speaker expects that if an objection is raised to the package consisting of (8.3.4), (8.3.5), and (8.3.4), it will be directed at (8.3.4).

When someone denies (8.3.3) (saying, for instance, "The king of France isn't bald"), Grice wants to say that normally the denial will be taken to apply only to the at-issue component of Russell's package. This, he tentatively suggests, could provide the basis for claiming that utterances of the negation of (8.3.3) implicate the existential component, (8.3.4), in many contexts. (Grice does not have much to say about the uniqueness component. This is more challenging because one also has to add an account of implicitly restricted quantification so that, for instance, 'the book' can amount to 'the item among the things now salient in the conversation that is a book'.)

Presupposition is approached in a different way by Robert Stalnaker in a series of papers beginning in 1970, invoking the idea of common ground. Stalnaker is a pragmatic theorist: Instead of working with the presuppositions of sentences, Stalnaker (1970) begins with the attitudes of the participants in a conversation. Pragmatic presupposition, for Stalnaker, is a relation between a conversational agent and her idea of the common ground. At any stage of a conversation, a participant presupposes what she takes for granted and supposes other participants in the conversation to take for granted. (Actually, this formulation will need to be modified; what is really wanted here is mutuality. See Section 8.6.)

Stalnaker's *speaker presuppositions* can be represented by a set of possible worlds: the possibilities that a speaker treats as open. In the simplest, and perhaps the most usual case, speakers believe their presuppositions. But Stalnaker allows cases in which speakers presuppose things they don't believe. (This can happen, for instance, when people indulge in pretense for conversational purposes.) In general, any merely private belief – something the speaker doesn't suppose to be shared by the audience – can't be a presupposition.

Stalnaker's next two papers, Stalnaker (1973, 1975), take into account the linguistic work on the topic that by then had begun to appear: especially, Kiparsky and Kiparsky (1971); Karttunen (1973, 1974). This early linguistic work treats presupposition as a relation between sentences and propositions. For instance, the following pair of sentences are not interchangeable:

(8.3.7) Agnes agreed to the proposal before Bert did.
(8.3.8) Bert agreed to the proposal, and Alice agreed to it before Bert did.

They share the content that a certain event occurred before another, but (8.3.8) claims explicitly what (8.3.7) presupposes – that Bert agreed to the proposal. A denial of (8.3.7) – "No, Alice didn't agree to the proposal before Bert did" – still carries the thought that Bert agreed. But if Bert didn't agree at all, this can be a reason to deny (8.3.8).

So Sentence (8.3.7) is related to *two* propositions: the proffered content and the accompanying thought that Bert actually agreed.

Karttunen (1974) proposed a pragmatic account of sentence presupposition along the following lines: It is felicitous to utter (8.3.7) only in contexts where it's accepted that Bert agreed to the proposal. Stalnaker (1973) entertains a similar idea. But later, Stalnaker (2002) has second thoughts about this, mainly because of difficulties having to do with accommodation.

(Accommodation does raise genuine problems; see Section 8.7.) This leads Stalnaker to doubt the theoretical value of sentence presupposition. But still later, he admits that 'even', at least, calls for an explanation that depends somehow on semantics; see Stalnaker (2014: 75–77), as well as Simons (2005). Contemporary pragmatic theorists generally agree that different examples of presupposition may call for different sorts of explanations, though they may differ on which cases are best classified as pragmatic and which as semantic.

Common ground is an important part of any account of presupposition. It is central, of course, for Stalnaker. Later work of Karttunen's (in collaboration with Stanley Peters), Karttunen and Peters (1975, 1979), explicitly relates presupposition to common ground, which they characterize as what all participants are justified in taking for granted.

Also at about this time Herbert H. Clark, a psycholinguist, began a train of thought that, within a few years, led him to recognize the centrality of common ground; see Haviland and Clark (1974). In the introduction to Clark (1992), Clark describes the interests that grew out of these works as follows: (1) common ground, (2) collaborative processes (and how collaboration can go beyond Gricean cooperation), (3) audience design (how utterances are tailored to their audiences), and (4) coordination of meaning. This inventory gives a good idea of how the idea of common ground suggests research topics that can be investigated in psychology laboratories.

Clark and Marshall (1981) concentrates on the conditions under which definite reference is appropriate, showing that these depend on the common ground. The paper makes a vivid and convincing case for the importance of *mutuality* for the common ground, and relates mutuality to arbitrary iterations of agent attitudes. Supposing that *knowledge* is the relevant attitude, Clark and Marshall show that for something to be mutual for a group, not only must the members of the group know it, but know that they all know it, and know that they all know that they all know it – and they even manage to construct examples that support further iterations. We return to this important theoretical point in Section 8.6. A later paper, Clark and Carlson (1982), identifies discourse context with common ground and continues to stress its mutuality. For a more recent survey of the ideas, see Clark (2005).

Stalnaker's conception of common ground moved in a similar direction. Like Clark, Stalnaker (2002) stresses the importance of mutuality for conversational common ground. The chief difference between Stalnaker and Clark is the attitude that is taken to be mutual. For Clark, it is knowledge. For Stalnaker, although in many cases it can be identified with belief, more accurately it is what is accepted for the sake of the conversation. Stalnaker points out, for instance, that conversants don't always challenge a contribution to the conversation that they don't believe – for instance, they may wish to be polite or choose not to interrupt the flow of conversation. Likewise, Stalnaker thinks that in idle conversation some mutual beliefs may be suspended – allowing, for instance, platitudes about the weather to masquerade as new information.

8.4 Accommodation

David Lewis, in Lewis (1979c), was the first author to single out the phenomenon of accommodation for systematic discussion. But others had noticed it earlier, in connection with indirect speech acts and presupposition – see Searle (1975a); Karttunen (1974). The term itself, and an appreciation of how general the phenomenon is, is due to Lewis, who characterizes it as follows.

> If at time t something is said that requires component s_a of conversational score to have a value in range r if what is said is to be true, or otherwise acceptable, and if s_a does not have a value in the range r just before t, and if such-and-such further conditions hold, then at t the score-component takes some value in the range r.

The standard example of presupposition accommodation illustrates the phenomenon. Suppose it's a conversational requirement on simple definite NP-s like 'my sister' that they are not to be used unless the existence of their reference is part of the common ground. But clearly, I can felicitously utter (8.4.9) even when my audience has no idea whether I have a sister.

(8.4.9) Sorry, I can't have lunch with you; I have to meet my sister at the airport.

Pragmatic theorists can see these examples as a source of consternation. Natural and plausible pragmatic rules – rules that were actually proposed in the literature – turn out to have commonplace counterexamples. Lewis, on the other hand, is delighted to show how widespread accommodation is, without any hint that he sees it as problematic; in fact, he appeals to accommodation in his arguments against skepticism and to defend his view that performatives are true or false. Evidently, there can be a wide range of reactions to the phenomenon.

Thomason (1990) argues that accommodation in fact does raise methodological problems for pragmatic theory but that nevertheless we have to live with the phenomenon. Accommodation is a form of cooperation and is not confined to language: We accommodate others when we recognize the plans on which they are acting and automatically act to remove perceived obstacles. Plan recognition is a fundamental part of language understanding. So, if there were pragmatic rules involving the common ground, we would have to expect apparent violations of these rules to occur through accommodation. If we wish to have pragmatic rules at all, their status will be peculiar: They must not only be defeasible but routinely violated.

Commentators on Grice haven't noticed that his theory of implicature also has this peculiarity. He believes that conversational implicatures are often induced by "flouting" a conversational maxim. So his maxims, too, must be anomalous social rules that are often, if not routinely, violated to achieve an effect.

This does place pragmatic theory in a peculiar position. The challenge to pragmatic theorists is to find sound methods of justifying rules, when these rules are commonly "observed in the breach."

The status of accommodation has often been debated, and many different views are in play. For further references, see Zeevat (1992); Beaver (1999); Stalnaker (2002); Simons (2003); Thomason et al. (2006); von Fintel (2008).

8.5 Conversational Score and Ingredients of Common Ground

The common ground must record information that is overtly conveyed and accepted in a conversation. But it should obviously do more than this. For instance, if something perspicuous happens while the parties are talking to one another – to use an example of Stalnaker's, if a goat happens to show up – this will normally become part of the common ground. As well as introducing the accommodation phenomenon, Lewis (1979c) provided an extensive inventory of components of the common ground, suggesting the following six ingredients.

1. Presuppositions. Here, Lewis follows Stalnaker, differing from him only in stressing the importance of accommodation. (See Section 8.4.)

2. Permission. In an earlier paper, Lewis (1979b), Lewis borrowed from deontic logic the idea that what is permissible for an agent is a set of worlds – those in which the agent acts according to its obligations – and considers how verbal instructions from an authority can change this boundary. He now adds to that thought the idea that the set of permissible worlds is part of the common ground. Although Lewis doesn't think of it this way and has a quite different account of illocutionary force, there are the makings here of a theory of mood: Declarative sentences shift the presuppositions, while imperatives and permissions shift the obligations. A more modern and more sophisticated account of imperative mood along these lines can be found in Portner (2004).

3. Definite Descriptions. Lewis wishes to account not only for complex descriptions like 'the cat over there in the corner' but for simple ones like 'the cat'. Unqualified definite descriptions clearly raise problems for Russell's theory, and Lewis chooses to invoke *salience* in addressing these difficulties, as well as a "domain of discourse," which he does not say much about. The idea is that the salience of an object can be changed: by the environment, or by speakers who point the object out or mention it. So 'the cat' will refer at a given stage of a conversation to the most salient cat at that stage. (Lewis does not address what happens if there is no most salient cat and so elects to set aside the problem of how to provide a general and unified theory of definite NPs.)

Salience, then, becomes another component of the common ground, in the form of designated elements of the domain of discourse.

4. Coming and Going. 'Come' and 'go' are linked to a perspective or reference point and indicate motion toward or away from that location. For details, Lewis refers to an earlier work, Fillmore (1997). This reference point can be shifted by discourse acts, and again accommodation is in play. So a location – which may be different from the actual location of the speaker – is added to the list of common ground elements.

5. Vagueness. In Lewis (1970b), Lewis proposed to address vagueness by means of an idea identical to van Fraassen's theory of supervaluations. (Lewis doesn't mention van Fraassen or cite van Fraassen (1966), and seems to have arrived at the idea independently.) This application of supervaluations seems to have occurred to several people – Kamp (1975) and Fine (1975) are examples – and is still one of the most popular approaches to vagueness. See Section 13.3.

Lewis called a way of making a vague term precise a "delineation." For instance, a delineation for 'cool' would be a precise temperature separating things that are cool from things that aren't. The idea, then, is that what is genuinely true is what is true on all acceptable delineations. Since different standards of precision are appropriate in different contexts (where a standard of precision is a – possibly rank-ordered – set of delineations), this is yet another component of the common ground.

6. Relative Modality. Due mainly to Angelika Kratzer (who had interacted with Lewis at an early stage in her work), linguists have accepted the idea that modals (and especially 'can' and 'must') involve a *modal base* and a *preference ordering*; see Portner (2009); Kratzer (2012). The modal base determines a background set of possible worlds – the alternatives, epistemic or practical, that are considered open. The preference ordering ranks these alternatives appropriately (either epistemically, in terms of something like likelihood, or practically, in terms of something like value or utility). Lewis argues that the modal base is part of the common ground and can be changed by contributions to the conversation, adding that – as in the case of vagueness – it is easier to expand the set of possibilities than to contract it, so that the skeptic has a rhetorical edge.

At this point, a strategy for approaching the philosophical problems of skepticism begins to emerge in Lewis' paper. He argues that whoever wishes to propose higher standards of precision has a rhetorical edge in a conversation and attributes whatever plausibility skeptical arguments may have to this rhetorical advantage. Unsurprisingly, it is this strategy that many philosophers found most interesting about Lewis (1979c); it has generated an extensive literature. See Preyer and Peter (2005); DeRose (2009); Egan and Weatherson (2011).

The inventory of common ground elements is open-ended; it isn't hard to think of more items.

In particular, if assertions aim to enlarge what is presupposed, and commands aim to enlarge what is obligatory, it makes sense to propose that questions aim to add a prominent and current item to a list of *questions under discussion*. This important idea seems to have originated with Roberts (1996) and now is widely used in linguistic and computational accounts of discourse; see, for instance, Ginzberg (2012).

But why stop at these three types of illocutionary acts? (See Section 10.1 for a discussion of this term, due to J. L. Austin.) We could say, for instance, that the common ground contains a list of public agent commitments to courses of action and that promising aims to add a commitment to this list or that the common ground contains information about instances of gratitude, condemnation, and sympathy and that thanking, blaming, and condoling add appropriately to this list. If we do this systematically, the common ground could easily become implausibly inflated – and yet this idea provides an attractive account of illocutionary acts. Without accepted tests and criteria for inclusion in common ground, it is difficult to be sure where common-ground inflation should end.

Lewis' idea that salience serves to fix the reference of simple definite NPs like 'the cat' is plausible – but what sort of things are salient? If we say that salience attaches to perceptible individuals, we lack a sufficiently general theory of the phenomenon: Mental episodes, qualities, fictional characters, and in fact just about anything that can be talked about can be salient.

Salient references can be introduced in many ways: by the environment, by pointing, and by complex definite as well as indefinite noun phrases, as in:

(8.5.10) A cat lives upstairs from me. Last night the cat kept me awake all night.

Examples of this sort, of course, are the inspiration of Discourse Representation Theory; see Kamp and Reyle (1993). And Strawson mentioned the phenomenon much earlier in Strawson (1959: 18), classifying the phenomenon as "identification relative to a story."

This raises a further problem: Sentences like (8.5.10) are meaningful even if the upstairs neighbor has no cat; he likes to play cat videos with loud soundtracks. In that case, (8.5.10) is meaningful, even though it is false. And 'the cat' doesn't refer here to any individual at all, so we can't appeal to a salient individual to explain why the two-sentence discourse is meaningful.

Lauri Kartunnen introduced the thought that an indefinite noun phrase can introduce a *discourse referent*, which can then be coreferenced to later noun phrases, and especially to pronouns and simple definite descriptions; see Karttunen (1971). This idea was incorporated in later, more elaborate theories of coreferentiality: Hans Kamp's Discourse Representation Theory and Irene Heim's File Change Semantics; see Heim (1988); Kamp and Reyle (1993).

It's tempting and natural to say that discourse referents should be part of the common ground. However, discourse referents are syntactic – or perhaps mental – items and don't map in any simple way to actual individuals. We can iterate knowledge attributions, saying that Ann knows that Bob knows that Charlie is sick. But we can't iterate acquaintance, such as Ann's acquaintance with Charlie. For this and other reasons, mutuality for individuals is less clear than mutuality for propositions. Explicating this notion is even more perplexing when it becomes a matter of the mutuality of discourse referents.

8.6 Mutuality

As we saw, early theorists who recognized the common ground acknowledged that it is mutual but differed as to how to characterize this mutuality. The simplest idea would be that what is mutual is believed by all participants. A more sophisticated idea is that it is what not only is believed by all participants but is believed by all participants to be believed by all participants. This is the beginning of a series that can in principle be carried on indefinitely.

Introducing some terminology, let's say that ϕ is (strictly) mutual for an attitude $[B]$ and group $\mathcal{G}$ if for all finite series $a_1, a_2, \ldots, a_n$ of members of $\mathcal{G}$, $[B, a_1][B, a_2] \ldots [B, a_n]\phi$ is true. For instance, if $\mathcal{G} = \{a, b\}$ and the attitude is knowledge, ϕ is mutual for $\mathcal{G}$ if a knows ϕ, b knows ϕ, a knows that b knows ϕ, a knows that a knows ϕ, b knows that a knows ϕ, b knows that b knows ϕ, a knows that b knows that a knows ϕ, etc. (Some authors call this *common knowledge*. We use the term 'mutual' because sometimes 'common knowledge' merely refers to what every member of a group knows.)

Herbert Clark and Catherine Marshall devised an increasingly complex series of scenarios intended to show that – at least until they become too difficult to process – these iterations are required by the conversational common ground. Here are the fourth and fifth (and last) of their examples.

> **Version 4.** On Wednesday morning Ann and Bob read the early edition of the newspaper, and they discuss the fact that it says that *A Day at the Races* is showing that night at the Roxy. Later, Ann sees the late edition, notes that the movie has been corrected to *Monkey Business*, and marks it with her blue pencil. Still later, as Ann watches without Bob knowing it, he picks up the late edition, and sees Ann's pencil mark. That afternoon, Ann sees Bob and asks, "Have you ever seen the movie showing at the Roxy tonight?"
>
> **Version 5.** On Wednesday morning Ann and Bob read the early edition of the newspaper and discuss the fact that it says that *A Day at the Races* is playing that night at the Roxy. Later, Bob sees the late edition, notices the correction of the movie to *Monkey Business*, and circles it with his red pen. Later, Ann picks up the newspaper, sees the correction, and recognizes Bob's red pen mark. Bob happens to see her notice the correction

> and his red pen mark. In the mirror Ann sees Bob watch all this, but realizes that Bob hasn't seen that she has noticed him. Later that day, Ann sees Bob and asks, "Have you ever seen the movie showing at the Roxy tonight?" (Clark and Marshall 1981: 12–13)

In the fourth example, Ann knows that Bob knows what movie is playing, but Bob does not know that Ann knows that Bob knows this. In the fifth example, Ann knows that Bob knows that Ann knows what movie is playing, but Bob doesn't know that Ann knows that Bob knows that Ann knows this. The conclusion is that in both of these cases, support is lacking for the definite reference in the final question.

Many people agree with these judgments although the agreement is somewhat shaky due to the difficulty of reasoning with even moderately long knowledge iterations. But theoretical considerations from many different areas – bargaining theory, game theory, formal models of communication and multiagent systems, and the requirements of social and linguistic conventions – independently support the need for mutuality. For bargaining, see Aumann (1976). For game theory, see Geanakopolos (1994) and Aumann (1995). For communication and multiagent systems, see Fagin et al. (1995). For conventions, see Lewis (1969). (This last work did much to familiarize philosophers with mutual attitudes. But Lewis himself didn't stress – perhaps didn't even mention – mutuality in connection with common ground.)

For any attitude that the members of a group may have, we can define the mutual-in-$\mathcal{G}$ version of this attitude. But what is the special attitude that is associated with the conversational common ground? Although people often speak of knowledge or belief, Stalnaker shows convincingly in Stalnaker (1970) that the right attitude is acceptance for the sake of a conversation, an ad hoc attitude that the participants construct to track what has been established in the course of a conversation. But what attitudes should the participants take away for themselves from a conversation? Should the participants believe what has been said, or find it probable? Do they know it?

Conversations can be evidence for what people believe, find probable, and know. In that respect, they are not importantly different from other sources of evidence. In deciding, for instance, whether we should believe what someone has said – regardless of whether we accept it for purposes of the conversation – we will want to take into account the speaker's veracity, the plausibility of what was said, and similar considerations.

8.7 Grounding and Dynamics of Common Ground

To be at all useful in conversation – some would say, for coordinated, successful conversation to be possible at all – common ground has to be initialized and maintained by the participants.

Clark and Schober (1989) distinguish *communal* and *personal* factors in the initial common ground. We can reach reliable conclusions about the information that can be expected to be shared by certain groups of people; for instance, we can assume that someone who lives nearby will be familiar with the local geography. Personal factors have to do with people with whom we have interacted. To these factors, we can add *environmental* influences. These originate in the mutually perceivable environment of the group.

Modifying a suggestion that was made in Thomason (1998), an agent A will be able to initialize an ad hoc common ground for a conversation with another agent B if A's beliefs are labeled with social features that indicate who can be supposed to share them. For instance, there might be a category of beliefs that A obtained as a graduate student in physics and that any graduate student in physics might be expected to obtain. If A knows that B obtained a graduate degree in physics, these beliefs can be added to the initial common ground. The initialization mechanism, then, depends on two things. (1) Conversants stock a fairly elaborate set of belief-relevant features – that is, of features from which it can be inferred that agents will have certain beliefs. When they acquire beliefs, they track the belief-relevant features under which the belief was acquired. (2) Conversants must be able to classify agents according to the belief-relevant features they possess. The shared features can then be used to construct an ad hoc attitude. It will be reasonable to assume at the outset of the conversation that this attitude is mutual.

In fact, the conditions for securing mutuality, at the beginning or at any later stage of a conversation, have to be defeasible. Often in the course of a conversation, the participants discover a misalignment in the common ground, and must diagnose it and make repairs. This suggests that a nonmonotonic logic would be appropriate for formalizing the reasoning that underlies mutuality. See, for instance, Brewka et al. (1997); Strasser and Antonelli (2015). Thomason (2000) shows that with appropriate defaults (for instance, an initializing default to the effect that whatever agent A accepts for the sake of the conversation, agent B also accepts for the sake of the conversation), although mutuality itself may not be achieved, the participants will suppose that it has been.

In practice, conversational participants seem to be well aware that coordination may fail in many ways, and that they deploy many mechanisms to detect and repair miscoordinations, such as clarification requests and clarification subdialogs. The term 'grounding' was coined for this phenomenon in Clark and Schaefer (1987). The purpose of grounding, they say, is to ensure that "the speaker and addressees mutually believe that the addressees have understood what the speaker meant [according] to a criterion sufficient for current purposes." Later publications, including Clark and Brennan (1991) discuss the phenomenon. For discussions of how grounding has influenced the design of automated conversational agents, see Traum (1999); Traum and

Larsson (2004). Grounding provides strong evidence that speakers and hearers are aware of the need for mutuality and take pains to ensure that it is achieved.

8.8 Conclusion

Much can be learned about conversation by treating it as a cooperative activity, in which agents track each other's attitudes and act as if many of these attitudes are shared. What is meant by "sharing" can be modeled using technical ideas that involve iterated attitudes: iterations such as "Speaker 1 accepts that Speaker 2 accepts that Speaker 1 accepts that ϕ."

Presupposition, according to pragmatic theories, is fundamentally a kind of conversational acceptance of this sort. Following David Lewis, many other items can be incorporated in the common ground, and this can be used to account for many other features of conversation. But the conversational dynamics of presupposition and other elements of the common ground is complicated by the accommodation phenomenon. Accommodation challenges the status of pragmatic rules or "rules of conversation," making them appear to have regular and unremarkable exceptions.

9 Implicature and Figurative Speech

9.1 Two Branches of Pragmatics

Pragmatics studies the use of language. Usually, this means the use of language to communicate – but there are many ways to theorize about usage. We saw in Section 7.1 that logically minded philosophers, such as Carnap and Reichenbach, considered pragmatics to be more or less confined to the study of indexical expressions. This is by no means a trivial topic, but it ignores many factors that inform the use of language, concentrating only on the components of context that are needed to interpret a fairly narrow inventory of expressions: 'I', 'here', tenses, and (perhaps) most modals, among others. There is room for disagreement about what should be included in this list, but however liberal the criteria for inclusion, as long as we stick to the spirit of the logical tradition we will continue to invoke a *knowledge-lean* conception of context that treats it as a function delivering appropriate semantic values for a fixed set of terms. And it will minimize the role of pragmatic reasoning because – as long as it assumes that speakers and hearers know the meanings of expressions employed and the context in which they find themselves – the only reasoning task it requires is the application of a known function to known arguments.

This conservative approach to pragmatics has the advantage of being congenial to linguistic theorizing. To the extent that core linguistic theory invokes reasoning procedures, these are processes like parsing that are limited in scope and are not *knowledge-rich* – that is, they do not depend on massive amounts of real-world knowledge. Limiting the scope of reasoning about context makes it easy to formulate pragmatics as an extension of formal semantics; in fact, it can easily be absorbed into dynamic semantics. See, for instance, Chierchia (1995); van Benthem (1996); Muskens et al. (2011). On the other hand, this makes it hard to see what pragmatics is good for, what its value might be as an independent area of linguistic theory.

The narrow conception of context and reasoning excludes many important aspects of language use from the scope of pragmatics. Even simple utterances are ambiguous; complex utterances are astonishingly ambiguous. Mechanical disambiguation by computers uses machine learning and knowledge in the form of large corpora. Human disambiguation, as in 'They drank the port', seems to bring common sense to bear in ways that are not very well understood, but that certainly involve learning and world knowledge.

The process known to computational linguists as "natural language understanding" draws even more heavily on world knowledge and common sense. Understanding a text (or a conversational item) involves far more than disambiguating its component sentences – even if the disambiguation is correct. Children's stories illustrate the phenomenon. Consider the following text, taken from the beginning of *Sleeping Beauty* (Grimm and Grimm 1884):[1]

(9.1.1) A long time ago there were a king and queen who said every day, "Ah, if only we had a child," but they never had one.
But it happened that once when the queen was bathing, a frog crept out of the water on to the land, and said to her, "Your wish shall be fulfilled, before a year has gone by, you shall have a daughter."
What the frog had said came true, and the queen had a little girl who was so pretty that the king could not contain himself for joy, and ordered a great feast. He invited not only his kindred, friends and acquaintances, but also the wise women, in order that they might be kind and well-disposed towards the child. There were thirteen of them in his kingdom, but, as he had only twelve golden plates for them to eat out of, one of them had to be left at home.

A reader who understands this story will be able to make the following inferences, as well as many others.

(9.1.2)
(i) The king and queen were married to each other.
(ii) The king and queen had a kingdom.
(iii) The king and queen had no children.
(iv) The king and queen wanted to have a child.
(v) The queen was bathing in a pond or stream or lake, not in a bathtub.
(vi) The pond or stream or lake contained water.
(vii) There was land by the pond or stream or lake.
(viii) The frog predicted that the king and queen would have a child.
(ix) The king was pleased that the child was pretty.
(x) The king ordered a feast because he was pleased.
(xi) The king invited guests from his kingdom to the feast.
(xii) The king wanted the wise women to be well-disposed to his daughter.
(xiv) There were thirteen wise women in the kingdom.
(xv) Twelve wise women were invited.
(xvi) One wise woman was not invited.

These inferences are encouraged, and intended, but they all require the reader to reason beyond the literal text. They all – except perhaps for the one about the location of the queen's bath – are immediate and automatic. And they are not easy to classify. Philosophers would call (9.1.2i–iv) conversational implicatures but would probably be puzzled about the rest. Most of

[1] This following example parallels a similar one, presented in Lehnert (1988).

the examples on this list differ from those that usually are used to illustrate conversational implicature in the philosophical literature and don't match well with philosophical attempts to define the phenomenon. Many of them involve the resolution of anaphora or ellipsis.

Such examples illustrate how pervasive interpretive inference is. Pragmatic inference is commonplace and indispensable because human communication does not work well when too much is made explicit. The following revision of *Sleeping Beauty* is not only horribly awkward, but more difficult to understand than the original.

> A long time ago there were a king and queen. They were married. They had a kingdom. They said every day, "Ah, if only we had a child," but they never had a child.
>
> Once the queen was bathing in a pond. The pond contained water and there was land by the pond. A frog crept out of the water in the pond onto the land by the pond, and said to the queen ...

To put a thought into words while avoiding this sort of awkwardness, a speaker has to decide what to leave out. Roughly, the rule seems be "if the hearer will automatically infer something I mean to convey even if it is omitted from my utterance, I should leave it out." It is the hearer's or reader's task to fill in the resulting gaps correctly.

Pragmatic inference does many things: It resolves ambiguity, ellipsis, and anaphora, it detects metaphor and other tropes, and it constructs implicit meanings, like (9.1.2i–xvi). Usually, these things take place efficiently, automatically, and simultaneously, and no doubt are integrated with one another and with other automatic linguistic processing tasks. More rarely, and usually when an anomaly or impasse is detected, they can be slow and under conscious control. In this respect – allowing for automatic as well deliberative processing – pragmatic inference resembles many other forms of reasoning; see, for instance, Kahneman (2011).

If all goes well and a communicative transaction is coordinated, the meanings that a hearer or reader infers will coincide with those that a speaker or author meant to communicate. We need a neutral term for these reconstructed meanings: Let's call them *pragmatic augmentations*. Examples (9.1.2.i–xv) are plausible cases of pragmatic augmentation: A reader who does not make these inferences has not understood the author's communicative intentions.

Recall Grice's notion of conversational implicature from Section 6.2.2. Implicatures (as the term is used by philosophers these days) are, roughly, conclusions any reasonable linguistically competent interpreter would draw that are licensed in part, but not entirely, by the literal content of the utterance.

How do conversational implicatures fit into the more general picture of pragmatic inference? In particular, how do they align with the process of pragmatic augmentation? Not very well. Typical examples of pragmatic augmentation, like the ones in the *Sleeping Beauty* example, don't conform well with Grice's tests for conversational implicature. And they can't be naturally explained by the conversational maxims, the theoretical apparatus that provides Grice's rational reconstruction of implicature. The reasoning that generates implicatures has to be triggered somehow, and the only trigger Grice supplies is a hypothetical anomaly: "if this additional thought were not intended, the utterance would violate a maxim." But, as we said, inferences like those in Example (9.1.2) are automatic. It's highly implausible to say that they involve a detected anomaly, because this, you would expect, would precipitate a slower reasoning process that is deliberative and conscious. So those who are interested in an account of the actual reasoning, either for psychological or computational purposes, will probably have to look elsewhere.

Part of the problem with the philosophical tradition beginning with Grice is attention to constructed examples designed to illustrate what is perceived as important for philosophical purposes. This neglects many cases of pragmatic augmentation. And part of the problem is the challenge of how to provide the basis for an adequate and explanatory theory: a theory that could predict, at least in some cases, that something is *not* conversationally implicated. This challenge is common to all approaches to pragmatics; it is not peculiar to philosophy or to Grice.

Philosophers would classify (9.1.2i) as an implicature but would exclude (9.1.2vi) and might hesitate about many of the other fifteen inferences. The difference has to do in part with the extent to which the inference depends on speakers' intentions. Regardless of what the author may have intended, ponds can be expected to contain water. But in fact most kings are not married to most queens, so when the reader infers (9.1.2i), she is relying on the fact that the author would not use the first sentence of (9.1.1) without intending to convey that this king and this queen are married to each other.

This difference is related to Grice's *cancelabilty* test for implicature, which was mentioned in Section 6.2 and was illustrated with an implicature associated with 'try'. The idea is that if an inference can be canceled, either by changing the context or by explicit denial, it is, *ceteris paribus*, an implicature. (Grice, and the subsequent literature, do not go into detail about the sort of possibility that is associated with *cancelability*, but we will assume that the inference is cancelable if it can be explicitly contradicted without making the discourse anomalous and incoherent.) Although this test works well in many cases, Grimm's fairy tale illustrates ways in which it can break down. (9.1.2iv) resembles standard examples of conversational implicature, but it would be impossible to add a disclaimer ("but actually the king and queen didn't want a child") to the story without rendering the narrative anomalous and unintelligible. And although (9.1.2ii) is cancelable ("Actually, the king and queen were disinherited and had no kingdom") this augmentation cancels a defeasible expectation about natural regularities rather than an expectation concerning speaker intentions.

Philosophers' examples are often skewed in favor of the relatively rare cases in which the reasoning is conscious. One of Grice's first examples, and one of the most famous, involves a testimonial for a student seeking a position that reads "Mr. X's command of English is excellent, and his attendance at tutorials has been regular." The letter is anomalous, and the reader must pause and think to work out the inference that the writer has a poor opinion of the candidate's academic qualifications. No doubt Grice favored this example because he felt that the reasoning behind implicatures was in principle rationalizable. When the reasoning process is conscious and explicit, we can observe the rational process.

Linguists and cognitive scientists interested in implicature should be cautious about adopting the methodology of philosophers who have written on the subject. In this section, we have seen some of the features that make this methodology problematic. (1) Philosophers have relied for the most part on constructed rather than naturally occurring examples. Three paragraphs of the *Sleeping Beauty* tale have revealed many inferences that don't fit comfortably into the philosophical menagerie; this suggests that examples chosen to illustrate a particular theory may leave much of the ground uncovered. (2) We have seen that implicature, as Grice characterized it and as most philosophers think of it, presents an incomplete picture of pragmatic conclusion-drawing: It is part of the wider phenomenon of pragmatic augmentation. (3) Implicature may not be a natural inferential category. It resists characterization, it can be difficult to separate cases of pragmatic augmentation that are implicatures from those that are not, and it might be dangerous to separate implicature-drawing from disambiguation, anaphora resolution, and other pragmatic inferencing processes. (4) Most pragmatic augmentation is fast and automatic, though sometimes it can be slow and reflective. A methodology that seeks first to explain pervasive, automatic cases of augmentation might well be more successful than one that begins with the examples that philosophers have found important.

9.2 Implicature

The last section was intended to put the study of implicature into perspective for linguists and other nonphilosophers and to suggest that the philosophical tradition may not provide the best basis for a scientific study of this topic. Now we'll look more closely at what philosophers – and especially Paul Grice – have said about implicature.

9.2.1 Philosophical Origins of Implicature

In Grice's work, the idea of implicature originates in his rejection of the philosophical conclusions that J. L. Austin drew from linguistic usage. So it serves larger philosophical goals. In Section 6.2, we mentioned an epistemological issue – the status of phenomenalism. This theory holds that all our empirical knowledge is based on sense impressions – incorrigible evidence about how things seem to us. J. L. Austin criticizes the theory by pointing out that it is peculiar to speak of the things we ordinarily know by direct experience in terms of seeming. When someone sees a red book in plain sight on the desk in front of her, in ordinary light and under ordinary circumstances, it would be absurd for her to say "I seem to see a red book," or "that book looks red to me."

Grice addresses this objection in Grice (1961), written six years before he delivered the William James Lectures at Harvard. This is the first place in the philosophical literature that the notion of implicature appears, though in 1961 Grice does not use the term 'implicature' but speaks of "implication." He begins by considering several case studies in which "something might be said to be implied as distinct from being stated." These are (1) the sense of contrast that accompanies 'but', (2) innuendo in a recommendation letter, and (3) the thought accompanying uses of 'or' that the alternatives are open possibilities. (All three examples are repeated in Grice [1989a], a later and more definitive version of the theory.)

With the idea in place that there can be systematic "implications" of this kind, Grice can return to the philosophical issue – the status of phenomenalism – and can argue that Austin's point depends on conflating literal meaning with implicature: 'I seem to see a red book' can be literally true, even though using it in normal circumstances is anomalous because it implicates that there is some doubt about the matter when there plainly is no such doubt.

Grice (1989a) remains motivated by philosophical concerns. He wishes to undermine the assumption, made unquestioningly by "formalists" and "informalists" alike – by the likes of both Carnap and Austin – that natural languages and the formal languages studied by logicians are fundamentally different. Grice sets out to argue that the core terms of modern symbolic logic – especially 'or', 'and', 'not', and 'if' – do not have meanings that differ from their literal meanings in ordinary language. The hope, of course, is that apparent discrepancies having to do with the use of these expressions can be explained away using the same strategy that Grice applied to 'seem to see' in Grice (1961).

9.2.2 Grice on Meaning and Implicature

Grice's "Logic and Conversation," the first of his William James Lectures, Grice (1989a: 22–57), is the most influential of his works in pragmatics – partly because it is more readable than many of his other works and partly because the work has obvious philosophical payoffs. It is there that Grice characterizes conversational and conventional implicature, discussing examples and attempting to ground conversational implicatures in rational cooperation.

We believe that the subsequent emphasis on implicature and conversational maxims gives a distorted impression of the theoretical significance of Grice's ideas. Grice's account of implicature looks tentative. Although he frequently returned to other ideas to rework them, apparently he didn't do this with implicature. And what he has to say about it is likely to mislead non-philosophical readers interested in pragmatics. For that reason, we will begin with the two components of his theory that we consider most important: speaker meaning and linguistic meaning.

Grice on Meaning

In Dennett and Steglich-Petersen (2008), a collection of facetious definitions of philosophers' names, 'Grice' is defined as "conceptual intricacy." The definition is apt. Like many philosophers, Grice practices a dialectical method in which ideas are proposed, criticized, and revised – and usually made more complicated. And he does this recursively. After several rounds, the formulations can become quite baroque. Grice was a virtuoso at this sort of dialectic, and we have to be prepared for complexity in studying his work. We will avoid this Gricefulness when we can and will emphasize the core ideas that we believe are of lasting importance for linguists and philosophers. But some complexity will be unavoidable.

Grice has two things in mind when he speaks of "meaning": (1) literal meaning (or "meaning in the favored sense,") and (2) speaker meaning (or "non-natural meaning"). The former originates in linguistic conventions. The latter arises in intentions and intention recognition, uses general-purpose reasoning that is not especially linguistic, and is, in some sense, rational.

Most of what Grice has to say about literal meaning is found in Grice (1968) and Grice (1982). Linguists and philosophers would expect this to center on syntactic structures and their interpretation. But, though Grice was certainly acquainted with formal semantics, he doesn't make use of it in his written work. This may have been because he had foundational doubts about this style of semantics, but certainly it was also a matter of taste; Grice was more at home with philosophical analysis than with logical theories.

Grice is consistently general about the vehicles of conventional meaning in his work. These can be gestures as well as other signals, and – in the case of linguistic vehicles – can of course be simple (words) or complex (phrases). Utterance types – for instance, sentence types – have *timeless meanings*. Instead of treating these as functions from contexts to intensions, as formal semanticists do, Grice uses paraphrase: The timeless meanings of 'I don't have a penny' might be, roughly, (1) "I have no money" and (2) "I have no pennies."

Timeless meanings, Grice believes, are a matter of convention, but he has little to say about what linguistic conventions are or how they arise in a community. Lewis (1969) puts flesh on this idea in a way that is broadly compatible with Grice's program, in that it takes speaker attitudes as fundamental. Unlike Grice, however, Lewis appeals to game theory in his explanations.

To take contextual effects into account, Grice distinguishes (unqualified) timeless meanings from *applied* timeless meanings. These too are a matter of paraphrase; on an occasion where 'I' refers to Bill Gates, an applied timeless meaning of 'I don't have a penny' might be "Bill Gates has no pennies."

Opposed to timeless meanings are meanings that arise when a speaker ("utterer") U communicates something. If U uses a conventional vehicle (say, a declarative sentence) to do this, there will be two sorts of occasional meanings. These are (1) what the sentence literally means on the occasion, and (2) what the speaker means. This corresponds to the common-sense distinction between (1) what someone literally says and (2) what people imply without explicitly saying. Without intuitions about these matters, we would be unable to distinguish literal from implicit meanings, and terms like 'innuendo', 'intimation', and 'insinuation' would make no sense. Exploiting these intuitions, which are remarkably robust, we are able to communicate things without taking full responsibility for them, and – if we're careful – to recognize when things are being communicated to us in this oblique way.

What S means on a given occasion is determined by selecting meanings for the words in S, together with linguistic rules, and invoking an appropriate contextualization of the indexicals in S. For instance, the occasional meaning of 'I don't have a penny' might be

(9.2.3) that Bill Gates doesn't have any money at time t.

In terms of formal semantics, this meaning is a proposition, because 'that'-clauses like (9.2.3) are associated with propositions. But Grice doesn't include propositions in his theoretical apparatus or deploy formal semantic rules, simply saying things like "S means that . . . ."

Of course, linguists and philosophers used to formal semantics would find it natural to replace these ideas about linguistic meaning with ideas deriving from Montague's work: (1) begin with a syntactic structure of a sentence together with disambiguated words, (2) use compositional semantic rules to arrive at a character, i.e. at a function from contexts to propositions, and (3) associate a context with an utterance occasion and apply the character to this context. This procedure will deliver the proposition that the sentence literally means on that occasion. Such a revision does no fundamental violence to what Grice has to say about literal meaning, and in fact it fills in a bothersome gap in his account: how to get from a timeless meaning of a sentence (if indeed such things are paraphrases) to the proposition that is literally meant by the sentence on a given occasion. It is hard to see how to do this without using semantic rules to assign "timeless" intensional meanings (which can be identified with characters) to sentences.

What a speaker means on a given occasion is a different matter. Grice characterized speaker meaning (which he calls "non-natural meaning," or "meaning-NN") in Grice (1957) and returned to this topic on several later occasions, reexamining and revising the ideas. Natural meaning is causal; when rain clouds mean that it will rain, this is a matter of natural meaning. Using a suite of examples of meaning to contrast the two, Grice decides that the crucial difference between non-natural and natural declarative meaning is (roughly) an intention to create a belief by a plan that involves the recognition of that very intention. (For more about this, see Section 11.2.)

For instance, suppose H says 'You owe me $500' and U responds by uttering 'I don't have a penny', meaning that U can't pay H at t (proposition p). Proposition p is not the literal meaning, so H has to work it out by somehow inferring that this is what U meant to convey – that is, H must recognize U's intention I to communicate p. The peculiar communicative intention I that U had, then, was to make H believe p by recognizing I. If the intention is successful, H, on hearing the utterance, asks what intention U must have had in saying 'I don't have a penny' and concludes (1) that U wouldn't have addressed the issue unless U meant to communicate that U can't pay, so (2) this is what U must have meant, and trusting U's sincerity (3) forms the belief that U can't pay.

The details of Grice's account of speaker meaning can be challenged; some of the criticisms and Grice's responses can be found in Grice (1982). But these details are less important than the central ideas, which surely are correct. These are

(i) What a speaker means on a given occasion can differ in various ways from what the speaker's words literally mean.

(ii) Communication of these speaker meanings is accomplished by recognition of the speaker's intentions.

(iii) Successful communication of speaker meanings requires reasoning, by both the speaker and the hearer. Moreover, the reasoning used by the two must be deeply similar. Uttering a sentence offers a variety of alternative speaker meanings to the hearer, who must select one of these alternatives. For communication to be successful, the speaker must frame her utterance so that the alternative that will seem best to the hearer will be the one she intends to convey.

Cooperation and the Conversational Maxims

These ideas raise a single question to glaring prominence: What exactly is the reasoning that allows a speaker to plan and a hearer to recognize speaker meanings? Whether Grice himself sought to address this issue is not entirely clear. He suggested a reconstruction of the reasoning, but he never made claims about the actual reasoning processes that do, or even should, allow hearers to determine what speakers mean. Nonetheless, many of his followers have taken him to be making such claims, and in what follows we will do the same.

The hearer's reasoning – even if it isn't deductive – is based on evidence, and draws conclusions about the speaker meanings that are in play when an utterance is made. According to Grice, the evidence consists in the literal meaning of the sentence that is uttered, together with information about the context. And it is constrained by a *principle of cooperation* and uses four *conversational maxims* that help to specify how the principle can be applied. So we have two further central ideas.

(iv) Hearers use the literal meaning of a sentence and information about the conversational context to infer speaker meanings.

(v) Inference of speaker meanings is constrained by the principle of cooperation and uses the four conversational maxims.

Recall Grice's cooperative principle, which was discussed in Section 8.1: "Make your conversation such as is required, at the stage at which it occurs, by the accepted purpose or direction of the talk exchange in which you are engaged" (Grice 1989b: 26). As we said, the terms of Grice's formulation are of little use in characterizing the reasoning. To work with Grice's principle, we would need first to identify, at each point in a conversation, what the accepted purpose is, and second to identify the conversational contributions that would be compatible with a given purpose.

But Grice's four conversational maxims provide guidance that is somewhat more explicit (Grice 1989a: 26–27):

Quantity:

i. Make your contribution as informative as is required (for the current purposes of the exchange).

ii. Do not make your contribution more informative than is required.

Quality: Try to make your contribution one that is true.

i. Do not say what you believe to be false.

ii. Do not say that for which you lack adequate evidence.

Relation: Be relevant.

Manner: Be perspicuous.

i. Avoid obscurity of expression.

ii. Avoid ambiguity.

iii. Be brief (avoid unnecessary prolixity).

iv. Be orderly.

How do these ideas relate to conversational implicature? (Grice 1989a: 30) characterizes conversational implicature as follows;

> A man who (by, in, when) saying (or making as if to say) that *p* has implicated that *q*, may be said to have conversationally implicated that *q*, provided that (1) he is presumed to be observing the conversational

> maxims, or at least the Cooperative Principle, (2) the supposition that he is aware that, or thinks that, *q* is required in order to make his saying or making as if to say *p* (or doing so in *those* terms) consistent with this presumption; and (3) the speaker thinks (and would expect the hearer to think that the speaker thinks) that it is in the competence of the hearer to work out, or grasp intuitively that the supposition mentioned in (2) is required.

In other words, Grice characterizes conversational implicature in terms of implications that are to be explained, and that can be explained, by the assumption that the speaker is observing the conversational maxims (or at least the cooperative principle). Sometimes readers take this to be an official definition of conversational implicature, but it could also be thought of as a claim about adequacy: that the maxims and the cooperative principle somehow suffice to explain Grice's examples of conversational implicature, and others like them.

How are conversational implicatures related to Grice's notion of speaker meaning? Most of the pragmatic theorists who borrow heavily from Grice – the "neo-Griceans" – treat conversational implicatures as things the speaker means. And in fact, all of Grice's examples of implicatures are thoughts that, plausibly, the speaker intends to convey. Remarkably, however, Grice does not commit himself explicitly to this, nor does he explain his reluctance on this point. There are commentators on Grice – for instance, Saul (2002) – who feel that there are counterexamples to this claim. Whether or not Grice would have accepted Saul's examples, it seems that he had doubts on this matter.

How good in fact are the conversational maxims at explaining presumptive conversational implicatures? Often, the maxims will provide plausible explanations. For instance, there is a *scalar implicature* associated with

(9.2.4) Some students failed.

Usually, an utterance of this sentence will implicate that not all students failed. The rationale appeals to the maxim of quantity: If all students failed, the speaker would be violating maxim (1i) in saying (9.2.4). Therefore (assuming the speaker is cooperative and knows whether all students failed), she knows that not all students failed, and (since she herself can reproduce this rationale) can be taken to intend to communicate this.

But even though Grice's maxims are sound admonitions, they don't provide helpful guidance. Telling someone to say as much as is required and to be orderly and relevant is a bit like telling a would-be investor to buy low and sell high. Although good communication should satisfy the conditions enumerated in the maxims, the maxims don't provide any detail about how the reasoning accomplishes this. Even worse, the maxims often fail at the much easier task of enabling after-the-fact explanations of specific implicatures. Example (9.2.4) illustrates this. The Gricean explanation depends crucially on the assumption that the speaker knows whether all students failed. But the implicature persists even when we have no special reason to suppose that the speaker knows this. If Anna has talked to some students about how well they did on an examination, and it's plain that she didn't talk to all of them, when she says (9.2.4) she nevertheless implicates that not all students failed. This and other difficulties are discussed in Davis (1998: 77–87).

The maxim of quantity is the most successful of Grice's maxims. Uses of this maxim can be defended against many of Davis' criticisms by invoking the *question under discussion*, (Roberts 1996; Ginzburg 2012). The quantity maxim then says: "make your contribution contribute as much as you truthfully can to the question under discussion." Although this helps to some extent, it is hard to have much confidence in the general idea of conversational maxims, in light of Davis' searching critique.

Not-At-Issue Content and Conventional Implicature

The landscape of meaning is complicated by the fact that an utterance can involve not one propositional content but a configuration of propositional contents, which contribute in different ways to what is communicated. This is another idea that goes back to Frege, who produced a classification of effects of this kind in Frege (1956). (For a systematic discussion of Frege's ideas on this topic, and their relation to modern pragmatics, see Horn [2007].)

For our purposes, Frege's category of *Andeutungen*, or intimated thoughts, is of special importance. Here are some of the cases Frege had in mind.

(9.2.5) 'The rider reined in his horse' versus 'The rider reined in his steed', Frege (1956: 295).

(9.2.6) 'Alfred has not come' versus 'Alfred has not come yet', Frege (1956: 295).

(9.2.7) 'Ernest is poor and honest' versus 'Ernest is poor but honest', Frege (1956: 296).

Many later philosophers have followed Frege in claiming that in all of these sentence pairs the same sense or proposition is expressed, but that the second version adds a subsidiary thought. In Example (9.2.7), for instance, what is intimated is that there is a contrast of some sort between Ernest's poverty and his honesty.

Frege's idea that some sentence contents are intimated, as a matter of linguistic convention, has evolved into the modern idea of *multidimensional* semantics. The linguistic evidence for multidimensionality is based primarily on the observation that some parts of sentence content are *at issue*, while others are not.

We discussed at-issueness briefly in Section 8.3; the idea is that the at-issue content of an utterance is prominent and easily deniable, while not-at-issue content is backgrounded in various ways. In Simons et al. (2010), what is at issue is characterized as what bears on the question under discussion. Not-at-issue content is often less crisp than at-issue content and harder to paraphrase. 'But' and 'steed' are good examples of this – you can say, for instance, that 'but' involves some sort of contrast, but it's hard to refine this characterization further, and there are counterexamples even to this very vague and general formulation. Some not-at-issue content, as in 'I couldn't get the damned car to start' is emotive.

The content of sentences is determined compositionally. So, if we have decided to split content into at-issue and not-at-issue dimensions, we have to investigate the compositional characteristics of the not-at-issue component. This is known as the *projection problem*, and initially was associated with presuppositions; see, for instance, Beaver (1996).

This can be illustrated with negation. Consider Frege's first example and its negation:

(9.2.8) The rider reined in his steed.
(9.2.9) The rider didn't rein in his steed.

According to the two-dimensional story, (9.2.8) will have two semantic components: (1) the proposition that the rider reined in his horse x and (2) The proposition that x was high-spirited. And the meaning of (9.2.9) also will consist of two semantic components, and both must be characterized compositionally in terms of the semantic components of (9.2.8).

If we identify propositions with sets of possible worlds, the negation of a proposition X is just its set theoretical complement, the set containing whatever is not in X. This remains unchanged in the two-dimensional case – the at-issue content of (9.2.9) is the complement of the set of worlds in which the rider reined in his horse. On the other hand, just like (9.2.8), its negation (9.2.9) intimates that the horse was high-spirited. So the not-at-issue content of the negative is the same as the not-at-issue of the positive sentence. This is one typical projection pattern: at-issue projection follows the one-dimensional composition rule, and not-at-issue projection is inert. But there are other, more complicated patterns. Multi-dimensional semantics was first presented in Karttunen and Peters (1975). For a more recent and extended discussion of not-at-issue content, see Potts (2005).

Grice's examples of *conventional implicature* are cases of not-at-issue content. In Grice (1989a: 45), he cites 'therefore', and has much the same thing to say about it that Frege said about 'but'. 'Therefore', Grice says, has the same meaning ("in the favored sense") as 'and'. But 'He is an Englishman, therefore he is brave' carries the additional thought that Englishmen are brave, that bravery follows somehow from being an Englishman.

It is easy to see why conventional implicatures are conventional; there is a lexical difference between 'and' and 'therefore' (and 'but'), and this difference is a matter of linguistic convention. The cancelability test confirms this: You can't say "He is an Englishman, therefore he is brave – but I don't mean to say that being an Englishman has anything to do with being brave" without contradicting yourself.

On the other hand, Grice doesn't explain why he thinks conventional implicatures are implicatures – he doesn't say what conventional and conversational implicatures are supposed to have in common. And it is hard to see what they do have in common. It is true that often both conversational and conventional implicatures serve as *intimating devices* – they often express not-at-issue content. But this is not always true: A conversational implicature can be the main point of an utterance, as in

(9.2.10) I didn't tell you I'd be late for dinner,

said by a wife to her husband at breakfast. This implicates that the wife will be late for dinner, and the implicature is the principal, at-issue content that is communicated. If the husband replies 'That's going to be inconvenient' he means it will be inconvenient that she will be late.

Not only is the term "conventional implicature" problematic, but the linguistic phenomena at stake in intimated content are controversial. (For instance, Bach [1999] denies that there is such a thing as conventional implicature.) For useful thoughts on the data and how to classify them, see Tonhauser et al. (2013).

9.3 Speaker and Hearer

Grice's definition of speaker meaning characterizes it in terms of speakers' attitudes – meanings are a matter of what the speaker intends. Likewise, his conversational maxims are admonitions to the speaker. On the other hand, Grice (1969: 86), characterizes implicature in terms that center on the hearer:

> what is implicated is what is required that one assume a speaker to think in order to preserve the assumption that he is observing the Cooperative Principle (and perhaps some conversational maxims as well).

As we said in Section 9.2.2, Saul (2002) constructs examples where what is implicated is not speaker-meant; these examples involve cases of misunderstanding and exploit the discrepancy between Grice's speaker-based and hearer-based accounts. Perhaps it would be most useful to say that speaker- and hearer-oriented accounts of both meaning and implicature are available along Gricean lines. Hearer meaning would be what the hearer takes the speaker meaning to be. Speaker implicature would be what the speaker takes the hearer implicature to be. You could then maintain that what is speaker-implicated is speaker-meant, and what is hearer-implicated is hearer-meant. If conversation is successful, of course, what the speaker means will coincide with what the hearer takes her to mean. Then the distinction will collapse and we can simply say that normally (and we can hope that successful communication is normal) implicatures are meant, regardless of whether one takes the speaker's or the hearer's point of view.

This way of looking at things links together Grice's two most significant contributions to pragmatics. And it is theoretically useful, because it makes the connection between sentence meaning and speaker meaning the central topic of pragmatics, treating implicature as a more, or perhaps less, important special case.

9.4 Pragmatic Reasoning

Like other forms of reasoning, pragmatic reasoning moves from premises to conclusions. For the hearer, the reasoning is abductive, the premises are the utterance (including body language) and the context of utterance, and the conclusion is a bundle of items to be added to the common ground – and not, as Grice suggested, to the hearer's beliefs. For the speaker, the reasoning is planning or reasoning from ends to means, the premises are a goal about what needs to be added to the common ground and the context of utterance, and the conclusion is an utterance. The reasoning leads, for both the speaker and the hearer, to assumptions about pragmatic augmentations: information that will be added to the literal meaning of the language that is used in an utterance.

In discussing Grice's conversational maxims, we indicated that an adequate theory of pragmatic augmentation must do more than to supply plausible after-the-fact explanations of conversational implicatures. It should *predict* these implicatures and provide an accurate model of how the reasoning works. The model should be compatible with, and if possible confirmed by, psychological testing, and it should be *implementable* in the form of automated conversational systems. Without this third feature, it is hard to see how a theory of reasoning could actually be tested and refined in light of evidence. Grice's own approach to reasoning was highly idealized, and he may have disputed the value of this more empirical methodology. But that seems to lead to a less ambitious and promising approach to the problems.

It is difficult to say how long it will be until computer scientists produce genuinely lifelike conversational agents. But there has been steady progress in this area. Although a theory to support this technology doesn't yet exist, several candidates for a reasoning architecture have been proposed that could provide the basis for such a theory: *Relevance Theory*, *DICE* (Discourse in Common Sense Entailment), and *Weighted Abduction*.

Relevance Theory was introduced in Sperber and Wilson (1986b) and was refined and elaborated in later work by Sperber, Wilson, and their associates. Their model of reasoning combines deduction with hypothesis formation. These reasoning processes are limited by cognitive effort; the idea is that they will stop after expectations of diminishing value and increasing effort attach to the body of inferences. The process may be guided by expectations about speaker intentions but, if so, Sperber and Wilson (1986b) is not very explicit about this aspect of the reasoning. The success of the process depends on the ability of speakers to manage their contributions so that the inferences that are to be communicated will be those that will be produced by this inferential process.

Inference is certainly the cognitive mechanism that produces pragmatic augmentations, including implicatures. And the components of inference to which Sperber and Wilson draw attention are likely to be part of any successful account of the reasoning – especially, semantic parsing, intention recognition, and abduction or reasoning to the best explanation. (Deduction may be less important, because there are ways to use abduction to do the useful work of deduction.)

But, as we said, a theory of pragmatic augmentation needs to be testable, and this requires specific predictions about pragmatic inferences that are actually derived from the model. This requirement leads inevitably to a computational project: A testable theory would have to provide the specification of a computer program for a conversational agent. If the topic of conversation is limited to a specific task domain, such agents are feasible: see, for instance, the papers in Howes and Larsson (2014) and other SEMDIAL proceedings, and Stent and Bangalore (2014). Although their capacity for pragmatic augmentation is very limited, it is likely that this capacity will emerge eventually, if not soon. At that point, theories of pragmatic augmentation could be tested by implemented computational agents. Evidence of this kind would almost certainly require revisions in all the available theories, including Relevance Theory.

The idea that there is a tradeoff in pragmatic reasoning between the quantity and quality of the results and the computational time and effort required to achieve them is certainly correct and no doubt applies to every sort of real-time reasoning. However, in itself it doesn't seem to provide a very promising model of pragmatic reasoning, where the hearer's task is to infer what the speaker means to communicate. The problem is that, in itself, it doesn't narrow the search space enough for efficient solutions; this seems to require a more definite goal to guide the search and to indicate when it can be stopped, and this is more likely to emerge from expectations about speaker's intentions.

Relatively little work has been done to implement Relevance Theory; the only example we know of is Poznański (1992). Until the ideas are tested more thoroughly, it is hard to see if the inferential problems can be overcome.

Discourse in Commonsense Entailment was introduced in Asher and Lascarides (2003). This architecture is an extension of Hans Kamp's Discourse Representation Theory, designed to include reasoning about discourse connections and pragmatic augmentation. Like Relevance Theory, DICE uses deductive inference, but here the inference is nonmonotonic or defeasible, an innovation that makes it much easier to formulate workable rules of inference. It shares the problem of using forward inference without a plausible stopping rule. However, there have been sustained efforts to implement and test DICE in dialogue systems, and these may produce solutions to that problem.

Weighted abduction has been explored by Jerry Hobbs in work beginning with Hobbs et al. (1993). The idea is to use reasoning to the best explanation to support pragmatic inference, and to implement this using extensions of the programming language PROLOG. The strong point of Hobbs' architecture is that it integrates pragmatic reasoning with other forms of linguistic reasoning – not only pragmatic inferencing such as ellipsis resolution, but parsing. Since PROLOG begins with a goal and ends when the reasoning has achieved this goal, this architecture does not have a problem with stopping the inferencing. But Hobbs has not gone beyond providing case-by-case explanations of inferences, and, as far as we know, the ideas have not been tested in a working conversational agent.

It may surprise some readers to see this section begin with philosophical ideas and end with computational architectures and their implementation and testing. But there is a good reason for this shift in emphasis. Grice was certainly right that pragmatic augmentation is a pervasive feature of human communication. But the reasoning is simply too complex to be captured either by philosophical analysis or a deductive system with rules that can be spelled out in a few pages. The reasoning makes massive use of real-world knowledge, and so is not suited for the methods in the philosophical toolbox. Computers, on the other hand, can incorporate large knowledge bases and inference rules that are far more complex than anything that can be written by philosophers or anyone else. And computational dialogue systems can be tested by observing how they perform in conversations with humans. This is the only methodology that promises to deal adequately with the problems of pragmatic inference.

9.5 Figurative Speech

When speakers use figurative language they mean something beyond (or something altogether different from) what their words mean on the occasion. This is a matter of *pragmatic displacement* rather than pragmatic augmentation. Classical rhetoric catalogs many figurative devices:

Allusion: Saying 'He made me an offer I couldn't refuse', recalling *The Godfather* and meaning, perhaps in jest, that he used a threat to persuade me.

Synecdoche: Saying 'Brussels insists on the measure' meaning that officials in Brussels on behalf of the European Union insist on the measure.

Hyperbole: Saying 'That train goes faster than the speed of light' meaning that the train is considerably faster than normal trains.

Meiosis: Saying 'I've had a bad day' when I lost both legs in an accident.

Irony: Saying 'This was the perfect ending' after a dismally unentertaining show is interrupted by a fire alarm.

The orthodox Gricean view classifies all of these as implicatures. Grice (1989a) suggests that irony, metaphor, synecdoche, and hyperbole are conversational implicatures where the first maxim of Quality ('Do not say what you believe to be false') is flagrantly violated and the audience must look for an alternative interpretation of the speaker's utterance. But this can't be right in general. If a decision made by EU officials is in the news, it is probably also true literally that Brussels is in the news – but saying 'Brussels is in the news' would nonetheless convey something other than this literal truth.

The specific interpretations associated with figurative speech seem to be driven by expectations of cooperativity and rationality that aren't easily accounted for by Grice's maxims. This is why many theories (e.g. Sperber and Wilson 1986a; Bezuidenhout 2001; Carston 2002; Recanati 2004) have turned instead to accounts of figurative speech that allow optional pragmatic processes (such as free enrichment or loosening) to generate the communicated from the linguistically encoded content.

By far the most widely discussed form of figurative speech is *metaphor*. Metaphor pulls together meanings from distinct domains. Often the resulting package combines incompatible elements: In this case a metaphor will be an instance of what is called in rhetoric an oxymoron, in philosophy a category mistake, and in linguistics a clash of selectional features. But not all metaphors are anomalous, or even false. Hills (1997) mentions the example of Lois Lane metaphorically saying in a moment of gratitude 'Clark Kent is Superman'. Metaphors diverge from ordinary cases of semantic anomaly in serving a communicative purpose – they invite an interpretation; the interpreter is to discover a connection (sometimes called *analogy*) between the object (sometimes called *tenor*) and the attributed feature (sometimes called *vehicle*). The analogy is often elaborated to obtain a sustained rhetorical effect, as illustrated by Will Ferrell's commencement address at Harvard in 2003:

> I graduated from the University of Life. All right? I received a degree from the School of Hard Knocks. And our colors were black and blue, baby. I had office hours with the Dean of Bloody Noses. All right? I borrowed my class notes from Professor Knuckle Sandwich and his Teaching Assistant, Ms. Fat Lip Thon Nyun. That's the kind of school I went to for real, okay?

Metaphors are indispensable – they are the primary means whereby we can go beyond limitations of the languages we speak. In Walton (1993), Kendall Walton uses the following example,

(9.5.11) Crotone is on the arch of the Italian boot.

To explain without the help of a map where Crotone is located is a difficult task; language is ill-suited to convey this sort of information. To say, for example, that Crotone is about 420 kilometers south-east of Naples on the shore of the Ionian Sea would be more precise but less useful for virtually everyone.

Successful metaphorical speech is *figuratively true*. How can we understand this notion? Walton claims that figurative truth is truth in (or according to) a fiction. 'Sherlock Holmes lives in Baker Street 221b' is false (Sherlock Holmes does not literally exist and neither does 221b Baker Street). But it's true in Conan Doyle's novels. Similarly, (9.5.11) is false (not only is Italy not literally a boot, boots don't literally have arches) but true in an ad hoc fiction suggested by the speaker's utterance.

The Sherlock Holmes fiction and the Italian boot fiction are games of make-believe, where the addressees are invited to imagine various things. What is true in a fiction is what participants in the game can be expected to imagine, according to the rules of the game. These rules are complex. Some fictional truths are explicitly stipulated: Conan Doyle says in the novel that Holmes lives in Baker Street 221b, while the speaker who produces (9.5.11) invitingly presupposes that Italy is a boot. Accordingly, we should not construe speaker presupposition as belief. Following Stalnaker (2002) we should say that presupposition is a kind of acceptance – taking something to be true for a specific purpose. Fiction can be such a purpose. But fictional truths are only partially fictional; they are permeated with regularities we project from our own real world. That's why it is true in Conan Doyle's story that Holmes lives near Melcombe Street (something that is never mentioned in the novels) and why it is true in the ad hoc make-believe generated by someone who utters (9.5.11) that Reggio Calabria (a town a speaker may never have heard of) is on the toe of the Italian boot.

Both of these fictions employ real-world objects to help us generate fictional truths – Baker Street and Italy. These entities function somewhat like props on the stage aiding imagination. But the significance of the props within the two fictions is different. The Holmes fiction exploits the audience's knowledge of the prop to flesh out a content ("this is where one might expect to find bachelor lodgings of the sort Holmes and Watson occupy"); the boot fiction exploits a content to inform about the prop ("this is the part of Italy where Crotone is to be found"). For Walton, metaphor is make-believe of the second, *prop-oriented* kind.

The view that metaphor is prop-oriented make-believe has encouraged some philosophers to argue that various seemingly nonmetaphorical claims are best construed as metaphorical. Consider for example:

(9.5.12) 'Napoleon could have won the battle of Waterloo' is true only if there is a possible world where Napoleon won the battle of Waterloo.

Since 'Napoleon could have won the battle of Waterloo' is (let's suppose) true, and, since in the actual world Napoleon lost, the truth of (9.5.12) seems to require the existence of at least one merely possible world. But if (9.5.12) is only figuratively true, merely possible worlds need not be any more real than Sherlock Holmes. Yablo (1996) suggests that metaphor creeps into semantics this way. For any way things could be, we pretend that there is a possible world where things are that way. This make-believe is a rigorous sort of fiction: It is closed under logical consequence and validates the instances of the T-schema. Thus, it follows that (9.5.12) is true in the semantic fiction. The enterprise is prop-oriented – the props are sentences of English. The point of engaging with the semantic fiction is to gain better insight into how the truth-conditions of the props are compositionally determined.

Yablo is concerned to make possible worlds palatable to philosophers who have ontological worries about them. A philosopher can resort to possible worlds for metaphysical purposes and even use them to arrive at insights into modality, without believing in their existence.

Metaphors are abundant in natural languages, and the good ones often enjoy fossilization as picturesque idioms, like 'domino effect', 'in a nutshell', or 'tunnel vision'. Even a cursory look at the history of compound words will reveal that many probably started their lives as metaphors. This fact has encouraged some philosophers to call into question the dominant pragmatic views on metaphor and argue that metaphor is a semantic phenomenon.

On semantic accounts, metaphorical truth is a kind of truth and depends on the facts, though the dependence is not quite that of literal truth. (On standard views, truth in a fiction is *not* a kind of truth – it is just something that is taken to be true whatever its actual truth-value may be.) Stern (2000) proposes an account that locates metaphorical interpretation in logical form. When used metaphorically, an expression is a kind of complex indexical whose semantic value is assigned by the context of utterance as long as it satisfies some linguistically encoded constraints. For instance, the metaphorical interpretation of (9.5.13) invokes an operator in the logical form taking the vehicle of the metaphor ('is a fish') in its scope and delivering a modified interpretation, in the context of utterance – in this case, the property of being a good swimmer.

(9.5.13) Michael Phelps is a fish.

One advantage of adding such an operator to the logical form of the sentence is that it provides a way to explain why metaphorical and literal interpretations fail to coordinate. (For a critical assessment of the relevant data and of Stern's theory in general, see Camp [2005].)

Perhaps the most significant difficulty in making sense of metaphor is that its interpretation allows for a certain amount of flexibility. We think of assessments of literal meaning as a matter of identifying the very thought the speaker meant. But there may not even be a specific, identifiable thought corresponding to metaphorical meaning, as argued in (Davidson 1978: 46–47):

> When we try to say what a metaphor "means," we soon realize there is no end to what we want to mention … How many facts are conveyed by a photograph? None, an infinity, or one great unstatable fact? Bad question. A picture is not worth a thousand words, or any other number. Words are the wrong currency to exchange for a picture.

Whether or not this is right, metaphorical language often requires hard work on the part of the interpreter, as Fogelin (1988) stresses. Indeed, much of the pleasure we take in literary metaphor derives from a cooperative project that is very like meaning construction. If the reader is not producing a metaphorical content, what is she doing, and how can she tell when the work is well done? After all, there are right and wrong, better and worse interpretations of metaphor. Metaphor interpretation is constrained – the interpreter must discover the point of the metaphor and, if she does not, she fails to understand the utterance. Semantic accounts tend to predict too little flexibility, while pragmatic accounts typically allow too much. To find the right balance continues to be a challenge for linguists and philosophers alike.

9.6 Conclusion

Pragmatics used to be called the wastebasket of semantics but would have been better likened to an untamed jungle neighboring the better-regulated and more orderly gardens of linguistic theory. Modern pragmatics, which actually began and developed over roughly the same period as formal semantics, may still harbor some tangled patches, although much of it is now orderly and well cultivated.

Work on pragmatic augmentation is still heavily influenced by the ideas of Paul Grice, but it has been supplemented by accounts capable of making detailed predictions (work on scalar implicatures is an example) and by important new ideas (such as the question under discussion). We can expect more developments of this kind as the burden shifts from philosophy to linguistics and as new modeling techniques from computational linguistics are brought to bear on pragmatic reasoning.

Nevertheless, areas of pragmatics remain that are far closer to philosophy than to linguistics. Metaphor and figurative language is one of these; some of the best work on this topic has been done by philosophers more concerned with aesthetics and philosophy of art than with philosophy of language. Another is the relation between linguistic meaning and usage, a topic which we discuss in Section 11.4.

10 Assertion and Other Speech Acts

10.1 Locution, Illocution, Perlocution

In the *Port Royal Logic*, Antoine Arnauld and Pierre Nicole summarize the traditional doctrine of judgment as follows: "After conceiving things by our ideas, we compare those ideas and, finding that some belong together and others do not, we unite and separate them. This is called *affirming* or *denying*, and in general *judging*" (Arnauld and Nicole 1996: 82).

Judgments, thus conceived, simultaneously perform two tasks: They *relate* two ideas (usually those of the subject and of the predicate, but the doctrine is often extended to cover other cases as well) and they *assess* their relation, either assenting or dissenting. So, for example, in judging whether 1343 is a prime number, one is supposed to be uniting or separating two items: the idea of 1343 and the idea of a prime number.

But what if one has no opinion on the matter? It seems that one could simply entertain the thought that 1343 is a prime number without taking a stand on its truth-value. Arguably, this is exactly what you were doing just a moment ago, when you read and understood the expression '1343 is a prime number' as part of the previous sentence. Since, we assume, you did not know that 1343 is 17 times 79, you refrained from affirming or denying that 1343 is a prime number. It now seems that the two tasks the traditional doctrine of judgment lumps together should be kept separate. It is one of Frege's enduring achievements in philosophy to make this point with great clarity.

Frege (1956) insisted on a sharp distinction between apprehension and affirmation, and gave them a common object: the thought. Judging that 1343 is a prime number involves first apprehending the thought that 1343 is a prime number, and second affirming the truth of this thought. These two mental acts correspond to the two parts of the Fregean symbol '⊢' (Frege 1967: 11–12): the horizontal '-' represents the first, the vertical '|' the second. In apprehending a thought – say, the thought that 1343 is a prime number – we direct ourselves to a content which unites the contents of the subject and the predicate. Here we have the modern notion of a proposition: something that has a truth-value that is independent of our act of apprehension.

As Frege (1960a) points out, once we separate apprehension from affirmation, we no longer need to distinguish affirmation and denial as two forms of judgment. We can think of negation as an operation on content, which means that denying that 1343 is a prime number can be seen as simply affirming that 1343 is not a prime number. For Frege, all judgment involves affirmation – an inner act of assenting to an apprehended proposition that can be outwardly manifested in an act of asserting that proposition by uttering a sentence that expresses it.

Asserting that 6343 is a prime number must be distinguished both from uttering the sentence '6343 is a prime number' and from convincing someone that 6343 is a prime number. The former can be thought of as a possible means, the latter as a possible goal of the assertion. Uttering '6343 is a prime number' does not require assertion – after all, this sentence is uttered whenever one utters 'I don't think 6343 is a prime number'. And convincing someone that 6343 is a prime number requires more than assertion – the hearer may be skeptical, even though 6343 is indeed a prime number.

Following Austin (1962b), we can say that uttering '6343 is a prime number' is a *locutionary act*, while convincing someone that 6343 is a prime number is a *perlocutionary act*. The locutionary act is a public presentation of a content by means of a linguistic expression; the perlocutionary act requires that the audience should react to the presentation of the content in a specific way. Assertion is something in between. Along with commanding, promising, asking, excusing, naming, and much else, it is what Austin called an *illocutionary act*. Illocutionary and perlocutionary acts are not always easy to distinguish. Austin famously said that illocutionary acts are performed *in* a locutionary act, while perlocutionary acts are performed *by* a locutionary act. But ordinary speech is not always careful about this: 'In uttering these words he warned me that the enemy is coming' is just as fine as 'By uttering these words he warned me that the enemy is coming'. Illocutionary acts are often expressed by verbs taking just a subject and a complement clause, while the verbs standing for perlocutionary acts often take an extra argument for the addressee. But there are plenty of exceptions – 'tell', 'warn', 'advise', and 'thank' all express illocutionary acts but still take an argument for the affected person.

Austin concedes – and this is a major source of complication – that illocutionary acts themselves require at least one effect: securing uptake. Austin (1962a: 116) says: "I cannot be said to have warned an audience unless it hears what I say and takes what I say in a certain sense." Austin may or may not be right about warnings, but assertions, promises, and commands can certainly be made without the audience recognizing them.

Austin's illocutionary acts generalize the Fregean notion of assertion – a linguistically manifested act of affirming a proposition. But, despite the fact that this is often assumed, illocutionary acts don't require language use, and illocutionary content is not invariably propositional. In the next two subsections, we will try to establish these points.

10.1.1 Language and Illocution

Gestures can perform illocutionary acts, and can even be spontaneous, with no need for a convention: As long as the speaker means something in behaving in a certain way, she can be performing an illocutionary act. A child can run down a grocery store aisle, abruptly stop in front of shelves stuffed with boxes of Cinnamon Toast Crunch cereal, turn back and smile at her father. This is a perfectly good way to ask for the treat – no better and no worse than loudly saying "Can I please have the sweet cereal?" Even silence can serve as a vehicle for an illocutionary act; there is such a thing as silent assent. We normally expect illocutionary acts to involve locutions (speaking or writing), because illocutionary acts involve presentation of content, and language is an exceptionally good vehicle for this. But when there is another way to make the content salient we can and often do bypass language.

The realization that illocutionary acts needn't involve language raises questions about the role of conventions in illocution. Some of Austin's classic examples of illocutionary acts – marrying and naming a ship – are paradigmatically conventional. But could one make an assertion or a request without there being an established practice of doing so? If this required uttering some linguistic expression, the answer would of course be negative – without conventions there is no linguistic communication. However, since nonlinguistic assertions and requests are possible, the answer to this question is far from trivial: For influential opposing views on this matter see Strawson (1964) and Searle (1969).

While speech is not essential to illocution, illocution does seem to be essential to speech. Wittgenstein (1953) describes a simple language consisting only of four words: 'block', 'pillar', 'slab', and 'beam', used by a builder to communicate with an assistant. The builder calls out one of the words, the assistant picks up the appropriate item and brings it to the builder. This can, Wittgenstein claims, constitute a "complete primitive language," and there is no doubt such a system could indeed be employed in coordinating behavior. But the reason for this is precisely that the builder's utterances are not mere *locutionary* acts. They are commands (or requests – we don't know enough about the context to tell which) to fetch an item of the sort picked out by the word uttered, and the fact that this is how they are to be taken must be common ground between the speaker and the audience. If things go smoothly, the builder also performs the perlocutionary act of enticing the assistant to bring him the item he needs. But a mutually understood system of communication could be in place even if a perverse assistant always refused to obey the builder. The assistant couldn't refuse except as a response to an understandable illocutionary act.

There are language games simpler than Wittgenstein's that do not involve illocutionary acts at all. Keiser (2016b) mentions the example of a community that uses a dead language exclusively to tell ancient stories to each other that they do not believe to be true. They are clearly not making assertions, and it is arguable that they are not even performing illocutionary acts. All they do is call each other's attention to contents by means of bare locutionary acts. While this seems correct, it does not show that the community could have this as their *only* language – presumably they would need another one for their ordinary interactions. The moral, then, is that we should qualify the claim that illocution is essential to language use. While it is possible for a community to use a language without using it to perform illocutionary acts, it doesn't seem possible for them to use a language without also performing illocutionary acts.

10.1.2 Illocution and Propositional Content

Some authors assume that illocutionary acts must always have propositional content. Searle (1975b: 344), for instance, represents each illocutionary act as having the form F(p), where F indicates the force of the act and p its propositional content. This is too restrictive, since there are convincing counterexamples to the claim that the content of an illocutionary act is always propositional. For instance, we typically ask questions by uttering interrogative sentences, and, on standard semantic views, these don't express propositions. Interrogative sentences are typically taken to express collections of their answers; see, for instance, Hamblin (1958); Karttunen (1977); Groenendijk and Stokhof (1984).

So, if answers are propositions, it follows that questions are not. And if referring and predicating are illocutionary acts, their corresponding locutions are utterances of sentence components, rather than of whole sentences. When I say "6343 is a prime number," I make an assertion. But I also refer to a number and predicate a property of that number. To insist that all illocutionary acts must have propositional content would make the status of reference and predication problematic.

Those who dislike nonpropositional illocutions might insist upon a sharp distinction between the content of the expression uttered (locutionary content) and the content of the act performed in uttering the expression (illocutionary content). Perhaps when I utter 'Shit', the illocutionary content is that I curse the situation; when I utter 'Hi', the illocutionary content is that I greet you; and when I utter 'Sorry', the illocutionary content is that I apologize for what I have done. Queries are second-order illocutionary acts: They are requests that the addressee perform a first-order illocutionary act – to make an assertion that answers a question. Then, one might suggest, the illocutionary content of my utterance of the interrogative 'Who is coming to the party tonight?' is the proposition that I request that you tell me who is coming to the party tonight.

But these maneuvers won't do. The proposal is, in effect, to load the force of the act into its content. The immediate consequence of this is that different kinds of illocutionary acts can never share their content, a deeply unintuitive result. One person can assert what another has previously conjectured and can command what others can only request; I can promise to do something and you can predict that I won't do it, and so on.

10.2 Performatives and Constatives

That we can do things with words was a quintessential philosophical discovery – something everyone always knew but no one had seriously thought about until a philosopher pointed out how puzzling it was. The right person utters the right words at the right time and *thereby* the baby is baptized, the couple is wed, the bet is wagered, the contract is sealed, the order is placed, the title is bestowed. These are completely ordinary facts, hardly worth mentioning until they are juxtaposed with another set of completely ordinary considerations: No matter who utters what and when, *just by that*, no egg will be fried, no roof will be fixed, and no desk will be cleared. Saying so doesn't make it so – except when it does.

Credit goes to Austin (1961) and Austin (1962a) for drawing the relevant distinction. When I say to the waiter 'I order the halibut' I am not telling him what I am doing – I am just doing it. When I watch myself on a video and narrate the events as they unfold, I might choose to utter the same sentence but then I am not placing an order – I am describing what I did when the recording was made. The first utterance is what Austin called a *performative*, the second a *constative*.

The declarative sentences used in making performative utterances are special: They are always in present tense, never in progressive aspect, and they often have a first-person subject and a verb from a class of "performative verbs" characterizing the action performed. Performatives that involve sentences of this sort are called *explicit* (e.g. ordering by uttering 'I order the halibut'); the others are called *implicit* (e.g. ordering by uttering 'I'd like the halibut' or 'I will have the halibut'). Finally, performatives can be *indirect* – e.g. 'Can I have the halibut?' Sentences normally used in performative utterances also have constative uses, except when they contain a special adverb or prepositional phrase, such as 'hereby', 'herewith', or 'with these words'.

Austin (1962a: 149) claims that there are well over a thousand "performative verbs" in a concise English dictionary. Austin seems to be assuming that performativity is a lexically encoded feature, but another possibility is that performativity is instead determined by contextual clues and by the actual content of the verb. Verbs that denote natural changes or states, by their very nature, are hardly likely to have performative uses, while verbs that denote conventional states or changes often do. Think, for instance, of the difference between (10.2.1) and (10.2.2).

(10.2.1) You're tired!
(10.2.2) You're fired!

Although in practice we can easily tell the difference between performative and constative utterances, theoretically the distinction is hard to pin down. As Austin (1961: 246) himself points out, there are cases that are very hard to categorize: Saying 'I am sorry about the mess' seems to be halfway between the performative use of 'I apologize for the mess' and the constative use of 'I feel bad about the mess'. But the greatest threat to the distinction is not the existence of utterances that exhibit an "unfortunate hovering" between the performative and the constative. It is, rather, that there is no obvious way to articulate the nature of the distinction.

It won't do to say that we *do* things when we utter performatives and *describe* things when we utter constatives: describing is a kind of doing. To say that performatives bring about new states of affairs while constatives report on existing ones won't do either: Any act brings about a new state of affairs. If the right person in the right circumstances utters 'I hereby name this ship the *Queen Elizabeth*', a state of affairs of something having been named comes to be. And similarly, if the right person in the right circumstances utters 'I hereby claim that this ship is the *Queen Elizabeth*' a state of affairs of something having been claimed comes to be.

Austin's last word about the distinction is this:

> What then finally is left of the distinction of the performative and constative utterance? Really, we may say that what we had in mind here was this: (a) With the constative utterance, we abstract from the illocutionary (let alone the perlocutionary) aspects of the speech act, and we concentrate on the locutionary: moreover, we use an over-simplified notion of correspondence with the facts ... (b) With the performative utterance, we attend as much as possible to the illocutionary force of the utterance, and abstract from the dimension of correspondence with the facts. (Austin 1962a: 144–145)

Austin's suggestion is suggestive but not particularly clear. Consider uttering the sentence 'I want the halibut' as a constative (addressing a friend at the table talking about who will order what) and as a performative (addressing the waiter and making the order). Does the speaker in the first case really concentrate on the correspondence between his words and the fact that he wants the halibut, while abstracting from what sort of illocutionary act he is performing? Does the speaker in the second case really attend to the illocutionary act and abstract from any correspondence between his words and the world? And, even if this shift were to occur, could it really explain the difference between the two cases?

A better way to think about the feature that separates performatives from constatives originates with a famous example from Anscombe (1963: 56):

> Let us consider a man going round a town with a shopping list in his hand. Now it is clear that the relation of this list to the things he actually buys is one and the same whether his wife gave him the list or it is his own list; and that there is a different relation where a list is made by a detective following him about. If he made the list itself, it was an expression of intention; if his wife gave it him, it has the role of an order. What then is the identical relation to what happens, in the order and the intention, which is not shared by the record? It is precisely this: if the list and the things that the man actually buys do not agree, and if this and this alone constitutes a mistake, then the mistake is not in the list but in the man's performance (if his wife were to say:"Look, it says butter and you have bought margarine", he would hardly reply: "What a mistake! we must put that right" and alter the word on the list to "margarine"); whereas if the detective's record and what the man actually buys do not agree, then the mistake is in the record.

There are two different ways to use a list of items. The shopper's way is to try to match the world to the list – making sure that everything named on the list shows up in the shopping cart. The detective's way is to try to match the list to the world – making sure that everything in the shopping cart ends up named on the list. The two lists might be indistinguishable in appearance but they guide the behavior of their users in different ways, which accounts for the contrast Anscombe stresses: If there is a mismatch between the contents of the list and the content of the shopping cart, the shopper is supposed to change the latter, the detective is supposed to change the former. While this is not Anscombe's own terminology, the distinction came to be called *direction of fit*: The shopper's list has a world-to word direction of fit, the detective's list has a word-to-world direction of fit.

What exactly is the difference between the two lists? In the first place, it lies in how they are made. The shopper's list was issued as a request, the detective's list is penned as a report. They share content (that the shopper buys such-and-such items) but they differ in force. The source of the difference can be traced even further. The mental states that came to be manifested in creating the two lists can themselves be said to have different directions of fit: The request expresses a desire or an intention (satisfied just in case the world comes to match its content), while the report expresses a belief or a guess (true just in case its content matches the world). This distinction lines up with the traditional division of mental states into *conative* (or practical) and *cognitive* (or theoretical) ones.

Direction-of-fit accounts of the performative–constative distinction offer a different perspective on why performatives are often seen as incapable of truth or falsity. If truth is correspondence between words and facts, we might talk about two kinds of truths: the ones made true by a corresponding fact and the ones that seek to make corresponding facts hold. This idea goes back as far as Thomas Aquinas:

> When therefore things are the measure and rule of the mind, truth consists in the equation of the mind to the thing, as happens in ourselves. For according as a thing is, or is not, our thoughts or our words about it are true or false. But when the mind is the rule or measure of things, truth consists in the equation of the thing to the mind; just as the work of an artist is said to be true, when it is in accordance with his art. Now as works of art are related to art, so are works of justice related to the law with which they accord. (McDermott 1993: *Summa Theologicae* Part I, Question 21, Article 2)

On this view, our reluctance to call wishes or promises true when they are fulfilled would reflect a preference for a narrower conception of truth – the one that consists in conformity to mind-independent facts.

Searle and Vandervecken (1985: 52–53) use direction of fit to distinguish among four types of speech acts:

(i) **Word-to-world direction of fit**: Success of speech act requires that the content of the utterance match a preexisting fact (e.g. 'This ship is named *The Donald*'.)

(ii) **World-to-word direction of fit**: Success of speech act requires that a fact be brought about to match the content of the utterance (e.g. 'If only this ship were named *The Donald*!')

(iii) **Double direction of fit**: Success of speech act requires that a fact be brought about to match the content of the utterance *by virtue* of the fact that the content is taken to match a fact (e.g. 'I hereby name the ship *The Donald*'.)

(iv) **Empty direction of fit**: Success of speech act requires no fit between the content of the utterance and a fact (e.g. ' Hail to *The Donald*!').

Constatives belong to category (i). The peculiar feature of classic performatives – that saying that something is the case makes it the case – is a characteristic of category (iii). I say something whose truth requires a fact, which comes to exist precisely because what I said is taken to be true. Of course, for this to work, the relevant fact must be one whose existence depends solely on my authority (to name, to marry, to apologize, etc.) and others' willingness to acknowledge my exercise of this authority on the given occasion. The point of the speech act is to bring about a fact; the mechanism is to speak as if the fact already obtained.

10.3 Assertion

Constative speech acts can normally be reported using 'say' combined with a 'that'-clause, but this is a rather imperfect test. Some performative speech acts can also be reported this way; for example, if to order the halibut I utter 'I want the halibut', the waiter can subsequently report my order to the cook by uttering 'He said that he wants the halibut'. And some constative speech acts cannot be reported this way. For example, if I utter 'I want the halibut' to order the halibut, I suggest that I am in the mood for halibut – but the waiter cannot correctly report my order to the cook by uttering 'He said that he is in the mood for halibut'. (If he did make such a report, I could legitimately object as follows: 'I didn't say that; I was ordering the halibut because it was the only thing on the menu that wasn't red meat.)

Not all constative speech acts are assertions. Instead of asserting that something is the case one might, for example, *suppose*, *conjecture*, or *imply* that it is. A supposition lacks the "all things considered" character of assertion – it is made for the sake of some limited purpose. A conjecture lacks the evidential basis of assertion – it is made on less than conclusive grounds. And an implication lacks the explicitness of assertion – it relies on the addressee's reasoning. For these reasons, philosophers prefer to use the somewhat artificial 'assert' for the paradigm constative speech act.

Lewis (1981: 37) presents a simple and compelling picture of how assertion works in its paradigmatic uses: "I know, and you need to know, whether A or B or . . .; so I say a sentence that I take to be true-in-English, in its context, and that depends for its truth on whether A or B or . . .; and thereby, if all goes well, you find out what you needed to know." The act does not always have this effect – if I utter 'It is raining' on a theater stage or during language class, my utterance won't help anyone to find out what the weather is like. Lewis' point is that we can transfer knowledge by means of assertion – provided "all goes well." And he mentions some of the things that need to go well: The speaker must have knowledge if he is to transfer it and must find a sentence that can express what he knows. Other things that Lewis doesn't mention are fairly obvious: The hearer must understand the assertion and she must trust the speaker.

While it seems clear that knowledge can be transmitted through assertion, *how* this happens may call for explanation. Suppose it is true that p and the speaker knows this. He asserts that p and the hearer understands his assertion. Suppose further that the hearer trusts the speaker, so she comes to believe that p. The question is why this true belief counts as knowledge. For the hearer to know that p she must have some reason for her belief. She may not be able to articulate her reason, but if she is she might say something like this: "Given that the speaker asserted that p he presumably knows that p, and that is good enough for me." But why is the hearer entitled to think that the speaker knows that p, given that he asserted that p?

Perhaps this question has a simple answer, along the following lines. Conversations often have widening the scope of what is mutually known among the participants as their goal, and when this is so, the goal is usually mutually known. In such conversations it would be uncooperative to assert that p if the speaker did not know that p, and since the hearer is entitled to think the speaker is cooperative, she is also entitled to think the speaker knows that p if she asserted that p. As far as it goes, this is plausible, but the simple answer has problems explaining a phenomenon known as *Moore's Paradox*.

Moore (1990: 211) noticed the curious fact that one cannot assert (10.3.3) felicitously even though such an assertion might be true:

(10.3.3) It's raining but I don't know it.

Suppose that it started to rain just after I came inside. I may then mistakenly think the weather has not changed, and then (10.3.3) would be true about me. *You* can express this truth now without impropriety, uttering 'It is raining but you don't know it' and *later on* I can too, uttering 'It was raining but I didn't know it'. But for me at the time there seems to be no faultless way to say such a thing.

Assertion contrasts with supposition with regard to this Moorean feature. There is nothing whatsoever wrong with supposing (say, for the sake of argument) that (10.3.3) is the case. We can imagine someone locked up in an underground room saying this:

(10.3.4) Let's suppose that it's raining.

Conjecturing that (10.3.3) is the case seems also possible:

(10.3.5) – What's your best guess about the weather in Dublin?
– Oh, it's raining. But, of course, I don't know this.

One may reasonably hope that, if we understand the source of the peculiar sort of infelicity associated with (10.3.3), we can gain insight into why assertion enables us to transfer knowledge. The literature on Moore's Paradox is enormous; in what follows we will look at three of the most influential types of approaches.

10.3.1 Implication

Moore (1990: 209–210) offers the following diagnosis of why I cannot without absurdity say about myself that it is raining but I don't believe it, even though someone else can:

> Now though, according to me, there's no difference between what's *meant* by the sentence he uttered assertively and what's *meant* by the sentence I utter assertively, and both express what may perfectly well be true; there is a difference between what I *imply* by uttering assertively the words 'it's raining' and what you imply by uttering the same words at the same time in the same place. Namely I *imply* that I believe it's raining and *not* that you do; you imply that you do not that I do.

If we wish to explain the analogy to knowledge, we might say that in asserting (10.3.3), one implies not only that one believes that it's raining but also that one *knows* it. Anyone who asserted that it is raining but he does not know that it is would then imply that he knows that it is raining and assert that he does not know this. So, while the proposition expressed by (10.3.3) is perfectly coherent, asserting that proposition is not.

According to this idea, asserting that p can be used to transfer knowledge of p because trusting the speaker requires believing not only what he asserts but also what he implies. When a speaker asserts p the trusting hearer will come to believe both that p and that the speaker knows that p, and since the latter is reason for the former, the hearer may come to know that p.

The exact sense in which someone making an assertion implies that he believes what he asserted is not easy to pin down. There is no obvious conventional way to link some feature of the assertion with the alleged implication. The indicative mood of the sentence that is uttered is the only remotely plausible candidate, but it is at best a defeasible indicator: Indicative sentences are frequently used to perform speech acts other than assertions – not only other constative speech acts, like conjectures and suppositions, but also performatives, like promises, permissions, baptisms, and bets. Moreover, as Williamson (1996a) has stressed, conventional ties must be to some extent arbitrary, but the link between asserting and knowing does not seem to be.

Ruling out conventionality, one might suggest that the implication Moore identifies is a conversational implicature. Asserting what one does not know violates Grice's Maxim of Quality: Try to make your contribution one that is true, and hence, try to avoid saying what you do not believe or lack adequate evidence for. But there are problems with the idea that in asserting that p one conversationally implicates that one knows that p.

First, it is not clear that Grice's maxim prohibits asserting what one does not know – it all depends on what counts as "adequate evidence." Suppose I bought a lottery ticket and that I know that the chances of this particular ticket winning are less than one in a hundred million. On many views, this would count as perfectly adequate evidence that the ticket won't win. Nonetheless, intuitively, one does not know of this (or any other) particular ticket that it won't win. Second, conversational implicature is supposed to be cancelable, which means that explicit cancelations should be felicitous. But (10.3.3), an explicit cancelation of the alleged implicature, is definitely *not* felicitous. And finally, Grice (1975: 41–42) explicitly rejects this proposal:

> When I speak of the assumptions required in order to maintain that the Cooperative Principle and maxims are being observed on a given occasion, I am not thinking of assumptions that are nontrivially required; I do not intend to include, for example, an assumption to the effect that some particular maxim is being observed. This seemingly natural restriction has an interesting consequence with regard to Moore's "paradox." On my account, it will not be true that when I say that *p*, I conversationally implicate that I believe that *p*; for to suppose that I believe that *p* (or rather think of myself as believing that *p*) is just to suppose that I am observing the first maxim of Quality on this occasion. I think this consequence is intuitively acceptable; it is not a natural use of language to describe one who has said that *p* as having, for example, "implied,"

> "indicated," or "suggested" that he believes that *p*; the natural thing to say is that he has expressed (or at least purported to express) the belief that *p*. He has of course committed himself, in a certain way, to its being the case that he believes that *p*, and while this commitment is not a case of saying that he believes that *p*, it is bound up, in a special way, with saying that *p*.

The heart of Grice's objection is that the connection between assertion and belief is *direct*: When I make an assertion, I commit myself to believing what I asserted just as straightforwardly as I commit myself to what I asserted. No special reasoning is required to figure this out; any appeal to the cooperative principle or to the maxims would be otiose. The reasoning seems equally compelling if we replace 'believe' with 'know' in the last two sentences of the above quotation.

10.3.2 Expression

According to Grice, in asserting that it is raining, I neither assert nor imply that I know (or believe) that this is so; rather, I express or at least purport to express this attitude. He is perfectly right that this manner of speaking is very natural; the question is what expressing an attitude amounts to. Grice follows the passage we quoted by promising to clarify his view when he discusses the function of the *indicative mood*. Grice (1968: 123) makes good on the promise. There Grice proposes that by the indicative mood of a sentence uttered the speaker means that she believes what she says.

This idea won't do: Indicative sentences are used to perform a plethora of speech acts besides assertions, and hence, assigning a special type of speaker meaning to all occurrences of the indicative mood is hopeless. But if we are charitable we can (somewhat tentatively) read Grice as gesturing towards an account of *force*, not of what we would nowadays call mood. It goes as follows: For a speaker to assert that p is (perhaps among other things) to express a belief (or perhaps knowledge) with the content that p; this in turn is for her to mean that she believes (or knows) that p. If we combine the analysis of speaker meaning from Grice (1957) with this, we get the following:

> By uttering x the utterer U asserted that p iff for some audience A, U uttered x intending
>
> i. S intends that A believe (or know) that S believes (or knows) that p,
> ii. S intends that A recognize i.,
> iii. S intends that A believe (or know) that S believes that p in part because ii.

This account explains the infelicity of (10.3.3). When a speaker asserts that it is raining but she does not know it she means that she knows this. This yields a contradiction in what the speaker means, without a contradiction in what she says. The possibility of knowledge transfer rests on the fact that a trusting hearer believes what the speaker means; when a speaker asserts that p a trusting hearer will believe that the speaker knows that p, which is a reason for the hearer to believe that p.

Grice's intention-based account of assertion and others that are similar in spirit have been criticized on the basis of requiring rather complex intentions from speakers. (Varieties of an intention-based account of assertion have been proposed by Searle [1969: 47], Bach and Harnish [1979: 42], and Recanati [1988: 183].) But assertion seems like a relatively simple matter, and it is doubtful that it requires anything so sophisticated as an intention that someone should know that one knows that something is the case. More importantly, when I assert that it is raining, typically I mean to inform someone about the weather; I do not mean to convey information about my own mental life. Speakers acknowledge that their addressees will learn a great deal about their mental life in the course of conversation, and they accept this as an inevitable by-product of communication. But it seems wrong to say that asserting that it is raining consists in part in an intention to inform others about one's own mind.

Finally, there is a more specific problem: Speakers seem to be able to lie even if they know that the addressee knows that they are lying. Just consider Frank Pentangeli in the second Godfather movie. At a senate hearing he asserts, contrary to his earlier confession, that he knows nothing about criminal activities involving Michael Corleone. Frank has presumably no intention to get anyone to believe that he believes what he says, but his speech act still seems to be a *bona fide* assertion.

For an argument that tries to cast doubt on this intuition, see Keiser (2016b). Pagin (2011) uses similar examples to argue that there is no limit to the calculations of a deceptive speaker. If this is right, expression-based accounts of Moore's Paradox cannot work.

10.3.3 Requirement

One might avoid the pitfalls of intention-based views, by linking assertion to knowledge through some sort of social *requirement*. The idea goes back at least to Peirce (1933: 547):

> every assertion involves an effort to make the intended interpreter believe what is asserted, to which end a reason for believing it must be furnished. But if a lie would not endanger the esteem in which the utterer was held, nor otherwise be apt to entail such real effects as he would avoid, the interpreter would have no reason to believe the assertion.

It is a platitude that, in many cases, one who asserts p is accountable for this act – if it turns out that p is false, or poorly supported by evidence, or disbelieved by the speaker, etc. there will be consequences for the speaker's social standing. But Peirce makes a stronger claim: that one who makes an assertion is *always* accountable in this way. If Peirce is right, we can think of the consequences as the enforcement mechanism whereby society upholds the norms of assertion.

It is by no means clear that Peirce's strong claim is true – in casual conversations people frequently exaggerate, indulge in bullshit, and even lie without apparently violating social norms. Peirce must say either that what people are doing in casual conversation is not really assertion, or that in these settings the norms of assertion are set aside or overridden. For criticism of the idea that assertion is governed by norms specific to it see Pagin (2016).

Philosophers who believe assertion is governed by norms might try to distinguish assertions from other constative speech acts by appeal to these norms. Perhaps, for example, we are not accountable for the falsehood of our suppositions, and our culpability for false conjectures and implications is less (or at least different in kind) than our culpability for false assertions. But it is not easy to be precise as to what responsibilities the speaker of an assertion undertakes. According to Brandom (1994), someone who makes an assertion authorizes her addressees to assert anything that follows from what she asserted (and hence, bears some responsibility for those assertions) and to request justification for what she asserted (and hence, bears some responsibility for providing such a justification). This seems too strong. Suppose the addressee comes to believe something false that follows from what the speaker said but she does not rely on the speaker's assertion. In fact, she promptly forgot what the speaker said and her belief arose entirely because of her own shoddy thinking. Is the speaker still responsible? Suppose the speaker refuses to provide justification for a claim that is perfectly obvious. In fact, the speaker knows that the hearer has no doubts about the truth of the claim – she is just stonewalling. Did the speaker violate a norm by refusing to provide justification? It is quite possible that the way in which and the extent to which we hold each other responsible for assertions is subject to much cultural variation.

Things could be clearer if we could isolate certain norms as *constitutive* of assertion. Constitutive norms are the ones which makes the practice what it is; they can be contrasted with *regulative* norms which merely constrain engagement in an already-existing practice. It is, for example, a constitutive rule of soccer that the goalkeeper is not allowed to deliberately handle the ball outside the goal box, while it is a regulative rule that the goalkeeper should use his hands inside the goal box to prevent a goal. The difference is best appreciated not by considering cases where the two rules are *disobeyed* but rather cases where they are *disregarded.* A game where players pay no heed to the first rule would be something other than soccer, while a game where the second is flouted would be soccer badly played.

According to one view, assertion has no constitutive norms; see Maitra (2011). Again this seems too strong. A practice where speakers paid no attention to whether they are understood or whether what they say is relevant would surely not count as assertion. But these sorts of constitutive norms apply to communication across the board and cannot be used to distinguish assertion from other speech acts. The constitutive norms that are often claimed to specifically apply to assertion are *epistemic* in character – which is no surprise if we believe that one (and perhaps the only) function of assertion is to enable the transfer of knowledge. Williamson (1996a) suggested the following norm of assertion:

> **Knowledge norm of assertion:** One must assert that p only if one knows that p.

If there is such a norm it immediately explains why (10.3.3) is infelicitous. Suppose one asserts that it is raining but one does not know it. Supposing the speaker obeyed the knowledge norm, it follows that she knows that it is raining and that she does not know that it is raining, which is a contradiction. So, (10.3.3) cannot be used to make an assertion without violating the knowledge norm. Moreover, since knowing p requires that one believe p and that one should have evidence for p, the infelicity of (10.3.6) and (10.3.7) are also accounted for:

(10.3.6) It's raining but I don't believe it
(10.3.7) It's raining but I have no evidence for it

To account for the possibility of knowledge transfer via assertion is also straightforward. For a hearer to trust a speaker who made an assertion is to believe that he did not violate the knowledge norm. Believing this, the hearer can conclude that the speaker knows what he says, which in turn gives the hearer reason to believe it.

10.4 Expressivism

In Section 0.3 we briefly discussed Ayer's expressivism and its chief discontent, the Frege-Geach problem. According to Ayer, ethical, aesthetic, and religious terms fail to contribute anything to the content of sentences in which they occur. Their function is to express the emotions of the speaker without stating that the speaker has those emotions:

> if I say to someone, 'You acted wrongly in stealing that money', I am not saying anything more than if I had simply said, 'You stole that money.' In adding that this action is wrong I am not making any further statement about it. I am simply evincing my moral disapproval of it. It is as if I had said, 'You stole that money', in a peculiar tone of horror, or written it with the addition of some special exclamation marks. The tone, or the exclamation marks, adds nothing to the literal meaning of the sentence. It merely serves to show that the expression of it is attended by certain feelings in the speaker. If now I generalize my previous statement and say, "Stealing money is wrong," I produce a sentence which has no factual meaning – that is, expresses no proposition which can be either true or

> false. It is as if I had written 'Stealing money!!' – where the shape and thickness of the exclamation marks show, by a suitable convention, that a special sort of moral disapproval is the feeling which is being expressed. (Ayer 1936: 107)

The Frege–Geach objection is the following challenge: If (10.4.8) is neither true nor false, how can we account for the intuitive validity of inferences in which it occurs as a premise, like (10.4.8)?

(10.4.8) Stealing is wrong.

(10.4.9) Stealing is wrong; if stealing is wrong then so is robbery; so robbery is wrong.

The natural thing to say is that any instance of *modus ponens* is valid, even if it contains sentences that are neither true nor false. But there are two problems with this response. First, it is not clear what counts as an instance of *modus ponens* if we allow sentences that are neither true nor false. Should we say this is equally an instance?

(10.4.10) There are cookies in the drawer. If there are cookies in the drawer then go ahead and take some. So go ahead and take some.

Second, the account makes validity itself problematic. The emotivist certainly cannot say that the inference (10.4.8) is valid because it is truth-preserving. But if valid inferences needn't preserve truth, what exactly do they need to preserve?

To answer the Frege–Geach problem a number of philosophers have attempted to devise an alternative semantics for evaluative sentences – a semantics that does not assign truth-conditions to them but is capable of underpinning logical inference. But, on reflection, it is not clear that this is the best line of defense. Ayer says two things about 'Stealing is wrong' – that it lacks factual meaning (and hence, truth-conditions) and that sincerely uttering it is like sincerely uttering 'Stealing money!!' with a particular intonation (and hence, expressing moral disapproval). But the connection between the semantic claim and the pragmatic one is obscure. It seems that the first is supposed to provide support for the second (if 'Stealing is wrong' has no truth-value then one cannot use it to make an assertion, so in uttering it one must be doing something else), but the second can obviously stand on its own and is compatible with the idea that the sentence can be true or false. This would avoid the Frege–Geach problem without making revisionary claims about semantics. (David Lewis recommends this approach to performatives in Lewis [1970b].)

Expressivists of the purely pragmatic sort will, of course, say that in sincerely uttering 'Stealing is wrong', one expresses moral disapproval of stealing. And as long as we don't assume any particular account of what it is to express disapproval, this is uncontroversial – just as uncontroversial as saying that in sincerely uttering 'It is raining' one expresses a belief. A minimal version of this purely pragmatic expressivism would say that expression of disapproval is *all* the speaker is doing in sincerely uttering 'Stealing is wrong'. In particular, she does not express the belief that stealing is wrong *in addition* to a disapproval of stealing. The difficulty with this is that presumably, making such an utterance would not require the speaker to believe that stealing is wrong, in which case we would expect sincere utterances of (10.4.11) to be unproblematic. But they aren't.

(10.4.11) Stealing is wrong but I don't believe that it is.

Some pragmatic expressivists concede that sincere utterances of 'Stealing is wrong' are assertions but insist that they are to be distinguished from ordinary assertions. All assertions express beliefs, but beliefs are not a homogeneous class of mental states. Ordinary assertions express cognitive states (with a mind-to-world direction of fit), while evaluative assertions express conative states (with a world-to-mind direction of fit) or affective states (with no direction of fit). (See Blackburn [1984] and Gibbard [2003].) So, in asserting that stealing is wrong, one expresses a belief that *is* a disapproval.

This may seem to remove the issue from the domain of pragmatics – whether disapproval is a kind of belief seems clearly a question for psychology. But consider:

(10.4.12) Stealing is wrong but I don't disapprove of stealing.

Woods (2014) has claimed that (10.4.12) is not paradoxical, or if it is, its oddity is of a lesser sort than that of (10.4.11). Asserting that stealing is wrong but one does not disapprove of it would be making an intelligible claim – acknowledging the existence of a norm and at the same time dissociating oneself from it. But if this is right, in asserting that stealing is wrong one hasn't quite expressed disapproval of stealing.

There is a real intuition behind expressivism: What one is doing in sincerely uttering 'Stealing is wrong' is different from what one is doing in sincerely uttering 'Stealing is common'. But the difference is elusive. Whether it is a matter of psychology, pragmatics, or semantics remains a controversial issue.

10.5 Conclusion

While linguists have always recognized distinctions of sentential mood, it took a long time to get clear about its function. What declarative, interrogative, or imperative mood indicates is not what the speaker is saying but, rather, what she is doing in saying what she is saying. Following Searle, we might call this the speech act she is performing.

The correlation between mood and speech act is complicated: In natural languages there are only a handful of the former devices, but in human interactions there are hundreds of the latter. We need a theory if we are to make some progress in explaining how people figure out what speech act a speaker is performing when she is uttering a sentence.

Philosophers have focused most of their recent attention on the speech act of assertion. What makes assertion unique among speech acts is its capacity to transfer knowledge. If I know something and I assert it, you can come to know it too – this much is uncontroversial. But the mechanism is puzzling. In trusting my assertion, you can come to believe its content, but what makes this belief knowledge? Here is an idea: In asserting that p, I implied or otherwise meant that I know that p, and so, by trusting me, your belief qualifies as knowledge too. Here is another: It is common knowledge that it is a norm that one should not assert what one does not know, and so, knowing that I did not violate this norm is enough for you to come to know what I asserted.

What makes the theory of speech acts a very complex affair is that apparently we can perform multiple speech acts simultaneously. Perhaps in saying 'Can you pass the salt?' one isn't only making a request, one is also asking a question – as attested by the fact that someone could respond to the question saying 'No. Sorry, I cannot reach that far'. Perhaps in saying 'What he did was an outrage' one isn't only expressing disapproval, but one is also making an assertion – as attested by the fact that someone can agree with it saying 'That is true'. And perhaps – contra Austin – in saying 'I order the halibut' one isn't just ordering the halibut but also asserting that one is doing that – as attested by the fact that it would be infelicitous to add to such order '... but I don't know this'. If this is right, the connection between the mood of the sentence uttered and at least one associated speech act might be straightforward. Unfortunately, this would not help much in explaining how speakers manage to identify the *other* speech act.

PART III

Meaning as a Philosophical Problem

11 Meaning and Use

11.1 The Use Theory

Semantics, as it is generally practiced today, can appear to be a purely descriptive enterprise, tasked with assigning the correct meaning to each expression of a language. What makes the task problematic is that natural languages have infinitely many expressions and that we don't have a particularly clear idea of what meaning is. Compositionality helps with the first difficulty: It ensures that by specifying the meanings of lexical items and compositional rules that project those meanings up the syntactic tree, we can determine what all other expressions mean. Extensions help with the second problem: Whatever meanings are, they determine extensions in various contexts and various circumstances. If we can find suitable abstract entities that do this, we can model an important aspect of meaning.

But nontriviality does not guarantee that a project is worth undertaking. If you want to know what a certain sentence of Urdu means, just ask a native speaker and she will tell you – no need to wait until semanticists construct a viable theory of meaning for a fragment of Urdu that includes your sentence. If semanticists who work on Urdu merely did this on a larger scale, gathering and systematizing data about what the words, phrases, and sentences of Urdu mean, the theory would only yield information that roughly 70 million of us already have. And even if semantic theories make important predictions, we should not expect to use such a theory to adjudicate disagreements between native speakers about the meaning of some complicated expression. Though perhaps at some point in the future we might employ a well-confirmed comprehensive semantic theory this way, it is hard to believe that this is the sole benefit we should hope to gain from semantic theorizing.

So, what is the purpose of semantics? Here is a natural response: Like other scientific theories, semantics is supposed to provide *explanations* for certain phenomena. Explanations, at a first approximation, are satisfactory answers to *why*-questions. Physics explains why falling bodies on Earth accelerate at the same rate; chemistry explains why water expands upon freezing; biology explains why some people but not others have hemophilia, etc. Semantic theories, when successful, explain why linguistic expressions mean just what they do. Such explanations are worth having even if we obtain no new predictions about what means what.

There are many forms such semantic explanations might take, but the most straightforward idea is that they trace syntactic structure. So, for example, we might say that 'Socrates runs' has its meaning M because it has a certain syntactic structure, because its lexical components 'Socrates' and 'run' have the meanings M′ and M″, and because there is a semantic rule that tells us that expressions with such a structure and lexical components have M as their meaning. Let's call this a *compositional explanation* of the meaning of 'Socrates runs'.

Compositional explanations bottom out at lexical meaning – if we want to ask why words mean what they do, we will need to turn to explanations of a different sort. Dictionaries often try to capture the meaning of a word by providing a synonym, but these entries aren't explanatory – no one thinks that 'repel' means in English what it does because 'repulse' means in English what it does. Definitions may explain the meanings of technical terms. The word 'isotope' was coined in 1913 by Frederick Soddy, and to this day it remains a technical term of chemistry – thus it is not far-fetched to say that it means what it does because "each of two or more forms of the same element that contain equal numbers of protons but different numbers of neutrons in their nuclei" means what it does. After all, it is linguistic stipulation performed by means of this definition (or something close to it) that once bestowed meaning on the word 'isotope'. On the other hand, it would be odd to suggest that the word 'acceleration' means what it does because "the rate of change of velocity per unit of time" means what it does. The word comes from Latin, 'accelerate' was used in English well before Newton, and there is no reason to assume that physicists hijacked the old word and replaced its meaning with a new one. Rather, it seems that they left the meaning of 'acceleration' as they found it and simply discovered what acceleration was.

Even in cases when the definition of a word does explain its meaning, it can only do so by appealing to the meanings of other words. If we want to avoid circular explanations in semantics, the meanings of at least some words must be accounted for in a different way. This is the point where appeal to *use* becomes very tempting. As Wittgenstein (1953: §43) famously writes in the *Philosophical Investigations*, "[f]or a large class of cases – though not for all – in which we employ the word 'meaning' it can be defined thus: the meaning of a word is its use in the language."

Appeal to use is ubiquitous in dictionaries. One of the entries for 'hello' in the *Oxford English Dictionary* is that it is "used as a greeting or to begin a telephone conversation," for 'very' that it is "used for emphasis," for 'here' that it is "used when pointing or gesturing to indicate the place in mind," for 'why' that (with a negative) it is "used to make or agree to a suggestion," and so on. Dictionary entries specifying use are explanatory in ways definitions rarely and mere synonyms never are: It makes perfect sense to say that a word has such-and-such a meaning because it is used in a certain way.

In its most radical form, the use theory of meaning identifies the meaning of every expression of a language with its use among speakers of the language. Whether anyone has ever held such a view is doubtful. In any case, the view is clearly false for the simple reason that in any interesting language there are meaningful sentences that have never been used. A sensible but bold use-theory would identify only the meanings of words, or perhaps just a subclass of words, with their use.

But what about sentences? These, Ryle (1961: 228–229) argues, don't even have uses.

> Equating the notion of the meaning of a word with the notion of the use of that word, [some philosophers] go on without apparent qualms to talking as if the meaning of a sentence could equally well be spoken of as the use of that sentence. We hear, for example, that nonsensical English sentences are sentences that have no use in English; as if sentences could be solecisms.

Whether or not Ryle is right about this, the meanings of complex expressions can be accounted for by appealing to semantic rules. If there are words whose meanings aren't identified with their uses, those can be explained by appealing to the meanings of certain sentences in which they occur as constituents. Many use theorists are even less sanguine: They allow that use could always be distinct from meaning, insisting only on the claim that the former explains the latter, not the other way around.

So, what *is* the use of a word? At a first approximation, it is a certain pattern or regularity. Wittgenstein sought to illustrate word usage with examples of *language games*: mini-languages employed for specific purposes. Here is the classic example, mentioned in Section 10.1.1, Wittgenstein (1953: §2):

> The language is meant to serve for communication between a builder A and an assistant B. A is building with building-stones: there are blocks, pillars, slabs and beams. B has to pass the stones, and that in the order in which A needs them. For this purpose they use a language consisting of the words"block," "pillar," "slab," "beam". A calls them out; – B brings the stone which he has learnt to bring at such-and-such a call. – Conceive this as a complete primitive language.

Here, the relevant regularities are easy to describe – for example, whenever A utters 'block', B brings him a block. Of course, there are situations when the regularity breaks – for example, when there is too much noise to hear or no more blocks to fetch. One of the tasks a use theory faces is to explain why such situations should be viewed as exceptions rather than counterexamples. It cannot simply be that they are rare: It could be that A and B work in a noisy environment where supplies run out all the time, in which case A's utterances would frequently (perhaps even usually) not be followed by the appropriate response from B. Still, it does not seem that the meaning of 'block' would in any way be affected by this. If use is to explain meaning, it must be a *robust* regularity – one that permits exceptions and could persist even if some of the particular events that constitute it were different.

Spelling out what makes the relevant regularities robust is not the only challenge for a use theory. Another would be avoiding *circularity*. When we say that 'block' is used by A to instruct B to bring him a block, we characterize the use in terms of the very word whose meaning we seek to explain. Identifying the use of 'block' independently of its meaning is hard. Suppose the blocks, pillars, slabs, and beams are all laid out in the southern corner of the lot where the building project is taking place. Then, in a sense, whenever B hears an utterance he does the same thing: He goes to the southern corner, picks up something, and carries it to A. And yet, we need to distinguish what he does when he picks up a block from what he does when he picks up something else. But now, suppose some of the blocks are in the southern corner of the lot and others in the northern corner. Then when B brings A a block he can do either of two things: He can go to the southern lot, pick up a block, and carry it to A, or he can go to the northern corner, pick up a block, and carry it to A. And yet, we need to count both of these as the same response.

If both of these challenges are met we have identified the *role* 'block' plays within Wittgenstein's tiny language game. In this game, the roles of 'block', 'pillar', 'slab', and 'beam' are very similar. But, Wittgenstein (1953: §12) argues, once we look at more complex cases, we realize that the roles words play are disparate:

> Think of the tools in a tool-box: there is a hammer, pliers, a saw, a screw-driver, a rule, a glue-pot, glue, nails and screws. – The functions of words are as diverse as the functions of these objects. (And in both cases there are similarities.)
>
> Of course, what confuses us is the uniform appearance of words when we hear them spoken or meet them in script and print. For their application is not presented to us so clearly.

Wittgenstein doesn't deny that we can ask what words signify, but he does object to the thought that in positing a single interpretation function $[\![\cdot]\!]$, we uncover the meanings of expressions – something uniform that they have in common. On the other hand, without a common format for meaning assignment, it is hard to see how we could use our characterizations of the uses of words in explaining the meanings of complex expressions in which they occur. Wittgenstein himself would not be bothered by this: His version of use theory is really an antitheory, one that explicitly eschews explanation. In this regard, the use theory developed in Horwich (1998) is a true contemporary heir of Wittgenstein's legacy. But those of us who wish to preserve the explanatory promise of semantics need to do precisely what Wittgenstein warns against: identify a common role our words have in language in virtue of which they have their meanings.

Much of the initial appeal of use-theories of meaning came from the idea that use must be a regularity of observable public *behavior*, and thus it promises explanations of meaning that are free of appeals to allegedly obscure mental states and processes. It is the lure of behaviorism that is largely responsible for Wittgenstein's assessment that there is at most a loose family resemblance among the uses of words. We are often advised to "look and see" whether the uses of words have anything important in common – but what we can see is of course only how speakers using the words behave, not what is going on in their minds. As behaviorism gave way to functionalism in the philosophy of mind, use-theories of meaning that openly allow appeal to mental states and processes started to emerge in the philosophy of language.

Some post-behavioristic philosophers have suggested that the common role words play in our language is a matter of inference. Consider the introduction and elimination rules for conjunction in natural-deduction proofs. The former allows us to infer $\phi \wedge \psi$ from ϕ and ψ; the latter to infer both ϕ and ψ from $\phi \wedge \psi$. These jointly capture the inferential role of $\wedge$ in formal languages of classical logic – which amounts to its use in proofs. Of course, when it comes to the English word 'and', things get much more complicated – after all, 'and' can conjoin noun phrases and sometimes gives rise to collective readings. It shows up in nondeclaratives, and for these there is no straightforward notion of inference. Nonetheless, some theorists find it reasonable to hope that with appropriate rules we can capture the inferential role of this word, that this role can be then identified with its use among English-speakers, and that it can explain the meaning of 'and' in English.

The identification of use with inferential role has quite a bit of plausibility for many functional words in natural languages. It is more problematic if one tries to extend it to content words. To do so, one must consider what Sellars (1953) calls *material inferences*. These are inferences like "It's raining; therefore the streets will be wet" or "I am releasing a piece of chalk; therefore it will fall." Contrary to longstanding philosophical dogma, Sellars thinks these are not enthymemes – their validity does not rest on implicit generalizations that serve as missing premises. Rather, they spell out part of the inferential role of the words 'rain' and 'fall', respectively. On this sort of view, understanding a word consists in knowing its inferential role, which in turn is nothing more than knowing how to employ the word in reasoning – knowing which validities one should accept. For a contemporary defense of this view, see Brandom (2000).

More generous views about the roles of words in language accept sources of meaning other than inferential know-how. *Conceptual role semantics* is an example of such a view, though it deals not only with language but with thought as well. Proponents of conceptual role semantics place no restrictions on the sorts of reasoning that can figure in their explanations. Perceptual inferences and action-guiding decisions certainly count as reasoning, as well perhaps as noninferential mental processes such as categorization, association, and imagination.

The credibility of such a theory of meaning depends on how many types of roles it allows words to play. The more roles it provides, the more credible it will be. But this trend makes it harder to combine the theory with compositional explanations. There is a delicate balance to maintain, and opponents of conceptual role semantics exploit this weakness. Fodor and Lepore (2001), for instance, argue that meanings cannot be conceptual roles because the conceptual roles of complex expressions are not determined by the conceptual roles of their parts. This is a cogent criticism of theories that seek to identify meaning with conceptual roles. But many conceptual role theorists are more modest: They only claim that the conceptual roles of some words can explain their meanings and that these explanations can then be fed into compositional explanations of the meanings of complex expressions.

Use-theories of meaning are rarely more than bare sketches. To fill out the picture we need to say more about what uses are and how they interact with other practices. In particular, we theorists need to address two questions. First, what exactly are various linguistic expressions used for? What sorts of roles do they play in language? To say that they are used in inferencing seems too restrictive; to say that they are used in reasoning seems too permissive. Second, what regularities can be components of meaning? If A pushes B, then B will fall, and it may even be that A uses the pushing to make B fall. And yet, the event consisting of A's pushing of B has no meaning. On the other hand, if A utters a word to get B to bring him a block, as in Wittgenstein's language game, then the event is an utterance, and is meaningful.

In the next two sections we will consider two influential attempts that aim to address these issues – one due to Paul Grice and the other to David Lewis. In the last section, we ask whether there is a way to mold the two programs into a single theory.

11.2 Grice's Program

Back in Section 5.1 we mentioned the distinction drawn in Augustine of Hippo (1995) between natural and conventional signs: The former are those which signify "apart from any intention or desire of using them as signs," while the latter "are those which living beings mutually exchange in order to show, as well as they can, the feelings of their minds, or their perceptions, or their thoughts." Words clearly belong in the second category, and a post-behaviorist use theorist might even agree with the suggestion that their function is to display for others the contents of one's own mind. There is even a hint here about what all word meanings might have in common: signifying an intention or desire.

Paul Grice's program in the philosophy of language can be seen as an attempt to turn this intriguing but vague idea into a genuine explanatory theory. Grice continued to refine his theory for decades; the main milestones are Grice (1957, 1968, 1969, 1982).

First, he replaces Augustine's distinction with a different but closely related division between *natural meaning* and *non-natural meaning*. He directs our attention to linguistic differences between two usages of 'meaning' to introduce the distinction with examples along the following lines:

(11.2.1) Those spots mean that the patient has measles.
(11.2.2) Those three rings mean that the bus is full.

The former attributes natural meaning to the spots on the patient; the latter non-natural meaning to the rings of the bell. The most striking differences between these sentences involve factivity and agency: (11.2.1) entails that the patient has measles, while (11.2.2) does not entail that the bus is full; (11.2.2) entails that someone meant by those rings that the bus is full, while (11.2.1) does not entail that someone meant by those spots that the patient has measles.

A natural thought (one that Grice nonetheless does not endorse explicitly) is that while (11.2.1) is about a relation between facts, (11.2.2) describes a relation between an agent and a proposition. This suggestion is further supported by the different paraphrases these sentences permit:

(11.2.3) The fact that the patient has those spots means that he has measles.
(11.2.4) ? The fact that the bell has been rung three times means that it is full.
(11.2.5) ? What is meant by those spots is that the patient has measles.
(11.2.6) What is meant by those three rings is that the bus is full.

Grice also observes that only reports of non-natural meaning can be paraphrased using quotation marks:

(11.2.7) ? Those spots mean 'the patient has measles'.
(11.2.8) Those three rings on the bell mean 'the bus is full'.

This suggests that the non-natural meaning of the rings is, but the natural meaning of spots isn't, of the same type as the meaning of a linguistic expression. It is this commonality that encourages us to take seriously the fundamental idea of the Gricean program: "the meaning (in general) of a sign needs to be explained in terms of what users of the sign do (or should) mean by it on particular occasions" (Grice 1957: 217). If we understand what it is for three rings to mean on a particular occasion that the bus is full, perhaps we can move from there to understanding what 'the bus is full' means, and from understanding sentences of this type we might be able to get to the meaning of 'full'.

How does Grice fill in the details in this explanation of linguistic meaning? First, he sets out to define what it is for someone (the utterer) to mean something by a certain act (an utterance). Such acts require an audience: someone to whom the act is directed. In the declarative case the utterer, Grice suggests, intends that the audience should come to have a belief. But this primary intention is not enough: Iago drops a handkerchief to get Othello to believe that Desdemona was unfaithful, but he did not mean anything by his act. This is because Iago wishes to conceal his primary intention – he does not have the secondary intention that Othello should recognize his intention to get Othello to believe that Desdemona was unfaithful. In fact, he (probably) has the opposite secondary intention: that Othello should not believe that he intends him to believe that Desdemona was unfaithful.

So meaning seems to require a primary and a secondary intention. But this is still not sufficient: When Herod presents the head of John the Baptist to Salome, he (i) intends her to believe that St. John is dead and (ii) intends this intention to be recognized. And yet, he does not mean anything by his act. In this example, the secondary intention plays no role in creating the belief – Herod does not have the tertiary intention that Salome should believe that John is dead because she recognizes that he intends her to come to believe this. In fact, he (probably) has the opposite tertiary intention: that Salome should believe that John is dead because she can clearly see that he is.

Combining these three communicative intentions, Grice arrives at his famous three-pronged analysis of when an utterer means something by a declarative act.

> By uttering x the utterer U meant that p iff for some audience A, U uttered x intending
> (i) that A should believe that p,
> (ii) that A should recognize (i), and
> (iii) that (i) should be fulfilled because (ii) is fulfilled.

This is one of several famous attempts to define a philosophically important notion. Like the others – Plato's definition of knowledge as justified true belief, Hume's definition of causation as counterfactual dependence of effect upon cause, and Tarski's definition of logical truth as truth in all models – Grice (1957) is a source of controversy as well as insight.

Some critics reject outright Grice's intuition that the tertiary intention is necessary. When someone utters 'I can speak in a squeaky voice' in a squeaky voice, she arguably means that she can speak in a squeaky voice, but – having just displayed her ability – she presumably does not intend that her audience should come to believe this just because they recognize that this is what she intends. (This example is attributed to Neil Smith in Neale (1992). A similar example is discussed in Schiffer (1972) and in Recanati (1986): someone yells "I am here.")

Or consider an interpreter translating the words of a speaker delivering a moving speech. Suppose the interpreter does everything to make it clear to the audience that she fully identifies with the content of the speech. Then, the audience may well conclude that the interpreter meant just what the speaker did. At the same time, the interpreter presumably does not intend to produce a belief in the audience simply because they recognize that she intends them to do so – after all, it is clear to the audience that she is translating.

There are also examples that suggest that the analysis is too weak: The definition rules out the possibility that someone who means something by her utterance should hide her primary intention, but not the possibility that she should hide her secondary intention. Adding a clause that says that the utterer intends her secondary intention to be recognized by the audience won't really get rid of the problem, since then we still need a guarantee that the utterer isn't hiding *this* intention. The standard counterexamples along these lines came from Strawson (1964) and Schiffer (1972). Grice acknowledged that this is a problem. In Grice (1969) and Grice (1982) he tentatively suggested a fix – adding a clause that rules out any intention to deceive the audience with regard to the intentions that constitute the utterer's meaning. There are other proposals to avoid the regress, including appeals to mutual attitudes as in Schiffer (1972) and reflexive intentions as in Bach and Harnish (1979).

Other problems are directed to the first clause of the definition. Sometimes a speaker means something but does not intend to produce a belief with the same content (e.g. because she knows that the audience already has such a belief, or because she knows that there is no way they will adopt such a belief). In response to these sorts of counterexamples to the original analysis of utterer's meaning, Grice (1968) replaces (i) with (i′):

> (i′) that A should believe that U believes that p.

This is a significant change. On the original view, what someone means by an utterance is typically a proposition about the world outside the speaker; on the amended view, it is always a proposition about the speaker's own mind. This is a return to the old Augustinian idea that communication is a way in which people make aspects of their mental lives accessible to others, a view that was popularized by Locke (1975: 478):

> To make words serviceable to the end of communication, it is necessary . . . that they excite in the hearer exactly the same idea they stand for in the mind of the speaker. Without this, men fill one another's heads with noise and sounds; but convey not thereby their thoughts, and lay not before one another their ideas, which is the end of discourse and language.

The new definition avoids many counterexamples but not all. A bald-faced liar does not intend that her audience should believe that she believes her lie. Her aim is simply putting a certain proposition "on record," to make a feigned commitment available for later reference. The same example is used in Keiser (2016a) to support a revision of Grice's definition. Neale (1992) relies on different examples, such as the case of a speaker trying to remind an addressee of something that is common knowledge between them. In this case intending that the hearer should believe that the speaker believes what he means by his utterance would be pointless.

It appears that, at least in some cases, someone's primary intention in meaning that p could be nothing more than calling attention to the thought that p. Neale (1992: 550) proposed that (i) should be replaced by (i″):

> (i″) that A should actively entertain the thought that p (or the thought that U believes that p).

Grice made several attempts to generalize his definition to cover utterances whose force is not assertive. A speaker who utters 'Sit down!' normally doesn't mean the same thing as one who utters 'You are sitting down'. To capture the difference, Grice posited that ascriptions of utterer's meaning always use complements with *mood indicators*, that mood indicators are associated with propositional attitude types, and that those types feature in the specification of the primary intention. Thus, suppose $*_\psi$ is a mood indicator associated with the propositional attitude ψ. Then we can generalize (i″) in the following way:

> (i‴) that A should actively entertain the thought that $*_\psi$p (or the thought that U ψ's the thought that p)

There are many questions about this sort of generalization. Is it reasonable to think that there is always some (perhaps silent) mood indicator within complements of 'mean'? Do all moods correspond to some propositional attitude? What would it be to entertain the imperative-marked thought that the hearer should sit down? Is it different than entertaining the indicative-marked thought that the hearer should sit down? Grice addresses none of these, and his followers usually drop the ambition to handle nonassertive utterer's meaning altogether. To simplify the presentation we will do the same.

Let us now turn to how utterer's meaning is supposed to explain word meaning. Grice (1968) provides an intriguing outline. The first step is to define the meaning of a unstructured complete utterance type within an idiolect:[1]

> *Step 1:* For utterer U, the unstructured complete utterance type X has as one of its meanings 'p' iff U has in her repertoire the procedure to utter a token of X when by the utterance she means that p.

For example, suppose that nodding my head has 'I agree' in my idiolect as one of its meanings. According to Grice's analysis, this is true just in case I

[1] The definition of Grice (1968: 126) does not actually appeal to utterer's meaning, only to simple intentions. But that is because Grice believes that his definition entails the one given here. To clarify the structure of Grice's explanations, it is better to make explicit the connection between unstructured utterance type meaning in an idiolect and utterer's meaning.

have in my repertoire a procedure to perform a token of the head nodding type when by performing this act I mean that I agree. Head nodding might also mean other things in my idiolect (e.g. that I acknowledge the presence of someone) and there might be other procedures in my repertoire that mean the same thing (e.g. uttering the word 'yes').

Grice sought to explicate the crucial notion of having a procedure in one's repertoire in terms of having a standing readiness to perform the procedure if the conditions are right. Of course spelling out what it is for the conditions to be right would be a formidable task: A lewd gesture may well have a definite meaning in the idiolect of someone who would not be ready to make the gesture under virtually any circumstances. But this may just be a general problem with dispositions: Protecting a glass with bubble wrap does not make it any less fragile than it was when unprotected, but the protected glass would not break if it were dropped.

The next step of analysis turns from idiolects to public languages. This is crucial, for Grice accepts Wittgenstein's contention that within idiolects it makes no sense to speak of incorrect uses: What head nodding means in U's idiolect is irrelevant in deciding what it means when U nods to an addressee. Utterer's meaning is a matter of having certain intentions, and having those intentions (or at least having them rationally) depends on whether the utterer can (rationally) expect her audience to recognize them. Here is Grice's proposal:

> *Step 2:* For group G the unstructured complete utterance type X has as one of its meanings 'p' iff there are some (many) members of G such that
> (a) for them X has as one of its meanings 'p', and
> (b) for them having this meaning for X is conditional on the assumption that some (other) members of G also have this meaning for X.

In other words, for an English speaker U (but not for, say, a speaker of Bulgarian) the meaning of head nodding is 'U agrees' because for some (many) English speakers this is the meaning of the gesture in their idiolects and because this being so is conditional on the assumption that it is so for some (other) English speakers. Think of this as Grice's attempt to capture the idea that the meaning of head nodding is *conventional* among English speakers.

Let's turn now to meanings for structured complete utterance types. Here Grice helps himself to a robust notion of compositionality: He assumes that the meanings of complex utterance types are determined by the meanings of their constituent utterance types and the procedures for assembling those utterance types. Then the constituent utterance procedures and the procedure for combining constituents determine a resultant procedure for the combination. This yields the following generalization of Step 1:

> *Step 3:* For utterer U the structured complete utterance type X has as one of its meanings 'p' iff U has in her repertoire the resultant procedure to utter a token of X when by the utterance she means that p.

For example, suppose in my idiolect the sentence 'Socrates is perplexed' means that Socrates is perplexed. For Grice, this is because I have in my repertoire a resultant procedure to utter a token of 'Socrates is perplexed' when by the utterance I mean that Socrates is perplexed. Maybe I have never uttered such a sentence – perhaps I think Socrates is a know-it-all who is just faking perplexity. Never mind, as long as 'Socrates' and 'perplexed' have a certain meaning in my idiolect and as long as I have a procedure for predication in my repertoire, I am guaranteed to have this resultant procedure in my repertoire as well. Once we have this notion, we can use Step 2 to account for meanings of structured complete utterance types within public languages.

The final step seeks to define the meanings of incomplete utterance types (structured or unstructured). Grice proposes that the meanings of these can be specified in terms of the meanings of certain canonical complete utterance types in which they occur as constituents. The details are complex, and he only works out the case of the meanings of adjectives. Somewhat simplified, the definition goes as follows:

> *Step 4:* For utterer U the incomplete adjectival utterance type X means '…' iff U has in her repertoire the procedure to predicate X on a name when by the utterance she means that the referent of the name is … (where the two lacunae represented by dots are identically completed).

Thus, 'perplexed' means 'flabbergasted' in my idiolect just in case I have in my repertoire a procedure to predicate 'perplexed' of names when by my utterance I mean that the referent of the name is flabbergasted. Again, we can use Step 2 to define the meanings of incomplete utterance types in public languages.

It might seem that Grice's explanations are circular: In Step 3, he explains a meaning of 'Socrates is perplexed' in my idiolect by appealing to a meaning of 'perplexed' in my idiolect; then he turns around and in Step 4 explains a meaning of 'perplexed' in my idiolect by appealing to certain sentences (among them the sentence 'Socrates is perplexed') having a certain kind of meaning. But this isn't a genuine circularity: 'perplexed' is used, not mentioned in the explanation. Step 4 does not appeal to a meaning of 'Socrates is perplexed', or to any other specific sentence of this form.

Let's sum up by returning to the two questions we associated with use-theories at the end of the previous section and see how Grice attempts to answer them. The first question was what linguistic expressions are supposed to be used for. Grice argues that their function is to facilitate meaning things. More precisely, as speakers of a language we are equipped with certain procedures to combine unstructured linguistic expressions and to utter the resulting expressions meaning various things by those utterances. The second question concerned what distinguishes the regularities that constitute the use of a linguistic expression from those that don't. Part of Grice's answer to the second question follows from his answer to the first: The use of an expression is a procedure for employing utterances to mean things. But this isn't the full answer, because use can be correct or incorrect, and for a procedure to have such a normative characteristic there must be a standard of some sort to which it must conform. Grice nodded in the direction of an explanation of the normativity of use (see Step 2 above) but did no more than this.

11.3 Lewis' Program

Theories of linguistic meaning face two choice points. First, there is the question whether to explain the meanings of expressions bottom-up (beginning with words and proceeding to phrases and sentences) or to start higher up (with sentences, language games, or entire languages) and proceed downwards. Then, there is the question whether to begin with what expressions mean for individual speakers and then explain meaning for populations or to take public meanings as fundamental. David Lewis sides with Wittgenstein about the first question – meaning is to be explained top-down – but with Grice about the second – the individual perspective on meanings gets priority.

What Lewis calls a *language* is just a set of expressions paired with their interpretations. Sometimes (e.g. when there are infinitely many expressions) we might need to specify a language through a recursive procedure – a grammar. Languages can be associated with infinitely many different grammars and, according to Lewis, there is no objective ground for preferring one grammar over the others. If we opt for descriptions of languages in terms of simple compositional grammars, this is merely a matter of convenience. The answer to the question why a particular word or a sentence has a particular meaning for a population is always the same: "Because the expression belongs to a language the population uses and because that language pairs that expression with that meaning." This is the Wittgensteinian aspect of Lewis' view.

It makes little sense for Lewis to ask why an expression has a meaning in a language. All that can be said is that a language is a set of ordered pairs, and this particular ordered pair happens to be one of its members. On the other hand, it makes perfect sense to ask why a language is the language of a certain population. The answer is that there is a convention among members of the population sustained by a common interest in communication. Lewis then proceeds to explain what this convention is in terms of individual attitudes – preferences and expectations – of the members of the population. This is the Gricean aspect of the theory.

Although the Wittgensteinian aspect is straightforward, the Gricean component is challenging. It requires a general theory of conventions, explaining how they are grounded in the attitudes of individuals. Then it needs to show how languages and linguistic meanings can be explained as specific sorts of conventions. The first part of this philosophical project is pursued in Lewis

(1969: Chapters 1–3); the second in Lewis (1969: Chapters 4–5) and in Lewis (1975).

Let's start with conventions. At a first approximation, they are patterns of behavior people exhibit and expect others to exhibit. Moreover, they are patterns almost no one wants to be left out of. The following three conditions emerge from various formulations in Lewis (1969: Chapters 2–3).

> Suppose that the behavior of members of a population P when they figure as agents in a recurrent situation S exhibits a regularity R. This regularity is a *convention* iff in any instance of S among members of P,
>
> (i) almost every agent conforms to R,
> (ii) almost every agent expects almost every agent to conform to R,
> (iii) almost every agent prefers to conform to R on the condition that the others do.

This is a good beginning, but a crucial element is missing; the conformity must have a special sort of reason. Consider drinking behavior. People drink when they are thirsty if drink is available – a regularity that clearly satisfies this definition. But it satisfies it trivially – almost everyone prefers to drink when thirsty if others do because they prefer this unconditionally. Satisfying thirst is not a convention, because people would act to satisfy their thirst regardless of what they expect others to do.

The challenge is to characterize the reason why some regularities are conventional. Here, it is useful to appeal to *games*. Economists think of games as problems of interdependent decision-making. A game involves a group of agents, each with a range of possible actions. When the group acts, with each individual in the group choosing an action, the result will be an outcome. The members of the group are equipped with preferences for the possible outcomes and choose their individual actions with these preferences in mind. A *strategy* is a recipe for guiding an individual's behavior in a game.

It is helpful to think of conventions as the *coordinated strategies* that emerge from certain sorts of cooperative games. Here is a simple example. You and your friend enter a small lunch place and want to sit down at a table with just two chairs – one facing the window and another facing the room. You both prefer the chair facing the window a little and you both prefer sitting in different chairs a lot. In this situation there clearly are two outcomes that make sense for you and your friend – the ones where you sit in different seats. Game theorists call such solutions *proper coordination equilibria* and clarify the sense in which equilibria "make sense:" In an equilibrium everyone does worse if anyone unilaterally switches her choice.

Crucially, there are two such equilibria in our game: the two outcomes where each of you gets a different chair. (If your friend unilaterally switches her choice, or if you do, the two of you wind up in the same chair, and this is the worst outcome.) Although each of you prefers a different equilibrium, it is far more important to coordinate on one solution: If each of you follows your weak preference for the seat facing the window, you will both be very unhappy with the outcome. Games of this sort create an urgent practical problem: how to produce a consensus on a single group strategy. If you choose to sit in one seat, incorrectly expecting your friend to sit in the other, your uncoordinated choices will lead to an outcome that is far worse for everyone.

A *coordination problem*, then, involves a game where coincidence of preferences predominates and where there are multiple proper coordination equilibria. A solution to a coordination problem is a group strategy that leads to a proper coordination equilibrium.

We can now repair our definition. The idea is to specify in clause (iii) that conformity is preferred because it provides a solution to a coordination problem. (See Lewis [1969: 42].)

> (iii′) almost everyone prefers to conform to R on the condition that the others do, since S is a coordination problem and uniform conformity to R is a proper coordination equilibrium in S.

The problem of coordinating highway driving illustrates how this idea helps. American drivers solve the problem by driving on the right; driving on the left is another solution. In fact, almost everyone driving on American highways drives on the right and expects almost everyone to do the same. They prefer to drive on the right provided the others are doing the same. Because they expect others to drive on the right, they end up with a categorical preference to drive on the right.

But the American solution is arbitrary. There is another coordination equilibrium: driving on the left. Because American drivers' preference for driving on the right depends crucially on the solution this provides to the coordination problem, their preference is conditional on expectations about other drivers. When these expectations change – when they find themselves expecting others to drive on the left, as British drivers do, they themselves will prefer to drive on the left.

Game theory does not pretend to be a theory of either the actual behavior or the conscious reasoning of human agents. It is a theory of what is rational. If agents in general act rationally, it can account for the strategies they use in decision-making, whether or not these strategies are outcomes of conscious reasoning. In using game theory to account for conventions, what matters is whether the conventions arise from strategies that provide solutions to a recurring decision problem that are optimal in light of conditional preferences that can plausibly be attributed to the members of a group. Whether they recognize that this is in fact an explanation of their behavior is neither here nor there.

On the other hand, if the best way to account for a pattern of behavior appeals only to instinct, to blind habit, or to fear of punishment, then conformity to the pattern is not a matter of convention, no matter how people rationalize their behavior to themselves.

So far so good, but a problem remains. Suppose everyone drives on the right and expects everyone else to do the same. And suppose this is so because everyone wants to drive on the right for the reasons given in (iii′). But suppose also that everyone has the false belief that everyone else drives on the right for the wrong reason (a reason such as blind habit or fear of punishment). Then, driving on the right would still not be a convention – people would be expecting others to conform for the wrong reason. The situation is similar if no one has this false belief but everyone believes that everyone else has it, if no one believes that anyone has it but everyone believes that everyone else believes that everyone else has it, and so on.

Lewis addresses this difficulty by appealing to the notion of *mutuality* that was discussed in Section 8.6. He modifies the definition once more, demanding that the fulfillment of conditions (i), (ii), (iii′) should be *mutual knowledge*. This means that everyone knows that they are fulfilled, everyone knows that everyone knows that they are fulfilled, everyone knows that everyone knows that everyone knows that they are fulfilled, etc.

The appeal to mutual knowledge creates an epistemological challenge – how can agents acquire mutual attitudes? Though commentators disagree about how difficult this challenge is, the postulation of mutuality is indispensable for both game theory and for game-theoretic explanations of mutuality. For more about this topic, see Thomason (2000); Vanderschraaf and Sillari (2009).

Although the final account of conventionality in Lewis (1969: 78) is rather complex, involving several refinements, we will not pursue the details further here. As matters stand today, we don't have a generally accepted definition of convention: Lewis himself offered a different definition in Lewis (1975), and philosophical debate on the topic hasn't converged on a single proposal. But virtually all proposals follow Lewis' central insight: that conventions are regularities that are best explained as solutions to a coordination problem.

The definition of 'convention' is free of terms like 'should', 'required', 'correct', or 'good', and in this sense conventions are not inherently normative. Nonetheless, they are regularities to which we believe we ought to conform. If I belong to a certain population that conforms to a convention, then I have (probable) reason to believe that everyone expects me to conform to this regularity and that in so doing I would answer to everyone's preferences. Thus, *ceteris paribus*, I ought to conform. (See Lewis [1969: 97–98].)

Lewis sought to account for non-natural meaning in terms of conventions. His claim is that for someone to mean something by an utterance is for the utterance to be a conventional signal within a certain system. Let's use his classic example to see how this works.

Paul Revere has a plan. If he sees the redcoats coming by land he warns people that they are coming by land, if he sees that they are coming by sea he warns people that they are coming by sea, and if he sees that they are not coming he does nothing. In other words, his plan is to make what he does dependent on what he sees – a hallmark of rationality. Alas, Paul Revere has a problem. To see well he should be in the belfry, and to warn people effectively he should be in the saddle.

Since he can't be in both places, he recruits a sexton to help. But now a group of two people is involved, and he needs a plan for the group. A good group plan would allocate the seeing part of the task to the sexton and the warning part to Revere. But Revere's warning must be coordinated with what the sexton sees. If Revere, sitting in the saddle, can see the sexton in the tower, we now have a three-step group plan. First, the sexton sees what the redcoats are doing. Second, depending on what he has observed, he does one of two things that Revere can observe. Third, Revere will warn people, and the warning will depend on what he has seen the sexton do.

This division of labor creates a coordination problem: to pick plans for the sexton and for Revere which align, so that carrying them out jointly is equivalent to carrying out the original plan. Of course, many actions are available to the sexton, but let's assume that we are interested in only two: hanging one lantern and hanging two, and that the sexton has two plans for observing the redcoats and signaling:

S1: Hang one lantern if you see the redcoats coming by land and two lanterns if you see them coming by sea.

S2: Hang one lantern if you see the redcoats coming by sea and two lanterns if you see them coming by land.

Revere has two plans for observing the sexton's signal and warning:

R1: Warn the people that the redcoats are coming by land if you see one lantern and that they are coming by sea if you see two lanterns.

R2: Warn the people that the redcoats are coming by land if you see two lanterns and that they are coming by sea if you see one lantern.

Revere and the sexton want the people to be warned correctly. So they (greatly) prefer two plan combinations: S1+R1 and S2+R2, and they (greatly) disprefer the other two: S1+R2 and S2+R1. This, then is a coordination problem with the two equilibria S1+R1 and S2+R2, both of them equally good. Lewis calls such coordination problems *signaling problems*.

As we know from Longfellow's poem, the sexton and Paul Revere agreed to adopt one of these two solutions: S1+R1, or "[o]ne if by land, and two if by sea." Their agreement establishes a *conventional signaling system* Σ.

Conventional signaling systems give rise to *conventional meanings*; for instance, Σ supports a conventional meaning for the two-lantern signal. If we wish to characterize what this meaning is, we can do it in two ways – we can think of the signal as a declarative ("The redcoats are coming by land") or as an imperative ("Warn the people that the redcoats are coming by land!").

Dec: Hanging two lanterns in the belfry means in Σ that the redcoats are coming by sea iff hanging two lanterns is performed if the redcoats are coming by sea.

Imp: Hanging two lanterns in the belfry means in Σ to warn the people that the redcoats are coming by sea iff hanging two lanterns is performed if Revere is to warn the people that the redcoats are coming by sea.

How can we tell whether a particular signal in a signaling system has declarative or imperative meaning? This depends on the character of the plans for the sender and the receiver. Let's say that a plan to respond to what one sees is *discretionary* if it leaves room for deliberation. A signal has declarative meaning iff the sender's plan is nondiscretionary and the receiver's is discretionary. It has imperative meaning when the sender's plan is discretionary and the receiver's is not. When both plans are nondiscretionary, there is no good way to tell whether it's imperative or declarative.

For example, when a police car flashes its light at you, its driver has a discretionary plan but you don't – which is why the signal has an imperative meaning, to wit, 'Stop your car!' But when a regular car flashes its light at you, its driver does not have a discretionary plan but you do – which is why the signal has a declarative meaning, to wit, 'Your headlights are off'.

Lewis develops a connection between meaning in conventional signaling systems and Grice's notion of speaker meaning. He argues that, by giving a conventional signal in normal conformity to a convention, one must mean something in Grice's sense, i.e. in the sense of the original three-pronged definition given in Grice (1957). This is because "[t]he intention with which I do U can be established by examining the practical reasoning that justifies me in doing it. I need not actually go through that reasoning to have an intention; actions done without deliberation are often done with definite intentions" (Lewis 1969: 155). Whether or not Lewis' argument works in general, it's plausible that ordinarily, conventional signals will be meant in Grice's sense.

The converse, however, certainly fails: If I am trying to deceive you, or I am mistaken about the prevailing conventions, or I expect my audience to be mistaken about the prevailing conventions, I can mean something by an utterance without being in normal conformity to any convention.

It is tempting to view languages as conventional signaling systems, to define the meanings of declarative and imperative sentences along the lines of (*Dec*) and (*Imp*), and then to seek to characterize the meanings of words and phrases by abstracting them from the meanings of sentences in which they occur. But, as Lewis stresses, natural languages are quite different from signaling systems. Signals in a signaling system are used for a single purpose: to enable the transfer of information. They often leave little room for choice: Either the utterer or the audience is expected to act without discretion. Their expressive power is circumscribed: There are no resources for generalization. Lewis thinks that it's hopeless to try to base linguistic meaning on signaling conventions; it's more promising to characterize languages in the abstract way mentioned above and then to specify conventions linking populations to them.

According to Lewis' original view, in Lewis (1969: 177), a population uses a language L just in case a *convention of truthfulness in L* obtains in the population, sustained by a common interest in communication. (Lewis credits the idea of conventions of truthfulness in a language to Stenius [1967].) What is the convention of truthfulness in L? There is a negative part: trying not to utter sentences that are not true in L. There is also a positive part: occasionally uttering sentences of L.

Is it a matter of convention that we aim at making true utterances? No, and Lewis does not say that it is. The alternative to truthfulness in L is truthfulness in a different language L′ that solves the same coordination problem – to transmit a certain unit of information from utterer to audience. As long as we seek solutions to this problem, truthfulness itself has no alternative and is thus not a convention.

Like Grice's definition, Lewis' account of a population's language has been criticized in several ways, and – like Grice – Lewis has offered different formulations of the idea. On Lewis' later view, what makes a language L the language of a population is no longer that the convention of truthfulness in L obtains in it, but rather that the convention of truthfulness and trust in L does. Such a convention involves some language users making utterances in L, trying not to utter anything that is false in L, and some users coming to believe that the sentences uttered are true in L.

11.4 Linguistic Meaning and Language Use

Often, what you would expect to be simple turns out to be extraordinarily challenging when it is viewed through the lens of philosophy. The relation between linguistic usage and linguistic meaning is like this. Obviously, the language that a speech community shares is determined by usage: As the usage changes, characteristics of the language, including semantic characteristics, track the change. And if everyone used 'tail' to mean what 'leg' actually means, then 'tail' would *mean* 'leg' and 'Donkeys have four tails' would be true.

What is the usage–meaning relation? Use theorists have a simple answer to this question – they are the same – but have less success in producing an alternative to the theories of meaning deployed by formal semanticists. Usage is no clearer a starting point for a theory than meaning, and determining whether two uses are the same seems to depend on prior intuitions about meaning. But those for whom usage and linguistic meaning are different face the challenge of explaining how they are related.

Grice's and Lewis' accounts of the relation both seek to ground linguistic usage in a speech community in the attitudes and practices of the members of the community. But they meet the challenge of compositionality differently. Lewis appeals to familiar truth-conditional theories of compositionality and relates this to usage by a practice of truthfulness. Grice suggests, perhaps tentatively, that uses themselves can be composed.

Grice's utterer's meaning and Lewis' notion that conventions are mutually known strategies for coordinating actions in a community are attractive and powerful ways of clarifying linguistic usage. Several authors, including Schiffer (1972) and Bennett (1976) have been encouraged to make this clarification the basis of a detailed explanation of how linguistic usage determines meaning.

These accounts all subscribe in one way or another to two claims: that the meanings of complex expressions are somehow determined compositionally and that usage determines linguistic meaning: The meaning of a declarative sentence is what speakers in the community usually would use it to assert. But this generalization is undermined by pragmatic augmentations in which speakers regularly use a sentence to mean something that differs from its linguistic meaning, or from its "meaning in the favored sense."

The literal meaning of 'She took out her keys and unlocked the door', for instance, is quite different from what speakers normally use it to mean because the normal usage includes the thought that she used the keys to open the door. And in fact, compositional rules can produce meanings for sentences that are very different from what the sentences are generally used to mean. Compositionality, together with the meanings of 'outdo', 'forget', and of the reflexive construction, predict that 'I outdid myself' should mean that I did better than I in fact did, and that 'I forgot myself' should mean that I didn't remember myself. And perhaps this in fact is what the sentences do literally mean. But that is not what is normally meant when they are used.

David Lewis seems to have realized the challenge that regular pragmatic augmentations raise for attempts to ground theories of linguistic meaning in terms of use. He considers (Lewis 1975: 28) the following objection to his theory: "Suppose that the members of a population are untruthful in their language £ more often than not, not because they lie, but because they go in heavily for irony, metaphor, hyperbole, and such. It is hard to deny that the language £ is used by the population." He replies by distinguishing truthfulness from literal truthfulness.

> I claim that these people are truthful in their language £ though they are not *literally truthful* in £. To be literally truthful in £ is to be truthful in another language related to £, a language we can call literal-£. The relation between £ and literal-£ is as follows: a good way to describe £ is to start by specifying literal-£ and then to describe £ as obtained by a certain systematic departure from literal-£. This two-stage specification of £ by way of literal-£ may turn out to be much simpler than any direct specification of £. (Lewis 1975: 28)

This is a peculiar way of stating the common view that – though maybe the meanings of words are highly constrained by their usage – the linguistic meanings of complex expressions are determined compositionally. And compositionality appeals to intuitions about linguistic meaning that are more or less independent of pragmatic effects, much as intuitions about syntax are more or less independent of intuitions about meaning. Pragmatic augmentation can associate divergent meanings with these utterances, and these augmentations can depend in complex ways on the context. According to this view, the relation between linguistic meanings and utterer's meanings may be constrained in various ways, but it will not be as if the former is determined by the latter. As Lewis says, if pragmatic augmentations are pervasive, the specification of linguistic meaning is obtained first, and utterer's meanings are then derived as deviations from the linguistic meaning.

For Lewis, languages are mathematical abstractions that pair expressions with meanings. To associate a language with a speech community is to say that it is a good explanation of the community's linguistic practices. Lewis starts with a simple formulation of the relation between a language £ and a community. This formulation – even if it is framed in terms of truth – supposes that linguistic meanings and utterance meanings are identical or near-identical. This makes Lewis look like a use theorist.

But when the community indulges enough in pragmatic augmentations, he treats utterer's meanings as "translations" of the linguistic meanings. This no longer subscribes to the idea that usage determines linguistic meaning: It presents a much more complex picture of the relation between linguistic meaning and usage. At this point, we might ask if our own linguistic practices support Lewis' simple picture or whether they make it impossible to maintain the idea that linguistic meaning is based on usage. This question would be difficult to answer, even if we had good statistics on the frequency of pragmatic augmentation. But, given the systematicity and pervasiveness of conversational implicatures, augmentation does seem to pose a serious threat to any straightforward use theory.

11.5 Conclusion

Use theories seem attractive, partly, because of the prima facie plausibility of the idea that linguistic meanings are grounded in patterns of meaningful usage and, partly, because a usage-based theory might avoid the relentlessly abstract and formal apparatus of the logic-based approaches to linguistic meaning.

A semantic theorist who wishes to make usage fundamental must choose whether to begin with usage of words or of sentences, and with the usage of individuals or of a speech community. But however this is decided, the gap between words and sentences and between individual usages and community patterns of use is not easily closed. It is surprisingly difficult to maintain a usage-based approach to meaning that goes beyond the meanings of simple words and is faithful to linguistic evidence and intuitions.

12 Externalism and Internalism

12.1 Two Theses about Meaning

Skepticism about semantics has many forms. Perhaps the most influential goes back to the American linguist Leonard Bloomfield. The concern is that the universality of ordinary language pushes the theory of meaning towards the theory of everything:

> The situations which prompt people to utter speech include every object and happening in the universe. In order to give a scientifically accurate definition of meaning for every form of a language, we would have to have a scientifically accurate knowledge of everything in the speaker's world. The actual extent of human knowledge is very small compared to this. (Bloomfield 1933: 139)

You can think of Bloomfield's problem as a conflict between two theses about linguistic meaning. The first is that to understand a linguistic expression is to know its meaning; the second is that the meaning of a linguistic expression settles what in the world the expression is about. If both theses hold, the knowledge of someone who understands a word must fix what the word designates. For example, if ordinary speakers understand 'arthritis' or 'water' then their knowledge settles that the former picks out arthritis and not some other ailment and that the latter picks out water and not some other liquid. But then, one might think, to capture what ordinary speakers know, a scientific theory of meaning should distinguish arthritis and water from other things. And yet, it seems preposterous to think that it is the job of semanticists to pronounce on matters of medicine or chemistry.

There is a simple way for a working semanticist to avoid Bloomfield's worry: do not trouble with the meanings of words, except for a small number of closed-class lexical items, like 'every', 'might', 'and', and 'the'. Contemporary formal semantics takes this approach, concentrating on the problem of how meanings are assigned to syntactic structures, assuming an arbitrary association of lexical items with meanings of appropriate types. But this is a way of keeping the difficulty at arm's length, rather than a solution. Bloomfield's problem remains as a philosophical and foundational issue, and as a challenge for anyone who thinks that semantics should concern itself with how words take on meanings.

We will work with the following reformulations of the two theses, simplifying things by concentrating on declarative sentences:

(i) *Understanding/meaning:* If a speaker understands a sentence in a language, she knows that the sentence has a certain meaning in that language.

(ii) *Meaning/truth-conditions:* A meaning of a sentence determines a set of conditions under which it is true.

These two theses seem plausible. In fact, many philosophers are committed to stronger claims: e.g. that the meaning of an unambiguous sentence is precisely what anyone who understands the sentence must know about it, or that the meaning of an unambiguous declarative sentence is exhausted by its truth-conditions. But all we need to generate Bloomfield's problem are the relatively weak claims (i) and (ii).

We present two arguments based on examples introduced in Burge (1979) and Putnam (1975), although their examples will be put to a slightly different use here. The arguments are not air-tight – in fact, we will discuss ways of evading them in the next section – but they are formidable. They are presented in the form of a *reductio ad absurdum*: (i) and (ii), together with seemingly obvious assumptions, lead to something like a contradiction.

12.1.1 The Arthritis Argument

Felix is a speaker of English who has an inflammation in his thigh. He sincerely utters the following sentence:

(12.1.1) I have arthritis.

The sentence, as uttered by Felix is unambiguously false in English: Arthritis is a condition exclusively of the joints. Imagine a language, Twin English, that differs from English only in how the word 'arthritis' is used. Unlike English speakers, speakers of Twin English employ the word to refer to all instances of joint or bone ailment.

Suppose Felix has a molecule-by-molecule duplicate, Twin Felix, who is a speaker of Twin English. Example (12.1.1) is unambiguously true as uttered by him: What speakers of Twin English call 'arthritis' is a condition that can affect the thigh. By (ii) it follows that (12.1.1) has different meanings in English and Twin English. Let's call these two meanings M_1 and M_2, respectively. There is no reason to deny that Twin Felix knows that (12.1.1) has M_2 as a meaning, so let's say he does. Since he is a duplicate of Felix, it is reasonable to assume that whatever he knows Felix knows too. So, Felix also knows that (12.1.1) has M_2 as a meaning.

Since Felix is a normal English speaker who just happens to be mistaken about where arthritis can occur, we may assume that Felix understands (12.1.1) in English. By (i) it follows that he knows that (12.1.1) has M_1 as a meaning. But let's say that while Felix is not given to philosophical reflection he does have a good command of English – it never occurred to him that there are languages where the sentences he knows have different meanings, but he is well aware that (12.1.1) is unambiguous in the language he speaks. Then it would seem very odd to say that he knows that (12.1.1) has two distinct meanings. But if he doesn't we have a contradiction.

Perhaps the most obvious way to block the argument is to deny that someone could understand (12.1.1) in English while falsely believing that arthritis can be in the thigh; Crane (1991) and Segal (2000) advocate this response.

This may work for 'arthritis' but probably not for all other words we could use in its stead. A general response would have to insist that any meaningful word has a definition and a speaker can never understand a sentence if she is mistaken about the definition of any word that occurs in the sentence. To understand 'Whales were hunted for their oil', one could not believe that whales are fish; to understand 'Hurricanes are common in Florida', one could not believe that winds of 70 miles per hour are hurricanes; to understand 'My brother plays in a symphony orchestra', one could not believe that the piano can be part of a symphony orchestra, and so on. But if understanding a sentence is this demanding, then Bloomfield definitely has a point; a theory of meaning for English would come dangerously close to the theory of everything.

Ordinary linguistic understanding is social: It does not require speakers to be experts, only that they should defer to those who are. Felix counts as understanding (12.1.1) in English in part because he tends to defer in just this way. When an English-speaking doctor tells him that this sentence is false, he is *inclined* to concede that he was mistaken. Of course, he might not *actually* concede the point, but this is a different matter: People can be stubborn and irrational and this may override the inclination to defer. The point is that if Felix thinks he is an expert and owes deference to no one when it comes to (12.1.1) then, arguably, he really does not understand the sentence. Our knowledge of words, then, piggy-backs on the knowledge of others – but this does not mean it is not genuine understanding.

We have now arrived at the conclusion that there is no easy answer to the arthritis argument: The tension between (i) and (ii) is genuine.

12.1.2 The Water Argument

Oscar is a speaker of English around 1750 who sincerely utters the following sentence (pointing at a glass of water in front of him):

(12.1.2) This is water.

The sentence as uttered is unambiguously true in English. Now, imagine a planet, Twin Earth, that differs from Earth only in that wherever Earth has H_2O, Twin Earth has a superficially indistinguishable substance with a different chemical composition, XYZ. Imagine that Oscar has a molecule-by-molecule duplicate, Twin Oscar, who inhabits Twin Earth and is a speaker of Twin English.[1]

Suppose that somehow a glass of H_2O shows up in front of Twin Oscar. He points at it and utters (12.1.2). The sentence as uttered by Twin Oscar is unambiguously false: 'water' in Twin English refers to XYZ and what Twin Oscar is pointing at is not XYZ. By (ii) it follows that (12.1.2) has different meanings in English and Twin English. Let's call these two meanings M_1 and M_2, respectively. There is no reason to think that either Oscar or Twin Oscar fails to understand (12.1.2) in their own language: The fact that they are ignorant of the chemical composition of what they call 'water' does not seem like an obstacle. By (i) it follows that Oscar knows that (12.1.2) has M_1 as a meaning and Twin Oscar knows that (12.1.2) has M_2 as a meaning. Since they are duplicates, it is reasonable to assume that whatever one knows the other knows as well. But let's say that while Oscar is not given to philosophical reflection, he does have a good command of English – it never occurred to him that there are languages where the sentences he knows have different meanings, but he is well aware that (12.1.2) is unambiguous in the language he speaks. Then it would seem very odd to say that he knows that (12.1.2) has two distinct meanings. But if he doesn't we have a contradiction.

Perhaps the most obvious way to resist this argument is to claim that XYZ is really water, albeit a different kind of water from H_2O. As Mellor (1977: 302–303) writes: "It is indeed quite plain to my Fregean eye that in 1950, as in 1750, 'water' had the same extension on Twin Earth as it had here."

But this goes against fairly strong intuitions. We surely don't want to say that a forged \$20 bill is a \$20 dollar bill, so why grant that a liquid is water just because it is superficially indistinguishable from water? To be water is no more a matter of appearances than being a \$20 bill. (It might be more promising to say that there is no fact of the matter about this; cf. LaPorte (1996) and LaPorte (1998). But then it is not entirely clear what we should think about understanding (12.1.2).)

Many things have a hidden nature: Something could *appear* to be a kind of thing, even to noncasual observers, without *being* that kind of thing. In this sense, arguably, water and a \$20 bill both have a hidden nature: The former has to have the right sort of makeup (being mostly a collection of H_2O molecules), the latter has to have the right sort of history (going back to some facility operated by the Bureau of Engraving and Printing).

[1] It may seem as if this is a lot to imagine. For instance, Oscar and his twin could not be perfect duplicates, since Oscar's body is largely made of H_2O and Twin Oscar's of XYZ. This and others like it are genuine worries, but to concentrate on the main argument we will set them aside. Putnam has other versions of this argument (e.g. one that replaces 'water' with 'aluminum') that does not have this particular problem. We will assume here, with most authors, that these details do not affect the force of Putnam-like examples.

12.1.3 Comparison

The arthritis and water arguments have a similar structure. They both rely on the intuition – which is plausible enough – that subtle differences in the environment may affect the truth-value of a sentence without affecting a normal speaker's understanding of it. In the first case, these differences involve the use of a word, while in the second they involve the underlying nature of its referent. In both cases, we discover a conflict between (i) and (ii) – between the thesis that understanding requires knowledge of meaning and the thesis that meaning determines truth-conditions.

Rejecting either of the principles about meaning would not be easy – they both seem fundamental to our semantic theorizing. If (i) is false, it seems odd that a theory of meaning relies almost exclusively on judgments of speakers who are presumed to understand their language. And if (ii) is false then it seems misguided for a theory of meaning to employ truth as one of its basic notions.

The two examples also point in opposite directions. It is natural to agree that in Burge's example the meaning of (12.1.1) shifts between English and Twin English – after all, speakers of Twin English use 'arthritis' in a different way and differences in use often lead to differences in meaning. By contrast, the natural thing to say is that the meaning of (12.1.2) is the same in English and Twin English. At the time of utterance (i.e. around 1750) no one would have been able to distinguish H_2O and XYZ, so a difference in meaning would have to be a difference that eludes all English and Twin English speakers. To account for Putnam's case we are pulled towards rejecting (ii), but then to account for Burge's we would still need to reject (i). This seems doubly unappealing.

In the next section we will look at two ways one could resist the arguments for the incompatibility of our two theses. Neither is really convincing, but they do show the direction in which solutions to our predicament might be sought.

12.2 Two Attempts to Block the Arguments

Let's consider two assumptions in the arguments of the previous section. The first was made explicit: On the basis of the fact that they are duplicates we claimed that there is no difference between what Felix and Oscar know and what their twins do. The second was tacit: We have taken it for granted that 'meaning' is used in the same sense in the two theses whose incompatibility the arguments seek to show.

Let's consider the first assumption first. What could Felix know that Twin Felix does not? It seems that anything about arthritis itself that Felix might know – that it is sometimes an inflammation, that it is typically in the limbs, that it causes pain, that a lot of elderly people have it, etc. – his duplicate on

Twin Earth would know too. What might differentiate their epistemic situation is linguistic knowledge about the word 'arthritis'. Consider the following sentence:

(12.2.3) 'Arthritis' is an English word.

It seems quite reasonable to assume that Felix could know what this expresses in English. Not so for Twin Felix. He knows what (12.2.3) expresses in Twin English but that is not the same: In Twin English 'English' refers to Twin English! Twin Felix never heard of English, so he certainly does not know that the words he is familiar with belong not only to his language but also to English. Call this the *language response*.

There are at least two reasons to be dissatisfied with this response. For one thing, it is insufficiently general: Even if it disarms the Arthritis Argument, it cannot really be used against the Water Argument. There is no prima facie plausibility to the claim that Oscar and Twin Oscar speak different languages, so Twin Oscar presumably does know that 'water' is an English word. For another, it allows proponents of the Arthritis Argument to retrench after making a concession. They can allow that Felix and Twin Felix can differ in what they know about English but claim that they are identical in their knowledge, at least where this knowledge does not concern any particular language. With this weaker assumption the argument still goes through. Suppose we grant that both Felix and his twin understand 'I have arthritis' and let's say that M_1 is the meaning of this sentence in English and M_2 its meaning in Twin English. Felix knows that M_1 is a meaning of the sentence. Likewise, Twin Felix knows that M_2 is a meaning of the same sentence. What they know does not concern any particular language – it just matches a meaning with an expression. Thus, given that they are duplicates, we might still want to maintain that Felix must also know that M_2 is a meaning of the sentence, and similarly Twin Felix must know that M_1 is a meaning of the sentence. And this is still implausible: If they have never thought about alternative meaning assignments, it seems that both Felix and Twin Felix should think that 'I have arthritis' has a single meaning.

Let's consider then the second assumption of the two arguments. Since Kaplan (1989), it is customary to distinguish between two notions of meaning – character and content. If a sentence is free of indexicals, the two differ only nominally: Character is a constant function that assigns the same content to all contexts of utterance. But what if 'water' is an indexical that picks out H_2O when used by an inhabitant of Earth and XYZ when used by an inhabitant of Twin Earth? The content of 'This is water' (uttered pointing at a glass of H_2O) would then be different when uttered by Oscar and his twin, even if the character they both know is the same. Call this the *indexical response*.

At first, one might think that this maneuver is ad hoc – there is no independent evidence for the claim that 'water' is an indexical. Competent speakers are well aware that words like 'I', 'here', and 'now' pick out different things in different contexts, but they would be surprised to hear this about 'water'. If the proposal is correct, ordinary speakers exhibit a certain *semantic blindness*.

Objections of this sort are raised regularly whenever linguists or philosophers posit surprising or hidden indexicality. But the complaint is not particularly convincing: Linguistic competence requires the ability to pass judgments about meaning or truth-conditions in ordinary contexts. Cross contextual evaluations are rare and overt judgments regarding the indexicality of an expressions are theoretical. Ordinary speakers are largely blind to the workings of language; the idea that they may be unreliable about the presence of indexicality is not unreasonable. According to many of our best current semantic theories, many expressions are context sensitive: Context helps in identifying the domain of quantifier phrases, the flavor of modal auxiliaries, the degree of gradable adjectives, and much else.

Putnam himself has suggested that we should accept that words like 'water' are indexicals. Putnam (1970: 188) called these words *natural kind terms* and characterized them as follows:

> A natural kind term ... is a term that plays a special kind of role. If I describe something as a lemon, or as an acid, I indicate that it is likely to have certain characteristics (yellow peel, or sour taste in dilute water solution, as the case might be); but I also indicate that the presence of these characteristics, if they are present, is likely to be accounted for by some "essential nature" which the thing shares with other members of the natural kind. What the essential nature is is not a matter of language analysis but of scientific theory construction; today we would say that it is chromosome structure, in the case of lemons, and being a proton-donor, in the case of acids.

While the general idea is clear, there are a number of things that are slightly off about this characterization. When I call a manifestly green lemon a lemon I do not indicate, absurdly, that *it* is likely to have a yellow peel. Such an indication would require an addressee-directed intention of some sort, and it is highly implausible that in using the word 'lemon' one always tries to convey information about the color of lemon peel. Moreover, it is not even true that lemons are likely to have yellow peels – most lemons are green because most lemons are unripe. So, it might be closer to the truth to say that speakers of English use 'lemon' presupposing (not indicating!) that lemons (not any particular lemon!) typically (not likely!) have yellow peels and also that this general fact follows from the essential nature of lemons. We might then hypothesize that these presuppositions are lexically encoded.

In general, for any natural kind term T, speakers who understand it presuppose that whatever items T applies to typically exhibit some manifest properties $M_1, M_2, \ldots M_n$, and do this because they share an underlying property – because they are things of the same kind. Here we have an explicit list of manifest properties, together with the claim that they are associated with some underlying property. So speakers who understand *T* and who accept such a presupposition must know the list of manifest properties that typify *T*, but they needn't know which underlying property accounts for this fact. If its typical manifest properties $M_1, M_2, \ldots M_n$ can have alternative accounts, in terms of different underlying properties, it's plausible to say that *T* is an indexical. It will refer to different things in contexts where different underlying properties are salient.

This is the case with 'water' in Putnam's example: We can account for the typical transparency, odorlessness, potability, of a quantity of liquid either by its being H_2O, or (Putnam assumes) by its being XYZ. On Earth, the former account is right; on Twin Earth, the latter. So if the presuppositions of both Oscar and Twin Oscar are correct, they refer to different stuff using the word 'water'. (For this to work it is crucial to assume that the disjunctive property of being *either* H_2O *or* XYZ is not what underlies being typically transparent, odorless, potable, etc. If it were, we would have to conclude that H_2O and XYZ are both water.)

The indexical response seems like a reasonable way to disarm the Water Argument, but it works less well when it comes to the Arthritis Argument. As it turns out, 'arthritis' does not refer to a single disease, but is an informal way to talk about more than a hundred different types of conditions. What these conditions have in common is that they are all typically manifested in joint pain. As far as we know there isn't a single underlying property – a specific etiology – that accounts for this. If 'arthritis' were a natural kind term it would be defective: The presupposition it encodes would be false, and hence, it would fail to apply to anything at all. It would be a term like 'phlogiston' or 'unicorn'. So, evidently, 'arthritis' is not a natural kind term.

This leads to another problem. Use of an empty indexical (a demonstrative accompanied by a pointing gesture that aims at nothing, a use of '20 billion years ago' assuming the Big Bang was the beginning of time approximately 13.8 billion years ago, a use of 'you' within an utterance addressed at no one, etc.) is deeply infelicitous in a context where its emptiness is common ground. Even though 'water' is not a defective natural kind term and it never was, in 1750 it was still an open possibility that it might be. It could have turned out, for example, that the liquid in rivers and lakes on Earth is a mixture of H_2O and XYZ, just as air turned out to be a mixture. Had this happened, arguably, uses of 'water' would still not have become deeply infelicitous. Rather, we would have simply dropped the presupposition of common underlying nature and continued to use 'water' to refer to the stuff in rivers and lakes. Arguably, this is what happened to 'jade'. When in 1863 Alexis Damour discovered that some of the ornamental stones we used to call 'jade' are aluminum-rich pyroxene (jadite) while the rest are a magnesium-rich amphibole (nephrite), we did not stop using the term.

In other words, there is a significant respect in which 'water' does not behave the way indexicals do. The difference is diachronic: It concerns what happens to a word over time if a certain discovery is made. Still, it is important enough to undermine the conjecture that 'water' (or, for that matter, any other natural kind term) is an indexical.

In principle, both the linguistic and the indexical response block the arguments of the previous section. The former works better against the Arthritis Argument, the latter against the Water Argument. But in the end, neither response is entirely satisfactory.

12.3 Externalism

The attempt to disarm the Arthritis Argument by arguing that, unlike Felix, his twin does not know that 'arthritis' is an English word falters because it is not radical enough. The example is too specialized and it can be easily sidestepped by rephrasing the argument. But the insight behind the example can be used to formulate a much more satisfactory response.

Twin Felix does not know that 'arthritis' is an English word because he doesn't know there is such a language as English. He doesn't know this because he doesn't speak it and never encountered anyone who does. In fact, he never had a thought about English – the thoughts he would express using the word 'English' are all about Twin English. Once we get this far, we might make a further step and consider whether he ever had thoughts about arthritis itself. Twin Felix is in some sense familiar with arthritis, since he presumably knows people who suffer from this condition. But when he uses the word 'arthritis', he talks about a different ailment – tharthritis. Perhaps Felix and his twin are always thinking about different ailments because they associate different concepts with the word 'arthritis', which in turn is due to the fact that they are are members of different linguistic communities.

This idea extends naturally to Oscar and his twin. Oscar has the concept of water and uses it to think about H_2O; Twin Oscar has the concept of thwater and uses it to think about XYZ. Now it looks as if their mental lives are very different. The beliefs, hopes, expectations, and desires Oscar expresses using the word 'water' in sentences are mental states that Twin Oscar never had, even though he expresses *his* beliefs, hopes, expectations, and desires using identical sounding sentences in circumstances that for them (and everyone else at the time) would be indistinguishable.

All this goes against deeply entrenched intuitions and a long philosophical tradition about the mind that is sometimes called *internalism*. Internalists hold that mentality – how one represents the world to oneself and what it is like for one to have those representations – is an intrinsic matter. They are committed to the idea that the only way our environment can influence our mental life is by making a difference to what goes on inside us. Assuming physicalism, molecule-by-molecule duplicates are intrinsically the same; assuming internalism, they are also mentally identical.

It is natural to say that when we see a movie, we might be frightened by a bear; when we hallucinate, we might see a dagger; and when we dream, we might believe that we are swimming in the ocean. It is also tempting to take those claims at face value: When we are really taken in by the movie, when the hallucination is perfectly vivid, and when we dream as we normally do, then our mental states are the *same* as the mental states we would have if we were really attacked by a bear, presented with a dagger, or were swimming in the ocean. Moreover, as Descartes (1996: AT VII.22) suggested, we might want to say that if "some malicious demon of the utmost power and cunning has employed all his energies in order to deceive me," then I would still have the emotions, perceptual experiences, and beliefs that in fact I have, even though most of those mental states would radically misrepresent reality. This is what internalists believe.

The conclusion Putnam (1975) drew from Oscar's predicament was that "meanings ain't in the head," more precisely, that the meanings of certain linguistic expressions are not determined by the intrinsic makeup of people who understand those expressions. Assuming such speakers can use those expressions literally – intending to convey precisely what the expressions themselves mean – it follows that the contents of some mental states are not determined by what is inside the head. Assuming mental states are individuated by their contents, then *externalism* – the opposite of internalism – follows. And once we have come this far, the reasonable thing to do is to embrace a fairly thoroughgoing externalism – one that extends far beyond mental states about water and other natural kinds. (McGinn [1977] was probably the first to make the point that Putnam's position leads to externalism not just about linguistic meaning but about mental content in general.) The argument presented by Burge (1979) used Felix's predicament to go directly to this conclusion, without specifically considering linguistic meaning.

Externalism is a fairly popular view among philosophers – in part, because of its potential to answer the skeptic. Putnam (1981) presented a complex argument in favor of the claim that we know a priori that external world skepticism of the most radical sort is false.

Putnam uses a thought experiment to make his point. Consider the hypothesis that you are a brain in a vat connected to a supercomputer. Your brain is stimulated by electrical impulses, and you have simulated experiences qualitatively indistinguishable from those you might have when you look at a glass of water. What exactly would your belief be about? If we think – as seems rather plausible – that the reason Twin Oscar has no beliefs about water is that he never interacted with the stuff, then we should think the same about this hypothetical scenario. Your belief that there is water in front of you might be about your own experiences, or about the electrical stimuli causing those experiences, or perhaps about aspects of the computer program that are responsible for the pattern of electrical stimuli. (Putnam's own argument is formulated in terms of linguistic meaning, not mental content, and accordingly, it is more complex. This version of the argument appears in Tymoczko [1989], Ebbs [1989], and Brueckner [2003].) No matter which of these is correct, the belief that there is water in front of you would be true: You do have water-experiences, there are also electrical stimuli causing those experiences, and there are also aspects of a computer program generating those electrical stimuli. This is odd: Surely, we want to say that if you were a brain in a vat your beliefs wouldn't be true! The conclusion we are supposed to draw is that the initial assumption – that you are a brain in the vat – is incoherent.

This is a striking argument, but it does not quite defeat skeptical doubt. The usual way the skeptic argues is this: "You know you have hands only if you know that the thought you would express by the sentence 'I have hands' is true. But for all you know you could be a brain in the vat, in which case this thought would not be true. So, you don't know whether you have hands." If Putnam is right, this version of skepticism is out: If you were a brain in the vat, the thought expressed by 'I have hands' would be different, but it would still be true. But the skeptic who is an externalist can run the following argument instead: "You know you have hands only if you know that the thought you would express by the sentence 'I have hands' is about your hands (and not about your own experiences, electrical stimuli, or aspects of a computer program). But, for all you know, you could be a brain in the vat, in which case this thought would not be about your hands. So, you don't know whether you have hands."

Some philosophers have an answer to this latter version of the argument. In order to know that some of my beliefs are about water, it is enough if I know that I believe that water is wet. And I do know that – I am aware of my belief, and being aware of a belief is sufficient to know what the belief is. Let's call this last thesis *transparency*. We can use transparency against the externalist skeptic: Since I know that I believe that water is wet, I can conclude that I have a belief about water, and since brains in vats don't have such beliefs, I can prove that I am no brain in the vat. Of course, if I am a brain in the vat, I have an equally compelling argument proving something I would express by saying 'I am not a brain in the vat'. The conclusion would be impeccable, but it would not say what this sentence says in English. If I were an envatted brain, I would not have beliefs about brains and vats. Like all other thoughts we might be inclined to describe as being about external objects, these too would be about electrical stimuli, or aspects of a computer program, or perhaps about nothing at all.

Is the skeptic refuted? Assuming externalism and transparency I can prove that *I* am not a brain in a vat. But the proof may not convince the skeptic. The argument relies on the premise that I believe that water is wet, but *he* doesn't believe that water is wet.

Is the skeptic crazy in refusing to trust his senses? This is not obvious. We often revise beliefs we form on the basis of experiences when someone points out that those experiences are compatible with the falsity of those beliefs. You think you met Tweedledee, I point out that he looks just the same as his twin brother Tweedledum, you suspend your belief – nothing could be more reasonable than that. It is hard to show that the skeptic shouldn't react in an analogous way when he considers that his experiences could be qualitatively the same even if he lacks the belief that water is wet.

So, the proof may not convince a rational skeptic. Even worse, many philosophers have argued that the two premises it relies on, externalism and transparency, are incompatible with one another. Perhaps the most famous argument to this effect concerns *slow switching*. Imagine that one night while he is sound asleep, secret agents move Oscar to Twin Earth, and they dispose of his twin. When he wakes up, Oscar will of course notice no difference and keep saying things like 'There is water in that glass over there' but his claims will be false: What's over there is XYZ, and XYZ is not water. However, over time, as he interacts with XYZ, the word 'water' in his mouth will eventually come to refer to XYZ (perhaps after a period of referential indeterminacy). This is not so far-fetched: Evans (1973: 11) describes a similar reference shift that actually happened involving the name 'Madagascar'. Apparently the name 'Madageiscar', first recorded in Marco Polo's memoirs, is a corrupted transliteration of the name of the Somali port Mogadishu which Marco Polo managed to confuse with the island.

Back on Earth, before the slow switch, at time t Oscar believed that water was wet at t, and given transparency, he knew that he believed this. Given externalism, after the switch, at time t′ Oscar does not have any beliefs about water, so he does not believe that water was wet at t, and hence, he does not know that he believes this. So, it looks as if Oscar knew something before the switch that after the switch he no longer knows. And yet, it seems strange to say that there is anything that Oscar has *forgotten*. (The slow switching argument has many versions. This one is due to Boghossian [1989].)

There aren't many places where an externalist can resist this argument. She might concede that people undergoing slow switching no longer know what they believe, and hence, that transparency is only normally true. But then all we have is an argument against the skeptic that is sound only if we assume conditions are normal – which is not much of a victory. Most skeptics think the external world probably exists – it's just that we don't know that it does. (This is like a lottery: You know your ticket almost certainly will lose, but you don't know that it will lose.)

The most promising way to respond to slow switching is to say that it operates with an overly simple view of memory. For instance, we can question the tacit premise that remembering p entails knowing p. (Bernecker [2010: Chapter 3] argues this. Williamson [2000] disagrees: He argues that knowledge is the weakest factive mental state.) Suppose I am asked about the name of a student in my class last year and, to be sure, I check on the course website.

When asked why I checked I might say "I remembered his name, but I wasn't sure." If I wasn't sure, perhaps I didn't really know.

Alternatively, the externalist could say that we can lose knowledge without forgetting. Suppose you are driving and on the side of the road you see a barn. Based on that, you come to know that there is at least one barn nearby. As you drive on, you enter an area with lots of fake barns – facades that look from the road just like barns. You continue to believe that there is at least one barn in the area, thinking you have a lot of new evidence for your belief. But now your evidence is inadequate, and as a result your belief is arguably no longer knowledge. And yet, you forgot nothing. Of course, you could know that there is at least one barn nearby if you continued to base your beliefs solely on what you saw first. But you don't, and that's the problem.

Whether externalism gives us a good argument against external world skepticism remains controversial. But it is beyond doubt that externalists can at least resolve the tension between the theses we began with: that those who understand a sentence know what it means and that meanings determine truth-conditions.

12.4 Narrow Content

Like the language response to Putnam's example, the indexical response fails because it is not radical enough. Indexicalists think the problem with the Water Argument is equivocation: What someone who understands a sentence knows determines a character for the sentence, and any content of the sentence will determine a set of conditions under which it is true. But there is no single notion of meaning that does both. The trouble is that 'water' doesn't behave like a normal indexical – its content does not seem to vary with the context of *utterance*.

If Oscar relocates to Twin Earth, his word 'water' will continue to refer to water – at least initially. But the content of 'water' is sensitive to the *context of common use*, the circumstances in which Oscar's linguistic peers generally employ the word. The reason Oscar will eventually use 'water' to refer to XYZ if he spends enough time in his new environment is that he becomes a member of a different community that uses this word to pick out a different thing. Because of this, he finds himself in a new context of common use. The same can be said of Felix: If he were to travel to his Twin Earth he would eventually become a member of a different speech community, and then he would find himself in a new context of common use, employing 'arthritis' to refer to tharthritis.

To overcome the shortcomings of the indexical response we need to distinguish between two kinds of content: one that is sensitive to the context of common use, and one that isn't. Content that is insensitive to the context of common use can be *narrow* – i.e. content that does not depend on anything outside the head. Felix and his twin both associate the same narrow content with 'arthritis', and the beliefs they express uttering 'I have arthritis' also share narrow content. But what determines the truth-conditions of their beliefs is content that is sensitive to the context of common use. This content is *wide* – it is content that depends on what is outside the head. This is why the beliefs that Felix and his twin express uttering 'I have arthritis' differ in wide content. The same holds for Oscar and his twin: The beliefs they express when they utter 'This is water' while pointing at a glass filled with H_2O share narrow content but not wide content.

Externalists will, of course, object to this diagnosis. They work with a single notion of content – the wide one. They agree that the beliefs of duplicates are *similar* in many respects but they don't think there is a sense in which they are *identical*. And since positing another kind of content unquestionably has theoretical costs, we should see whether there are good reasons to believe in narrow content.

Advocates of narrow content often invoke causal considerations; the classic version of this argument is in Fodor (1988). Mental states play a crucial role in causally explaining behavior, and they do so in virtue of the content they have. There is a glass of water in front of Oscar and he reaches out his hand for it. What caused his behavior? The natural response is that it was caused, in part, by his belief that the glass contains water and his desire to drink water. There is a glass of XYZ in front of Twin Oscar and he too reaches out his hand for it. It seems clear that the causal explanation should be the same. But if all content is wide, this isn't so: Twin Oscar has a different belief and a different desire than Oscar.

Externalists object to this sort of argument because it seems to confuse causal explanations with causation itself. Causation is plausibly local: Features of the environment can affect an agent's behavior only by affecting her intrinsic properties. But in providing causal explanations, we must describe causes and effects, and it is here that the environment could make a difference. Burge (1989) uses the example of a heart. What it is to be a heart is defined extrinsically to the heart itself: The heart is an organ that pumps blood. We could have an intrinsically indistinguishable organ whose function is to pump waste, but this would not mean that in causally explaining a particular heart murmur we must ignore its proper function.

Another major reason to believe in narrow content is that without it we seem to be forced to deem apparently rational beliefs irrational. The classic example is due to Kripke (1979).

Pierre grows up a monolingual French speaker never leaving France. He frequently utters 'Londres est joli' and he apparently believes what he says. Later he moves to London, learns English, and frequently utters 'London is not pretty' in all sincerity. He never realizes that the city he calls 'Londres' in French is the same as the city he calls 'London' in English, so he never sees any reason to change either of these beliefs.

If there is only one kind of content and it is wide, we must say unequivocally that Pierre has contradictory beliefs. And yet, it does not seem that he is guilty of any kind of irrationality. Kripke himself did not offer a resolution to this puzzle – in fact, he suggests that the puzzle shows a place where "our normal practices of interpretation and attribution of belief are subjected to the greatest possible strain, perhaps to the point of breakdown" (1979: 283) It is easy to imagine versions of this puzzle involving arthritis or water – Pierre may sincerely assent both to 'L'arthrite est guérissable' and to 'Arthritis is not curable' or to 'L'eau est somptueux' and to 'Water is not sumptuous'.

The tension is eased if we say that 'Londres' and 'London' share their wide but not their narrow content and that considerations of rationality concern the latter, not the former. But this suggestion is problematic. Suppose someone were to tell Pierre that his beliefs concern the same city. Then, clearly, Pierre would be rationally required to abandon at least one of these beliefs. But if rationality is a matter of narrow content, this would be hard to explain: Narrow content does not determine reference, so learning that 'Londres' and 'London' refer to the same city should prima facie make no difference to the rationality of holding both beliefs. In any case, externalists often concede that in order to assess the rationality of Pierre's beliefs we do need to distinguish between two kinds of content, but they maintain that both of those contents are wide. On the one hand, there is the proposition expressed by 'London is pretty' given the way things actually are (i.e. given that there is one city named both 'Londres' and 'London'). On the other, there is the proposition that would be expressed by this sentence if things were as Pierre takes them to be (i.e. if there were two cities, one named 'Londres' and another named 'London'). (For arguments that the latter is still wide content, see Stalnaker [1989] and Stalnaker [1990].)

Perhaps the most interesting considerations in favor of narrow content are those that seek to show that the *linguistically relevant* notion of content is narrow. Chomsky (2000) presents a number of influential arguments to this effect. One of them concerns London. (For some reason, this city beats out all others in philosophers' examples.) 'London', Chomsky says, can be used to talk about a particular place near the River Thames but also about a political institution which could, in principle, be relocated. But no place could be at another place.

Why not say that 'London' is ambiguous, that there is '$London_1$' which refers to a place and '$London_2$' which refers to an institution? Well, there are different sorts of ambiguities, so we should say which kind of ambiguity is at stake here. 'London' is not *homonymous* like 'bank' – its two contents are not only associated with a single spelling but are intimately related. So much so that the same ambiguity shows up with all city names in many (perhaps all) human languages. Moreover, the link between the two contents of city names isn't the usual loose kind that we find with *polysemous* words like 'giant'.

We call certain mythical monsters of human appearance and prodigal size, such as Goliath or Enceladus, giants. We also call ordinary people of extraordinary size, such as Manute Bol or Gheorghe Muresan (both 7-7), giants. But we would not coordinate occurrences of 'giant' the way we coordinate occurrences of 'London':

(12.4.4) Giants are mythical creatures, and many of them are basketball players.
(12.4.5) London is near the ocean, but if sea levels rise it may have to move.

The fact that (12.4.5) is an acceptable (and perhaps true) sentence is remarkable, and it is the core of Chomsky's case for narrow content. Note that the occurrence of the pronoun 'it' is anaphoric on the occurrence of 'London', which means that their interpretation is linked. We must find some sort of meaning for these occurrences to share. And yet, given what the sentence says, it seems clear that their reference cannot be the same. Hence the need for narrow content in semantics.

Chomsky has plenty of other examples that illustrate the same point. 'Book' can refer to physical tokens or abstract types, but we can say "The book I just read hardly fits onto my shelf, and yet it is sold at every airport." 'Door' can refer to wooden frames or the opening they enclose, and yet we can say 'The door I just passed through was painted green'. And so on.

Chomsky (2000: 128) directly challenges Putnam's argument for externalism with the following example:

> Suppose cup_1 is filled from the tap. It is a cup of water, but if a tea bag is dipped into it, that is no longer the case. It is now a cup of tea, something different. Suppose cup_2 is filled from a tap connected to a reservoir in which tea has been dumped (say, as a new kind of purifier). What is in cup_2 is water, not tea, even if a chemist could not distinguish it from the present contents of cup_1. The cups contain the same thing from one point of view, different things from another; but in either case cup_2 contains only water and cup_1 only tea.

It is interesting to compare this case with that of Kripke's Pierre. There too, the intuitive diagnosis is that Londres and London are the same city from one point of view (i.e. ours) but different cities from another point of view (i.e. Pierre's). There too, it was tempting to say that Pierre believes of Londres only that it is pretty and of London only that it is not. In both cases narrow content can be called to the rescue: Perhaps Pierre associates different narrow contents with 'Londres' and 'London' even though their wide contents (from our point of view) are the same, and perhaps we associate different narrow contents with 'the liquid in cup_1' and 'the liquid in cup_2' even though their wide contents (from the chemist's point of view) are the same.

Externalists would challenge this diagnosis in both cases by stressing that the two points of view do not have the same status. Our perspective is superior to Pierre's because we know a crucial thing he does not: that Londres and London are identical. So, semantics should take our judgment seriously and discard his, and we should assign one and the same content to 'Londres' and 'London'. Similarly, one might suggest that the perspective of the chemist trumps that of ordinary folk when it comes to the issue of what is and what isn't water. So, semantics should respect the chemist's judgment that 'the liquid in cup_1' and 'the liquid in cup_2' pick out the same thing.

At the heart of Chomsky's resistance to externalism is his rejection of semantic deference. We should defer to chemists when it comes to the nature of water but they hold no special authority when it comes to *the meaning* of 'water'. Things are different with 'H_2O', a technical term whose syntax and compositional semantics is different from anything we find in English, and whose lexical constituents have meanings stipulated by chemistry. For Chomsky, understanding a natural language is a strictly individual capacity, one that is independent not only of its speakers' social embedding but even of their communicative aims. Technical terms are not really parts of natural languages, only of their artificial extensions.

Chomsky (1986) distinguishes between two conceptions of the nature of human languages. On the first, commonly held view, languages are abstract entities, representable as sets of expression types paired with their meanings. Language thus construed is a social category: It belongs to a population on account of the fact that its members use the expressions of the language in a way that conforms to some convention. It is natural to see the convention as tied to communication and somehow involving truth – perhaps it is a convention of aiming to utter sentences that are true in the language and of taking the sentences uttered as true in the language, as Lewis (1975) suggested – which leads one to a conception of meaning that determines truth-conditions, and then to externalism. Chomsky calls languages construed in this way *E-languages*. He rejects this conception, sometimes saying that there are no E-languages, sometimes suggesting that there are such things but their individuation is interest-relative. Either way, he thinks they are not subject to systematic theorizing. If linguistics is to be a science, it must have a different subject matter.

For Chomsky, linguistic theory is about the language faculty – a module of the human mind. Language, then, is a psychological category: It belongs to an individual, and it is acquired as a result of biological maturation, not in the course of getting attuned to some social convention. Chomsky calls languages understood in this way *I-languages* and characterizes them with three *i*'s. I-languages are individuated in terms of their grammars, and grammars aren't simply lists of expression with their meanings. They are, rather, procedures (or what Church [1941] called *functions in intension*) to generate the expressions (with their meanings) in a particular way. This is the first *i*. I-languages are states of our language faculty which can vary from speaker to speaker and can change even within a single individual over time. They are thus not vernaculars or dialects but *idiolects* – the second *i*. And finally,

I-languages are states of the mind whose properties supervene on facts about the brain. The relevant facts, Chomsky maintains, are *internal* – they are independent of the social or physical environment. This is the third *i*.

Chomsky's notion of an I-language is an attractive package but it is nonetheless important to see that the three *i*'s don't have to go together. Most linguists who individuate languages in terms of grammars nevertheless think that the languages they study are shared by a population of speakers. Hence, they feel that they are not seeking merely to provide the empirically correct pairing of expressions and meanings for the idiolect of a single speaker. If some individual variations can be neglected, there will be natural classes of idiolects, and it is these that many would regard as the proper subject matter of linguistics.

Moreover, even if we view the study of language as part of individual psychology, we are not forced to accept internalism. The mental states that constitute the language faculty may include attitudes whose content is to be individuated widely. (Ludlow [2013] develops a conception of language that holds on to the first two of the Chomskian *i*'s but rejects the third.)

12.5 Conclusion

Semantics has two aims: to account for the fact that speakers of a language by and large understand the words, phrases, and sentences they use and to say how these words, phrases, and sentences relate to various aspects of the world they are about. It is because of the first aim that we rely on judgments of ordinary speakers and it is because of the latter that we talk about reference and truth in the theory of meaning. Bloomfield's problem is the worry that it may be impossible for a single theory to achieve both of these aims.

Considerations based on examples due to Burge and Putnam bring the problem in focus. If the meaning of a sentence determines its truth-conditions then it seems inevitable that the meaning must depend on factors external to the mind of individual speakers. Felix understands the word 'arthritis', but the intension of this word depends on social facts he is unaware of; Oscar understands the word 'water', but the intension of this word is fixed by chemical facts he knows nothing about.

Externalists seek to reconcile the tension by embracing the bold thesis that many mental states are individuated widely: Even if we fix the the total brain state of a person, what she believes, expects, wants, imagines, etc. remains unsettled. What ultimately fixes what someone knows when she understands a sentence can be something she is completely unaware of: for instance, how people whom she never met use the sentence, or the undiscovered nature of something mentioned by the sentence.

Internalists, on the other hand, think that Bloomfield's problem is insurmountable. For them, there are two notions of meaning: What you grasp when you understand a sentence is one thing, and what determines the truth-conditions of that sentence is another. Accordingly, there are two theories of meaning: one that studies how sentences are matched with mental representations and another that studies how those representations are connected with objects, properties, facts, and whatever else might be found in the inventory of the universe.

13 Paradox and Vagueness

13.1 The Threat of Paradox

Linguistic semantics shares with mathematics the honor of having its foundations infested with paradoxes. The discovery of the Russell Paradox in 1901 interrupted decades of progress in clarifying the mathematical foundations of the calculus, showing that very natural assumptions about sets could lead to a contradiction. The paradoxes affecting semantics, however, have been known from ancient times, long before such things as set theory and semantics had occurred to anyone; in fact, the Liar Paradox may have been mentioned as early as the sixth century BCE.

When Alfred Tarski set himself the task of putting semantics on a rigorous basis, with truth a central component of the theory, the status of the Liar Paradox, as well as the related semantic paradoxes that were discovered much later, changed. They were seen not as philosophical conundrums, but as real impediments to a mathematical project:

> all attempts to characterize this meaning [of semantic concepts] in a general and exact way miscarried. And what is worse, various arguments in which these concepts were involved, and which seemed otherwise quite correct . . . led frequently to paradoxes and antinomies. (Tarski 1944: 346)

We discussed in Section 1.2.5 Tarski's notion of a semantic metalanguage. Tarski's theorem on truth, which we will address in Section 13.2, implies that an adequate semantic metalanguage must be different from its object language, and in particular must support a different and more powerful truth predicate. Moreover, there is no single comprehensive semantic metalanguage but an unending hierarchy of metalanguages: the Tarski hierarchy. This is how Tarski overcame the challenge presented by the semantic paradoxes.

The vagueness of "ordinary language" was often cited by philosophers and logicians who felt that natural and formal languages were fundamentally different and that, because of this difference, semantic theories of natural languages would be misguided and futile. Some of these skeptics may have had in mind something worse: the Sorites Paradox, which provides a short and easy path from vagueness to inconsistency.

The founders of formal semantics were more optimistic. They seem to have regarded these difficulties as challenges that could be, or even had been, solved by developments in logic. Years ago, an author of this book (Rich Thomason) heard Richard Montague explicitly deny that the Liar Paradox was a problem for natural language semantics. He never addressed the problem directly in his work but probably had in mind the Tarski hierarchy. As for vagueness, Montague had this to say in Staal (1969: 280), responding to a question from Michael Dummett:

> Mr. Dummett has also called attention to the existence of vagueness, which is a more difficult thing to handle. What is needed is an exact development of the model theory of vague languages ... I still suspect that some such [many-valued logical] treatment is possible, perhaps within the context of the much richer many-valued (including Boolean-valued) logics that are today available. (Indeed, Professor Tarski tells me that some interesting work on vagueness has just been done at Berkeley by a student named Joseph Goguen.)

Lewis (1970b) says nothing about the semantic paradoxes. But, like Montague, he classifies vagueness as a technical problem. Earlier, in Lewis (1969), he had recommended excluding vagueness from semantics, by thinking of natural languages as (ideally) precise. Uncertainty will then arise about which of a large class of perfectly precise languages to associate with a speaker, or with a population. This pragmatic uncertainty would then be the source of vagueness. (This idea would have trouble accounting for "hedges" like 'somewhat', which apparently shift the vagueness contours of adjectives and so seem to require a language-internal treatment.)

Later, however, Lewis (1970b: 64–65) reconsiders this idea, and suggests a semantic solution that is different from the continuum-valued approach of Goguen (1969). Apparently independently, he recommends a version of van Fraassen's supervaluational theory, first presented in van Fraassen (1966). Consider all the *precisifications*, or reasonable ways of making the vague terms in a language precise – Lewis calls these "delineations." Each precisification yields a bivalent interpretation of the language, which supports compositional rules and will assign either $\top$ (true) or $\bot$ (false) to each sentence in each model, relative to a context of utterance. We then say that a sentence is true (absolutely) if it is true according to all precisifications, false (absolutely) if it is false according to all precisifications, and neither true nor false otherwise. We can obtain a quantitative theory of degrees of truth by introducing a measure over the set of precisifications: The larger the set of precisifications on which a sentence is true, the closer its degree of truth to 1; the smaller the set of precisifications, the closer its degree of truth to 0.

In their early work on natural language semantics, Montague and Lewis represent two ways of dealing with paradoxes: (1) seek to convert them to technical problems or (2) ignore them. The second strategy should actually be attractive to linguists. No working scientist wants to get entangled in paradoxes – leave them to the philosophers! This can be a useful division of labor, but, as we will see, it is harder to maintain it in the case of vagueness.

13.2 The Semantic Paradoxes

Modern logicians and philosophers almost unanimously formulate the Liar and other semantic paradoxes, including the *Grelling Paradox*, the *Curry Paradox*, and the *Yablo Paradox*, as metalinguistic: They rely on mechanisms for referring to sentences. Here, we only discuss the Liar. The Liar Paradox can be formulated most easily by creating a name for a sentence and using the name in that very sentence:

(13.2.1) Sentence (13.2.1) is not true.

Though this certainly looks peculiar, there is no appeal to anything objectionable here. A sentence is displayed and named by giving it a reference number, which is then used to refer to the example sentence. We have been doing this sort of thing throughout this book.

For our purposes, the significant thing about (13.2.1) is that, as we show in detail below, it produces the following contradictory equivalence:

(13.2.2) Sentence (13.2.1) is true if and only if (13.2.1) is not true.

We can generalize what is going on here, and at the same time show that trying to deal with the semantic paradoxes by removing the resources that lead to self-reference is unworkable. Let's say that a language *supports self-reference* if for any syntactic (that is, for any sentence-applicable) predicate P of the language, there is a formula ψ_P that is true if and only if $P(\psi_P)$. This means that for any syntactic predicate of the language, we can construct a sentence saying of itself that it has the predicate. A language equipped with a truth predicate and negation will express the predicate of being untrue and, if it supports self-reference, will then produce the Liar sentence (13.2.2).

Using the methods of *arithmetization* and the *diagonal construction*, Kurt Gödel showed that any theory that can express a minimal amount of arithmetic will support self-reference. (See Montague [1962] for details.) Therefore, in denying self-reference to a theory, we are denying it the ability to talk about numbers and their properties. This is far too high a price to pay; we must write off the idea of restricting self-reference.

The Liar Paradox is the inspiration for a famous theorem about truth that was proved in Tarski (1936). To understand the theorem, we return to Tarski's Convention T, which was mentioned in Section 1.2.5. Here, L is any language, and ML is any language that (1) contains first-order logic, (2) contains L, and (3) is capable of naming the formulas of L.

(13.2.3) If ϕ is a formula of L and α is a name of ϕ in ML, then $T(\alpha) \leftrightarrow \phi$ is true in ML.

If ML has no predicate T satisfying (13.2.3), then it has no way of capturing truth in L. On the other hand, such a predicate, if available, will do the job of capturing this concept.

Assume that L supports self-reference, and as before let ML contain L as well as a truth predicate for L satisfying (13.2.3). Now, suppose L and ML to be identical. $\neg T$, the negation of T, is also a predicate of L. Since L supports self-reference, there is a sentence ψ of L saying of itself that it satisfies $\neg T$, so that (13.2.4) must be true in L, where β is a name in L of ψ.

(13.2.4) $\psi \leftrightarrow \neg T(\beta)$ is true in L.

It's an immediate consequence of (13.2.3) that:

(13.2.5) $\psi \leftrightarrow T(\beta)$ is true in L.

But (13.2.4) and (13.2.5) can't both be true. At this point we have a contradiction. So the hypothesis that L = ML is false, and we have shown that if L supports self-reference then L cannot contain its own truth predicate.

To understand this proof is to realize that those who thought that the Liar Paradox somehow shows natural languages to be inconsistent were misguided in several ways. It may not even be correct to say that a *language* is inconsistent, because for inconsistency we need an inferential structure. Here, for instance, is what Tarski had to say about this point.

> Our everyday language is certainly not one with an exactly specified structure. We do not know precisely what expressions are sentences, and we know even to a smaller degree which sentences are to be taken as assertable. Thus the problem of consistency has no exact meaning with respect to this language. (Tarski 1944: 349)

Suppose, however, that we say a natural language is inconsistent if claims in it that are taken for granted by the population of its competent speakers are inconsistent. Then, as competent speakers of the English language, *we ourselves* will be inconsistent if English is. As we'll see, a few logicians have been driven to this conclusion, but for most of us it is unacceptable.

Finally, as we have stated Tarski's theorem, it has nothing to do with consistency or with the more basic notion of what is provable. It has to do only with *what can be expressed* in a language: The theorem states that no language can express its own truth predicate.

Tarski's theorem, is after all a theorem – and its proof leaves very little room for evasion. Despite that, an enormous, longstanding and ongoing effort has been dedicated to the semantic paradoxes, and claims to have avoided their unwelcome consequences in one way or another are abundant. Before turning to these efforts, let's examine the baseline solution. This is simply to accept the Tarski hierarchy in some form.

What is the Tarski hierarchy? It is simply the hierarchy of metalanguages that emerges from Tarski's theorem. Begin with a self-reference supporting language L_0. Tarski showed that an adequate metalanguage L_1 for L_0 must be different, and more powerful than L_0. For the same reason, there will be a metalanguage L_2 for L_1 that is different from both L_1 and L_0. And the hierarchy continues indefinitely; in fact, it extends through the transfinite ordinal numbers of set theory. Exactly how these metalanguages are formulated is not important. They can contain their object languages and a new truth predicate, or they can quantify over the sets denoted by predicates of their object languages (in which case the metalinguistic hierarchy is the same as the hierarchy of type theory), or they can characterize a family of models of their object languages.

Mathematical logicians seem to have little or no difficulty in working with this solution. For one thing, the distinction between object language and metalanguage was firmly fixed in the first four decades of the twentieth century; this was mentioned in Section 1.2.1. For another, work in set theory, proof theory, and recursion theory has familiarized logicians with many sorts of hierarchies: hierarchies of sets, of axiomatic theories of consistency, and of degrees of computability. A mathematical logician must learn to think of important logical notions as relative to a language, and to live with hierarchies.

Philosophers have been less comfortable with Tarski's baseline solution. The Tarski hierarchy is unintuitive, is motivated by technical considerations, and is philosophically worrisome. Perhaps the most obvious worry is that it seems to deny to semantic theoreticians a language in which they can work. If a logical, philosophical, or linguistic semanticist wishes to speak generally about truth in all languages, there is no way to do this.

The nature of truth is a perennial philosophical topic, going back at least to Plato's *Theaetetus*, and it continues to attract the attention of philosophers. Although the philosophical community was at first reluctant to accept Tarski's ideas about truth, most contemporary philosophers who are interested in the topic treat it as a starting point: But for philosophers, it tends to be a point of departure. Typical philosophical studies of the topic begin by stating Tarski's approach and then developing an alternative. There are many book-length works meeting this description, including Chapuis and Gupta (2000), Maudlin (2004), Beall and Armour-Garb (2005), Bolander et al. (2006), Field (2008), Richard (2008), Lynch (2009), and Ebbs (2009), as well as many, many articles.

Probably there is no single source for philosophers' discontent with Tarski's baseline. But one important component may be the idea that there ought to be a single standpoint from which to do philosophy. For some philosophers, this is common sense or ordinary language. And for some, it is science, while others find it in some preferred version of metaphysics. In any case, there would be a language associated with the philosophical enterprise. But Tarski's theorem seems to show that this language would be incapable of expressing its own truth; for that, another language would be required, and another standpoint. The impossibility of a universal metalanguage seems to leave us with no privileged philosophical perspective.

Since the Tarski hierarchy is based on a mathematical theorem, the options available for work of this kind are limited. There are two basic alternatives. Either you can weaken Tarski's criterion for the adequacy of a semantic metalanguage, or you can embrace the contradiction. The first alternative is by far the most popular, and is often (but not always) combined with a nonclassical logic: for instance, a logic that allows truth-value gaps. Kripke (1975) was an influential signpost in this direction, inspiring an extensive subsequent literature on the topic. There is a mathematical side to this work that is interesting and important; for an overview and references, see Halbach and Leigh (2014). But from the perspective of a philosopher wishing to avoid the Tarski hierarchy and who believes that concepts such as truth and negation should be expressible, this trend is less satisfactory than it appears to be at first glance: It induces other, equally unpalatable "revenge hierarchies." Kripke's approach, for instance, does not allow a language to define its own negation and so induces a hierarchy of metalanguages with increasingly expressive negation operators.

Dialethic approaches allow some sentences to be both true and false, in the same context and the same sense. These solutions too require modifications to classical logic. Here, the source of the difficulty is the principle that anything whatever is a logical consequence of a contradiction; $(\phi \wedge \neg\phi) \rightarrow \psi$ is a logical truth. Obviously, then, in classical logic any contradiction would be disastrous. So the dialethists appeal to *paraconsistent* logics, which do not have this feature. The leading proponent of this idea is Graham Priest: see, for instance, Priest (2002).

Context-dependency can be added to the mix of responses to the semantic paradoxes. Contextualist approaches accept the Tarski hierarchy or an alternative, but claim that attributions of truth are context-dependent. There is little or no direct linguistic evidence for this, but sometimes there is a compelling theoretical need for postulating context dependence without such evidence, and this may be such a case. This idea opens an attractive possibility for disarming the proof of Tarski's theorem – perhaps it involves a concealed change of context. See, for instance, Glanzberg (2004). Unfortunately, this strategy depends on a further claim: that the relevant sort of context-dependence is ineliminable. If there is a two-place predicate "true in c" relating a sentence to a context, Tarski's theorem can then be reproduced for truth relative to c_0, where c_0 is an arbitrary, fixed context. In this case, the contextualist solution collapses to Tarski's baseline or to a variant of it. While the appeal to context may well be legitimate, the claim that truth in L can only be discussed in context-sensitive metalanguages is less plausible.

In Section 13.1 we indicated that the semantic paradoxes might lie on one side of a useful division of labor between linguists and other theoreticians interested in semantics – perhaps linguists can safely ignore these matters and leave them to others. This seems reasonable. The metalinguistic Liar Paradox relies on combinations of 'true' with direct discourse, and such combinations are rare in natural languages. More importantly, although linguists claim to be interested in all languages, they mean all human languages, or maybe all possible human languages. This is not the same as the family of metalanguages generated by Tarski's theorem. As long as linguists confine themselves to a metalanguage for all human languages – where human languages don't include the technical apparatus of semantic theory – they can appeal comfortably to the baseline solution that the Tarski hierarchy affords.

The Liar Paradox has been known from ancient times, but the metalinguistic version of it is relatively new; until recently it was formulated using indirect discourse, as in (13.2.6). There is no mention of a sentence here; instead, the example involves what the Greek philosopher Eubulides *said*, so that it makes use of a propositional attitude.

(13.2.6) Eubulides said that what he was then saying is false.

This version of the Liar Paradox can be produced in intensional logic, the most common logical framework used in linguistic semantics. So perhaps it is less easy to ignore. Prior (1961) formalizes it as follows.

(13.2.7) $\forall p(\mathrm{Say}(E,p) \to \neg p)$

Notice that the formalization differs from the English version. There is no appeal to a notion of falsity; instead a quantifier and a variable 'p' of propositional type is used to formulate a general sentence. Example (13.2.7) implies 'If E said that snow is white then snow isn't white', 'If E said that 4 is an even number then 4 isn't an even number', and infinitely many sentences like this.

The problem is that Example (13.2.7) implies (13.2.8), which says that E must have then said something true. (The reason is that if everything E said then were false, then (13.2.7) would be false, i.e. something E then said would have to be true. So something E said then must not have been false.)

(13.2.8) $\exists p[\mathrm{Say}(E,p) \wedge p]$

On the other hand, Example (13.2.7) *says* that E said something false. So the example implies that E said at least two things, one of them true, and the other false.

Unlike the metalinguistic Liar, this paradox doesn't produce an outright contradiction. But it does yield the peculiar consequence that some things just can't be said without also saying something else. And this is not only true of saying: It also is true of writing, thinking, hoping, explicitly saying, and any propositional attitude. Because of this feature, (13.2.7) is often classified as an *empirical paradox*.

If propositions are identified with sets of possible worlds, the reasoning of the paradox must be accepted, along with the conclusion that, in some cases, one can't have an attitude towards a single proposition. The consequences of the indirect discourse paradoxes for more fine-grained theories of propositions are less well understood. Genuine contradictions may be lurking here, because to treat attitudes as relations to syntactically structured objects may make it possible to reproduce the metalinguistic paradoxes, but there may be ways of avoiding these paradoxes that are not available for the metalinguistic Liar Paradox. See Cresswell (1985).

Although these consequences should be disturbing, even to linguists, they are, it seems, far more logical in nature than linguistic. Even if this family of paradoxes is closer to home than the metalinguistic paradoxes, perhaps semanticists can comfortably leave them to logicians.

13.3 Vagueness and the Sorites Paradox

13.3.1 The Vagueness Phenomenon

There are many reasons to be puzzled about whether something is true, even when we're certain of the relevant facts. A sentence can contain indexicals and we may be uncertain about the context, or it can be ambiguous and we can be uncertain about which of several senses is in play. Vagueness also induces uncertainty about truth, but this uncertainty persists even for disambiguated sentences in well-specified contexts.

Let's imagine an elderly woman who owns a car and uses it for errands. She often drives 3 miles to shop. Much less often, she drives as much as 50 miles for special occasions. She finds it easy to say that a 3-mile trip is not long, and that a 50-mile trip is long. If we ask her about a 26-mile trip she may hesitate. Or, if we ask her this on different occasions, her judgments may be inconsistent: Sometimes she says this is a long trip, sometimes that it isn't.

We may be able to help her with her hesitation, perhaps eliciting the opinion that, after all, a 26-mile trip is long. But then she is likely to remain uncertain about 23 miles and to lose patience with us if we persist. We may also be able to help with the inconsistency, pointing out that when she says it's long, she is thinking about her dislike of driving; when she says it's short, she is thinking of how pleasant the cafe is at the end of the drive. But this sort of help, too, has its limitations, because of course she can think of both of these things at once.

13.3.2 The Sorites Paradox

In daily life, like the elderly driver, we often encounter borderline cases. Like her, we can hesitate or contradict ourselves. But this doesn't prevent vague concepts from playing a useful and even indispensable role in our reasoning. We can confidently judge in many cases whether a trip is long or short, and this will guide us in deciding whether to include it in our plans. If we find ourselves unable to judge such things, that too can be helpful – it means we can simply ignore this issue in making our decision and must either look for other reasons or decide capriciously.

Sometimes, however, we are forced to resolve a vague question. This happens in the law, where judgments must not be capricious and yet can involve the application of a vague rule. Is a certain pornography store actually near an elementary school? If I persuade you to hand over your money by threatening you with a coffee cup, is it armed robbery? To decide such cases, the legal system resorts to arbitrary precision: anything less than 1000 yards from a school is near the school; a coffee cup is not a weapon. Many such determinations are incorporated in the law, through court decisions and explicit legislation. Anyone will agree that these precisifications are to some extent arbitrary. But this is not in itself a reason to object to them, as long as they are uniform and public.

Vagueness becomes treacherous only when we begin to theorize about it. The problematic character of vagueness surfaced as early as the fourth century BCE, with the discovery (attributed to Eubulides of Miletus) of the *Sorites Paradox*, or the "paradox of the heap." The difficulty is this: One grain of sand certainly doesn't make a heap, and adding a grain to an accumulation that isn't a heap can't make a heap. So, no matter how many grains of sand an accumulation may contain, it will not be a heap: There are no heaps of sand.

This ancient version produces the paradox in its most challenging form. 'Heap' is an unregimented term – it is connected to ordinary perception and interests, and there are no conventional measurement techniques that refine it further. Michael Dummett argues forcefully in Dummett (1975) that some words are closely connected to ordinary perception, in such a way that their extensions can't differ for perceptually indistinguishable items. If 'heap' is such a word, and it's impossible – at least in the critical region of reasonable doubt about whether we are dealing with a heap – to discern the difference between an accumulation of n and n+1 grains of sand, then both these accumulations must be heaps if either is. And of course we must agree that *one* grain doesn't make a heap. Now the paradoxical conclusion is inevitable. We have, say, 100,000 true statements $\neg\text{Heap}(n) \leftrightarrow \neg\text{Heap}(n+1)$, as well as $\neg\text{Heap}(1)$. Using only *modus ponens* (99,999 times), we reach the conclusion $\neg\text{Heap}(100{,}000)$: 100,000 grains of sand can't make a heap.

At this point, some theorists feel that classical logic should be abandoned. The two most attractive ways of doing this are (1) supervaluations and (2) many-valued logic, especially logics that use real numbers as truth-values. Fine (1975) is the standard reference for the first idea, while Goguen (1969), Dubois et al. (2007), and Smith (2008) discuss versions of the second. (Goguen's article is an early appearance of the theory, Dubois et al. describe the version of the approach known as "fuzzy logic," and Smith provides a book-length presentation, with a useful survey of the leading theories of vagueness.)

There are many similarities between approaches (1) and (2). Both allow us to introduce degrees of truth, something that seems welcome in connection with vagueness. Both block the Sorites argument, but in ways that create a certain amount of discomfort: Many-valued logics make *modus ponens* invalid, while Supervaluations make $\exists n[\neg\text{Heap}(n) \wedge \text{Heap}(n+1)]$ fully true.

The supervaluation technique preserves the validities of classical logic, including excluded middle, $\phi \vee \neg\phi$, but rejects bivalence – the principle that either ϕ or $\neg\phi$ is true, for any formula ϕ. A third idea, which retains both excluded middle and bivalence, claims that vagueness is a matter of ignorance. This theory is presented and defended in Williamson (1996b). A supervaluationist can say that although $\exists n[\neg\text{Heap(n)} \wedge \text{Heap(n+1)}]$ is fully true, there nevertheless is no n such that ¬Heap(n) and Heap(n+1) are both true. But an ignorance theorist is committed to bivalence and so to the existence of such a number and to the claim that of two indiscernable piles of sand, one is a heap and the other is not. The virtue of this last approach is logical simplicity; the disadvantage is implausibility.

Any of these choices could easily be combined with a semantic theory of natural languages. The epistemic theory, of course, would require no adjustments at all. But supervaluations and many-valued logics are straightforward modifications of classical logic that could easily be combined with intensional type theories of the sort that are most commonly used in formal semantics.

Although these choices are readily available, another alternative might well be preferable to semanticists – to use a logic without truth-value gaps, either ignoring the problem of vagueness entirely or simply accepting the fact that the theory must assign semantic values that are to some extent arbitrary to some lexical items.

This alternative is more attractive than it might seem at first, for two reasons. First, most work in contemporary formal semantics concentrates on the interpretation of complex expressions and functional words, ignoring the problem of how to provide specific interpretations for content words. Although there are some vague function words (e.g. prepositions like 'next to', determiners like 'many', auxiliaries like 'must'), vagueness is primarily associated with content words.

Second, vagueness is closely related to, if not identical to, multiplicity of semantic truth-conditions. If we agree that an expression is vague if resolving the relevant ambiguities and contextual factors will not suffice to decide between equally plausible semantic assignments, then we have to say that logical maneuvering will not eliminate vagueness. Whether we use supervaluations or many-valued logic, there will, for instance, be a definite number n such that it will be false that n grains makes a heap, but neither true nor false that n+1 grains does. But the selection of this n is arbitrary; equally good theories will pick different values of n. (This is sometimes referred to as the problem of *higher-order vagueness*.)

Of course, context can help to reduce ambiguity. But context can't eliminate it entirely. Even if we agree that for our purposes 'long' is to apply to trips that a certain woman might make, and furthermore that it is sensitive to her current interests and preferences, this will not uniquely divide distances into those that qualify and those that don't. Vagueness, in the form of equally good interpretive alternatives, seems to be as unavoidable in semantics as it is in the law; somehow we need to learn to live with it.

Perhaps, then, vagueness offers no compelling reasons for adopting a nonstandard logic. Alternative logics do not eliminate the element of arbitrariness, and much, if not all, of the work that is done by measures over precisifications or by many-valued logic is done at least as well by a degree semantics for vague lexical items.

13.3.3 The Semantics of Degree

Many vague words – here, 'heap' may be an exception – are measurable. That is, it is plausible to think of their meanings as a matter of degree, where *degrees* are indices associated with a measurement class or scale, indices that somehow are ordered. (See, for instance, Cresswell [1976].) Gradable adjectives (adjectives that admit a comparative form) are perhaps the most common examples. In a given context, then, an adjective such as 'long' will relate an individual to a degree of length.

Degree theory interprets a phrase 'x is $[_{\text{ADJ}}\alpha]$' relative to a context, by assigning it a precise range of degrees. Regimenting the meaning of a gradable adjective like 'long' in this way eliminates any vagueness it might have. But this doesn't prevent the approach from accounting for semantic data that are closely related to vagueness. In fact, Christopher Kennedy calls his theory a "grammar of vagueness." (See Kennedy [2007].)

For instance, the approach can characterize ways in which context can influence how a range of degrees is assigned to a gradable adjective. According to Kennedy, context affects an adjective like 'expensive' by providing a comparison class; roughly, 'expensive' means "expensive to a degree exceeding the norm imposed by class C," while 'pretty expensive' means "expensive to a degree appreciably exceeding the norm imposed by C." So 'x is pretty expensive' entails 'x is expensive'. An adjective like 'straight' falls into a different class, so that 'x is pretty straight' entails 'x is not straight'. These results about entailment align with similar entailments that are predicted by formal semantic theories. But they interact with considerations about vagueness.

13.4 Conclusion

The semantic paradoxes, as well as the Sorites, have preoccupied philosophers for a very long time, without anything like an entirely satisfactory solution having emerged. Although both paradoxes are closely related to questions of meaning, linguistic theories of meaning can be deployed without requiring a solution that meets the standards of philosophy.

The semantic paradoxes can be addressed by enforcing a clear separation of object language and metalanguage. If metalinguistic expressions like direct discourse 'true' are not included in the object language, these paradoxes will not arise.

Vagueness is harder to ignore, but can be addressed by accepting the necessity of a certain amount of arbitrary regimentation in the semantics of words. Such regimentation seems to be unavoidable, does little or no harm, and even can support the development of something very like a theory of vagueness.

Glossary

$\bot$ A truth-value: "the false". 25

$\exists$ Logical notation for the existential quantifier: logical 'exists'. 10

$\forall$ Logical notation for the universal quantifier: logical 'every'. 10

λ **abstraction** See "Lambda abstraction". 46

$[\![\ ]\!]$ The semantic evaluation operator, taking an expression η to its semantic value $[\![\eta]\!]$. 45

$\neg$ Logical notation for negation: logical 'not'. 10

$\top$ A truth-value: "the true". 25

$\ulcorner\ \urcorner$ Corner quotes. Special notation introduced by Willard V.O. Quine, applicable to expressions containing syntactic metavariables. For example, $\ulcorner(\phi \vee \psi)\urcorner$ is the result of concatenating '(', ϕ, '$\vee$', ψ, and ')' in that order. Contrast this with '$(\phi \vee \psi)$', which is the result of concatenating '(', 'ϕ', '$\vee$',' ψ', and ')' in that order. We use corner quotes in this book for a different purpose. 5

$\vee$ Logical notation for disjunction: logical 'or'. 5

$\wedge$ Logical notation for conjunction: logical 'and'. 10

a priori vs. a posteriori truth An a posteriori truth is one that cannot be known without relying on experience; an a priori truth is one that is not a posteriori. 70

abstract/concrete Philosophers do not agree on the precise characterization of this distinction, but it is always seen as exhaustive. Usually, something counts as abstract when it is not located in space and time and has no causes or effects. Paradigmatic abstract entities are the natural numbers. 7

accommodation The speaker manifestly presupposes something, the hearer adopts the same presupposition, and as a result, the common ground is expanded. 188

Aktionsarten Types of verbs that are useful in classifying how they interact with aspect and with certain adverbs. Zeno Vendler provided one of the most influential classifications. 99

analysis, philosophical An account that is intended to be philosophically explanatory. Usually, but not always, it is a concept or the meaning of an expression that is analyzed. Philosophical analysis proceeds by disclosing an underlying structure in the thing analyzed, often through definition or formalization. 113

anaphoric relation A relation between two occurrences of phrases where the semantic value of the one is inherited from that of the other; e.g. the relationship between 'Jill' and 'her' in the default interpretation of 'Jill loves her mother'. 73

behaviorism An approach to psychology, popular in the first half of the twentieth century, that avoided mentalistic theorizing and stressed direct relations between stimuli and behavioral responses. 241

binding relation A relation between two occurrences of phrases where the semantic value of the one depends on a semantic rule associated with the other; e.g. the relationship between 'Every woman' and 'her' in the default interpretation of 'Every woman loves her mother'. 88

bivalence A semantics is bivalent if it assigns exactly one truth-value to each sentence. A nonbivalent semantics that assigns neither truth-value to some sentences allows for *truth-value gaps*, and a nonbivalent semantics that assigns both truth-values to some sentences admits *truth-value gluts*. 12

character Context-independent meaning. David Kaplan modeled it as a function from contexts to intensions. 55

characteristic function The characteristic function of a set X inputs an object x and outputs the truth-value ⊤ if x belongs to X and the value ⊥ otherwise. 23

common ground What the conversational participants mutually take for granted. Many theorists take this to be what they all believe, and all believe they all believe, and all believe they all believe they all believe, ... Some theorists use knowledge in this definition; others use mere acceptance for the purposes of conversation. 182

compositionality, semantic The thesis that there is a function mapping the complete structure and the meanings of the ultimate constituents of any complex expression to the expression's meaning. 41

conceptual role semantics The view that the meaning of an expression is exhausted by its role in reasoning, broadly construed, including perceptual judgments and action-guiding decisions. 241

conditional A sentence consisting of a main clause and a subordinate clause that expresses a condition: 'If it snowed last night the streets are slippery' is a conditional. 26

content The decontextualized meaning of an expression that is supposed to be understood by competent speakers. It is usually assumed that content, together with the relevant facts of the world, determines extension. For instance, the content of a declarative sentence and real-world facts determine a truth-value. 26

context, of utterance The situation in which an utterance takes place. Normally modeled in formal semantics in one of two ways: as an n-tuple whose components are the semantic values of indexicals in a given context or as the common ground among the conversational participants. 165

correspondence theory, of truth Any account of truth that characterizes it as a relation between sentences and language-independent features of the way things are. 156

cross-world-identification The philosophical and logical question of how to track the same individual from one possibility to another. Also known as modal individuation. 109

definite description A term used mainly in philosophy, for definite noun phrases, especially those headed by the definite article. 9

dialethic logic Logic that makes room for true contradictions. 282

disposition Philosophical terminology for a property that consists in a tendency to undergo certain changes, conditional on a test condition. Solubility and elasticity, for example, are dispositions. 98

empiricism Radical empiricism holds that the acquisition and/or justification of all knowledge requires empirical evidence. Moderate empiricists exempt logical knowledge from this requirement. 14

enthymene An inference that depends on a missing, implicit premise. 241

expressivism The philosophical view that the primary function of moral and evaluative sentences is not to describe a matter of fact but rather to express an attitude or emotion. 15

extension A semantic value such as an individual or object, or a truth-value. More generally, semantic values constructed from these by forming sets and functions are considered to be extensions. The extension of a nonsentential expression is whatever contributes to the truth-values of declarative sentences in which it occurs as a constituent; in particular, the extension of a referring expression is the thing to which it refers. 1

extensional construction A construction whose semantic behavior can be entirely explained in terms of extensions. 1

force For Frege, a type of mental act directed at a content. For instance, one can wonder whether p is the case and then suppose or accept or reject p. For some speech act theorists, *illocutionary force* determines what speech act a content enters into – for instance, whether it is commanded or promised. 26

formal semantics The approach to the semantics of natural languages that makes extensive and systematic use of ideas from symbolic logic. 31

free variable A variable that is not bound by a quantifier. 23

function A rule that assigns a single output to certain fixed-length sequences of inputs. The fixed length is called the *arity* of the function, the inputs are the function's arguments, the outputs are its values. The domain of the function is the set of all its arguments; the range of the function is the set of all its values. Functions are often represented as sets of ordered tuples $\langle\langle x_1, \ldots, x_n\rangle, y\rangle$, such that for all $\langle\langle a_1, \ldots, a_n\rangle, b\rangle$ and $\langle\langle a_1, \ldots, a_n\rangle, c\rangle$, in the set, $b = c$. 1

functionalism In philosophy, functionalist theories of cognition countenance mental states and characterize them in terms of how they relate to each other as well as to perceptual and motor functions. 241

grounding The process of maintaining coordination in a conversation. Many conversational mechanisms, such as back-channeling and repetition, assist the grounding process. 194

iff Short for "if and only if". 72

implicature For Paul Grice, information conveyed by an utterance that is not part of what the speaker said. He distinguished *conventional* implicatures (encoded as part of the meaning of the expression uttered) and *conversational* implicatures (conveyed through a mechanism relying on the presumption of the cooperativity of the speaker). 161

indexical expression An expression whose semantic value is sensitive to the context of utterance. 166

individuation, modal The philosophical and logical question of how to track the same individual from one place, or time, or possible world to another. Also known as cross-world-identification. 109

inferential role semantics The view that the meaning of an expression is exhausted by its role in inferences. 241

inscrutability of reference The view that there are no empirical constraints on semantic theorizing beyond getting the truth-conditions of declarative sentences right, and hence, that there are equally good theories that disagree on the reference of words. 69

intension The intension of an expression is a function from possible worlds (and perhaps further parameters, such as times or places) to extensions. 1

intensional construction Used ambiguously in philosophy for either a construction whose semantic behavior can't be entirely explained in terms of extensions, or more narrowly for a subclass of these expressions whose semantic behavior can be explained in terms of intensions. 1

internalism versus externalism Internalism in the philosophy of mind is the view that mentality – how one represents the world to oneself and what it is like for one to have those representations – is an intrinsic matter. The environment makes a difference to what is on our minds only if it makes a difference to what is going on inside us. Externalism is the view that denies this. 266

lambda abstraction A method of providing an explicit name of a function from a description, involving a free variable, of how the function operates. For instance, $\lambda x\, x^2 + 2x + 1$ is the function that inputs a number and outputs the result of squaring it, adding the result of multiplying the number by 2 to this, and then adding 1. If 'x is red' refers to its truth-value $\top$ or $\bot$, then '$\lambda x\, x$ is red' refers to the function that returns $\top$ if 'x' refers to something red, else to $\bot$. 46

language game For Ludwig Wittgenstein, a practice of using a certain set of expressions following certain rules for certain ends. Wittgenstein saw language use in general as a patchwork of language games. 239

Liar Paradox In its ancient form, a Cretan says that all Cretans are liars. In its modern, metalinguistic form, a sentence says of itself that it is false or untrue. 277

locution versus illocution versus perlocution J. L. Austin distinguishes various acts associated with an utterance. The locutionary act is a public presentation of a content by means of a linguistic expression (e.g. the mere utterance of the sentence 'I am hungry'). The perlocutionary act involves an audience reaction (e.g. convincing someone that I am hungry by uttering 'I am hungry'). The illocutionary act usually involves a combination of content and force: Asserting that I am hungry is an illocutionary act, so is promising to buy someone lunch. Illocutionary acts do not depend on audience reactions. The precise lines between these acts are often hard to draw. 217

logical positivism The view that any meaningful claim that isn't logically true must be acquired through and/or justified by empirical evidence if it is true at all, and that this evidence must ultimately be reducible to sense impressions. 14

logically proper name For Bertrand Russell, a logically proper name refers to its referent without describing it. Speakers who understand such a name stand in a direct epistemic contact (Russell called this acquaintance) with its referent, and consequently cannot be mistaken about its existence or identity. 9

metamathematics The application of mathematics to mathematical theories themselves. 31

metasemantics The study of how and why a specific meaning is associated with a specific expression. 59

modal verbs A small class of verbs associated with some sort of necessity or possibility. In English, most modal verb are auxiliaries like 'must', 'may', 'should', 'might', and 'can'. 3

model A mathematical structure that provides domains for interpreting the expressions of a language and that enables a definition of truth for the sentences of a language. 3

model theory The mathematical study of models. 1

natural versus non-natural meaning Paul Grice distinguishes between meaning as inference of natural causes (as in 'Smoke means fire' or 'That coating of ice means that the walk is slippery') and meaning for the purposes of communication (as in 'He meant fire by his loud cry' or 'That sign means that the walk is slippery'). 201

naturalism Ontological naturalism is the view that science is the best guide to questions about what there is. Methodological naturalism is the view that the scientific method is the first and best way to examine questions of all kinds. 8

nominalism Traditionally, the philosophical view that there are no universals, that there is no single thing that many things have in common. In contemporary philosophical usage, the view that there are no abstract entities. 7

nonmonotonic logic A logic with a nonmonotonic consequence relation. This means that a conclusion that follows from a set of premises may no longer follow if new premises are added. 194

observation sentence A sentence that is closely tied to observation and can be verified or disconfirmed by competent speakers in a position to have the relevant observational experiences. 70

ontology The branch of metaphysics that deals with what kinds of things there are. 4

ordinary language philosophy A philosophical movement in the middle of the twentieth century that sought to solve or dissolve philosophical questions by reflection on the fine detail of the uses of certain expressions in everyday situations. Among its central figures were the late Ludwig Wittgenstein, Gilbert Ryle, J. L. Austin, and the early Peter Strawson. 151

performative utterance For J. L. Austin, a performative utterance is one whose point is the performance of some act, such as ordering, promising, naming, marrying, etc. It is to be distinguished from utterances whose point is to describe things. An utterance of 'I promise that I will come' is usually performative: The speaker makes a promise. But an utterance of 'I promised that I would come' is usually not performative: The speaker describes the making of a promise. 157

phenomenalism The philosophical view that all empirical truths are reducible to truths about actual and possible sense-data, or immediate sense impressions. 153

possible world A complete specification of a way things might be; a possibility. *Possible worlds semantics* is the standard way of dealing with modality and even intensionality in formal semantics. 104

pragmatics The study of the use of meaningful expressions. Linguistic pragmatics focuses for the most part on how presuppositions and implicatures arise when speakers utter declarative sentences. 1

productivity, linguistic The capacity of competent speakers of a language to understand expressions they have never encountered before. 41

proposition The intentional objects of belief and assertion. It is often thought that propositions are also the meanings of declarative sentences that are not context sensitive, but this is controversial. In formal semantics, propositions are often represented as sets of possible worlds. 7

propositional attitude A mental event, process, or state directed at a proposition. It is typically assumed that mental verbs taking clauses as complements (e.g. 'believe') express propositional attitudes; it is often assumed that mental verbs taking infinitival complements (e.g. 'want') also express propositional attitudes. 27

propositional logic The logic of languages whose sole logical constants are sentential connectives such as conjunction, disjunction, and negation. 45

psychological verb A verb indicating a mental state of some sort. 3

quantifier Logical constant used to express generalizations. In formal languages these are usually variable-binding devices, like the '∀' and '∃' of first-order logic. 6

radical interpretation A process whereby someone who lacks any prior knowledge of the meanings of expressions in the language and gathers evidence exclusively from observing competent speakers' interaction with the environment determines the meanings of expressions. In particular, radical interpretation does not rely on shared language or culture. 67

Russell Paradox A paradox in the theory of sets, which can be circumvented by type theory or by restrictions on the set-theoretic Axiom of Comprehension. The problem has to do with the set of all sets which are not members of themselves. Is it a member of itself? Both answers lead to an immediate contradiction. 277

semantic value An entity (or entities) that is associated with a linguistic expression and which serves to model some aspect of its meaning. In linguistic semantics, semantic values are often extensions or intensions. 36

semantics The systematic study of what expressions mean. Linguistic semantics focuses for the most part on a specific aspect of linguistic meaning: the truth-conditions of declarative sentences and the contributions the constituents of declarative sentences make to their truth-conditions. 1

sense-data The intentional objects of perceptions, supposed to be mind-dependent and to have all and only the properties they appear to have. It is controversial whether such things exist. 153

substitutivity, principle of The principle that interchanging an ultimate constituent within a complex expression with a synonym does not change the meaning of the complex expression. 49

supervaluation A valuation is an assignment of a truth-value to every sentence. A sentence that is not determinately true or false has many permissible valuations. A supervaluation is a partial assignment of truth-values to sentences that treats a sentence as true iff it is true on all permissible valuations and as false iff it is false on all permissible valuations. 278

Tarski hierarchy A series of metalanguages, each more powerful than its predecessor and each able to define truth in its predecessor. 277

teleological explanation An explanation of a phenomenon in terms of its function or purpose. 99

transitive verb, intensional A transitive verb whose object position is intensional; 'seek', 'imagine', and 'fear' are intensional transitive verbs. 107

truth-value For Frege, two objects to which sentences can refer: the True and the False. In logic they are often represented by '1' and '0'; we use '$\top$' and '$\bot$'. 25

variable Devices used in logical languages and programming languages to secure generality. Many linguists, especially those who believe in a level of "logical form," feel that variables also figure in natural languages. 6

Bibliography

Adams, Robert Merrihew. 1981. Actualism and Thisness. *Synthese*, **49**(1), 3–41.

Ahmed, Tarek Sayed. 2005. Algebraic Logic: Where Does It Stand Today? *The Bulletin of Symbolic Logic*, **11**(4), 465–516.

Aloni, Maria. 2001. *Quantification under Conceptual Covers*. Ph.D. Dissertation, University of Amsterdam, Amsterdam.

Anderson, Alan R. 1951. A Note on Subjunctive and Counterfactual Conditionals. *Analysis*, **12**, 35–38.

Anderson, Alan R., and Belnap, Nuel D. 1975. *Entailment: The Logic of Relevance and Necessity, Vol. 1*. Princeton, NJ: Princeton University Press.

Anderson, C. Anthony. 1977. *Some Models for the Logic of Sense and Denotation with an Application to Alternative (0)*. Ph.D. Dissertation, Philosophy Department, UCLA, Los Angeles.

Anscombe, G. E. M. 1963. *Intention*. 2 edn. Ithaca, NY: Cornell University Press.

Arlo-Costa, Horacio, and Egré, Paul. 2016. The Logic of Conditionals. In: Zalta, Edward N. (ed), *The Stanford Encyclopedia of Philosophy*. https://plato.stanford.edu/archives/win2016/entries/logic-conditionals/.

Armstrong, David. 1968. *A Materialist Theory of the Mind*. London: Routledge and Kegan Paul.

Arnauld, Antoine, and Nicole, Pierre. 1996. *Logic or the Art of Thinking*. Cambridge: Cambridge University Press. Translated by Jill Vance Buroker.

Asher, Nicholas, and Lascarides, Alex. 2003. *Logics of Conversation*. Cambridge: Cambridge University Press.

Atkin, Albert. 2013. Peirce's Theory of Signs. In: Zalta, Edward N. (ed), *The Stanford Encyclopedia of Philosophy*. Stanford Encyclopedia of Philosophy. http://plato.stanford.edu/archives/sum2013/entries/peirce-semiotics/.

Augustine of Hippo. 1995. *De Doctrina Christiana*. Oxford: Oxford University Press. Originally published 397–426 CE. Translated by R. P. H. Green.

Aumann, Robert J. 1976. Agreeing to Disagree. *Annals of Statistics*, **4**(6), 1236–1239.

Aumann, Robert J. 1995. Backward Induction and Common Knowledge of Rationality. *Games and Economic Behavior*, **8**(1), 6–19.

Austin, John L. 1946. Other Minds. *Proceedings of the Aristotelian Society*, **20**, 148–187.

Austin, John L. 1950. Truth. *Proceedings of the Aristotelian Society*, **24**, 111–128.

Austin, John L. 1956. Ifs and Cans. *Proceedings of the British Academy*, **42**, 109–132.

Austin, John L. 1956–1957. A Plea for Excuses. *Proceedings of the Aristotelian Society*, **57**, 1–30.

Austin, John L. 1961. Performative Utterances. Pages 233–252 of: Urmson, J. O., and Warnock, G. J. (eds), *Philosophical Papers*. 3 edn. Oxford: Oxford University Press. Edited transcript of an unscripted 1956 radio talk produced by the BBC.

Austin, John L. 1962a. *How to Do Things with Words*. Oxford: Oxford University Press. Edited by J. O. Urmson and G. J. Warnock.

Austin, John L. 1962b. *Sense and Sensibilia*. Oxford: Oxford University Press. Reconstructed posthumously from lecture notes by G. J. Warnock.

Ayer, Alfred J. 1936. *Language, Truth and Logic*. London: Victor Gollancz.

Bach, Kent. 1999. The Myth of Conventional Implicature. *Linguistics and Philosophy*, **22**(4), 327–366.

Bach, Kent, and Harnish, Robert M. 1979. *Linguistic Communication and Speech Acts*. Cambridge, MA: The MIT Press.

Bar-Hillel, Yehoshua. 1954. Indexical Expressions. *Mind, New Series*, **63**, 359–379.

Bar-Hillel, Yehoshua. 1963. Can Indexical Sentences Stand in Logical Relations? *Philosophical Studies*, **14**(6), 87–90.

Barwise, K. Jon, and Cooper, Robin. 1981. Generalized Quantifiers and Natural Language. *Linguistics and Philosophy*, **4**(1), 159–219.

Barwise, Jon, and Etchemendy, John. 1987. *The Liar*. Oxford: Oxford University Press.

Bealer, George. 1998. Propositions. *Mind, New Series*, **107**(425), 1–32.

Beall, J. C., and Armour-Garb, Bradley (eds). 2005. *Deflationism and Paradox*. Oxford: Oxford University Press.

Beaney, Michael. 2016. Analysis. In: Zalta, Edward N. (ed), *The Stanford Encyclopedia of Philosophy*, summer 2016 edn. https://plato.stanford.edu/archives/sum2016/entries/analysis/.

Beaver, David. 1996. Presupposition. Pages 939–1008 of: van Benthem, Johan, and ter Meulen, Alice (eds), *Handbook of Logic and Language*. Amsterdam: Elsevier.

Beaver, David I. 1999. Presupposition Accommodation: A Plea for Common Sense. Pages 21–44 of: Moss, Lawrence S., Ginzburg, Jonathan, and de Rijke, Maarten (eds), *Logic, Language and Computation, Vol. 2*. Stanford, CA: CSLI Publications.

Bell, David. 1987. Thoughts. *Notre Dame Journal of Formal Logic*, **28**(1), 36–50.

Bell, David. 1996. The Formation of Concepts and the Structure of Thoughts. *Philosophy and Phenomenological Research*, **56**(3), 583–596.

Bennett, Jonathan. 1976. *Linguistic Behaviour*. Cambridge: Cambridge University Press.

Bennett, Michael R., and Partee, Barbara H. 1982. *Toward the Logic of Tense and Aspect in English*. Bloomington, IN: Indiana University Linguistics Club.

Bermúdez, José L. 2001. Frege on Thoughts and Their Structure. *Logical Analysis and History of Philosophy*, **4**, 87–105.

Bernecker, Sven. 2010. *Memory: A Philosophical Study*. Oxford: Oxford University Press.

Bezuidenhout, Anne. 2001. Metaphor. *Midwest Studies in Philosophy*, **25**(1), 156–186.

Blackburn, Patrick, de Rijke, Maarten, and Venema, Yde. 2001. *Modal Logic*. Cambridge: Cambridge University Press.

Blackburn, Simon. 1984. *Spreading the Word: Groundings in the Philosophy of Language*. Oxford: Oxford University Press.

Bloomfield, Leonard. 1933. *Language*. New York: Holt, Rinehart and Winston.

Boër, Steven E., and Lycan, William G. 1986. *Knowing Who*. Cambridge, MA: The MIT Press.

Boghossian, Paul A. 1989. Content and Self-Knowledge. *Philosophical Topics*, **17**(1), 5–26.

Bolander, Thomas, Hendricks, Vincent F., and Pedersen, Stig Andur (eds). 2006. *Self-Reference*. Stanford, CA: CSLI Publications.

Brandom, Robert B. 1994. *Making It Explicit: Reasoning, Representing, and Discursive Commitment*. Cambridge, MA: Harvard University Press.

Brandom, Robert. 2000. *Articulating Reasons: An Introduction to Inferentialism*. Cambridge, MA: Harvard University Press.

Braun, David. 1998. Understanding Belief Reports. *The Philosophical Review*, **107**(4), 555–595.

Brentano, Franz. 1995. *Psychology from an Empirical Standpoint*. 2 edn. London: Routledge. Originally published in 1874. Translated by A. C. Rancurello, D. B. Terrell, and L. McAlister.

Brewka, Gerhard, Dix, Jürgen, and Konolige, Kurt. 1997. *Nonmonotonic Reasoning: An Overview*. Stanford, CA: CSLI Publications.

Bromberger, Sylvain. 1992. Types and Tokens in Linguistics. Pages 170–208 of: Bromberger, Sylvain (ed), *On What We Know We Don't Know*. Chicago, IL: University of Chicago Press.

Brueckner, Anthony. 2003. Trees, Computer Program Features, and Skeptical Hypotheses. Pages 217–226 of: Luper, Steven (ed), *The Sceptics: Contemporary Essays*. Burlington, VT: Ashgate.

Burge, Tyler. 1979. Individualism and the Mental. *Midwest Studies in Philosophy*, **4**(1), 73–121.

Burge, Tyler. 1989. Individuation and Causation in Psychology. *Pacific Philosophical Quarterly*, **70**(4), 303–332.

Camp, Elisabeth. 2005. Metaphors and Demonstratives: Josef Stern's, *Metaphor in Context*. *Noûs*, **39**(4), 715–731.

Cappelen, Herman, and Dever, Josh. 2013. *The Inessential Indexical: On the Philosophical Insignificance of Perspective and the First Person*. Oxford: Oxford University Press.

Cappelen, Herman, and Lepore, Ernest. 2005. *Insensitive Semantics: A Defense of Semantic Minimalism and Speech Act Pluralism*. Oxford: Blackwell.

Carnap, Rudolf. 1934. *Logische Syntax der Sprache Schriften zur wissenschaftlichen Weltauffassung*. Vienna: Verlag von Julius Springer.

Carnap, Rudolf. 1937. *The Logical Syntax of Language*. London: Kegan Paul Trench, Trubner. Translated by Amethe Smeaton, Countess von Zeppelin.

Carnap, Rudolf. 1942. *Introduction to Semantics*. Cambridge, MA: Harvard University Press.

Carnap, Rudolf. 1950. Empiricism, Semantics, and Ontology. *Revue Internationale de Philosophie*, **4**, 20–40.

Carnap, Rudolf. 1956. *Meaning and Necessity*. 2 edn. Chicago, IL: Chicago University Press. First edition published in 1947.

Carston, Robyn. 2002. *Thoughts and Utterances: The Pragmatics of Explicit Communication*. Oxford: Blackwell.

Carston, Robyn. 2012. Word Meaning and Concept Expressed. *The Linguistic Review*, **29**(4), 607–623.

Casati, Roberto, and Varzi, Achille C. 1999. *Parts and Places: The Structures of Spatial Representation*. Cambridge, MA: The MIT Press.

Castañeda, Hector-Neri. 1966. "He": A Study in Self-Consciousness. *Ratio*, **8**, 187–203.

Castañeda, Hector-Neri. 1969. Indicators and Quasi-Indicators. *American Philosophical Quarterly*, **4**(2), 85–100.

Chapuis, André, and Gupta, Anil (eds). 2000. *Circularity, Definition, and Truth*. New Delhi: Indian Council of Philosophical Research.

Chierchia, Gennaro. 1995. *Dynamics of Meaning: Anaphora, Presupposition, and the Theory of Grammar*. Chicago, IL: Chicago University Press.

Chisholm, Roderick. 1957. *Perceiving*. Ithaca, NY: Cornell University Press.

Chomsky, Noam. 1986. *Knowledge of Language: Its Nature, Origin, and Use*. New York: Praeger.

Chomsky, Noam. 2000. *New Horizons in the Study of Language and Mind*. Cambridge: Cambridge University Press.

Church, Alonzo. 1940. A Formulation of the Simple Theory of Types. *Journal of Symbolic Logic*, **5**(1), 56–68.

Church, Alonzo. 1941. *The Calculi of Lambda Conversion*. Princeton, NJ: University of Princeton Press. Annals of Mathematics Studies, Number 6.

Church, Alonzo. 1943. Carnap's Introduction to Semantics. *The Philosophical Review*, **52**(3), 298–304.

Church, Alonzo. 1950. On Carnap's Analysis of Statements of Assertion and Belief. *Analysis*, **10**, 97–99.

Church, Alonzo. 1951a. A Formulation of the Logic of Sense and Denotation. Pages 3–24 of: Henle, Paul, Kallen, Horace M., and Langer, Susanne K. (eds), *Structure, Method, and Meaning: Essays in Honor of Henry M. Scheffer*. New York: Liberal Arts Press.

Church, Alonzo. 1951b. The Need for Abstract Entities in Semantic Analysis. *Proceedings of the American Academy of Arts and Sciences*, **80**, 100–112.

Church, Alonzo. 1993. A Revised Formulation of the Logic of Sense and Denotation. Alternative (1). *Noûs*, **27**, 141–157.

Clark, Herbert. 1992. *Arenas of Language Use*. Chicago, IL: University of Chicago Press.

Clark, Herbert, and Carlson, Thomas B. 1982. Context for Comprehension. Pages 313–330 of: *Attention and Performance IX*. Mahwah, NJ: Lawrence Erlbaum Associates.

Clark, Herbert H. 2005. Pragmatics of Language Performance. Pages 365–382 of: Horn, Laurence R., and Ward, Gregory (eds), *Handbook of Pragmatics*. Oxford: Blackwell.

Clark, Herbert H., and Brennan, Susan E. 1991. Grounding in Communication. Pages 127–149 of: Resnick, Lauren B., Levine, John M., and Teasley, Stephanie D. (eds), *Perspectives on Socially Shared Cognition*. Washington, DC: American Psychological Association.

Clark, Herbert H., and Marshall, Catherine R. 1981. Definite Reference and Mutual Knowledge. Pages 10–63 of: Joshi, Arivind, Webber, Bonnie, and Sag, Ivan (eds), *Elements of Discourse Understanding*. Cambridge: Cambridge University Press.

Clark, Herbert H., and Schaefer, Edward F. 1987. Collaborating on Contributions to Conversations. *Language and Cognitive Processes*, **2**(1), 19–41.

Clark, Herbert H., and Schober, Michael. 1989. Understanding by Addressees and Overhearers. *Cognitive Psychology*, **21**, 211–232.

Code, Alan D. 1995. Potentiality in Aristotle's Science and Metaphysics. *Pacific Philosophical Quarterly*, **76**(3–4), 405–418.

Cohen, S. Marc. 2014. Aristotle's Metaphysics. In: Zalta, Edward N. (ed), *The Stanford Encyclopedia of Philosophy*. Stanford Encyclopedia of Philosophy. http://plato.stanford.edu/archives/sum2014/entries/aristotle-metaphysics/.

Collins, John. 2007. Syntax, More or Less. *Mind*, **116**(464), 805–850.

Cottingham, John, Stoothoff, Robert, and Murdoch, Dugald (eds). 1984. *The Philosophical Writings of Descartes*. Cambridge: Cambridge University Press.

Crane, Tim. 1991. All the Difference in the World. *The Philosophical Quarterly*, **41**(1), 1–25.

Crane, Tim. 1998. Intentionality as the Mark of the Mental. *Royal Instutute of Philosophy Supplement*, **43**, 229–251.

Cresswell, Max J. 1976. The Semantics of Degree. Pages 261–292 of: Partee, Barbara H. (ed), *Montague Grammar*. New York: Academic Press.

Cresswell, Max J. 1985. *Structured Meanings*. Cambridge, MA: The MIT Press.

Crimmins, Mark. 1995. Contextuality, Reflexivity, Iteration, Logic. Pages 381–399 of: Tomberlin, James E. (ed), *Philosophical Perspectives, Vol. 9: AI, Connectionism, and Philosophical Psychology*. Atasacadero, CA: Ridgeview Publishing Company.

Davidson, Donald. 1965. Theories of Meaning and Learnable Languages. Pages 3–17 of: Bar-Hillel, Yehoshua (ed), *Proceedings of the International Congress for Logic, Methodology, and Philosophy of Science*. Amsterdam: North-Holland.

Davidson, Donald. 1967. Truth and Meaning. *Synthese*, **17**(1), 304–323. Reprinted in Davidson (1984).

Davidson, Donald. 1968. On Saying That. *Synthese*, **19**, 130–146.

Davidson, Donald. 1969. True to the Facts. *Journal of Philosophy*, **66**(21), 748–764.

Davidson, Donald. 1973. In Defense of Convention T. Pages 76–86 of: Davidson, Donald (ed), *Inquiries into Truth and Interpretation*. Oxford: Oxford University Press.

Davidson, Donald. 1973. Radical Interpretation. *Dialectica*, **27**(3–4), 313–328. Republished in Davidson (1984).

Davidson, Donald. 1978. What Metaphors Mean. *Critical Inquiry*, **5**(1), 31–47.

Davidson, Donald. 1979. The Inscrutability of Reference. *Southwestern Journal of Philosophy*, **10**(2), 7–19.

Davidson, Donald. 1984. *Inquiries into Truth and Interpretation*. Oxford: Oxford University Press.

Davis, Wayne A. 1998. *Implicature: Intention, Convention, and Principle in the Failure of Gricean Theory*. Cambridge: Cambridge University Press.

den Dikken, Marcel, Larson, Richard, and Ludlow, Peter. 1996. Intensional 'Transitive' Verbs and Concealed Complement Clauses. *Revista de Linguistica*, **8**(1), 29–46.

Dennett, Daniel, and Steglich-Petersen, Asbjørn. 2008. *The Philosophical Lexicon, 2008 edition*. http://www.philosophicallexicon.com/.

DeRose, Keith. 1992. Contextualism and Knowledge Attributions. *Philosophy and Phenomenological Research*, **52**(4), 913–929.

DeRose, Keith. 2009. *The Case for Contextualism: Knowledge, Skepticism, and Context, Vol. 1*. Oxford: Oxford University Press.

Descartes, René. 1996. *Meditations on First Philosophy*. Cambridge: Cambridge University Press. English translation by John Cottingham.

Dever, Josh. 1999. Compositionality as Methodology. *Linguistics and Philosophy*, **22**(3), 311–326.

Dowty, David R. 1979. *Word Meaning in Montague Grammar*. Dordrecht: D. Reidel Publishing Co.

Dretske, Fred. I. 1980. The Intentionality of Cognitive States. *Midwest Studies in Philosophy*, **5**(1), 281–294.

Dretske, Fred I. 1981. *Knowledge and the Flow of Information*. Cambridge, MA: The MIT Press.

Dretske, Fred. 1995. *Naturalizing the Mind*. Cambridge, MA: MIT Press.

Dubois, Didier, Prade, Henri, and Godo, Lluís. 2007. Fuzzy-Set Based Logics—An History-Oriented Presentation of Their Main Developments. Pages 325–450 of: Gabbay, Dov M., and Woods, John (eds), *Handbook of the History of Logic, Vol. 8: The Many Valued and Nonmonotonic Turn in Logic*. Amsterdam: Elsevier Science Publishers.

Dummett, Michael. 1960. A Defense of McTaggart's Proof of the Unreality of Time. *The Philosophical Review*, **69**(4), 497–504.

Dummett, Michael A.E. 1975. Wang's Paradox. *Synthese*, **30**, 301–324.

Dummett, Michael. 1988. More about Thoughts. *Notre Dame Journal of Formal Logic*, **30**(1), 1–19.

Ebbs, Gary. 1989. Skepticism, Objectivity and Brains in Vats. *Pacific Philosophical Quarterly*, **73**(3), 239–266.

Ebbs, Gary. 2009. *Truth and Words*. Oxford: Oxford University Press.

Egan, Andy, and Weatherson, Brian. 2011. *Epistemic Modality*. Oxford: Oxford University Press.

Elbourne, Paul. 2011. *Meaning: A Slim Guide to Semantics*. Oxford: Oxford University Press.

Evans, Gareth. 1973. The Causal Theory of Names. *Proceedings of the Aristotelian Society*, **47**, 187–208. Supplementary Series.

Evans, Gareth. 1981. Understanding Demonstratives. Pages 280–304 of: Parett, Herman (ed), *Meaning and Understanding*. Oxford: Oxford University Press.

Evans, Gareth. 1983. *The Varieties of Reference*. Oxford: Oxford University Press.

Fagin, Ronald, Halpern, Joseph Y., Moses, Yoram, and Vardi, Moshe Y. 1995. *Reasoning about Knowledge*. Cambridge, MA: The MIT Press.

Feferman, Anita Burdman, and Feferman, Solomon. 2004. *Alfred Tarski: Life and Logic*. Cambridge: Cambridge University Press.

Field, Hartry. 2008. *Saving Truth from Paradox*. Oxford: Oxford University Press.

Fillmore, Charles. 1997. *Lectures on Deixis*. Stanford, CA: CSLI Publications.

Fine, Kit. 1975. Vagueness, Truth and Logic. *Synthese*, **30**(3–4), 265–300.

Fodor, Jerry A. 1988. *Psychosemantics: The Problem of Meaning in the Philosophy of Mind*. Cambridge, MA: MIT Press.

Fodor, Jerry A., and Lepore, Ernest. 2001. Why Meaning (Probably) Isn't Conceptual Role. *Mind and Language*, **6**(4), 328–343.

Fogelin, Robert. 1988. *Figuratively Speaking*. New Haven, CT: Yale University Press.

Forbes, Graeme. 1989. Indexicals. Pages 464–490 of: Gabbay, Dov, and Guenthner, Franz (eds), *Handbook of Philosophical Logic, Vol. 4*. Dordrecht: D. Reidel Publishing Co.

Forbes, Graeme. 2006. *Attitude Problems*. Oxford: Oxford University Press.

Foster, John A. 1976. Meaning and Truth Theory. Pages 1–32 of: Evans, Gareth, and McDowell, John (eds), *Truth and Meaning: Essays in Semantics*. Oxford: Oxford University Press.

Frege, Gottlob. 1892. Über Sinn und Bedeutung. *Zeitschrift für Philosophie und philosophische Kritik*, **100**, 25–50.

Frege, Gottlob. 1906. *Brief Survey of my Logical Doctrines*. Unpublished manuscript. Translated by P. Long and R. White in Frege (1979c), pp. 197–202.

Frege, Gottlob. 1918. Der Gedanke. *Beiträge zur Philosophie des deutschen Idealismus*, **1**, 58–77.

Frege, Gottlob. 1953. *The Foundations of Arithmetic*. 2 edn. Oxford: Oxford University Press. Originally published in 1884. Translated by J. L. Austin.

Frege, Gottlob. 1956. The Thought. *Mind, New Series*, **65**(259), 289–311. English translation by Peter T. Geach of Frege (1918).

Frege, Gottlob. 1960a. Negation: A Logical Investigation. Pages 117–135 of: Geach, Peter, and Black, Max (eds), *Translations from the Philosophical Writings of Gottlob Frege*. Oxford: Basil Blackwell. Originally published in 1915 as "Die Verneinung. Eine Logische Untersuchung."

Frege, Gottlob. 1960b. On Sense and Reference. Pages 56–78 of: Geach, Peter, and Black, Max (eds), *Translations from the Philosophical Writings of Gottlob Frege*. Oxford: Basil Blackwell. Originally published in 1892 as "Über Sinn und Bedeutung." Translated by Max Black.

Frege, Gottlob. 1967. Begriffschrift, a Formula Language Modeled on that of Arithmetic, for Pure Thought. Pages 1–82 of: *From Frege to Gödel: A Source Book in Mathematical Logic, 1879–1931*. Cambridge, MA: Harvard University Press. Originally published in 1879. Translated by Stefan Bauer.

Frege, Gottlob. 1979a. Logic. Pages 126–151 of: Hermes, Hans, Kambartel, Friedrich, and Kaulbach, Friedrich (eds), *Posthumous Writings*. Oxford: Blackwell. Translated by Peter Long and Roger White.

Frege, Gottlob. 1979b. On Concept and Object. Pages 182–194 of: McGuinness, Brian (ed), *Collected Papers on Mathematics, Logic, and Philosophy*. Oxford: Blackwell. Translated by Peter Geach and Max Black.

Frege, Gottlob. 1979c. *Posthumous Writings*. Oxford: Blackwell. Edited by Hans Hermes, Friedrich Kambartel, and Friedrich Kaulbach. Translated by Peter Long and Roger White.

Frege, Gottlob. 1980a. *The Foundations of Arithmetic*. Evanston, IL: Northwestern University Press. Originally published (in German) in 1884. Translated by J. L. Austin.

Frege, Gottlob. 1980b. *Philosophical and Mathematical Correspondence*. London: Blackwell. Edited by Gottfried Gabriel et al.

Frege, Gottlob. 1984. Compound Thoughts. Pages 390–406 of: McGuiness, Brian (ed), *Gottlob Frege: Philosophical and Mathematical Correspondence*. Chicago, IL: University of Chicago Press. English Translation by Hans Kaal of "Logische Untersuchengen, Dritter Teil: Gedankengefüge," originally published in 1923.

Gallin, Daniel. 1975. *Intensional and Higher-Order Logic*. Amsterdam: North-Holland.

Gamut, L.T.F. 1991a. *Logic, Language, and Meaning: Vol. 1: Introduction to Logic*. Chicago, IL: University of Chicago Press.

Gamut, L.T.F. 1991b. *Logic, Language, and Meaning: Vol. 2. Intensional Logic and Logical Grammar*. Chicago, IL: University of Chicago Press.

Garcia-Carpintero, Manuel. 2000. Indexicals as Token-Reflexives. *Mind*, **107**(427), 529–563.

Geach, Peter T. 1965. Assertion. *The Philosophical Review*, **74**, 449–465.

Geanakopolos, John. 1994. Common Knowledge. Chap. 40 of: Aumann, Robert, and Hart, Serigiu (eds), *Handbook of Game Theory, with Economic Applications, Vol. 2*. Amsterdam: North-Holland.

Gibbard, Allan F. 1975. Contingent Identity. *Journal of Philosophical Logic*, **4**(2), 187–221.

Gibbard, Allan F. 1990. *Wise Choices, Apt Feelings: A Theory of Normative Judgement*. Cambridge, MA: Harvard University Press.

Gibbard, Allen F. 2003. *Thinking How to Live*. Cambridge, MA: Harvard University Press.

Ginzburg, Jonathan. 2012. *The Interactive Stance: Meaning in Conversation*. Oxford: Oxford University Press.

Glanzberg, Michael. 2004. A Context-Hierarchical Approach to Truth and the Liar Paradox. *Journal of Philosophical Logic*, **33**(1), 27–88.

Glanzberg, Michael. 2007. Definite Descriptions and Quantifier Scope: Some Mates Cases Reconsidered. *European Journal of Analytic Philosophy*, **3**(2), 133–158.

Gödel, Kurt. 1931. Über formal unentscheidbare Satze der Principia Mathematica und verwandter Systeme I. *Monatschefte fur Mathematik und Physik*, **38**, 173–198.

Goguen, Joseph A. 1969. The Logic of Inexact Concepts. *Synthese*, **1969**(3–4), 325–373.

Goodman, Nelson. 1955. *Fact, Fiction and Forecast*. Cambridge, MA: Harvard University Press.

Grice, H. Paul. 1957. Meaning. *Philosophical Review*, **66**(3), 377–388. Reprinted in Grice (1989b), pp. 213–282.

Grice, H. Paul. 1961. The Causal Theory of Perception. *Proceedings of the Aristotelian Society*, **35**, 121–152.

Grice, H. Paul. 1968. Utterer's Meaning, Sentence-Meaning, and Word-Meaning. *Foundations of Language*, **4**(3), 225–242. Reprinted in Grice (1989b), pp. 117–137.

Grice, H. Paul. 1969. Utterer's Meaning and Intentions. *The Philosophical Review*, **78**(2), 147–177. Reprinted in Grice (1989b), pp. 86–116.

Grice, H. Paul. 1975. Further Notes on Logic and Conversation. Pages 113–127 of: Cole, Peter (ed), *Syntax and Semantics 9: Pragmatics*. New York: Academic Press. Reprinted in Grice (1989b).

Grice, H. Paul. 1981. Presupposition and Conversational Implicature. Pages 183–198 of: Cole, Peter (ed), *Radical Pragmatics*. New York: Academic Press. Reprinted in Grice (1989b).

Grice, H. Paul. 1982. Meaning Revisited. Pages 223–243 of: Smith, N. V. (ed), *Mutual Knowledge*. London: Academic Press. Reprinted in Grice (1989b), pp. 283–303.

Grice, H. Paul. 1986. Reply to Richards. Pages 45–106 of: Grandy, Richard E., and Warner, Richard (eds), *Philosophical Grounds of Rationality*. Oxford: Oxford University Press.

Grice, H. Paul. 1989a. Logic and Conversation. In: Grice, H. Paul (ed), *Studies in the Way of Words*. Cambridge, MA: Harvard University Press. The William James Lectures, delivered in 1967. Published with minor revisions.

Grice, H. Paul. 1989b. *Studies in the Way of Words*. Cambridge, Massachusetts: Harvard University Press.

Grimm, Jakob, and Grimm, Wilhelm. 1884. *Grimm's Household Tales*. London: G. Bell. Originally published, in German, 1819. Translated by Margaret Hunt.

Groenendijk, Jeroen, and Stokhof, Martin. 1984. On the Semantics of Questions and the Pragmatics of Answers. Pages 143–170 of: Landman, Fred, and Veltman, Frank (eds), *Varieties of Formal Semantics*. Dordrecht: Foris Publications.

Gupta, Anil. 1980. *The Logic of Common Nouns*. New Haven, CT: Yale University Press.

Halbach, Volker, and Leigh, Graham E. 2014. Axiomatic Theories of Truth. In: Zalta, Edward N. (ed), *The Stanford Encyclopedia of Philosophy*. https://plato.stanford.edu/archives/sum2014/entries/truth-axiomatic/.

Hale, Bob. 1987. *Abstract Objects*. Oxford: Basil Blackwell.

Halpern, Joseph Y., and Pucella, Riccardo. 2007. Dealing with Logical Omniscience. Pages 169–176 of: Samet, Dov (ed), *TARK '07: Proceedings of the 11th Conference on Theoretical Aspects of Rationality and Knowledge*. New York, NY, USA: Association for Computing Machinery.

Hamblin, Charles L. 1958. Questions. *Australasian Journal of Philosophy*, **36**(3), 159–168.

Harel, David, Kozen, Dexter, and Tiuryn, Jerzy. 2000. *Dynamic Logic*. Cambridge, MA: The MIT Press.

Haviland, Susan E., and Clark, Herbert H. 1974. What's New? Acquiring New Information as a Process in Comprehension. *Journal of Verbal Learning and Verbal Behavior*, **13**(5), 512–521.

Hawthorne, John. 2007. Context-Dependency and Comparative Adjectives. *Analysis*, **67**(3), 195–204.

Hawthorne, John, and Manley, David. 2012. *The Reference Book*. Oxford: Oxford University Press.

Heck, Richard. 2007. Meaning and Truth-Conditions. Pages 349–376 of: Greimann, Dirk, and Siegwart, Geo (eds), *Truth and Speech Acts: Studies in the Philosophy of Language*. London: Routledge.

Heim, Irene. 1988. *The Semantics of Definite and Indefinite Noun Phrases*. New York: Garland Publishing Company.

Heim, Irene, and Kratzer, Angelika. 1997. *Semantics in Generative Grammar*. Oxford: Blackwell.

Higginbotham, James. 1991. Belief and Logical Form. *Mind and Language*, **6**(4), 344–369.

Higginbotham, James, Pianesi, Fabio, and Varzi, Achille C. (eds). 2000. *Speaking of Events*. Oxford: Oxford University Press.

Hilbert, David. 1918. *Prinzipien der Mathematik*. Unpublished lecture notes by Paul Bernays. Blbliothek, Mathematisches Institut, Universität Göttingen.

Hilbert, David, and Bernays, Paul. 1934. *Die Grundlagen der Mathematik I*. Berlin: Springer-Verlag.

Hills, David. 1997. Aptness and Truth in Verbal Metaphor. *Philosophical Topics*, **25**(1), 117–154.

Hintikka, Jaakko. 1962. *Knowledge and Belief*. Ithaca, NY: Cornell University Press.

Hintikka, Jaakko. 1975. Impossible Worlds Vindicated. *Journal of Philosophical Logic*, **4**(4), 475–484.

Hobbs, Jerry, Stickel, Mark, Appelt, Douglas, and Martin, Paul. 1993. Interpretation as Abduction. *Artificial Intelligence*, **63**(1–2), 69–142.

Hodges, Wilfrid. 2001. Formal Features of Compositionality. *Journal of Logic, Language, and Information*, **10**(1), 7–28.

Horn, Laurence R. 2007. Toward a Fregean Pragmatics: *Voraussetzung, Nebengedanke, Andeutung*. Pages 39–69 of: Kecskes, Istvan, and Horn, Laurence R. (eds), *Explorations in Pragmatics: Linguistic, Cognitive and Intercultural Aspects*. Berlin: Mouton de Gruyter.

Horty, John F. 2009. *Frege on Definitions: A Case Study of Semantic Content*. Oxford: Oxford University Press.

Horwich, Paul. 1990. *Truth*. Oxford: Basil Blackwell.

Horwich, Paul. 1998. *Meaning*. Oxford: Oxford University Press.

Howes, Christine, and Larsson, Staffan (eds). 2014. *SEMDIAL 2015: Proceedings of the 19th Workshop on the Semantics and Pragmatics of Dialogue*. Gothenburg: Published online. http://flov.gu.se/digitalAssets/1537/1537599_semdial2015_godial_proceedings.pdf.

Huggett, Nick. 2010. Zeno's Paradoxes. In: Zalta, Edward N. (ed), *The Stanford Encyclopedia of Philosophy*. Stanford Encyclopedia of Philosophy. http://plato.stanford.edu/archives/win2010/entries/paradox-zeno/.

Hume, David. 1978. *A Treatise of Human Nature*. Oxford: Oxford University Press. Originally published in 1888. Edited by L. A. Selby-Bigge and P. H. Nidditch.

Irvine, Andrew David, and Deutsch, Harry. 2014. Russell's Paradox. In: Zalta, Edward N. (ed), *The Stanford Encyclopedia of Philosophy*, winter 2014 edn. Stanford Encyclopedia of Philosophy. http://plato.stanford.edu/archives/win2014/entries/russell-paradox/.

Jackendoff, Ray. 1997. *The Architecture of the Language Faculty*. Cambridge, MA: The MIT Press.

Jeffrey, Richard C. 1983. *The Logic of Decision*. 2 edn. Chicago, IL: University of Chicago Press.

Kahneman, Daniel. 2011. *Thinking, Fast and Slow*. New York: Farrar, Strauss and Giroux.

Kamareddine, Farouz, Laan, Twan, and Nederfelt, Rob. 2004. *A Modern Perspective on Type Theory: From its Origins until Today*. Dordrecht: Kluwer Academic Publishers.

Kamp, Hans. 1971. Formal Properties of 'Now'. *Theoria*, **37**(3), 227–273.

Kamp, Hans. 1975. Two Theories about Adjectives. Pages 123–155 of: Keenan, Edward L. (ed), *Formal Semantics of Natural Language*. Cambridge: Cambridge University Press.

Kamp, Hans. 1979. Events, Instants, and Temporal Reference. Pages 376–417 of: Bäuerle, Rainer, Egli, Urs, and von Stechow, Arnim (eds), *Semantics from Different Points of View*. Berlin: Springer-Verlag.

Kamp, Hans, and Reyle, Uwe. 1993. *From Discourse to Logic: Introduction to Modeltheoretic Semantics in Natural Language, Formal Logic and Discourse Representation Theory, Vol. 1*. Dordrecht: Kluwer Academic Publishers.

Kaplan, David. 1969. Quantifying In. *Synthese*, **19**(1–2), 178–214.

Kaplan, David. 1978. On the Logic of Demonstratives. *Journal of Philosophical Logic*, **8**, 81–98.

Kaplan, David. 1989. Demonstratives: an Essay on the Semantics, Logic, Metaphysics, and Epistemology of Demonstratives and Other Indexicals. Pages 481–563 of: Almog, Joseph, Perry, John, and Wettstein, Howard (eds), *Themes from Kaplan*. Oxford: Oxford University Press.

Karttunen, Lauri. 1971. *Discourse Referents*. Bloomington, IN: Indiana University Linguistics Club.

Karttunen, Lauri. 1973. Presuppositions of Compound Sentences. *Linguistic Inquiry*, **4**(2), 169–193.

Karttunen, Lauri. 1974. Presupposition and Linguistic Context. *Theoretical Linguistics*, **1**(1/2), 182–194.

Karttunen, Lauri. 1977. Syntax and Semantics of Questions. *Linguistics and Philosophy*, **1**(1), 3–44.

Karttunen, Lauri, and Peters, Stanley. 1975. Conventional Implicature in Montague Grammar. Pages 266–278 of: *Proceedings of the First Annual Meeting of the Berkeley Linguistics Society*. University of California at Berkeley, Berkeley, CA: Berkeley Linguistics Society.

Karttunen, Lauri, and Peters, Stanley. 1979. Conventional Implicature. Pages 1–56 of: Oh, ChoonKyo, and Dineen, David A. (eds), *Syntax and Semantics 11: Presupposition*. New York: Academic Press.

Keiser, Jessica. 2016a. Bald-Faced Lies: How to Make a Move in a Language Game without Making a Move in a Conversation. *Philosophical Studies*, **173**(2), 461–477.

Keiser, Jessica. 2016b. Coordinating with Language. *Croatian Journal of Philosophy*, **16**(2), 229–245.

Kemmerling, Andreas. 2011. Thoughts without Parts: Frege's Doctrine. *Grazer Philosophische Studien*, **82**, 165–188.

Kennedy, Christopher. 2007. Vagueness and Grammar: The Semantics of Relative and Absolute Gradable Adjectives. *Linguistics and Philosophy*, **30**(1), 1–45.

Kenny, Anthony. 1963. *Action, Emotion and Will*. London: Routledge and Kegan Paul.

Kenny, Anthony J. 2000. *Frege: An Introduction to the Founder of Modern Analytic Philosophy*. Oxford: Blackwell.

King, Jeffrey C. 2002. Designating Propositions. *The Philosophical Review*, **111**(3), 241–371.

King, Jeffrey C. 2007. *The Nature and Structure of Content*. Oxford: Oxford University Press.

Kiparsky, Paul, and Kiparsky, Carol. 1971. Fact. Pages 143–173 of: Bierwisch, Manfred, and Heidolph, Karl Erich (eds), *Progress in Linguistics: A Collection of Papers*. The Hague: Mouton.

Kleene, Steven C. 1952. *Introduction to Metamathematics*. New York: Van Nostrand.

Kolmogorov, Andrey N. 1956. *Foundations of the Theory of Probability*. New York: Chelsea.

Kratzer, Angelika. 2012. *Modals and Conditionals*. Oxford: Oxford University Press.

Kripke, Saul. 1972. Naming and Necessity. Pages 253–355 of: Harman, Gilbert, and Davidson, Donald (eds), *Semantics of Natural Language*. Dordrecht: D. Reidel Publishing Co.

Kripke, Saul. 1975. Outline of a Theory of Truth. *Journal of Philosophy*, **72**, 690–715.

Kripke, Saul A. 1979. A Puzzle about Belief. Pages 239–288 of: Margalit, Avishai (ed), *Meaning and Use: Papers Presented at the Second Jerusalem Philosophy Encounter*. Dordrecht: D. Reidel Publishing Co.

Kvart, Igal. 1993. Mediated Reference and Proper Names. *Mind*, **102**(408), 611–628.

Landman, Fred. 2000. *Events and Plurality*. Dordrecht: Kluwer Academic Publishers.

LaPorte, Joseph. 1996. Chemical Kind Term Reference and the Discovery of Essence. *Noûs*, **30**(1), 112–132.

LaPorte, Joseph. 1998. Living Water. *Mind*, **107**(426), 451–465.

Larson, Richard K. 2002. The Grammar of Intensionality. Pages 228–262 of: Preyer, Gerhard, and Peter, Georg (eds), *Logical Form and Language*. Oxford: Oxford University Press.

Lasersohn, Peter. 1995. *Plurality, Conjunction and Events*. Dordrecht: Kluwer Academic Publishers.

Lasersohn, Peter. 2006. Event-Based Semantics. Pages 316–320 of: Brown, Keith (ed), *Encyclopedia of Language and Linguistics, Vol. 4*. 2 edn. Amsterdam: Elsevier.

Lehnert, Wendy G. 1988. Knowledge-Based Natural Language Understanding. Pages 83–132 of: Shrobe, Howard E. (ed), *Exploring Artificial Intelligence*. San Mateo, CA: Morgan Kaufmann.

Lemmon, Edward John. 1966. Sentences, Statements, and Propositions. Pages 87–107 of: Williams, Bernard O., and Montefiore, Alan (eds), *British Analytical Philosophy*. London: Routledge. Reprinted in Rosenberg and Travis (1971).

Lepore, Ernest, and Ludwig, Kirk. 2007. *Donald Davidson's Truth-Theoretic Semantics*. Oxford: Oxford University Press.

Lewis, Clarence I. 1918. *Survey of Symbolic Logic*. Berkeley, CA: University of California Press.

Lewis, David K. 1968. Counterpart Theory and Quantified Modal Logic. *Journal of Philosophy*, **69**, 113–126.

Lewis, David K. 1969. *Convention: A Philosophical Study*. Cambridge, MA: Harvard University Press.

Lewis, David K. 1970a. Anselm and Actuality. *Nôus*, **4**(2), 175–188.

Lewis, David K. 1970b. General Semantics. *Synthese*, **22**(1–2), 18–67.

Lewis, David K. 1973. *Counterfactuals*. Cambridge, MA: Harvard University Press.

Lewis, David K. 1975. Languages and Language. Pages 3–35 of: Gunderson, Keith (ed), *Language, Mind, and Knowledge. Minnesota Studies in the Philosophy of Science, Vol. 7*. Minneapolis, MN: University of Minnesota Press.

Lewis, David K. 1979a. Attitudes *De Dicto* and *De Se*. *The Philosophical Review*, **88**(4), 513–543.

Lewis, David K. 1979b. A Problem about Permission. Pages 163–179 of: Saarinen, Esa, Hilpinen, Risto, Niiniluoto, Ilkka, and Hintikka, Merrill Province (eds), *Essays in Honour of Jaakko Hintikka*. Dordrecht, Holland: D. Reidel Publishing Co.

Lewis, David K. 1979c. Scorekeeping in a Language Game. *Journal of Philosophical Logic*, **8**(3), 339–359.

Lewis, David K. 1981. Index, Context, and Content. Pages 79–100 of: Kanger, Stig, and Öhman, Sven (eds), *Philosophy and Grammar: Papers on the Occasion of the Quincentennial of Uppsala University*. Dordrecht: D. Reidel Publishing Co.

Lewis, David K. 1986. *On the Plurality of Worlds*. Oxford: Basil Blackwell.

Lindström, Per. 1996. First-Order Predicate Logic with Generalized Quantifiers. *Theoria*, **32**(3), 186–195.

Locke, John. 1975. *An Essay Concerning Human Understanding*. Oxford: Oxford University Press. Originally published in 1689. Edited by Peter Niddich.

Ludlow, Peter J. 1999. *Semantics, Tense, and Time: An Essay in the Metaphysics of Natural Language*. Cambridge, MA: The MIT Press.

Ludlow, Peter. 2013. *The Philosophy of Generative Linguistics*. Oxford: Oxford University Press.

Lynch, Michael P. 2009. *Truth as One and Many*. Oxford: Oxford University Press.

Mackie, Penelope. 2006. *How Things Might Have Been: Individuals, Kinds, and Essential Properties*. Oxford: Oxford University Press.

Maitra, Ishani. 2011. Assertion, Norms, and Games. Pages 277–296 of: Brown, Jessica A., and Cappelen, Herman (eds), *Assertion: New Philosophical Essays*. Oxford: Oxford University Press.

Markosian, Ned, Sullivan, Meghan, and Emery, Nina. 2016. Time. In: Zalta, Edward N. (ed), *The Stanford Encyclopedia of Philosophy*. https://plato.stanford.edu/archives/fall2016/entries/time/.

Marsh, Robert C. (ed). 1956. *Logic and Language: Essays 1902–1950 by Bertrand Russell*. London: George Allen and Unwin.

Maudlin, Tim. 2004. *Truth and Paradox*. Oxford: Oxford University Press.

May, Robert. 1977. *The Grammar of Quantification*. Ph.D. Dissertation, Linguistics Department, Massachusetts Institute of Technology, Cambridge, MA.

May, Robert. 2006. Frege on Indexicals. *The Philosophical Review*, **115**(4), 487–516.

McDermott, Timothy (ed). 1993. *Thomas Aquinas: Selected Philosophical Writings*. Oxford: Oxford University Press.

McGinn, Colin. 1977. Charity, Interpretation, and Belief. *The Journal of Philosophy*, **74**(9), 521–535.

McGrath, Matthew. 2008. Propositions. In: Zalta, Edward N. (ed), *The Stanford Encyclopedia of Philosophy*. http://plato.stanford.edu/archives/fall2008/entries/propositions/.

Meinong, Alexius. 1981. On the Theory of Objects. Pages 76–117 of: Chisholm, Roderick (ed), *Realism and the Background of Phenomenology*. Atascadero, CA: Ridgeview. Originally published in 1904. Translated by Isaac Levi, D.B. Terrell, and Roderick M. Chisholm.

Mellor, D. Hugh. 1977. Natural Kinds. *The British Journal for the Philosophy of Science*, **28**(4), 299–312.

Mellor, D. Hugh. 1981. *Real Time*. Cambridge: Cambridge University Press.

Millikan, Ruth Garrett. 1984. *Language, Thought, and Other Biological Categories: New Foundations for Realism*. Cambridge, MA: The MIT Press.

Millikan, Ruth Garrett. 1993. *White Queen Psychology and Other Essays for Alice*. Cambridge, MA: The MIT Press.

Millikan, Ruth Garrett. 2005. *Language: A Biological Model*. Oxford: Oxford University Press.

Moltmann, Frederike. 2003. Propositional Attitudes without Propositions. *Synthese*, **135**(1), 77–118.

Montague, Richard. 1962. Theories Incomparable with Respect to Relative Interpretability. *Journal of Symbolic Logic*, **27**, 153–167.

Montague, Richard. 1968. Pragmatics. Pages 102–122 of: Klibansky, R. (ed), *Contemporary Philosophy: A Survey. I*. Florence: La Nuova Italia Editrice. Reprinted in *Formal Philosophy*, by Richard Montague, Yale University Press, New Haven, CT, 1974, pp. 95–118.

Montague, Richard. 1970. English as a Formal Language. Pages 189–224 of: Bruno Visentini et al. (eds), *Linguaggi nella Società e nella Tecnica*. Milan: Edizioni di Communità. Reprinted in *Formal Philosophy*, by

Richard Montague, Yale University Press, New Haven, CT, 1974, pp. 188–221.

Montague, Richard. 1974. The Proper Treatment of Quantification in Ordinary English. Pages 247–270 of: Thomason, Richmond H. (ed), *Formal Philosophy: Selected Papers of Richard Montague*. New Haven, CT: Yale University Press.

Moore, G. E. 1990. Moore's Paradox. Pages 207–212 of: Baldwin, Thomas (ed), *G. E. Moore: Selected Writings*. London: Routledge.

Morris, Charles. 1946. *Signs, Language and Behavior*. New York: Prentice-Hall.

Mostowski, Andrzej. 1957. On a Generalization of Quantifiers. *Fundamenta Mathematicae*, **44**(1), 12–36.

Muskens, Reinhard, van Benthem, Johan, and Visser, Albert. 2011. Dynamics. Pages 607–670 of: van Benthem, Johan, and ter Meulen, Alice (eds), *Handbook of Logic and Language*. 2 edn. Amsterdam: Elsevier Science Publishers.

Neale, Stephen. 1990. *Descriptions*. Cambridge, MA: The MIT Press.

Neale, Stephen. 1992. Paul Grice and the Philosophy of Language. *Linguistics and Philosophy*, **15**(5), 509–559. Review of *Studies in the Way of Words*, by H. Paul Grice.

Neale, Stephen. 2001. *Facing Facts*. Oxford: Oxford University Press.

Ninan, Dilip. 2013. Self-Location and Other-Location. *Philosophy and Phenomenological Research*, **87**(1), 301–331.

Nuchelmans, Gabriel. 1973. *Theories of the Proposition: Ancient and Medieval Conceptions of the Bearers of Truth and Falsity*. Amsterdam: North-Holland.

Nuchelmans, Gabriel. 1980. *Late-Scholastic and Humanist Theories of the Proposition*. Amsterdam: North-Holland.

Nuchelmans, Gabriel. 1983. *Judgement and Proposition. From Descartes to Kant*. Amsterdam: North-Holland.

Nute, Donald. 1984. Conditional Logic. Pages 387–439 of: Gabbay, Dov, and Günthner, Franz (eds), *Handbook of Philosophical Logic, Vol. 2: Extensions of Classical Logic*. Dordrecht: D. Reidel Publishing Co.

Ostertag, Gary. 2002. Descriptions and Logical Form. Pages 177–193 of: Jacquette, Dale (ed), *A Companion to Philosophical Logic*. Oxford: Blackwell.

Pagin, Peter. 2003. Communication and Strong Compositionality. *Journal of Philosophical Logic*, **32**(3), 287–322.

Pagin, Peter. 2011. Information and Assertoric Force. Pages 97–136 of: Brown, Jessica, and Cappelen, Herman (eds), *Assertion: New Philosophical Essays*. Oxford: Oxford University Press.

Pagin, Peter. 2016. Problems with Norms of Assertion. *Philosophy and Phenomenological Research*, **93**(1), 178–207.

Pap, Arthur. 1958. *Semantics and Necessary Truth: An Inquiry into the Foundations of Analytic Philosophy*. New Haven, CT: Yale University Press.

Parsons, Terence. 1990. *Events in the Semantics of English: A Study in Subatomic Semantics*. Cambridge, Massachusetts: The MIT Press.

Partee, Barbara. 1973. Some Structural Analogies Between Tenses and Pronouns in English. *Journal of Philosophy*, **70**(18), 601–609.

Partee, Barbara. 1984. Compositionality. Pages 325–343 of: Landman, Fred, and Veltman, Frank (eds), *Varieties of Formal Semantics*. Dordrecht: Foris Publications.

Peirce, Charles Sanders. 1906. Prolegomena to an Apology for Pragmaticism. *The Monist*, **16**, 492–546.

Peirce, Charles Sanders. 1933. *Collected Papers of Charles Sanders Peirce, Vols 3 and 4*. Cambridge, MA: Harvard University Press. Edited by Charles Hartshorne and Paul Weiss.

Perry, John. 1977. Frege on Demonstratives. *The Philosophical Review*, **86**(4), 474–497.

Perry, John (ed). 1993. *The Problem of the Essential Indexical: and Other Essays*. New York: Oxford University Press.

Peters, Stanley, and Westerståhl, Dag. 2006. *Quantifiers in Language and Logic*. Oxford: Oxford University Press.

Plantinga, Alvin. 1974. *The Nature of Necessity*. Oxford: Oxford University Press.

Poidevin, Robert Le, and MacBeath, Murray (eds). 1993. *The Philosophy of Time*. Oxford: Oxford University Press.

Poidevin, Robin Le. 2015. The Experience and Perception of Time. In: Zalta, Edward N. (ed), *The Stanford Encyclopedia of Philosophy*. http://plato.stanford.edu/archives/sum2015/entries/time-experience/.

Portner, Paul. 2004. The Semantics of Imperatives within a Theory of Clause Types. Pages 235–252 of: Watanabe, Kazuha, and Young, Robert (eds), *Proceedings from Semantics and Linguistic Theory XIV*. Ithaca, NY: Cornell University.

Portner, Paul. 2009. *Modality*. Oxford: Oxford University Press.

Potts, Christopher. 2005. *The Logic of Conventional Implicatures*. Oxford: Oxford University Press.

Poznański, Victor. 1992 (February). *A Relevance-Based Utterance Processing System*. Tech. rept. UCAM-CL-TR-246. University of Cambridge, Computer Laboratory.

Predelli, Stefano. 2006. The Problem with Token-Reflexivity. *Synthese*, **148**(5), 5–29.

Preyer, Gerhard, and Peter, Georg (eds). 2005. *Contextualism in Philosophy: Knowledge, Meaning, and Truth*. Oxford: Oxford University Press.

Priest, Graham. 2002. *Beyond the Limits of Thought*. 2 edn. Oxford: Oxford University Press.

Prior, Arthur N. 1959. Thank Goodness That's Over. *Philosophy*, **34**(128), 12–17.

Prior, Arthur N. 1961. On a Family of Paradoxes. *Notre Dame Journal of Formal Logic*, **2**, 16–32.

Prior, Arthur N. 1967. *Past, Present and Future*. Oxford: Oxford University Press.

Prior, Arthur N. 1968a. Changes in Events and Changes in Things. Pages 1–14 of: *Papers on Time and Tense*. Oxford: Oxford University Press.

Prior, Arthur N. 1968b. 'Now'. *Noûs*, **2**(2), 101–119.

Prior, Arthur N., and Fine, Kit. 1977. *Worlds, Times and Selves*. London: Gerald Duckworth and Company.

Pullum, Geoffrey, and Scholz, Barbara C. 2010. Recursion and the Infinitude Claim. Pages 113–138 of: van der Hulst, Harry (ed), *Recursion in Human Language*. Berlin: Mouton de Gruyter.

Pustejovsky, James. 1995. *The Generative Lexicon*. Cambridge, MA: The MIT Press.

Pustejovsky, James, and Boguraev, Branamir (eds). 1997. *Lexical Semantics: The Problem of Polysemy*. Oxford: Oxford University Press.

Putnam, Hilary. 1970. Is Semantics Possible? *Metaphilosophy*, **1**(3), 187–201.

Putnam, Hilary. 1975. The Meaning of "Meaning." Pages 131–193 of: Gunderson, Keith (ed), *Language, Mind, and Knowledge. Minnesota Studies in the Philosophy of Science, Vol. 7*. Minneapolis, MN: University of Minnesota Press.

Putnam, Hilary. 1981. *Reason, Truth and History*. Cambridge: Cambridge University Press.

Quine, Willard V. O. 1940. *Methods of Logic*. New York: Holt, Reinhart and Winston.

Quine, Willard V. O. 1948. On What There Is. *Review of Metaphysics*, **2**(5), 21–36.

Quine, Willard V. O. 1953a. Mr. Strawson on Logical Theory. *Mind*, **52**(248), 433–451.

Quine, Willard V. O. 1953b. Three Grades of Modal Involvement. Pages 65–81 of: *Proceedings of the XIth International Congress of Philosophy, Vol. 14*.

Quine, Willard V. 1956. Quantifiers and Propositional Attitudes. *The Journal of Philosophy*, **53**, 177–187.

Quine, Willard V. O. 1958. *Mathematical Logic*. Revised edn. Cambridge, MA: Harvard University Press.

Quine, Willard V. O. 1960. *Word and Object*. Cambridge, MA: MIT Press.

Quine, Willard V. 1969. Propositional Objects. Pages 139–160 of: Quine, Willard V. (ed), *Ontological Relativity and Other Essays*. New York: Columbia University Press.

Quine, Willard V. O. 1980. Reference and Modality. Pages 139–159 of: Quine, Willard V. O. (ed), *From a Logical Point of View*. New York: Harvard University Press.

Quine, Willard V. O. 1981. Five Milestones of Empiricism. Pages 67–72 of: Quine, Willard V. O. (ed), *Theories and Things*. Cambridge, MA: Harvard University Press.

Quine, Willard V. O. 1992. *The Pursuit of Truth*. Cambridge, MA: Harvard University Press.

Raffman, Diana. 1996. Vagueness and Context-Relativity. *Philosophical Studies*, **81**, 175–192.

Recanati, François. 1986. On Defining Communicative Intentions. *Mind and Language*, **1**(3), 213–241.

Recanati, François. 1988. *Meaning and Force: The Pragmatics of Performative Utterances*. Cambridge: Cambridge University Press.

Recanati, François. 2002. *Truth-Conditional Pragmatics*. Oxford: Oxford University Press.

Recanati, François. 2004. *Literal Meaning*. Oxford: Oxford University Press.

Reichenbach, Hans. 1947. *Elements of Symbolic Logic*. New York: MacMillan.

Richard, Mark. 1990. *Propositional Attitudes: An Essay on Thoughts and How We Ascribe Them*. Cambridge: Cambridge University Press.

Richard, Mark. 2008. *When Truth Gives Out*. Oxford: Oxford University Press.

Rini, Adriane A., and Cresswell, Max J. 2012. *The World-Time Parallel: Tense and Modality in Logic and Metaphysics*. Cambridge: Cambridge University Press.

Roberts, Craige. 1996. *Information Structure in Discourse: Towards an Integrated Formal Theory of Pragmatics*. Tech. rept. Linguistics Department, The Ohio State University, Columbus, OH. OSU Working Papers in Linguistics, *Vol. 49*. Edited by Jae-Hak Yoon and Andreas Kathol.

Roberts, Craige. 2002. Demonstratives as Definites. Pages 89–196 of: van Deemter, Kees, and Kibble, Riger (eds), *Information Sharing*. Stanford, CA: CSLI Publications.

Rochelle, Gerald. 1998. *Behind Time: The Incoherence of Time and McTaggart's Atemporal Replacement*. Aldershot: Ashgate.

Rosenberg, Jay F., and Travis, Charles (eds). 1971. *Readings in the Philosophy of Language*. Englewood Cliffs, NJ: Prentice-Hall.

Rothschild, Daniel, and Segal, Gabriel. 2009. Indexical Predicates. *Mind and Language*, **24**(4), 467–493.

Russell, Bertrand. 1905. On Denoting. *Mind, New Series*, **14**(56), 479–493.

Russell, Bertrand. 1910. On the Nature of Truth and Falsehood. Pages 116–124 of: *Philosophical Essays*. London: Longmans, Green.

Russell, Bertrand. 1910–1911. Knowledge by Acquaintance and Knowledge by Description. *Proceedings of the Aristotelian Society, New Series*, **11**, 108–128.

Russell, Bertrand. 1912. *Problems of Philosophy*. Oxford: Oxford University Press.

Russell, Bertrand. 1914. *Our Knowledge of the External World*. London: Allen and Unwin.

Russell, Bertrand. 1918–1919. Lectures on the Philosophy of Logical Atomism. *The Monist*, **28–29**, 495–527 and 190–222. Republished in Marsh (1956).

Russell, Bertrand. 1940. *An Inquiry into Meaning and Truth*. London: George Allen and Unwin.

Russell, Bertrand. 1957. Mr. Strawson on Referring. *Mind, New Series*, **66**, 385–395.

Ryle, Gilbert. 1949. *The Concept of Mind*. London: Hutchinson & Co.

Ryle, Gilbert. 1961. Use, Usage, Meaning. *Proceedings of the Aristotelian Society*, **35**, 223–231.

Rysiew, Patrick. 2016. Epistemic Contextualism. In: Zalta, Edward N. (ed), *The Stanford Encyclopedia of Philosophy*. The Stanford Encyclopedia of Philosophy. http://plato.stanford.edu/archives/spr2016/entries/contextualism-epistemology/.

Salmon, Nathan (ed). 1986. *Frege's Puzzle*. Cambridge, MA: The MIT Press.

Sartre, Jean Paul. 1971. *Sketch for a Theory of Emotions*. London: Methuen. Originally published in 1939. Translated by Philip Mairet.

Saul, Jennifer M. 2002. Speaker Meaning, What is Said, and What is Implicated. *Noûs*, **36**(2), 228–248.

Schein, Barry. 1993. *Plurals and Events*. Cambridge, MA: The MIT Press.

Schiffer, Stephen. 1972. *Meaning*. Oxford: Oxford University Press.

Schiffer, Stephen. 1996. Language-Created Language-Independent Entities. *Philosophical Topics*, **24**(1), 149–167.

Schneider, Erna. 1953. Recent Discussions on Subjunctive Conditionals. *Review of Metaphysics*, **6**, 623–649.

Scott, Dana S. 1970. Advice on Modal Logic. Pages 143–173 of: Lambert, Karel (ed), *Philosophical Problems in Logic*. Dordrecht: D. Reidel Publishing Co.

Searle, John. 1969. *Speech Acts: An Essay in the Philosophy of Language*. Cambridge: Cambridge University Press.

Searle, John R. 1975a. Indirect Speech Acts. Pages 59–82 of: Cole, Peter, and Morgan, Jerry L. (eds), *Syntax and Semantics, Vol. 3: Speech Acts*. New York: Academic Press.

Searle, John R. 1975b. A Taxonomy of Illocutionary Acts. Pages 344–369 of: Gunderson, Keith (ed), *Language, Mind, and Knowledge. Minnesota Studies in the Philosophy of Science, Vol. 7*. Minneapolis, MN: University of Minnesota Press.

Searle, John R. 1978. Literal Meaning. *Erkenntnis*, **13**, 207–224.

Searle, John R., and Vandervecken, Daniel. 1985. *Foundations of Illocutionary Logic*. Cambridge: Cambridge University Press.

Segal, Gabriel M.A. 2000. *A Slim Book about Narrow Content*. Cambridge, MA: The MIT Press.

Sellars, Wilfrid P. 1953. Meaning and Inference. *Mind*, **62**(247), 313–338.

Seuss, Dr. 1940. *Horton Hatches the Egg*. New York: Random House.

Simons, Mandy. 2003. Presupposition and Accommodation: Understanding the Stalnakerian Picture. *Philosophical Studies*, **112**(3), 251–278.

Simons, Mandy. 2005. Presupposition and Relevance. Pages 329–355 of: Szabó, Zoltán Gendler (ed), *Semantics Versus Pragmatics*. Oxford: Oxford University Press.

Simons, Mandy, Beaver, David, Tonhauser, Judith, and Roberts, Craige. 2010. What Projects and Why. Pages 309–327 of: Li, Nan, and Lutz, David (eds), *Proceedings from Semantics and Linguistic Theory XX*. Ithaca, NY: CLC Publications.

Sklar, Lawrence. 1976. *Space, Time, and Spacetime*. Los Angeles, CA: University of California Press.

Smith, Nicholas J.J. 2008. *Vagueness and Degrees of Truth*. Oxford: Oxford University Press.

Soames, Scott. 1988. Semantics and Semantic Competence. Pages 185–207 of: Schiffer, Stephen, and Steele, Susan (eds), *Cognition and Representation*. Boulder, CO: Westview Press.

Soames, Scott. 2002. *Beyond Rigidity: The Unfinished Semantic Agenda of Naming and Necessity*. Oxford: Oxford University Press.

Soames, Scott. 2010. *What is Meaning?* Princeton, NJ: Princeton University Press.

Sperber, Dan, and Wilson, Deirdre. 1986a. Loose Talk. *Proceedings of the Aristotelian Society*, **86**, 153–171.

Sperber, Dan, and Wilson, Deirdre. 1986b. *Relevance: Communication and Cognition*. Cambridge, MA: Blackwell.

Staal, Johan F. 1969. Formal Logic and Natural Languages (A Symposium). *Foundations of Language*, **5**(2), 256–284.

Stalnaker, Robert C. 1968. A Theory of Conditionals. Pages 98–112 of: Rescher, Nicholas (ed), *Studies in Logical Theory*. Oxford: Basil Blackwell.

Stalnaker, Robert C. 1970. Pragmatics. *Synthese*, **22**(1–2), 272–279.

Stalnaker, Robert C. 1973. Presuppositions. *Journal of Philosophical Logic*, **2**(4), 447–457.

Stalnaker, Robert C. 1975. Pragmatic Presuppositions. Pages 197–213 of: Munitz, Milton K., and Unger, Peter (eds), *Semantics and Philosophy*. New York: Academic Press.

Stalnaker, Robert C. 1976. Propositions. Pages 79–91 of: MacKay, Alfred, and Merrill, Daniel (eds), *Issues in the Philosophy of Language*. New Haven, CT: Yale University Press.

Stalnaker, Robert C. 1989. On What's in the Head. Pages 287–316 of: Tomberlin, James E. (ed), *Philosophical Perspectives 3: Philosophy of Mind and Action Theory*. Atascadero, CA: Ridgeview Publishing Company. Also available at http://www.jstor.org/journals/.

Stalnaker, Robert C. 1990. Narrow Content. Pages 131–146 of: Anderson, Charles A., and Owens, J. (eds), *Propositional Attitudes: The Role of Content in Logic, Language and Mind*. Stanford, CA: CSLI Press.

Stalnaker, Robert C. 1991. The Problem of Logical Omniscience, I. *Synthese*, **89**(3), 425–440.

Stalnaker, Robert C. 1997. Reference and Necessity. Pages 534–554 of: Wright, Crispin, and Hale, Bob (eds), *Blackwell Companion to the Philosophy of Language*. Oxford: Basil Blackwell.

Stalnaker, Robert. 2002. Common Ground. *Linguistics and Philosophy*, **25**(5–6), 701–721.

Stalnaker, Robert C. 2008. *Our Knowledge of the Internal World*. Oxford: Oxford University Press.

Stalnaker, Robert C. 2012. *Mere Possibilities: Metaphysical Foundations of Modal Semantics*. Princeton, NJ: Princeton University Press.

Stalnaker, Robert C. 2014. *Context*. Oxford: Oxford University Press.

Stalnaker, Robert C., and Thomason, Richmond H. 1968. Abstraction in First-Order Modal Logic. *Theoria*, **14**, 203–207.

Stanley, Jason. 2005. Semantics in Context. Pages 221–253 of: Preyer, Gerhard, and Peter, Georg (eds), *Contextualism in Philosophy: Knowledge, Meaning, and Truth*. Oxford: Oxford University Press.

Stanley, Jason, and Szabó, Zoltán Gendler. 2000. On Quantifier Domain Restriction. *Mind and Language*, **15**, 219–261.

Stenius, Erik. 1967. Mood and Language Game. *Synthese*, **17**(3), 254–374.

Stent, Amanda, and Bangalore, Srinivas (eds). 2014. *Natural Language Generation in Interactive Systems*. Cambridge: Cambridge University Press.

Stern, Josef. 2000. *Metaphor in Context*. Cambridge, MA: The MIT Press.

Stevenson, Charles L. 1944. *Ethics and Language*. New Haven, CT: Yale University Press.

Stone, Matthew. 1997. *The Anaphoric Parallel between Modality and Tense*. Tech. rept. IRCS-97-06. IRCS, University of Pennsylvania, PA. http://repository.upenn.edu/cis_reports/177/.

Stoppard, Tom. 1993. *Arcadia*. London: Faber & Faber.

Strasser, Christian, and Antonelli, G. Aldo. 2015. Non-Monotonic Logic. In: Zalta, Edward N. (ed), *The Stanford Encyclopedia of Philosophy*.

The Stanford Encyclopedia of Philosophy. http://plato.stanford.edu/archives/fall2015/entries/logic-nonmonotonic/.

Strawson, Peter F. 1950. On Referring. *Mind, New Series*, **59**(235), 320–344.

Strawson, Peter F. 1952. *Introduction to Logical Theory*. London: Methuen.

Strawson, Peter F. 1959. *Individuals: An Essay in Descriptive Metaphysics*. London: Methuen.

Strawson, Peter F. 1964. Intention and Convention in Speech Acts. *The Philosophical Review*, **59**, 439–460.

Szabó, Zoltán Gendler. 2000. Compositionality as Supervenience. *Linguistics and Philosophy*, **23**(5), 475–505.

Szabó, Zoltán Gendler. 2001. Adjectives in Context. Pages 119–146 of: Kenesei, István, and Harnish, Robert M. (eds), *Perspectives on Semantics, Pragmatics, and Discourse*. Amsterdam: John Benjamins.

Szabó, Zoltán Gendler. 2004. On the Progressive and the Perfective. *Noûs*, **38**(1), 29–59.

Szabó, Zoltán Gendler. 2005a. Expressions and Their Representations. *Philosophical Quarterly*, **49**(220), 145–163.

Szabó, Zoltán Gendler. 2005b. Sententialism and Berkeley's Master Argument. *Philosophical Quarterly*, **55**(220), 462–474.

Szabó, Zoltán Gendler. 2006. Sensitivity Training. *Mind and Language*, **21**(1), 31–38.

Szabó, Zoltán Gendler. 2010. The Determination of Content. *Philosophical Studies*, **148**(2), 253–272.

Tarski, Alfred. 1936. Der Wahrheitsbegriff in den formalizierten Sprachen. *Studia Philosophica*, **1**, 261–405.

Tarski, Alfred. 1944. The Semantic Conception of Truth and the Foundations of Semantics. *Philosophy and Phenomenological Research*, **4**, 341–375.

Tarski, Alfred, and Vaught, Robert L. 1956. Arithmetical Extensions of Relational Systems. *Compositio Mathematica*, **13**(2), 81–102.

Tenny, Carol, and Pustejovsky, James (eds). 2000. *Events as Grammatical Objects*. Cambridge: Cambridge University Press.

Thomason, Richmond H. 1980. A Model Theory for Propositional Attitudes. *Linguistics and Philosophy*, **4**, 47–70.

Thomason, Richmond. 1990. Accommodation, Meaning, and Implicature: Interdisciplinary Foundations for Pragmatics. Pages 326–363 of: Cohen, Philip R., Morgan, Jerry, and Pollack, Martha (eds), *Intentions in Communication*. Cambridge, MA: MIT Press.

Thomason, Richmond H. 1998. Intra-Agent Modality and Nonmonotonic Epistemic Logic. Pages 57–69 of: Gilboa, Itzhak (ed), *Theoretical Aspects of Reasoning About Knowledge: Proceedings of the Seventh Conference (TARK 1998)*. San Francisco, CA: Morgan Kaufmann.

Thomason, Richmond H. 2000. Modeling the Beliefs of Other Agents. Pages 375–473 of: Minker, Jack (ed), *Logic-Based Artificial Intelligence*. Dordrecht: Kluwer Academic Publishers.

Thomason, Richmond H., Stone, Matthew, and Devault, David. 2006. *Enlightened Update: A Computational Architecture for Presupposition and Other Pragmatic Phenomena*. http://web.eecs.umich.edu/~rthomaso/documents/prags/eu.pdf.

Thomason, S. K. 1984. On Constructing Instants from Events. *Journal of Philosophical Logic*, **13**(1), 85–96.

Thomason, S. K. 1989. Free Construction of Time from Events. *Journal of Philosophical Logic*, **18**(1), 43–67.

Tonhauser, Judith, Beaver, David, Roberts, Craige, and Simons, Mandy. 2013. Toward a Taxonomy of Projective Content. *Language*, **89**(1), 66–109.

Traum, David R. 1999. Computational Models of Grounding in Collaborative Systems. Pages 124–131 of: Brennan, Susan E., Giboin, Alain, and Traum, David R. (eds), *Working Papers of the AAAI Fall Symposium on Psychological Models of Communication in Collaborative Systems*. Menlo Park, CA: American Association for Artificial Intelligence.

Traum, David R., and Larsson, Staffan. 2004. The Information State Approach to Dialogue Management. Pages 325–354 of: van Kuppevelt, Jan, and Smith, Ronnie W. (eds), *Current and New Directions in Discourse and Dialogue*. Dordrecht: Kluwer Academic Publishers.

Travis, Charles. 1994. On Constraints of Generality. *Proceedings of the Aristotelian Society, New Series*, **94**, 165–188.

Tuomela, Raimo. 1995. *The Importance of Us*. Stanford, CA: Stanford University Press.

Tymoczko, Thomas. 1989. Brains Don't Lie: They Don't Even Make Many Mistakes. Pages 195–213 of: Roth, Michael D., and Ross, Glen (eds), *Doubting: Contemporary Perspectives on Skepticism*. Dordrecht: Kluwer Academic Publishers.

van Benthem, Johan. 1996. *Exploring Logical Dynamics*. Stanford, CA: CSLI Publications.

van Fraassen, Bas C. 1966. Singular Terms, Truth-Value Gaps and Free Logic. *Journal of Philosophy*, **3**, 481–495.

van Fraassen, Bas C. 1970. *An Introduction to the Philosophy of Time and Space*. New York: Random House. Available at https://www.princeton.edu/~fraassen/BvF.

van Lambalgen, Michiel, and Hamm, Fritz. 2005. *The Proper Treatment of Events*. Oxford: Blackwell.

Vanderschraaf, Peter, and Sillari, Giacomo. 2009. Common Knowledge. In: Zalta, Edward N. (ed), *The Stanford Encyclopedia of Philosophy*. http://plato.stanford.edu/archives/spr2009/entries/common-knowledge/.

Vendler, Zeno. 1957. Verbs and Times. *Philosophical Review*, **46**(2), 143–160.

Vlastos, Gregory. 1966. Zeno's Race Course. *Journal of the History of Philosophy*, **4**(2), 95–108.

von Fintel, Kai. 2008. What Is Presupposition Accommodation, Again? Pages 137–170 of: Hawthorne, John (ed), *Philosophical Perspectives 22, 2008: Philosophy of Language*. Oxford: Blackwell.

Wallace, David. 2012. *The Emergent Multiverse: Quantum Theory According to the Everett Interpretation*. Oxford: Oxford University Press.

Walton, Kendall L. 1993. Metaphor and Prop Oriented Make-Believe. *European Journal of Philosophy*, **1**(1), 39–57.

Westerståhl, Dag. 1998. On Mathematical Proofs of the Vacuity of Compositionality. *Linguistics and Philosophy*, **21**(6), 635–643.

Wetzel, Linda. 2014. Types and Tokens. In: Zalta, Edward N. (ed), *The Stanford Encyclopedia of Philosophy*. http://plato.stanford.edu/archives/spr2014/entries/types-tokens/.

Whitehead, Alfred North, and Russell, Bertrand. 1925–1927. *Principia Mathematica, Vol. 1*. 2 edn. Cambridge: Cambridge University Press.

Whitrow, Gerald J. 1980. *The Natural Philosophy of Time*. 2 edn. Oxford: Oxford University Press.

Williamson, Timothy. 1996a. Knowing and Asserting. *The Philosophical Review*, **105**(4), 489–523.

Williamson, Timothy. 1996b. *Vagueness*. London: Routledge.

Williamson, Timothy. 2000. *Knowledge and Its Limits*. Oxford: Oxford University Press.

Wittgenstein, Ludwig. 1953. *Philosophical Investigations*. New York: The Macmillan Company. Edited by G. E. M. Anscombe and Rush Rhees. Translated by G. E. M. Anscombe.

Woods, Jack. 2014. Expressivism and Moore's Paradox. *Philosopher's Imprint*, **14**(5), 1–12.

Wooldridge, Michael J. 2000. *Reasoning about Rational Agents*. Cambridge: Cambridge University Press.

Wright, Crispin. 1983. *Frege's Conception of Numbers as Objects*. Aberdeen: Aberdeen University Press.

Yablo, Stephen. 1996. How in the World? *Philosophical Topics*, **24**(1), 255–286.

Zadrozny, Wlodek. 1994. From Compositional to Systematic Semantics. *Linguistics and Philosophy*, **17**(4), 329–342.

Zeevat, Henk. 1992. Presupposition and Accommodation in Update Semantics. *Journal of Semantics*, **12**(4), 379–412.

Author Index

Subject Index